STEPHEN HASK

MW00633987

The Story of
DANIEL
THE PROPHET

ADVENTIST PIONEER LIBRARY

© 2023 **ADVENTIST PIONEER LIBRARY**
P. O. Box 51264
Eugene, OR, 97405
www.APLib.org

Originally published by the *Bible Trainig School, South Lancaster, Mass.*, 1908.

Published in the USA

January, 2023

ISBN: 978-1-61455-127-0

The original page numbers of the printed edition of this book are found within brackets throughout the text.

STEPHEN HASKELL

The Story of
DANIEL
THE PROPHET

"But go thy way till the end be: for thou shalt rest,
and stand in thy lot at the end of the days."
Dan. 12:13.

ADVENTIST PIONEER LIBRARY

STEPHEN NELSON HASKELL
1833–1922

CONTENTS

Daniel interpreting the dream.

AUTHOR'S PREFACE

THE world is flooded with fictitious reading of all grades. The unreal is presented in the most fascinating style while too often the living truths taken from God's Word are presented in a heavy, somber style. The Bible is the most interesting of all books. It is adapted to every mind. In the Story of Daniel the Prophet, a few of the interesting facts in regard to God's dealings with His people have been gathered into, a simple narrative.

The book is the result of much prayerful study. It is sent forth with an earnest prayer, that in the hands of the parents it may be the means of making the study of the Bible in the family a blessing to young and old; and that the teacher in the schoolroom may see precious rays of light flashing from its pages, pointing both teacher and pupil to the Great Divine Teacher.

God grant that as it falls into the hands of the careless and unbelieving, they may be influenced to read, and as they read, may behold the beauty of our God, and be led to worship toward His holy temple.

We trust that while its simplicity will attract many who might not be inclined to read a deep argumentative treatise, the most studious will find food for thought, and thus become better acquainted with the character of our Heavenly Father. Those who wish to enter into a more comprehensive study, will find that the marginal references open up many veins of precious ore in the deep mines of God's Word.

We earnestly pray that even the skeptic may not cast it aside; but that he may give it a careful reading, and while tracing the fulfilled prophecy in the history of the world, learn to prize the Word of God.

Throughout the entire book the special providence of God over those who are faithful to Him is brought out in clear contrast to the fate of those who ignore His guiding hand. The truth is the same, whether in the history of nations or individuals.

As the Story of Daniel the Prophet goes forth on its mission of love for the Great Master, may it prove a blessing to all classes, young and old, rich and poor, learned and unlearned.

S. N. H.

INTRODUCTION

THE prophecies of the Bible are like rare diamonds lying hidden in the solitude of the mine. The practiced eye of the prospector discovers the gems, and intuitively reads their value; and the skillful hand of the lapidary brings out their many-faced beauties in all their sparkling glory. Every facet shines like the sun. One can not exhaust a diamond; neither can one exhaust the prophecies. New facets remain to be polished, to add their brilliant reflection to the whole. In the prophecies as many features appear as there are different temperaments that men bring to their study.

The prophecy of Daniel is no exception. This book has lessons for all classes. Because the magnitude of the field of his vision is unlimited in extent, it may be studied from points of view which no man can number. The historian feasts upon his records. The chronologist delights in calculating his periods. The lover of the Messiah rejoices in the contemplation of the times and events that led to His first advent, and demonstrated His Messiahship. And the friend of God traces with pleasure the providential movements by which the course of events has been controlled, and men been put up, and cast down, just according as they have been instruments in God's hand to carry out His beneficent designs and purposes.

There are lessons in these respects for those who take an interest in such themes; but above, and greater than all, are the lessons to be drawn from Daniel's character,—his integrity, his devotion to duty, and his steadfastness in adhering to true principles, in the face of the greatest apparent danger, and in opposition to the dictates of worldly policy. These principles glow with undimmed luster through all his career, and have encouraged, comforted, and strengthened the servants of God in all ages.

Much has been written on the book of Daniel, and much more might be written, as long as principles of divine truth, and noble examples of adherence to them, form interesting and profitable themes of study. In the present work, lessons from this latter source have been especially drawn out. These will be found wonderful subjects for study, and many remarkable thoughts are presented on these points in the following pages. These are lessons which can be laid to heart with the most satisfactory and lasting profit. One who desires to master the philosophy of an acceptable Christian life, and the means and methods by which a close connection with God may be maintained, can find no more competent text-book than is furnished in the record of the experiences of the prophet Daniel. Do you wish to acquire a vivid sense of God's care for His people, and His constant remembrance of them, and the easy means He makes use of to accomplish His ends, you will find the subject fully exploited in the prophecy of Daniel.

Example is a powerful factor in the promotion of the Christian life. "Be ye followers of me," says Paul, "even as I also am of Christ." 1 Cor. 11:1. He exhorts Timothy to be an "example of the believers." 1 Tim. 4:12. What higher standard can be raised to attain unto, than is shown in Daniel's relation to God? for it is said of him that he was a "man greatly beloved." Such was the emphatic testimony borne from God by the angel Gabriel to Daniel, coming as he did immediately from the court of heaven and the presence of God.

The occasion on which these words were first spoken, shows what relation the man thus addressed maintained to God, and God to him. It was when the prophet, burdened with anxiety in regard to a previous vision which he had not understood, appealed to God for help. He had been seeking the Lord, by earnest prayer, to learn the meaning of it. An angel had been strictly enjoined to make Daniel understand all the matter. And now when the angel came to complete his mission, and make the prophet understand the vision, which he had been prevented by Daniel's illness from doing in its completeness in his previous interview (Dan. 8:27), he says: "O Daniel, I am now come forth to give thee skill and understanding. At the *beginning* of thy supplication the commandment came forth, and I am come to show thee; for thou art *greatly beloved*; therefore understand the matter and consider the vision." Dan. 9:22, 23. The angel asserts that one reason, perhaps the leading reason, why he had now come to give him skill and understanding, was that he was a man "greatly beloved."

Think of the circumstances of this case. God was imparting truth to make known to the world what was to come thereafter. He was making use of one of His servants for this purpose. The process was temporarily interrupted. But Daniel had fixed his heart on understanding all that God had to reveal; and he lifted up his petition to the only source from which help could come. Now mark the answer borne from the throne of the universe, by the hand of a mighty angel: "At the *beginning* of thy supplication, the commandment *came forth*." The commandment referred to, was the commandment, or instruction, to Gabriel, to go down to the earth, to this servant of the Lord, and clear up all doubts and uncertainty in his mind in regard to the truth on which he was perplexed.

Will anyone now raise the query, Does the Lord hear prayer? Is He attentive to the wants of His people? In view of this narrative how can we harbor the least vestige of doubt? No sooner does Daniel's prayer *begin* to ascend to the throne than instruction comes forth from God to Gabriel, to go down to the earth and complete his mission to the prophet. With alacrity he obeys. And the prophet says of him, "Being caused to fly *swiftly*." From the beginning of Daniel's prayer, as recorded in Daniel 9, to that point in the prayer when Gabriel appeared upon the scene (verse 20), could not have been over three minutes and a half, at the ordinary rate of speech. In this brief space of time the prophet's prayer ascended to heaven, it was heard, decision made, and the answer came. There is no loitering in heaven. The first faint whisper of want by the child of God, is instantly lodged upon the throne. The command to answer is given, and the return messenger is at once by the side of the prophet, with the response of comfort and joy. No earthly "rapid transit" can equal this. What a glimpse does this give us into the inner courts of the heavenly world! What a view of the divine telegraphy there employed, and waiting at the court's command! What assurance, encouragement, and comfort must these great facts impart to every true and trusting servant in the vineyard of the Lord!

In this story of Daniel, not only is one such incident given, but a whole series of them is woven together in this tapestry of truth. They begin with Daniel as prime minister in the court of the kingdom of Babylon—Babylon, the city of renown, clothed with such magnificence that inspiration has seen fit to describe it as the head of gold on the world's great representative image. Daniel 2. The Lord by the prophet has called Babylon "the glory of kingdoms, the beauty of the Chaldees' excellency." Isa. 13:19. In that city there were beauty, glory, and excellency combined in most striking and prolific forms.

Imagine a space (we must imagine it; for no such spot existed before, and has not existed since);—imagine this space containing two hundred and twenty-five square miles, situated in a fertile plain, wrought up by expert cultivation to the superb production of ornamental trees and shrubs, fragrant flowers, and substantial fruits, till the whole became a veritable paradise, as the garden of the Lord; imagine this space laid out in a perfect square, watered by the magnificent Euphrates, and surrounded by a wall eighty-seven feet thick and three hundred and fifty feet high, fifteen miles in length on each side, and the great square of the whole area of the city, subdivided into lesser squares by twenty-five streets running from each side of the city, parallel with the opposite walls, and at right angles with each other, and adorned with palaces, porticoes, columns, colonnades, towers, monuments, and hanging gardens, arrayed with everything that art could embellish or money and labor produce, to make a spot pleasant to the sight and touch and every bodily sense.

Such was Babylon, glowing in the light of the Syrian sun, and fanned by the blandest zephyrs that ever blew, when Daniel entered to serve the long period of seventy years in captivity. But he was a captive only to political power. He served the Lord, and was spiritually free. From this point through all the personal experience of the prophet, and on through the scenes opened to his mind by the spirit of prophecy, the divine narrative runs. These scenes and experiences are woven together in this book into one connected whole, and the spiritual and practical lessons to be drawn from them are hung like banners of light all along the way.

No one can rise from the study of the prophecies without the conviction being deeply graven upon his heart that the end of the Christian course well repays all the toil and effort of the heavenly journey. The words of the hymn well voice this sentiment:—

> "Then let us hope; 'tis not in vain;
> Though moistened by our grief, the soil;
> The harvest brings us joy for pain;
> The rest repays the weary toil.
> For they shall reap who sow in tears,
> Rich gladness through eternal years."

After his long service and all his trying cares, the word to Daniel was, "Thou shalt rest, and stand in thy lot at the end of the days." The outcome of the Christian service of the disciples in the latter days is expressed in a similar strain by the apostle John in the Revelation: "Blessed are the dead which die in the Lord from henceforth: yea, saith the Spirit, that they may rest from their labors; and their works do follow them." Rev. 14:13. To Daniel, "Go thou thy way till the end be: for thou shalt rest, and stand in thy lot at the end of the days." To John: "Surely I come quickly;" and "my reward is with me, to give every man according as his work shall be." Rev. 22:20, 21. Rest follows the labor; and the end will come. Then follows the remainder of the promise: "Thou shalt stand in thy lot." The rest is undisturbed, and the lot is sure.

What is the lot in which Daniel and all of like character are at last to stand? Who can describe it? for who can conceive of it? It must embrace the condition and all the circumstances of the people of God, when gloriously redeemed. And in reference to this, Paul utters the following living words: "Eye hath not seen, nor ear heard, neither have entered into the heart of man, the things that God hath prepared for them that love Him." 1 Cor. 2:9. That is, the boldest flight of the imagination, the most intense conception of the unseen glories of the heavenly world, have never formed, and can not form, in the human mind any tangible idea of what God has prepared and has in store for His people. "But God," the apostle continues, "hath revealed them unto us by His Spirit." Yes, the Spirit has revealed these things to those who are filled with that Spirit, and have received the Holy Ghost.

We are happy to give, by way of introduction, this word of commendation to this book, which has new phases for every earnest and spiritually minded reader; and which never grows old.

U. S.

Battle Creek, Mich., April, 1901.

A Word to the Reader

It has been with much prayer, and a deep sense of the importance of the subject, that these pages have been prepared. We are living in the closing scenes of this world's history. The Lord's own testimony, in the closing words of the book of Daniel, "Go thou thy way till the end be: for thou shalt rest, and stand in thy lot at the end of the days," should arrest the attention of all who are interested in preparing for the coming of Christ. Then the manner in which the Saviour Himself makes mention of the prophecies of Daniel should not be lightly passed by. He says, "When ye therefore shall see the abomination of desolation, spoken of by Daniel the prophet, stand in the holy place, (*whoso readeth, let him understand*)." Daniel the prophet is the only one in the Bible to whom the Lord addressed, through the angel Gabriel, the words, "Thou art greatly beloved." Such words to any living mortal in the flesh are worthy of consideration by the devout.

We invite a careful perusal of the contents of this work, with the prayer that the Lord will impress minds by His Holy Spirit. The book is not designed to arouse controversy or awaken discussion upon theories, but to tell the truth as it is in Jesus Christ. From the beginning to the end we have tried to tell the story of the prophet and his writings in a brief, simple style, to create a religious interest in the things of God. To the Bible student we have suggested thoughts, both in the story and by the side references, that will encourage study in the home and in the school.

Yours in the blessed hope,
S. N. H.

CHAPTER I

DANIEL AND HIS FELLOWS TESTED

ALTHOUGH Daniel lived twenty-five hundred years ago, he is a latter-day prophet.[1] His character should be studied, for its development reveals the secret of God's preparation of those who will welcome Christ at His appearing. His prophecies should be understood, for in them is the key which unlocks history to the end of time. The Saviour himself bore witness to this. When the disciples asked, "What shall be the sign of Thy coming, and of the end of the world?" He said, "When ye therefore shall see the abomination of desolation spoken of by [10] Daniel the prophet. . . whoso readeth, *let him understand.*" In this we have the divine permission to read and understand the prophecies of Daniel. These prophecies are intended, therefore, to warn a people of the coming of Christ.

True, it was once a sealed book, for the prophet was told to shut up the words, and seal the book "to the time of the end," "for at the time of the end shall be the vision." And again, "The words *are* closed up and sealed till the time of the end." But the time of the end has come. It began in 1798, and though "none of *the wicked* shall understand," yet "*the wise shall understand.*" With the book of Daniel in hand, and a heart open to hear the voice of God, man may come in touch with the Father of light. "He that hath an ear, let him hear what the Spirit saith."

Daniel begins the book with the simple statement that in the third year of the reign of Jehoiakim, king of Judah, 607 b. c., Nebuchadnezzar, the king of Babylon, came unto Jerusalem and besieged it; that in the siege, Jehoiakim was

Then said he, Knowest thou wherefore I come unto thee? Dan 10:20.

Now I am come to make thee understand what shall befall thy people in the latter days: for yet the vision is for many days. Dan 10:14.

Understand, O son of man: for at the time of the end shall be the vision. Dan 8:16, 17 Behold, I will make thee know what shall be in the last end of the indignation: for at the time appointed the end shall be. Dan 8:19. Matt. 24:3, 15. Luke 21:20 Consider what I say: and the Lord give thee understanding in all things. 2 Tim. 2:7. 1 Cor. 10:15 But thou, O Daniel, shut up the words, and seal the book, even to the time of the end: many shall run to and fro, and knowledge shall be increased. Dan 12:4

And he said, Go thy way, Daniel: for the words are closed up and sealed till the time of the end. Many shall be purified, and made white, and tried; but the wicked shall do wickedly: and none of the wicked shall understand; but the wise shall understand. But go thou thy way till the end be: for thou shalt rest, and stand in thy lot at the end of the days. Dan. 12:9, 10, 13

Dan. 8:26 1 John 2:27 Rev. 2:29

1. In the third year of the reign of Jehoiakim king of Judah came Nebuchadnezzar king of Babylon unto Jerusalem, and besieged it. 2. And the Lord gave Jehoiakim king of Judah into his hand, with part of the vessels of the house of God: which he carried into the land of Shinar to the house of his god; and he brought the vessels into the treasure house of his god. Dan. 1:1,2

---

[1] NOTE.—In the margin are many passages of scriptures that will direct the mind of the reader to those portions of the Bible which give light upon the story of Daniel the prophet. In the texts quoted, marks of ellipsis are omitted; and frequently several verses are cited in the reference, though only one or more are printed in full.

Lam. 4:12.
2 Kings 23:36.
2Kings 24:5.
2 Chron. 36:5-7

When the Most High divided to the nations their inheritance, when he separated the sons of Adam, he set the bounds of the people according to the number of the cildrens of Israel.

Deut. 32:8

given by the Lord into the hands of Nebuchadnezzar, but allowed to remain on the throne in Jerusalem, yet Nebuchadnezzar carried with him to Babylon, as tribute, a part of the vessels of the house of God, and, as hostages, some of the members of the royal household.

This act, with similar ones which followed in swift succession, was but the culmination of events which began years before. In order to appreciate this climax, it is essential that we study the causes which led to it. Since the captivity of Judah is an object lesson to people of the last generation, it is doubly necessary [17] that we trace the relationship between certain causes and results.

God had an object in calling the Jewish nation to separate themselves from other nations of the world. It was

They came to hear of the mighty
God that could heal the sick; but he
showed them only earthly treasure.

that his people might stand before the world as light-bearers. As a beacon set on a hill, Israel was to send beams of light to the world. The plan of education made [18] known to Israel through her prophets was the means of keeping that light burning. When this God-given plan was neglected, the light, as a candle deprived of the life-giving oxygen, burned dim. Then it was that the nation was pressed upon all sides by the foe. There is a Hebrew maxim which says that "Jerusalem was destroyed because the education of her children was neglected." The prophecies of Daniel and the connected history prove the truth of this maxim. It may be added that the Jews were restored to Jerusalem as the result of the proper education of a few Hebrew boys.

Just about one hundred years before the days of Daniel, Hezekiah was king of Judah. After a reign of thirteen years, he was on his deathbed, but he pleaded with God to lengthen his life. This was done, and fifteen years were added. On the king's recovery he was visited by ambassadors from Babylon, to whom he showed all his treasures. They came to hear of the mighty God, that could heal the sick: but he showed them only earthly treasure. He lost the opportunity to give them of the treasure of heaven. Then came a message from God by the hand of the prophet Isaiah, saying, "Behold, the days shall come, that all that is in thine house. . . shall be carried into Babylon; nothing shall be left." He was also at the same time told that his descendants should be eunuchs in the palace of the king of Babylon.

Here was portrayed the future captivity of the Hebrew race. The prophecy was placed on record, and repeated again and again by Jewish mothers as they taught their children. "Must my son be a captive in the court of a heathen [19] king? Then let me so train him that he will be true to the God of his fathers." There were other mothers who lightly let pass the thought, and the history of their sons' lives is recorded for our instruction.

Three years after his life had been saved, a son was born to Hezekiah. Notwithstanding the recent prophecy, Hezekiah and his wife, Hephzibah, failed to teach the

---

Acts 13:47, 48.

Isa. 42:6-7.

isa. 49:6.

1 Sam. 10:5-12; 19:23, 24.

Also in the third year of his reign he sent to his princes, even to Ben-hail, and to Obadiah, and to Zechariah, and to Nethaneel, and to Michaiah, to teach in the cities of Judah. And with them he sent Levites, even Shemaiah, and Nethaniah, and Zebadiah, and Asahel, and Shemiramoth, and Jehonathan, and Adonijah, and Tobijah, and Tob-adonijah, Levites; and with them Elishama and Jehoram, priests. And they taught in Judah, and had the book of the law of the LORD with them, and went about throughout all the cities of Judah, and taught the people.   2 Chron. 17:7-9

My people are destroyed for lack of knowledge: because thou hast rejected knowledge, I will also reject thee, that thou shalt be no priest to me: seeing thou hast forgotten the law of thy God, I will also forget thy children.   Hosea 4:6

At that time Merodach-baladan, the son of Baladan, king of Babylon, sent letters and a present to Hezekiah: for he had heard that he had been sick, and was recovered. And Hezekiah was glad of them, and shewed them the house of his precious things, the silver, and the gold, and the spices, and the precious ointment, and all the house of his armour, and all that was found in his treasures: there was nothing in his house, nor in all his dominion, that Hezekiah shewed them not.   Isa. 39:1,2

In those days was Hezekiah sick unto death. And Isaiah the prophet saind unto him, Thus saith the Lord, Set time house in order: for thou shalt die. Then Hezekiah prayed and wept sore. Then came the word of the Lord to Isaiah, saying, Go, and say to Hezekiah, I have heard thy prayer: behold, I will add unto thy days fifteen years.
          Isa. 38:1-5.

2 Kings 20:1-6

At that time Merodach-baladan, the son of Baladan, king of Babylon, sent letters and a present to Hezekiah: for he had heard that he had been sick, and was recovered. And Hezekiah was glad of them, and shewed them the house of his precious things, the silver, and the gold, and the spices, and the precious ointment, and all the house of his armour, and all that was found in his treasures: there was nothing in his house, nor in all his dominion, that Hezekiah shewed them not.   Isaías 39:1,2

Behold, the days come, that all that is in thine house, shall be carried to Babylon: and thy sons shall eunuchs in the place of theking Babylon.   Isa. 39:6,7.

2 Chron. 32:24-26.

For precept must be upon precept, precept upon precept; line upon line; here a little, and there a little.   Isa. 28:10.

O that thou hadst hearkened to my commandments! then had thy peace been as a river, and thy righteouness as the waves of the sea.
                                                Isa. 48: 18.

Manasseh was twelve years old when he began to reign, and reigned fifty and five years in Jerusalem. And his mother's name was Hephzi-bah. And he did that which was evil in the sight of the LORD, after the abominations of the heathen, whom the LORD cast out before the children of Israel.
                                                2 Reis 21:1-3

Even a child is known by his doings, whether his work be pure, and whether it be right.
                                                Prov. 20:11.

When he was twelve years old, they went up to Jerusalem after the custom of the feast. And he said unto them, How is it that ye sought me? wist ye not that I must be about my Father's business? And Jesus increasad in wisdom and stature, and in favor with God and man.
                                                Luke 2:42, 49, 52.
2 Chron. 33: 1-10.

The rod and reproof give wisdom: but a child left to himself bringeth his mother to shame. Correct thy son, and he shall give thee rest; yea, he shall give delight unto thy soul.   Prov 19:15-17

Gen. 18: 19.

2 Peter 3: 3,4.

Jer. 1: 2, 3.

Surely as a wife treacherously departeth from her husband, so have ye dealt treacherously with me, O house of Israel, saith the Lord.
                                                Jer. 3:20.

Deut. 28: 49-52.

Lo, I will bring a nation upon you from afar, O house of Israel, saith the Lord: it is a mighty nation, it is an ancient nation, a nation whose language thou knowest not, neither understandest what they say.   Jer. 5:15.

And the king commanded all the people, saying, Keep the passover unto the LORD your God, as it is written in the book of this covenant. Surely there was not holden such a passover from the days of the judges that judged Israel, nor in all the days of the kings of Israel, nor of the kings of Judah; Moreover the workers with familiar spirits, and the wizards, and the images, and the idols, and all the abominations that were spied in the land of Judah and in Jerusalem, did Josiah put away. And like unto him was there no king before him, that turned to the LORD with all his heart, and with all his soul, and with all his might.
                                                2 Reis 23:21-25.

young Manasseh in the way of truth. He was but twelve years of age when he came to the throne, but if he had been trained in the fear of God, he would not have chosen the worship of the heathen.

The youthful Christ at the same age settled not only His own destiny, but the destiny of the universe. When twelve years of age, standing by the temple in Jerusalem, His future work opened before Him, and He accepted His appointed mission. Why? Because Mary, His mother, had taught Him that heart service to God was His highest pleasure. Manasseh decided in favor of the heathen deities; did evil in the sight of God; and "for the sins of Manasseh" came the captivity of Judah.

At the age of twelve years, Christ made a decision which saved the world; at the same age Manasseh chose a course which brought ruin to the nation. In the training of your child are you Hephzibah or Mary?

The long reign of Manasseh passed, and the prophecy sent to Hezekiah was not yet fulfilled. Men began to wonder if it ever would come to pass. "Since the fathers fell asleep," said they, "all things continue as they were."

It was in the days of Josiah, the grandson of Manasseh, that Jeremiah prophesied. Through [20] this prophet, God pleaded with Jerusalem to return to Him. "Lo, I will bring a nation upon you from afar, O house of Israel, saith the Lord: it is a mighty nation, it is an ancient nation, a nation whose language thou knowest not." Thus was Babylon described, and Jerusalem's impending doom portrayed.

Josiah was spared the sight of the complete destruction of Jerusalem because of the reforms which he attempted. In his days there was kept by Judah, and by Israel also, the greatest Passover feast in the history of the nation. "Because thine heart was tender and thou hast humbled thyself before the Lord, ... behold I will gather thee unto thy fathers... and thine eyes shall not see all the evil which I will bring upon this place." In a peculiar way God gave Josiah an opportunity to avert the impending calamity. It was not yet too late to change the course of events. This opportunity was through the gifts of his sons. Josiah had three sons and one grandson, who were in turn seated on the throne at Jerusalem. Each, because of wrong training in youth, refused to take God at His word, and failing, hastened the final overthrow.

The three sons were Jehoahaz, Jehoiakim, and Zedekiah. The grandson was Jehoiachin, who preceded his uncle, Zedekiah. The fate of each is a solemn warning to people living at the end of time. He who might have been the light of heathen nations was swallowed up by Egyptian darkness. Jehoiakim, the second, who, properly trained, would have been so charged with the power of God that the heathen king would either have united his forces with the [21] king of Judah, or, opposing, would have been smitten as by a thunder-bolt, failing, paid tribute to Babylon. His capital was entered. Treasures from the house of God were ruthlessly torn from their place and dedicated to heathen worship. Youth—bright, promising youth—were taken from the royal family to serve the king of Babylon. Jehoiakim beheld this, but was powerless to interfere. His life was gone; he was not connected with the throne of God. His mother and his father made a fatal mistake, for they did not give him the training which God had commanded them to give. Neither did he profit by these mistakes, but educated his son in courtly manners and in the philosophy of the world; and as a result his son Jehoiachin languished nearly thirty-seven years in a prison in Babylon. This was another lamp without the oil another soul without the heavenly food; another son improperly trained to add to the disgrace of Judah. "Jerusalem was destroyed, because the education of her children was neglected."

Zedekiah, the third son of Josiah, had still an opportunity to save Jerusalem. Part of the treasures of this city were already in Babylon. Daniel and his companions had been in the court seventeen or eighteen years when Jeremiah came to Zedekiah with the words: "If thou wilt assuredly go forth unto the king of Babylon's princes, then thy soul shall live, and this city shall not be burned with fire.... Obey, I beseech thee, the voice of the Lord which I speak unto thee: so it

1 Chron. 3:15, 16.
2 Chron. 36:1-10.
2 Kings 23:30-34.

Jehoahaz was twenty and three years old when he began to reign; and he reigned three months in Jerusalem. And his mother's name was Hamutal. And he did that which was evil in the sight of the LORD. Jehoiakim was twenty and five years old when he began to reign; and he reigned eleven years in Jerusalem. And his mother's name was Zebudah. And he did that which was evil in the sight of the LORD. 2 Reis 23:31-37.

Surely at the commandment of the Lord came to this upon Judah, to remove them out of his sight, for the sins of Manasseh, according to all that he did; and also for the innocent blood that he shed. 2 Kings 24:1-4.

Jehoiachin was eighteen years old when he began to reign, and he did that which was evil in the sigh of the Lord. 2 Kings 24:8, 9, 17.

Nebuchadnezzar king of Babylon came against the city and his servants did besiege it. And he carried out thence all the trasures of the house of the Lord, and the treasures of the king's house, and he carried away all Jerusalem, and all the princes, and all the mighty men of valor. 2 Kings 24:10-16.

Evil-merodach king of Babylon in the year that he began to reign did lift up the head of Jehoiachin king of Judah out of prison; and he spake kindly to him, and set his throne above the throne of the kings that were with him in Babylon; and changed his prison garments: and he did eat bread continually before him all the days of his life. 2 Reis 25:27-29

Hebrew mother teaching her children.

shall be well unto thee, and thy soul shall live." In this time of peril, how did Zedekiah act? Did he deliver himself unto the Babylonians? God had commanded it; the city [22] would have been saved by it; his own soul would have been saved. Zedekiah pleaded a most human excuse, saying, "I am afraid."

In these three sons is revealed the weakness, the cowardice, the wickedness, and the final ruin of those trained for the service of the world and not for the service of God.

Living at the same time and in the same city with the princes already named, were others which the Scripture mentions by name. These were Daniel, Hananiah, Mishael, and Azariah, children of Judah, of the royal family—relatives of Jehoahaz, Jehoiakim, and Zedekiah.

At the first siege of Jerusalem, 607 B. C., Daniel was not over eighteen years of age; about the age of the prince Zedekiah, who afterward ruled in Jerusalem. Daniel had a godly mother who knew of the prophecy concerning the destruction of their city. She repeated to her son the words of God, that some day Hebrew children must stand in the heathen court at Babylon. Carefully did this mother teach her son to read the parchment scrolls of the prophets. The history of Israel was studied; the story of Nadab and Abihu was told and retold. The effect of strong drink was impressed upon the mind. The laws of his own being were studied. He knew that excess in eating and drinking would so dull the mind that the voice of God could not be heard.

The songs which these Hebrew children sang told the story of God's dealings with His people. It was in this manner that the image of God was engraven on their hearts. This education was not gained in the schools of the time, for they had departed from the plan of God; but [23] holy mothers, living close to the everlasting Father, led their children by precept and example, by word and song, to form characters that would stand the test.

It was the age when most of the young men in the capital of Judah were wild and reckless. They were excusing themselves because of their youth. But God chose from their midst certain ones whom He could trust in a foreign

2 Kings 24:17-20.

What time I am afraid I will trust in thee.
Psa. 56:3

Hear therefore, O Israel, and observe to do it; that it may be well with thee, and that ye may increase mightily, as the LORD God of thy fathers hath promised thee, in the land that floweth with milk and honey. Hear, O Israel: The LORD our God is one LORD: and thou shalt love the LORD thy God with all thine heart, and with all thy soul, and with all thy might. And these words, which I command thee this day, shall be in thine heart: and thou shalt teach them diligently unto thy children, and shalt talk of them when thou sittest in thine house, and when thou walkest by the way, and when thou liest down, and when thou risest up. And thou shalt bind them for a sign upon thine hand, and they shall be as frontlets between thine eyes. And thou shalt write them upon the posts of thy house, and on thy gates.
Deut. 6:3-9

When I call to remembrance the unfeigned faith that is in thee, which dwelt first in thy grandmother Lois, and thy mother Eunice; and I am persuaded that in thee also.
2 Timóteo 1:5

Do not drink wine nor strong drink, thou, nor thy sons with thee, and that ye may put difference between holy and unholy, and that ye may teach the children of Israel all the statutes which the Lord hath spoken.
Lev. 10:9-11.

Prov. 23:19-22.
Deut. 21:20, 21.

Then sang Moses and the children of Israel this song unto the Lord, and spake, saying, I will sing unto the Lord, for he hath triumphed gloriously: the horse and his rider hath he thrown into the sea. The Lord is my strength and song, and he has become my salvation: he is my God, and I will prepare him a habitation; my father's God, and I will exalt him. The Lord is a man of war: the Lord is his name.
Ex. 15:1-21

Judges 5:1-31.
Ps. 137:1-4
1 John 2:13, 14.
2 Kings 5:2-4.

The father of the righteous shall greatly rejoice: and he that begetteth a wise child shall have joy of him. Thy father and thy mother shall be glad, and she that bare thee shall rejoice.

Prov. 23:24, 25.

3. And the king spake unto Ashpenaz the master of his eunuchs, that he should bring certain of the children of Israel, and of the king's seed, and of the princes;
4. Children in whom was no blemish, but well favored, and skilful in all wisdom, and cunning in knowledge, and understanding science, and such as had ability in them to stand in the king's palace, and whom they might teach the learning and the tongue of the Chaldeans.
5. And the king appointed them a daily provision of the king's meat, and of the wine which he drank: so nourishing them three years, that at the end thereof they might stand before the king.
6. Now among these were of the children of Judah, Daniel, Hananiah, Mishael, and Azariah:

Dan. 1:3-6

Prov 23:1-3.

7. Unto whom the prince of the eunuchs gave names: for he gave unto Daniel the name of the Belteshazzar; and to Hananiah, of Shadrach; and to Mishael of Meshach; and to Azariah, of Abednego.
8. But Daniel purposed in his heart that he would not defile himself with the portion of the king's meat, nor with the wine which he drank: therefore he requested of the prince of the eunuchs that he might not defile himself.
9. Now God had brought Daniel into favor and tender love with the prince of the eunuchs.

Dan. 1:7-9.

land. Daniel and his three companions were snatched from the shelter of home, and with others were placed under the charge of Ashpenaz, master of the eunuchs in Babylon.

Now can be seen the results of the home training. Pure food, clean thoughts, and physical exercise placed them on the list of "children in whom was no blemish, but well-favored." But what of their intellectual ability? They had not been educated in the schools of Jerusalem, much less in those of Babylon. Was there not great danger that they lacked in the sciences or the essential branches? On examination, these four passed as "skillful in all wisdom, and cunning in knowledge, and understanding science," [24] and able to learn a difficult foreign language. God had fulfilled His promise in these children of the home school.

The crucial moment came when "the king appointed them a daily provision of the king's meat and of the wine which he drank." Daniel had unbounded confidence in the principles of temperance, not alone because he knew them to be scientifically true, but because they were God-given, and, in his case, had been put into practice. His edu- j cation had a Biblical foundation, and he knew that it was in harmony with true science. It was a life and death question; but the principles were divine, and he would obey, walk by faith, and leave the results with his Maker. "Daniel purposed in his heart that he would not defile himself with the portion of the king's meat, nor with the wine which he drank." The language of the prince of the eunuchs shows that there were other Hebrew youth who were selected, who did not make this request: "for," said the prince of the eunuchs, "why should he [the king] see your faces worse liking than the children which are of *your sort?*"

Daniel and his companions, after considering their dangerous and difficult position, took this matter to the Lord in prayer, and decided to be true to principle. Much was involved in this decision. If they sat at the king's table, they would partake of food which had been consecrated [25] to idols; and the Hebrew children would thus dishonor God, and ruin their own characters by removing the safeguard of temperance, and allowing themselves to be influenced by corrupt associations. Even at the cost of appearing singular, they decided not to sit at the table of the king. They might have reasoned that at the king's command they were compelled to partake of the food at the royal table which had been dedicated to an idol. But they determined not to implicate themselves with heathenism, and not to dishonor the principles of their national religion and their God. Surrounded by perils, after having made a most determined effort to resist temptation, they must trust the results with God.

With true courage and Christian courtesy, Daniel said to the officers who had charge over them: "Prove thy servants, I beseech thee, ten days; and let them give us pulse to eat, and water to drink. Then let our countenances be looked upon before thee, and the countenances of the children that eat the portion of the king's meat; and, as thou seest, deal with thy servants." It was no experiment with them; for they foresaw the result.

The officer hesitated. He feared that the rigid abstinence they proposed would have an unfavorable effect upon their personal appearance, and that, in consequence, they would lose favor with the king. The Hebrew children explained to the officer the effect of food upon the body; that overeating and the use of rich foods benumbs the sensibilities, unfitting mind and body for hard, stern labor. They urged most earnestly that they be allowed the simple diet, and [26] begged that they be given a ten-days' trial, that they might demonstrate by their own physical appearance at the end of that time the advantages of plain, nutritious food. The request was granted: for they had obtained favor with God and with men. It was an act of faith; there was no feeling of envy toward those who were eating of the king's meat. The minds of the four were filled with thoughts of love and peace, and they actually grew during those ten days.

God approved of their course; for, "at the end of ten days, their countenances appeared fairer and fatter in flesh than all the children which did eat the portion of the king's meat." The clear sparkle of the eye, the ruddy, healthy glow

Wine is a mocker, strong drink is raging: and whosoever is deceived thereby is not wise.
Prov. 20:1.

10. And the prince of the eunuchs said unto Daniel, I fear my lord the king, who hath appointed your meat and your drink: for why should he see your faces worse liking than the children which are of your sort? then shall ye make me endanger my head to the king.
11. Then said Daniel to Melzar, whom the prince of the eunuchs had set over Daniel, Hananiah, Mishael, and Azariah,
Dan.1:10, 11.

Commit thy way unto the Lord: trust also in him; and he shall bring it to pass. Ps. 37:5, 5

Who hath woe? who hath sorrow? who hath babbling? who hath wounds without cause? who hath redeness of the eyes? They that tarry long at the wine: they that go to seek mixed wine. Prov. 23:29-32

It is not for kings, O Lemuel, it is not for kings to drink wine; nor for princes strong drink: lest they drink and forget the law, and pervert the judgment of any of the afflicted.
Prov. 31:4, 5.

Isa. 5:11..

My son, keep the father's commandment, and forsake not the law of thy mother. When thou goest, it shall lead thee; when thou sleepest, it shall keep thee; and when thou awakest, it shall talk with thee.
Prov. 6:20-23

12. Prove thy servants, I beseech thee, ten days; and let them give us pulse to eat, and water to drink.
13. Then let our countenances be looked upon before thee, and the countenance of the children that eat of the portion of the king's meat: and as thou seest, deal with thy servants.
14. So he consented to them in this matter, and proved them ten days. Dan.1:12-14.

Hear, o my son, and receive my sayings; and the years of thy life shall be many. Prov. 4:10-12.

The wrath of a king is as messengers of death.
Prov. 16:14

Corn shall make the young men cheerful.
Zech 9:17.

Wherefore do you spend money for that which is not bread? and your labor for that which satisfieth not? hearken dilgently unto me, and eat ye that which is good, and let your soul delight itself in fatness.
Isa. 55:2.

The two tables.

of the countenance, bespoke physical soundness and moral purity. The Hebrew captives were thereafter allowed to have their chosen food.

The pulse and water which they then desired was not always the exclusive diet of Daniel, for on another occasion in his later life he said: "I ate no pleasant bread, neither came flesh nor wine in my mouth." But when entering upon the king's course of study and becoming connected with the royal court, he and his brethren voluntarily chose this simple, nourishing food. Likewise, when brought face to face with any difficult problem, or when desiring especially to know the mind of God, the record speaks of Daniel's abstinence from flesh food, wine, and food which tempt the appetite.

The character of Daniel is referred to by Ezekiel, who was a contemporaneous prophet, as representing those who will live just before the second coming of Christ. People will be called [27] to pass through experiences which require the keenest spiritual eyesight; therefore God asks them to give up all things which will in any way check the flow of the Holy Spirit through the mind. Herein lies the reason for strict adherence to the principles of health reform. Daniel and his companions gained the victory on the point of appetite. This was the avenue, and the only one, through which Satan was permitted to tempt Adam; and, had Adam proved true in the garden of Eden, and not eaten of the forbidden fruit, sin and suffering would never have been known. Appetite was the open door through which came all the results of sin, which, for six thousand years, have been so manifest in the human family.

As Christ entered upon the work of His ministry, He began where Adam fell, The first temptation in the wilderness was on the point of appetite. Here the Saviour bridged the gulf which sin had made. He redeemed the whole family of Adam, and wrought out a victory for the benefit of all who are thus tempted. In the last days God will prove His people as He proved Daniel. A voluntary self-control of appetite lies at the foundation of every reform,

It means much to be true to God. It embraces health reform. It means that the diet must be simple; it calls for

15. And at the end of ten days their countenances appeared fairer and fatter in flesh than all the children which did eat the portion of the king's meat.
16. Thus Melzar took away the portion of their meat, and the wine that they should drink; and gave them pulse.

Dan. 1:15, 16.

Ps. 42:11.
Isa. 58:8.

Beloved, I wish above all things that thou mayst prosper and be in health, even as thy soul prospereth.

3 John 1:2.

Dan. 10:3.

Though Noah, Daniel, and Job were in it, as I live, saith the Lord God, they shall deliver neither son nor daughter: they shall but deliver their own souls by their righteousness

Eze. 14:20.

Eze. 14:14-20.

Take heed to yourselves, lest at any time your hearts be overcharged with surfeiting, and drunkeness, and cares of this life, and that day come upon your unawares.

Luke 21:34.

Behold this was the iniquity of thy sister Sodom, pride, fullness of bread, and abundance of idleness was in her and in her daughters, neither did she strengthen the hand of the poor and needy.

Eze. 16:49.

The Lord God commanded the men, saying, Of every tree of the garden thou mayest freely eat: but of the tree of the knowledge of good and evil, thou shalt not eat of it: for in the day that thou eatest thereof thou shalt surely die.

Gen. 2:16, 17.

Gen. 3:17.

Then was Jesus led up of the Spirit into the wilderness to be tempted of the devil. And when he had fasted forty days and forty nights, he was afterward an hungered. And when the tempter came to him, he said, If thou be the Son of God, command that these stones be made bread. But he answered and said, It is written, Man shall not live by bread alone, but by every word that proceedeth out of the mouth of God. Matt. 4:1-4.

Prov. 16:32.

Every man that striveth for the mastery is temperate in all things.

1 Cor. 9:25.

Variety of food at one meal in Bible times.
Gen. 18:5-8.
Gen. 19:3.
Gen. 25:34.
Ruth 2:14.

1 Sam. 30:11, 12.
1 Kings 17:13-16.
1 Kings 19:5, 6.
2 Kings 4:42-44.
Matt. 14:18-29.
John 21:9, 12.

17. As for these four children, God gave them knowledge and skill in all learning and wisdom: and Daniel has understanding in all visions and dreams.
Dan. 1:17.

My son, if thou wilt receive my words, and hide my commandments with thee: yea, if thou criest after knowledge, and liftest up thy voice for understanding; if thou seekest her as silver, and searchest for her as for hid treasures; then shalt thou understand the fear of the Lord, and find the knowledge of God.
Prov. 2:1-5.

But ye hae an unction from the Holy One, and ye know all things. But the anointing which ye have received of him abideth in you, and ye need not that any man teach you: but as the same anointing teacheth you of all things, and is truth, and is no lie, and even as it hath taught, ye shall abide in him.
1 John 2:20, 27.

Howbeit when he, the Spirit of truth, is come, he will guide you into all truth: for he shall not speak of himself; but whatsoever he shall hear, that shall he speak: and he will show you things to come.
John 16:13.

18. Now at the end of the days that the king had said he should bring them in, then the prince of the eunuchs brought them in before Nebuchadnezzar.
19. And the king communed with them; and among them all was found none like Daniel, Hananiah, Mishael, and Azariah: therefore stood they before the king.
20. And in all matters of wisdom and understanding, that the king inquired of them, he found them ten times better than all the magicians and astrologers that were in all his realm.
Dan. 1:18-20.

Understanding is a wellspring of life unto him that hath it.
Prov. 16:22.

the exercise of temperance in all things. Too great a variety of food taken at the same meal is highly injurious; and yet, how often this is forgotten. Mind and body are to be preserved in the best condition of health. Only those who have been trained in the fear and knowledge of God, and who are true to principle, are fitted to bear responsibilities [28] in the closing work of the gospel.

Daniel and his companions passed through a strange school in which to become fitted for lives of sobriety, industry, and faithfulness. Surrounded with courtly grandeur, hypocrisy, and paganism, they exercised self-denial, and sought to acquit themselves so creditably that the Israelites, their down-trodden people, might be honored, and that God's name might be glorified.

These children had the Lord as their educator. They were connected with the Fountainhead of wisdom, by the golden channel, the Holy Spirit. They kept continually a living connection with God, walking with Him as did Enoch. They were determined to gain a true education; and, in consequence of their copartnership with the divine nature, they became in every sense complete men in Christ Jesus. While diligently applying themselves to gain a knowledge of the languages and sciences, they also received light direct from Heaven's throne, and read God's mysteries for future ages.

When at the end of three years, King Nebuchadnezzar tested the ability and acquirements of the royal princes whom he had been educating from other nations, none were found equal to the Hebrew youth, Daniel, Hananiah, Mishael, and [29] Azariah. They surpassed their associates tenfold in their keen apprehension, their choice and correct language, and their extensive and varied knowledge. The vigor and strength of their mental powers were unimpaired. Hence *they* stood before the king. "And in all matters of wisdom and understanding, that the king inquired of them, he found them ten times better than all the magicians and astrologers that were in all his realm."

These youth respected their own manhood, and their intrusted talents had not been enfeebled or perverted by indulgence of appetite. The good they wished to accomplish was ever in mind. They were faithful in the little things. God honored them; for they honored Him. God always honors adherence to principle. Among all the most promising youth gathered from the lands subdued by Nebuchadnezzar, the Hebrew captives stood unrivaled. Their regard for nature's laws and the God of nature was revealed in the erect form, the elastic step, the fair countenance, the untainted breath, the undimmed senses. It was not by chance that they attained to their marvelous wisdom. "The fear of the Lord is the beginning of wisdom." The foundation of the highest education is religious principle. Faith had been developed in childhood; and when these youth had to act for themselves, they depended upon God for strength and efficiency in their labors, and they were richly rewarded.

Where are the parents who to-day are teaching their children to control appetite, and to look to God as the Source of all wisdom? Our youth are daily meeting allurements to gratify [30] appetite. Every form of indulgence is made easy and inviting, especially in our large cities. Those who steadfastly refuse to defile themselves will be rewarded as was Daniel. The youth of today may bear a weighty testimony in favor of true temperance.

These principles, cherished, would fit young men who are rooted and grounded in the Scriptures, to enter worldly universities, and while taking a course of study, disseminate the truths of the gospel, and at the end of their course, come forth unsullied. There were consecrated youth among the Waldenses who entered worldly universities, and, while gaining their education, scattered the seeds of the Reformation. The papal authorities could not, by the most careful inquiries, find out who had introduced the so- called heresy; and yet the work had been accomplished, bearing fruit in the conversion of many who became leaders in the cause of Protestantism. Were these principles practiced, more young persons could be trusted as missionaries in responsible positions and in institutions of learning. Many will yet be called to stand before judges and kings. How are the children being educated?

1 Sam. 2:30.

When wisdom entereth into thine heart, and knowledge is plasant unto thy soul; discretion shall preserve thee, understanding shall keep thee: to deliver thee from the way of the evil man, from the man that speaketh froward things.
Prov. 2:10-12.

Prov. 13:15.
Luke 16:10.

The fear of the Lord is the beginning of wisdom: a good understanding have all they that do his commandments: his praise endureth forever.
Ps. 111:10.

And unto man he said, Behold, the fear of the Lord, that is wisdom; and to depart from evil is understanding.   Job 28:28.

Thou through thy commandments hast made me wiser than mine enemies: for they are ever with me. I have more understanding than all my teachers: for thy testimonies are my meditation.
Ps. 119:98-101.

Let us hear the conclusion of the whole matter: Fear God, and keep his commandments: for this is the whole duty of man.   Eccl. 12:13.

Train up a child in the way he should go: and when he is old, he will not depart from it.
Prov. 22:6.
They that understand among the people shall instruct many.   Dan. 11:33.

Seest thou a man diligent in his business? he shall stand before kings; he shall not stand before mean men.   Prov. 22:29.

But sanctify the Lord God in your hearts: and be ready always to give an answer to every man that asketh you a reason of the hope that is in you, with meekness and fear.
1 Peter 3:15.
21. And Daniel continued even unto the first year of King Cyrus.
Dan. 1:21.

That saith of Cyrus, He is my shepherd, and shall perform all my pleasure: even saying to Jerusalem, Thou shalt be built; and to the temple, Thy foundation shall be laid.

Isa. 44:28.

Isa. 45:1, 2.

The last words of the first chapter of Daniel are truly significant: "Daniel continued even unto the first year of King Cyrus." In other words, Daniel lived all the days of the Babylonian captivity,—over seventy years,—and had the pleasure of meeting that Cyrus whose name the prophet Isaiah had mentioned nearly two hundred years before he issued his wonderful decree for the deliverance of God's people. [31]

Chapter 2

A Controversy Between Truth and Error

"In the second year of Nebuchadnezzar, Nebuchadnezzar dreamed dreams," It is thus that we are introduced to the monarch of the greatest of earthly kingdoms in his own home. In chapter one, Nebuchadnezzar is referred to as the one who besieged Jerusalem; in chapter two he is spoken of as the ruler of every nation on earth. The kingdom which Nebuchadnezzar brought to the height of its glory can be traced in Bible history to its foundation. The history of Babylon is the story of the great controversy between Christ and Satan, begun in heaven, continued on earth, and which will end only when the stone cut out from the mountain without hands shall fill the whole earth.

Satan's accusation against God is that the Father is unjust. "But give me a fair chance," argued Lucifer, "and I can establish a kingdom on earth which will excel in glory the kingdom of God in heaven." He was granted the privilege of making a trial. The plains of Shinar were chosen; the people whom God told to fill the whole earth were gathered into a city. Babylon [32] grew, and its mighty walls, three hundred and fifty feet in height and eighty-seven feet thick, with the massive gates of brass, were designed to imitate the strength of the city of God. At the time of the founding of Babylon, Satan was still meeting with the council of the representatives of worlds, which was held at the gates of heaven. It was his design to counterfeit the plans of God. The earthly city was patterned after the heavenly. The Euphrates flowed through it as did the river of God through Paradise. The government was an absolute monarchy; a man occupied the throne, and as it grew, every knee of earth was caused to bow to its king. No power was tolerated above that of the monarch. Tyranny took the place of love. This is always true when man is exalted above God. It was to such a kingdom

1. And in the second year of the reign of Nebuchadnezzar Nebuchadnezzar dreamed dreams, wherewith his spirit was troubled, and his sleep brake from him.
Dan. 2:1.

Dan. 1:1.
Dan. 2:37, 38.
Jer. 27:6-11.

And Cush begat Nimrod: he began to be a mighty one in the earth. He was a mighty hunter before the Lord: wherefore it is said, Even as Nimrod, the mighty hunter before the Lord. And the beginning of his kingdom was Babylon, and Erech, and Accad, and Calneh, in the land of Shinar.
Gen. 10:8-10 [margin].

Gen. 11:9.
Isa. 14:12-14.

They said, Go to, let us build us a city and a tower, whose top may reach unto heaven; and let us make us a name, lest we be scattered abroad upon the face of the whole earth. Therefore is the name of it called Babel. Gen.11:1-9

Behold the land of the Chaldeans; this people was not, till the Assyrian founded it for them that dwell in the wilderness: they set up the towers thereof, they raised up the palaces thereof: and he brought it to ruin Isa. 23:13.

Jer. 50:58.
Now there was a day when the sons of God came to present themselves before the Lord, and Satan came also among them. And the Lord said unto Satan, Whence comest thou? Then Satan answered the Lord, and said, From going to and fro in the earth, and from walking up and down in it.
Job 1:6, 7.

that Nebuchadnezzar fell heir, and the beauty and power of the kingdom were increased by him in every possible way, until it was spoken of by the Lord as "Babylon, the glory of kingdoms, the beauty of the Chaldees' excellency."

Not only the power, but the wisdom also, of Nebuchadnezzar was exceedingly great. The king favored education, and during his reign Babylon was the educational center of the world. Every art and science was taught in the schools of Babylon. The wisdom of the ancients was made known to the students who sat at the feet of her magicians and wise men. They reveled in the study of astronomy and the higher mathematics. There were linguists who could teach the language of every nation. [33]

The king himself was highly educated, for it was he who examined the students on the completion of their course. Babylon was proud of her educational system; she trusted to it for salvation, but it was the cause of her ruin. "Thy *wisdom* and thy *knowledge,* it hath caused thee to turn away." God Himself speaks, saying: "Hath not God made foolish the wisdom of this world?" In the Babylonian court this was exemplified. Nebuchadnezzar and his counselors,—the wise men, astrologers, and soothsayers,—on one side, represented the education of the world, Daniel, a youth, not over twenty-one years of age, a Hebrew and a slave, was chosen by God to confound the wisdom of the mighty.

The Scriptures give the story in language that can be readily understood. But why did God give Nebuchadnezzar a dream? How could the God of heaven reveal truth to this heathen king? Doubtless He could not during his waking moments; but Nebuchadnezzar had contemplated the glory of his kingdom, and fell asleep with a longing desire to know its future. He knew that life was short. Soon he must die; what would the future be? It was God's opportunity, and while those eyes were closed to earthly things; while self was lost—dead, as it were—the future history of the world was spread before Nebuchadnezzar. On awaking, he found no language to express his thoughts. He who was acquainted with the world's wisdom knew not the language

---

Job 2:1, 2.
2 Chron. 18:18.

The Lord said unto him, Wherewith? And he said, I will go forth, and I will be a lying spirit in the moouth of all his prophets.
1 Kings 22:18-23.

Rev. 22:1, 2.

He who smote the people in wrath with a continual stroke, he that ruled the nations in anger, is persecuted, and none hindereth.
Isa. 14:3-7.

Behold I am against thee, O destroying mountain, saith the Lord, which destroyeth all the earth: and I will stretch out mine hand upon thee, and roll thee down from the rocks, and will make thee a burnt mountain.
Jer. 51:25.

Isa. 13:19.

Thy wisdom and thy knowledge, in hath perverted thee; and thou hast said in thine heart, I am, and none else beside me.
Isa. 47:10.

In all matters of wisdom and understanding, that the king inquired of them, he found them ten times better than all the magicians and astrologers that were in all his realm.
Dan. 1:17-20

Thou art wearied in the multitude of thy conseuls. Let now the astrologers, the stargazers, the monthly prognosticators, stand up, and save thee from these things that shall come upon thee. They shall not deliver themselves from the power of the flame.
Isa. 47:13, 14.

Where is the wise? where is the scribe? where is the disputer of this world? hath not God made foolish the wisdom of this world? For after that in the wisdom of God the world by wisdom knew not God, it pleased God by the foolishness of preaching to save them that believe. But we preach Christ crucified, unto the Jews a stumbling-block, and unto the Greeks foolishness; But unto them which are called, both Jews and Greeks, Christ the power of God, and the wisdom of God. Because the foolishness of God is wiser than men; and the weakness of God is stronger than men.
1 Cor. 1:18-25.

Yea, have ye never read, Out of the mouth of babes and sucklings thou has perfected praise?
Matt. 21:16.

of heaven. This he had never been taught. He tried to think what he had seen, but as his eyes again rested on the glory about him, the vision faded away. Earthly [34] things drew a veil over the things of God, and while he knew he had seen something, he knew not what it was.

The king demanded an interpretation, but the wisest men of the kingdom answered: "There is not a man upon the earth that can show the king's matter. . . . There is none other that can show it before the king, except the gods, whose dwelling is not with flesh." That the pretended knowledge of the wise men of Babylon might be exposed, the Lord had in His providence given Nebuchadnezzar this dream, and then allowed him to forget the details, while causing him to retain a vivid impression of the vision. The king was angered because the wise men requested him to tell them the dream, saying, "I know of certainty that ye would gain the time, because ye see the thing has gone from me." That is, they would be able to agree on some interpretation if the king could tell the dream. The king then threatened that if they failed to tell the dream, they should all be destroyed. The wise men urged that the requirement was most unreasonable; but the more they argued, the more furious the king became, and in his anger he finally "commanded to destroy all the wise men of Babylon."

This decree was made in the second year of Nebuchadnezzar's reign. He had ruled two years conjointly with his father, Nabopolassar, and two years alone; so Daniel and his fellows were serving their first year as wise men in the court of Babylon, having finished their three- years' course in the schools. They were therefore sought out by Arioch, the king's captain, to be slain. Daniel asked: "Why is the decree [35] so hasty from the king?" Then Arioch made the thing known to Daniel. Daniel alone had the courage to venture into the presence of the king, at the peril of his life, to beg that he might be granted time to show the dream and the interpretation. The request was granted.

"There are in the providence of God particular periods when we must arise in response to the call of God."

2. Then the king commanded to call the magicians, and the astrologers, and the sorcerers, and the Chaldeans, for to show the king his dreams. So they came and stood before the king.
3. And the king said unto them, I have dreamed a dream, and my spirit was troubled to know the dream.
4. Then spake the Chaldeans to the king in Syriack, O king, live forever: tell thy servants the dream, and we will show the interpretation. Dan. 2:2-4.
For what is your life? It is even a vapor, that appeareth for a little time, and then vanisheth away. James 4:14.

Why dost thou strive against him? for he giveth not account of any of his matters. For God speaketh once, yea twice, yet man perceiveth in not. In a dream, in a vision of the night, when deep sleep falleth upon men, in slumberings upon the bed; then he openeth the ears of men, and sealeth their instruction, that he may withdraw man from his purpose, and hide pride from man. Job 33:13-17

O the depth of the riches both of the wisdom and knowledge of God! how unsearchable are his judgments, and his ways past finding out! Rom. 11:33.

5. The king answered and said to the Chaldeans, The thing is gone from me: If ye will not make known unto me the dream, with the interpretation thereof, ye shall be cut in pieces, and your houses shall be made a dunghill.
6. But if ye show the dream, and the interpretation thereof, ye shall receive of me gifts and rewards and great honor: therefore show me the dream, and the interpretation thereof.
7. They answered again and said, Let the king tell his servants the dream, and we will show the interpretation of it.
8. The king answered and said, I know of certainty that ye would gain the time, because ye see the thing is gone from me.
9. But if ye will not make known unto me the dream, there is but one decree for you: for ye have prepared lying and corrupt words to speak before me, till the time be changed: therefore tell me the dream, and I shall know that ye can show me the interpretation thereof.
Dan. 2:5-9.
But the natural man receiveth not the things of the Spirit of God: for they are foolishness unto him: neither can he know them, because they are spiritually discerned. But he that is spiritual judgeth all things, yet he himself is judged of no man 1. Cor. 2:14, 15.

Four Hebrew Youth Bowed in Prayer.

10. The Chaldeans answered before the king, and said, There is not a man upon the earth that can show the king's matter: therefore there is no king, lord, nor ruler, that asked such things at any magician, or astrologer, or Chaldean,

11. And it is a rare thing that the king requireth, and there is none other that can show it before the king, except the gods, whose dwelling is not with flesh.

12. For this cause the king was angry and very furious, and commanded to destroy all the wise men of Babylon.

13. And the decree went forth that the wise men should be slain; and they sought Daniel and his fellows to be slain.

14. Then Daniel answered with counsel and wisdom to Arioch the captain of the king's guard which was gone forth to slay the wise men of Babylon:

15. He answered and said to Arioch the king's captain, Why is the decree so hasty from the king? Then Arioch made the thing known to Daniel.

16. Then Daniel went in and desired of the king that he would give him time, and that he would show the king interpretation.

Dan. 2:10-16.

Be not afraid of sudden fear, neither of the desolation of the wicked when it cometh. For the Lord shall be thy confidence. *Prov. 3:25, 26,*

17. Then Daniel went to his house, and make the thing known to Hananiah, Mishael, and Azariah, his companions;

The supreme moment had come to Daniel. For this very moment God had been giving him a preparation. From his birth every detail of his life had been pointing forward to this time, although he knew it not. His early education was such that at this moment when death stared him in the face, he could look up to God and claim His promise. Although Daniel when examined by Nebuchadnezzar had been accounted ten times wiser than his fellow students, he had not as yet been classed with the astrologers and wise men of Chaldea. Probably his youth and inexperience delayed such recognition. But God chooses the weak things of earth to confound the mighty, because the foolishness of God is wiser than men.

Four Hebrew youth bowed in prayer, and that [36] night "was the secret revealed unto Daniel." How could God talk with Daniel?—Because the Spirit of the Lord is with them that fear Him. Daniel's education had acquainted him with the voice of God. He was in the habit of seeing eternal things with the eye of faith. God showed Daniel the same things which He had revealed to Nebuchadnezzar, but which were hidden from him by the glamour of worldliness.

The song of praise which Tose from the lips of Daniel when the vision came, shows how self-forgetful he was, and how close his heart was knit to the heart of God.

The schools of Babylon developed pride, love of pleasure, haughtiness, and self-esteem. They fostered an aristocracy, and cultivated the spirit of oppression and slavery. Contrast with this the native simplicity, the courtesy, gentleness, and self-forgetfulness of the child of God as he enters the court and is introduced by Arioch.

Years before this, when Egypt was the educational center of the world, God taught Egyptian senators by the mouth of Joseph, a boy no older than Daniel. When Babylon had outgrown the counsels of Heaven, another

Hebrew meets the men of the schools. "Can not the wise men show the secret unto the king?"

Before Daniel was the king in his glory; around him stood the very teachers with whom he had studied three years. At this time were exemplified the words of the psalmist: "I have more understanding than all my *teachers;* for Thy testimonies are my meditation. I understand more than the ancients, because I keep Thy precepts."

Nebuchadnezzar was careworn from loss of [37] sleep, and in great anxiety because the dream troubled him; but Daniel was calm, conscious of his connection with God, the King of kings. Daniel now had opportunity to exalt his own wisdom, but he chose rather to give all the glory to God. He plainly told the king that it was beyond the power of man to reveal the dream or give the interpretation; "but there is a God in heaven that revealeth secrets, and maketh known to the king Nebuchadnezzar what shall be in the latter days." The king's mind was directed to God alone.

In one night God revealed the history of over twenty-five hundred years, and what the human historian requires volumes to explain is given in fifteen verses. The Scriptures explain themselves, and in divine records every word is well chosen and put in the proper setting.

In the image revealed to Nebuchadnezzar, the glory of the Babylonian kingdom is recognized by the Lord, and represented by the head of gold. But while giving due credit to the present state of things, the spirit of prophecy with equal candor points out to the self-exalted king the weakness of the institutions in which he has [38] placed his trust, and the inability of the Babylonian learning to save from impending destruction.

"Come down, and sit in the dust, O virgin daughter of Babylon, sit on the ground; there is no throne, O daughter of the Chaldeans; for thou shalt no more be called tender and delicate. Take the millstones and grind meal." From being master of all, Babylon must become the most humble servant. Because these people had disregarded the God of heaven, and had said, "None seeth me," evil would come

18. That they would desire mercies of the God of heaven concerning this secret; that Daniel and his fellows should not perish with the rest of the wise men of Babylon. Dan. 2:17, 18.

Let no man despise thy youth; but be thou an example of the believers, in word, in conversation, in charity, in spirit, in faith, in purity. 1. Tim. 4:12.

20. Daniel answered and said, Blessed be the name of God for ever and ever: for wisdom and might are his: 21. And he changeth the times and the seasons: he removeth kings, and setteth up kings: he giveth wisdom unto the wise, and knowledge to them that know understanding: 22. He revealeth the deep and secret things: he knoweth what is in the darkness, and the light dwelleth with him. 23. I thank thee, and praise thee, O thou God of my fathers, who hast given me wisdom and might, and hast made known unto me now what we desired of thee: for thou hast now made known unto us the king's matter. Daniel 2:19-23.

The secret of the Lord is with them that fear him; and he will show them his covenant. Psalm 25:12-14.

Rejoice in the Lord, O ye righteous: for praise is comely for the upright. Psalm 33:1.

24. Therefore Daniel went in unto Arioch, whom the king had ordained to destroy the wise men of Babylon: he went and said thus unto him: Destroy not the wise men of Babylon: bring me in before the king, and I will show unto the king the interpretation. 25. Then Arioch brought in Daniel before the king in haste, and said thus unto him, I have found a man of the captives of Judah, that will make known unto the king the interpretation. Daniel 2:24, 25.

26. The king answered and said to Daniel, whose name was Belteshazzar, Art thou able to make known unto me the dream which I have seen, and the interpretation thereof? 27. Daniel answered in the presence of the king, and said, The secret which the king hath demanded can not the wise men, the astrologers, the magicians, the soothsayers, show unto the king; 28. But there is a God in heaven that revealeth secrets, and maketh known to the king Nebuchadnezzar what shall be in the latter days. Thy dream, and the visions of thy head upon thy bed, are these; 29. As for thee, O king, thy thoughts came into thy mind upon thy bed, what should come to pass hereafter: and he that revealeth secrets maketh known to thee what shall come to pass. 30. But as for me, this secret is not revealed to me for any wisdom that I have more than any living, but for their sakes that shall make known the interpretation to the king, and that thou mightest know the thoughts of thy heart.

31. Thou, O king, sawest, and behold a great image. This great image, whose brightness was excellent, stood before thee; and the form thereof was terrible.

32. This image's head was of fine gold, his breast and his arms of silver, his belly and his thighs of brass.

33. His legs of iron, his feet part of iron and part of clay.

34. Thou sawest till that a stone was cut out without hands, which smote the image upon his feet that were of iron and clay, and brake them to pieces.

35. Then was the iron, the clay, the brass, the silver, and the gold, broken to pieces together, and became like the chaff of the summer threshing-floors; and the wind carried them away, that no place was found for them: and the stone that smote the image became a great mountain and filled the whole earth.

36. This is the dream; and we will tell the interpretation thereof before the king.

37. Thou, O king, art a king of kings: for the God of heaven hath given thee a kingdom, power, and strength, and glory.

38. And wheresoever the children of men dwell, the beasts of the field and the fowls of the heaven hath he given into thine hand, and hath made thee ruler over them all. Thou art this head of gold.

39. And after thee shall arise another kingdom inferior to thee, and another third kingdom of brass, which shall bear rule over all the earth.

40. And the fourth kingdome shall be strong as yron: forasmuch as yron breaketh in pieces and subdueth all things; and as yron that breaketh all these, shall it breake in pieces and bruise.

41. And whereas thou sawest the feete and toes, part of potters clay, and part of yron: the kingdome shalbe diuided, but there shalbe in it of the strength of the yron, forasmuch as thou sawest the yron mixt with myrie clay.

41. And as the toes of the feete were part of yron, and part of clay; so the kingdome shall be partly strong, and partly broken.

43. And whereas thou sawest yron mixt with myrie clay, they shall mingle themselues with the seede of men: but they shall not cleaue one to an other, euen as yron is not mixed with clay.

44. And in the daies of these Kings shall the God of heauen set vp a kingdome, which shall neuer be destroyed: and the Kingdome shall not be left to other people, but it shall breake in pieces, and consume all these kingdomes, and it shall stand foreuer.

45. Forasmuch as thou sawest that the stone was cut out of the mountaine without hands, and that it brake in pieces the yron, the brasse, the clay, the siluer, and the gold: the great God hath made known to the King what shall come to passe hereafter, & the dreame is certaine, and the interpretation thereof sure.

46. Then the King Nebuchadnezzar fell vpon his face, and worshipped Daniel, and commanded that they should offer an oblation, and sweet odours vnto him.

47. The King answered vnto Daniel and said, Of a trueth it is, that your God is a God of gods, and a

from unknown sources, and Babylon should be cut off. She would make a desperate effort to save herself by turning to her educators and wise men. "Let now the astrologers, the star-gazers, the monthly prognosticators, stand up and save thee from these things. . . . Behold, they shall be as stubble." When the trial came, there was nothing in all the realms of Babylon that could save it.

"The strength of nations and of individuals is not found in the opportunities and facilities that appear to make them invincible; it is not found in their boasted greatness. That which alone can make them great or strong is the power and purpose of God. They, themselves, by their attitude toward His purpose, decide their own destiny."

Nebuchadnezzar's kingdom lasted only until the reign of his grandson, when the second or inferior nation represented by the breast and arms of silver came upon the stage of action.

Medo-Persia took the place of Babylon; Grecia followed the Medo-Persian kingdom, while Rome, the fourth kingdom, was to be broken [39] into ten parts, which were to remain until the end of time. In the days of these kings the God of heaven would set up a kingdom which would never be destroyed nor conquered by any other people; it would break in pieces and consume all former kingdoms, and stand forever.

The image was a comprehensive outline of the world's history. The "glory of kingdoms" formed the head of gold, all following kingdoms deteriorated from Babylon as shown by the grade of metals forming the image. First gold, then silver, brass, and iron. In the latter part of the world's history, a marked change was revealed by the iron being mixed with miry clay. There were to be no more universal kingdoms ruled by men; when the power of the fourth kingdom was broken, it was to remain divided until the end. In place of one kingdom there would be several.

The clay mixed with iron also denoted the union of church and state. This combination is peculiar to the latter part of the world's history, to the feet and toes of the image.

Religion was the basis of government in the heathen nations; there could be no separation of the church and the

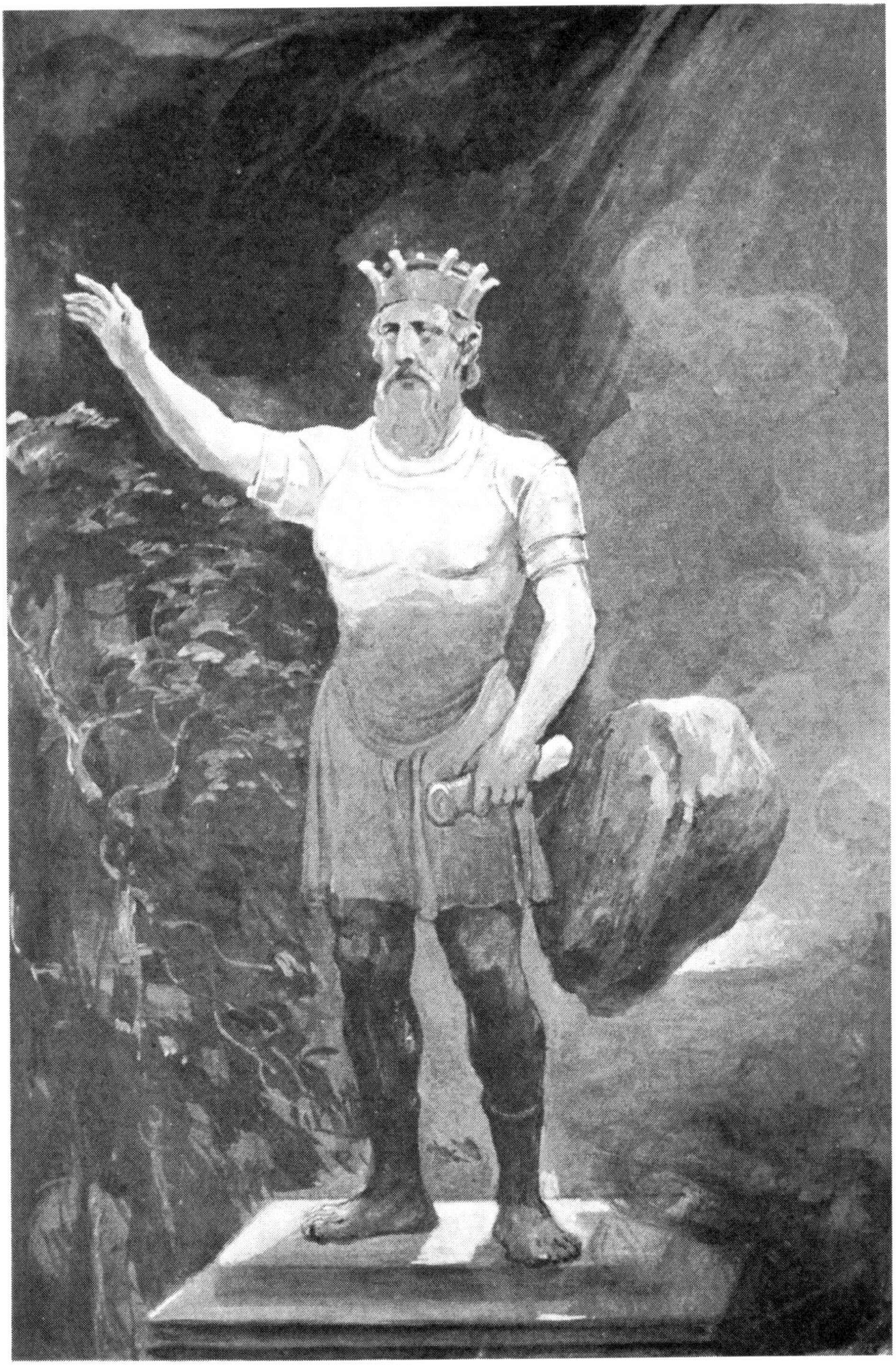

The image.

Lord of Kings, and a reuealer of secrets, seeing thou couldest reueale this secret.
48. Then the King made Daniel a great man, and gaue him many great gifts, & made him ruler ouer the whole prouince of Babylon, and chiefe of the gouernours ouer all the wise men of Babylon.
49. Then Daniel requested of the King, and he set Shadrach, Meshach, and Abednego ouer the affaires of the prouince of Babylon: but Daniel sate in the gate of the King."   Dan. 2:26-49.

The Gentiles shall come to thy light and kings to the brightness of thy rising   Isa. 60:3-5

Deut. 28:12, 13.

Deut. 15:6.

My people are destroyed for lack of knowledge.
Hosea 4:6.

Isa. 5:13.

Prov. 2:10, 11.

But as truly as I live, all the earth shall be filled with the glory of the Lord.   Num. 14:21.

Hab. 2:14

Thus saith the Lord, Let not the wise man glory in his wisdom, neither let the mighty man glory in his might, let not the rich man glory in his

state. When apostate Christianity united with the state, each remained in a sense distinct as the miry clay is separate from iron. The union continues until the stone smites the image upon the feet. The very fact that the "stone was cut out of the mountain without hands," shows that the last kingdoms on earth will not be overthrown by any earthly power, but that the God of heaven will bring upon them final destruction by giving them to the burning flames. [40]

The king listened to every sentence Daniel uttered when telling the dream, and recognized it as the vision which had troubled him. When Daniel gave the interpretation, he was certain that he could accept it as a true prophecy from the God of heaven. The vision had deeply affected the king, and when the meaning was given, he fell upon his face before Daniel in wonder and humility, and said, "Of a truth it is, that your God is a God of gods, and a Lord of kings, and a revealer of secrets, seeing thou couldest reveal this secret."

The youth of twenty-one was made ruler over all the provinces of Babylon, and chief governor over all the wise men of the kingdom. Daniel's companions were also given high positions in the government. It should be remembered that this dream as recorded in the second chapter of Daniel was given to Nebuchadnezzar in the second year of his sole reign. It was still during the lifetime of Jehoiakim, king of Judah.

It was in the providence of God that His people should carry the light of truth to all the heathen nations. What they failed to do in the time of peace, they must do in time of trouble. Babylon was the ruling power of the world; it was the educational center. The Jews were comparatively a small people; they lost the power of God by neglecting the education of their children; they failed to let their light shine. From their midst God took a few who were trained in the fear of the Lord, placed them in the heathen court, brought them into favor with the ruler of the world, so making Himself known to the heathen king,. He did even more; He revealed Himself to the king, and used these children [41] of His to prove that the wisdom of God excelled the wisdom of the Chaldeans. Having exalted true education,

He put Daniel and his companions at the head of that vast empire that the knowledge of the. God of heaven might go to the ends of the earth.

Having acknowledged the God of Daniel, Nebuchadnezzar was in a position to save Jerusalem instead of destroying it. It was because of these experiences that God could send word by His prophet a few years later that, should Zedekiah, king of Judah, deliver himself to the king of Babylon, Jerusalem would not be burned, and the world would receive the light of the gospel.

The history of the city of Babylon is put on record because it is God's object lesson to the world to-day. The book of Revelation, which is the complement of the book of Daniel, frequently uses the name Babylon, applying it to the modern churches. The relation of the Jews to the Babylon of Nebuchadnezzar is the same as that sustained by the remnant church, the true Israel, to the churches which, having known the truth, have rejected it.

The sins of ancient Babylon will be repeated to-day. Her educational system is the one now [42] generally accepted; her government, with its excessive taxes, its exaltation of the rich and the oppression of the poor, its pride, arrogance, love of display, its choice of the artificial in place of the natural, and the exaltation of the God of science instead of the God of heaven, is the one toward which the world of to-day is hastening.

As God called Abraham out of the idolatry of Chaldea, and made him the father of the Hebrew nation; as he delivered to that people a form of government that would exalt God; as he gave them commandment so to teach their children that the Jewish nation might become the teacher of nations and might be an everlasting kingdom, so to-day He calls forth a people from modern Babylon. He has entrusted to them principles of healthful living which will make them mentally and physically a wonder to the world. He has given them educational principles, which, if followed, wilt make them the teachers of the world, and finally bring them into the kingdom of God. And to them He has

riches. but let him that glorieth, glory in this, that hee vnderstandeth and knoweth me, that I am the Lord which exercise louing kindnesse, iudgement and righteousnesse in the earth: for in these things I delight, saith the Lord.

Jer. 9:23, 24.

And all nations shall serue him and his sonne, and his sonnes sonne, vntill the very time of his land come: and then many nations and great kings shall serue themselues of him.

Jer 27:7.

Then said Jeremiah unto Zedekiah, Thus saith the Lord the God of hostes, the God of Israel, If thou wilt assuredly goe foorth unto the king of Babylons Princes, then thy soule shall liue, and this Citie shall not be burnt with fire, and thou shalt liue, and thine house. But if thou wilt not goe foorth to the king of Babylons Princes, then shall this City be giuen into the hand of the Caldeans, and they shall burne it with fire, and thou shalt not escape out of their hand.

Jer 38:17-18:.

Babylon is fallen, is fallen, and all the grauen images of her Gods he hath broken unto the ground.

Isa 21:9.

And there followed another Angel, saying, Babylon is fallen, is fallen, that great citie, because she made all nations drinke of the wine of the wrath of her fornication. Rev 14:8.

Babylon hath beene a golden cup in the Lords hand, that made all the earth drunken: the nations haue drunken of her wine, therefore the nations are mad. Jer 51:7.

Rev. 17:4.

That thou shalt take up this proverb against the king of Babylo, and say, How hath the oppressor ceased! Isa. 14:4, margin.

And saying, Alas, alas, that great city, that was clothed in fine linnen, and purple and scarlet, and decked with gold, and pretious stones, and pearles: For in one houre so great riches is come to naught. Rev 18:16, 17.

Gen. 12:1.
Joshua 24:2, 3.
Deut. 6:6, 7.
Ps. 105:22.
Rev. 18:1-4.

For thou art an holy people unto the Lord thy God, and the Lord hath chosen thee to be a peculiar people unto himselfe, aboue all the nations that are vpon the earth. Thou shalt not eate any abominable thing. Deut 14:1-3.
Lev. 11:44.
1 Pet. 2:9.

Keep therefore and do them; for this is your wisdom and your understanding in the sight of the nations which shall hear all these statutes, and say, Surely this great nation is a wise and understanding people. For what nation is there so great, who hath God so nigh unto them, as the Lord our God is in all things that we call upon him for? Deut 4:5-8.

For many are called but few are chosen. Matt. 22:14.

delivered the principles of true government, which recognize the equal rights of all men, and which in the church organization binds all together —one body in Christ Jesus.

Only a few—four out of thousands—were true to these principles in the days of Daniel. How will it be to-day? [43]

CHAPTER 3

TRUE FREEDOM IN WORSHIP

"NEBUCHADNEZZAR the king made an image of gold." According to Usher's chronology, it had been twenty-three years since the dream as recorded in the second chapter of Daniel had been given to this same Nebuchadnezzar. As a result of the experience at that time, Daniel was made counselor, sitting in the gate of the king, and Shadrach, Meshach, and Abed-nego were appointed rulers in the province of Babylon. Many opportunities had presented themselves to these men of God, and they had kept the knowledge of their God before the people of Babylon. Jerusalem had in the meantime been destroyed. The Jews, as a nation, were scattered throughout the kingdom of Nebuchadnezzar; their king, Jehoiachin, languished in one of the prisons of Babylon. It was a time of sorrow and mourning for the chosen people of God. Could it be that they were forgotten by Him who smote Egypt, and led the hosts across the Red Sea? As far as human eyes could see, it was true. [44]

Nebuchadnezzar had been humbled when Daniel interpreted his dream; he had then worshiped God; but as the years passed, he lost the spirit which characterized true worship, and while in the mind acknowledging the God of the Jews, in his heart he was pagan still. He made an image of gold, patterning it as closely as possible after the image revealed to him in his dream, at the same time gratifying his own pride, for the entire figure was gold. There was no trace of the other kingdoms which were represented by the silver, the brass, the iron, and the clay in the dream. It stood on the plain of Dura, rising at least one hundred feet above the surrounding country, and visible for miles in every direction.

The decree was issued by Nebuchadnezzar, calling to the capitol the governors and rulers of provinces from all over the world. He, the ruler of kingdoms, thus showed his

1. Nebuchadnezzar the king made an image of gold, whose height was threescore cubits, and the breadth thereof six cubits; he set it up in the plain of Dura, in the province of Babylon.
2. Then Nebuchadnezzar the king sent to gather together the satraps, the prefects, the governors, the counselors, the treasurers, the judges, the justices, and all the officials of the provinces, to come to the dedication of the image which Nebuchadnezzar the king had set up.
3. Then were gathered the satraps, the prefects, the governors, the counselors, the treasurers, the judges, the justices, and all the officials of the provinces, to the dedication of the image that Nebuchadnezzar the king had set up. And they stood before the image that Nebuchadnezzar had set up.
4. Then a herald cried aloud, To you it is commanded, O people, nations, and languages,
5. That at what time you hear the sound of the horn, the pipe, zither, the lyre, harp, bagpipe, and all kinds of music, you shall fall down and worship the golden image that Nebuchadnezzar the king has set up.
6. And whoever does not fall down and worship, at that moment they will be thrown into the middle of a burning fiery furnace.
Dan 3:1-6.

Thou shalt love the Lord thy God with all thy heart, and with all thy soul, and with all thy strength, and with all thy mind; and thy neighbour as thyself."
Luke 10:27:.

No man can serve two masters: for either he will hate the one, and love the other; or else he will hold to the one, and despise the other. Ye cannot serve God and mammon.
Mat 6:24.

For whosoever exalteth himself, shall be abased.
Luke 14:11.

Let every soul be subject unto the higher powers. For there is no power but of God: the powers that be are ordained of God.
Rom 13:1.

Therefore at that time, when all the people heard the sound of the cornet, flute, harp, sackbut, psaltery, and all kinds of musick, all the people, the nations, and the languages, fell down and worshipped the golden image that Nebuchadnezzar the king had set up.
Dan 3:7.

Ps. 33:13-15.

For whatsoever things were written aforetime were written for our learning, that we through patience and comfort of the scriptures might have hope.
Rom 15:4.

Put them in mind to be subject to principalities and powers, to obey magistrates, to be ready to every good work.
Titus 3:1.

Thou shalt not make unto thee any graven image, or any likeness of any thing that is in heaven above, or that is in the earth beneath, or that is in the water under the earth: Thou shalt not bow down thyself to them, nor serve them: for I the LORD thy God am a jealous God, visiting the iniquity of the fathers upon the children unto the third and fourth generation of them that hate me.
Exo 20:4-5.
John 4:24.

And the LORD commanded me at that time to teach you statutes and judgments, that ye might do them in the land whither ye go over to possess it. Take ye therefore good heed unto yourselves; for ye saw no manner of similitude on the day that the LORD spake unto you in Horeb out of the midst of the fire: Lest ye corrupt yourselves, and make you a graven image, the similitude of any figure, the likeness of male or female, The likeness of any beast that is on the earth, the likeness of any winged fowl that flieth in the air, The likeness of any thing that creepeth on the ground, the likeness of any fish that is in the waters beneath the earth: And lest thou lift up thine eyes unto heaven, and when thou seest the sun, and the moon, and the stars, even all the host of heaven, shouldest be driven to worship them, and serve them, which the LORD thy God hath divided unto all nations under the whole heaven.
Deu 4:14-19: "
His own iniquities shall take the wicked himself, and he shall be holden with the cords of his sins.
Prov 5:22.

Rom. 6:23.

For the love of Christ constraineth us; because we thus judge, that if one died for all, then were all dead.
2Cor 5:14:.

authority. It was a great occasion, and subject kings and governors dared not disobey the mandates of this universal king.

Heaven was watching with intense interest, for this was the occasion when the highest worldly authority was to meet the government of God.

Babylon was not only the greatest and most powerful government in the days of Nebuchadnezzar, but it was a symbol of earthly governments of all time; and for that reason we have the record as given in the third chapter of Daniel.

As a king, he had a perfect right to call his subjects together. As subjects, it was the duty of those who were called, to obey.

When that great company had gathered [45] around the image on the broad plain, the voice of the herald was heard: "At what time ye hear the sound... of all kinds of music, ye fall down and worship the golden image...Whoso falleth not down and worshipeth shall the same hour be cast into the midst of a burning fiery furnace," "God is a spirit and they that worship Him must worship Him in spirit." But of spiritual worship, paganism is entirely ignorant. Except there be some form, some image before which they can bow, there can be, to them, no worship. It was wholly in accordance with the religion, the education, and the government of Babylon, for the king to erect an image such as he did. It was wholly in harmony with the custom—educational, religious, and civil—for the people in general to respect a command to worship such an image.

While it was in harmony with worldly government, it was not, however, according to the principles of the heavenly government. Hence it is that again, in the person of the Babylonian king, Satan is challenging the government of God. When Lucifer and his angels refused to bow before the throne of God, the Father did not [46] then destroy them. They were permitted to live until death should come as a result of the course they pursued. The Babylonian king, however, threatened utter destruction to all who refused to worship his golden image. The motive power in the heavenly government is love; human power, when exercised, becomes tyranny. All tyranny is a repetition of the Babylonian principles. We sometimes call it papal; it is likewise Babylonian. When the civil power enforces worship of any sort, be that worship true or false in itself, to obey is idolatry. The command must be backed by some form of punishment,—a fiery furnace,—and the conscience of man is no longer free. From a civil standpoint, such legislation is tyranny; looked at from a religious point of view, it is persecution.

The vast throng fell prostrate before the image, but Shadrach, Meshach, and Abed-nego remained erect. Then it was that certain Chaldeans, teachers in the realm, jealous of the position and power of these Hebrews, having waited for a chance to accuse them, said to the king, "There are certain Jews whom thou hast set over the affairs of the province of Babylon, . . . these men have not regarded thee."

Can it be, thought the king, that when the image is made after the pattern of the one shown me by the God of the Jews, those men, Shadrach, Meshach, and Abed-nego, have failed to worship at my command? Can it be possible that when I have elevated those men, who were only slaves, to high positions in the government, they disregard my laws? The thought rankled in the heart of the king. Self-exaltation brooks no opposition, and the men [47] were called forthwith into the presence of Nebuchadnezzar.

Can it be true, O Shadrach, Meshach, and Abed-nego, after all that has been done for you, that ye do not serve my gods nor worship the image which I have set up? The reason for making the image was doubtless explained, and another opportunity ofered them in which they might redeem the past offense. But if it was wilful disregard of authority, the law of the land should be enforced. The furnace was pointed to by the king as awaiting traitors and rebels.

What a test of the fidelity of these three companions of Daniel! They realized that they were in the presence of not only the richest monarch of earth, and that disobedience meant death, and before the assembled multitudes on the plain of Dura, but they were a spectacle to God, to angels, and to the inhabitants of other worlds. The whole

Choose you this day whom ye will serve.
Joshua 24:15.

The Spirit and the bride say, Come. And let him that heareth say, Come. And let him that is athirst come. And whosoever will, let him take the water of life freely. Rev 22:17.

8. Wherefore at that time certain Chaldeans came near, and accused the Jews.
9. They spake and said to the king Nebuchadnezzar, O king, live for ever.
10. Thou, O king, hast made a decree, that every man that shall hear the sound of the cornet, flute, harp, sackbut, psaltery, and dulcimer, and all kinds of musick, shall fall down and worship the golden image:
11. And whoso falleth not down and worshippeth, that he should be cast into the midst of a burning fiery furnace.
12. There are certain Jews whom thou hast set over the affairs of the province of Babylon, Shadrach, Meshach, and Abednego; these men, O king, have not regarded thee: they serve not thy gods, nor worship the golden image which thou hast set up.
Dan 3:8-12.

Settle it therefore in your hearts, not to meditate before what ye shall answer: For I will give you a mouth and wisdom, which all your adversaries shall not be able to gainsay nor resist. Luk 21:14-15.

For their redeemer is mighty; he shall plead their cause with thee. Prov 23:11.

13. Then Nebuchadnezzar in his rage and fury commanded to bring Shadrach, Meshach, and Abednego. Then they brought these men before the king.
14. Nebuchadnezzar spake and said unto them, Is it true, O Shadrach, Meshach, and Abednego, do not ye serve my gods, nor worship the golden image which I have set up?
15. Now if ye be ready that at what time ye hear the sound of the cornet, flute, harp, sackbut, psaltery, and dulcimer, and all kinds of musick, ye fall down and worship the image which I have made; well: but if ye worship not, ye shall be cast the same hour into the midst of a burning fiery furnace; and who is that God that shall deliver you out of my hands?
16. Shadrach, Meshach, and Abednego, answered and said to the king, O Nebuchadnezzar, we are not careful to answer thee in this matter.

Shadrach, Meshach, and Abed-nego, remained erect.

universe was watching with inexpressible interest to see what these men would do. The controversy was not between man and Satan, but between Christ and Satan, and eternal principles were at stake. Men were actors in the contest. They could stand as witnesses either for Christ or for Satan in this time of decision. Would they allow an unsanctified emotion to have possession of their lives, and compromise their faith? What could a religion be worth which admitted of compromise? What can any religion be worth if it does not teach loyalty to the God of heaven? What is there of any real value in the world, especially when on the very borders of eternity, unless it be God's acknowledgment of us as His children?

These Hebrew youth had learned from the history of God's dealings with the Israelites in times past, that disobedience brought only dishonor, disaster, and ruin; and that

17. If it be so, our God whom we serve is able to deliver us from the burning fiery furnace, and he will deliver us out of thine hand, O king.

Dan 3:13-17.

Isa. 43:10.
Matt. 10:32.
Matt. 16:26.
2 Chroni. 20:20.

18. But if not, be it known unto thee, O king, that we will not serve thy gods, nor worship the golden image which thou hast set up.

19. Then was Nebuchadnezzar full of fury, and the form of his visage was changed against Shadrach, Meshach, and Abednego: therefore he spake, and

the fear of the Lord was not only the beginning of wisdom, but the basis of all true prosperity. They therefore calmly and respectfully told the king that they would not worship his golden image, and that they had faith that their God was able to protect them.

The king was angry. His proud spirit could not tolerate this refusal to obey his decree. He ordered that the furnace be heated seven times - hotter than usual, and that the most mighty men of his army bind these three Hebrews and throw them into the fire. This was done, but God in this act began to vindicate His faithful children. The furnace was so exceedingly hot [49] that the mighty men who cast the Hebrews into the fire were themselves destroyed by the intense heat.

God suffered not envy and hatred to prevail against His children. How often have the enemies of God united their strength and wisdom to destroy the character and influence of a few humble, trusting persons! But nothing can prevail against those who are strong in the Lord. The promise is, "The wrath of man shall praise Thee."

God preserved His servants in the midst of the flames, and the attempt to force them into idolatry resulted in bringing the knowledge of the true God before the assemblage of princes and rulers of the vast kingdom of Babylon. "This is the victory that overcometh the world, even our faith.." All things are possible to those who believe. "What things soever ye desire, when ye pray, believe that ye receive them, and ye shall have them." God may not always work deliverance in the way that *we* think best, but He who sees everything from the beginning, knows what will bring honor and praise to His name.

Suddenly the king became pale with terror. He looked intently into the midst of the fiery furnace, and turned to those near him with the words, "Did we not cast three men bound into the midst of the fire?" They answered, "True, O king." The king then said, "Lo, I see four men loose, walking in the midst of the fire, and they have no hurt; and the form of the fourth is like the Son of God."

How did the king recognize the form of the Son of God? Evidently by the teachings of the [50] Jews in the court

commanded that they should heat the furnace one seven times more than it was wont to be heated.
20. And he commanded the most mighty men that were in his army to bind Shadrach, Meshach, and Abednego, and to cast them into the burning fiery furnace.
21. Then these men were bound in their coats, their hosen, and their hats, and their other garments, and were cast into the midst of the burning fiery furnace.
22. Therefore because the king's commandment was urgent, and the furnace exceeding hot, the flame of the fire slew those men that took up Shadrach, Meshach, and Abednego.

Dan 3:18-22.

For a just man falleth seven times, and riseth up again: but the wicked shall fall into mischief.
Prov 24:16.

Though he fall, he shall not be utterly cast down: for the LORD upholdeth him with his hand.
Ps 37:24.

Ps. 76:10.

And these three men, Shadrach, Meshach, and Abednego, fell down bound into the midst of the burning fiery furnace.   Dan 3:23.

When thou passest through the waters, I will be with thee; and through the rivers, they shall not overflow thee: when thou walkest through the fire, thou shalt not be burned; neither shall the flame kindle upon thee.   Isa 43:2.

1 John 5:4.
Mark 11:24.

24. Then Nebuchadnezzar the king was astonied, and rose up in haste, and spake, and said unto his counsellors, Did not we cast three men bound into the midst of the fire? They answered and said unto the king, True, O king.
25. He answered and said, Lo, I see four men loose, walking in the midst of the fire, and they have no hurt; and the form of the fourth is like the Son of God.
Dan 3:24-25.

Ps. 18:48.

Ye are our epistle written in our hearts, known and read of all men: Forasmuch as ye are manifestly declared to be the epistle of Christ ministered by us, written not with ink, but with the

Spirit of the living God; not in tables of stone, but in fleshy tables of the heart.

2Cor 3:2-3.

Now then we are ambassadors for Christ, as though God did beseech you by us: we pray you in Christ's stead, be ye reconciled to God.

2Cor 5:20.

Out of the abundance of the heart the mouth speaketh. A good man out of the good treasure of the heart bringeth forth good things.

Mat 12:34-35.

The angel of the LORD encampeth round about them that fear him, and delivereth them.

Ps 34:7.

He that loveth pureness of heart, for the grace of his lips the king shall be his friend.

Prov 22:11.

Let your light so shine before men, that they may see your good works, and glorify your Father which is in heaven.

Mat 5:16.

26. Then Nebuchadnezzar came near to the mouth of the burning fiery furnace, and spake, and said, Shadrach, Meshach, and Abednego, ye servants of the most high God, come forth, and come hither. Then Shadrach, Meshach, and Abednego, came forth of the midst of the fire.

27. And the princes, governors, and captains, and the king's counsellors, being gathered together, saw these men, upon whose bodies the fire had no power, nor was an hair of their head singed, neither were their coats changed, nor the smell of fire had passed on them.

28. Then Nebuchadnezzar spake, and said, Blessed be the God of Shadrach, Meshach, and Abednego, who hath sent his angel, and delivered his servants that trusted in him, and have changed the king's word, and yielded their bodies, that they might not serve nor worship any god, except their own God.

Dan 3:26-28.

of Babylon and in remembrance of his vision. Daniel and his companions had ever sought to bring before the king, the princes, and the wise men of Babylon, a knowledge of the true God. These Hebrews, holding high positions in the government, had been associated with the king; and as they were not ashamed of their God, they had honored and given glory to the Lord whenever opportunity afforded. The king had heard from their lips descriptions of the glorious Being whom they served; and it was from this instruction that he was able to recognize the fourth person in the fire as the Son of God. The king also understood the ministry of angels, and now believed that angels had interfered in behalf of these faithful men who would yield their bodies to punishment rather than consent with their minds to serve or worship any God but their own. These men were true missionaries. They held honored positions in the government, and at the same time let the light of the gospel shine through their lives. This miracle was one of the results of their godly lives.

With bitter remorse and feelings of humility, the king approached the furnace and exclaimed, "Shadrach, Meshach, and Abed-nego, ye servants of the most high God, come forth, and come hither." They did so, and all the hosts on the plain of Dura were witnesses to the fact that not even the smell of fire was upon their garments, and not a hair of their head had been singed. God had triumphed through the constancy of his faithful servants. The magnificent image was forgotten by the people in their wonder, and solemnity pervaded the assembly. [51]

What the Jews as a nation had failed to do in proclaiming the truth to the nations of the world, God accomplished under the most trying circumstances, with only three men. The story of the miraculous deliverance was told to the ends of the earth. The principles of religious liberty and freedom of conscience were known. The history of the Jews was passed from mouth to mouth as those unacquainted with the three Hebrews asked who they were and how they came into Babylon. The Sabbath was proclaimed. The story of Jewish

"He looked intently into the fiery furnace."

But before all these, they shall lay their hands on you, and persecute you, delivering you up to the synagogues, and into prisons, being brought before kings and rulers for my name's sake. And it shall turn to you for a testimony.

Luke 21:12-13.

They shall speak of the glory of thy kingdom, and talk of thy power; To make known to the sons of men his mighty acts, and the glorious majesty of his kingdom. Thy kingdom is an everlasting kingdom, and thy dominion endureth throughout all generations. The LORD upholdeth all that fall, and raiseth up all those that be bowed down.

Ps 145:11-14.

Having your conversation honest among the Gentiles: that, whereas they speak against you as evildoers, they may by your good works, which they shall behold, glorify God in the day of visitation.

1Pet 2:12.

Prov. 21:1.

Therefore I make a decree, That every people, nation, and language, which speak any thing amiss against the God of Shadrach, Meshach, and Abednego, shall be cut in pieces, and their houses shall be made a dunghill: because there is no other God that can deliver after this sort.

Dan 3:29.

Jer. 37:8-10.

Jer. 38:3.

Jer. 38:14-23.

Jer. 38:14-17.

education was made known. The glory of Babylon was for the time forgotten as the splendor of the heavenly kingdom and the principles of God's government became the absorbing theme. Without doubt some men dated their conversion from that day, and forces were set in operation which paved the way for the return of the Jews a few years later.

Again the heathen monarch is brought to acknowledge the power of the King of heaven. When Daniel interpreted the dream, worldly wisdom and the learning of the Babylonian schools fell before the simple gospel teaching as carried out by faithful mothers in Israel. When the three Hebrews were saved from the heat of the furnace, the principles of God's government —true Protestantism, as it would be called today—were proclaimed before the nations of the earth.

It was only a partial appreciation of these principles which Nebuchadnezzar at first gained; nevertheless it led to the decree that throughout the whole dominion, wherever a Jew might be living, no man should speak against the God of [52] Shadrach, Meshach, and Abed-nego. This gave freedom to every believer to worship unmolested. Satan, in attempting to destroy the Hebrews, had overstepped the bounds, and in place of the death of three, life was granted to thousands.

Usher's chronology gives the date of the issuing of this decree as twenty-six years after Daniel was carried captive to Babylon; but it is very probable that the exact date was the time the prophet Jeremiah told Zedekiah, king of Judah, if he would deliver himself into the hands of the king of Babylon's princes, Jerusalem would not be destroyed. Only a short time before the same prophet had come to Zedekiah, saying, "Thus saith the Lord; 'Deceive not yourselves, saying, The Chaldeans shall surely depart from us; for they shall not depart, for though ye had smitten the whole army of the Chaldeans that fight against you, and there remained but wounded men among them, yet should they rise up every man in his tent, and *burn this city with fire.*'"

No doubt it seemed strange to Zedekiah that the same prophet a little later, should come to him again saying, "Thus saith the Lord, the God of hosts, the God of Israel,

'If thou wilt assuredly go forth unto the king of Babylon's princes, then thy soul shall live, and this city *shall not be burned with fire;* and thou shalt live and thine house.'"

Zedekiah walked by sight and not by faith, and for lack of faith to believe God, he lost everything. His sight beheld only the Babylonian army and the Jews, and he feared to obey Faith would have led him to obey the command of God, irrespective of any [53] obstacles that sight may have presented.

God never commands us to perform impossibilities; He always with the command prepares the way, if we by faith will go forward and obey. If Zedekiah had only known that a decree had been issued in Babylon forbidding any one to *even speak a word* against the God of the Hebrews, he would, no doubt, have quickly obeyed.

God had made every provision to spare Jerusalem, the city of His choice, and the temple where His visible presence had abode for so many years. But Heaven's plans were frustrated by the doubting heart of the one whom God had trusted with the oversight of His work in the earth. In vain did the prophet of the Lord plead, "Obey, I beseech thee, the voice of the Lord which I speak unto thee." But Zedekiah's eyes were blinded by earthly things, he measured the message from God by his own mind. He saw only seeming contradiction in the message, which, if believed, carried the glad tidings of victory. If Zedekiah had gone forth to the Chaldeans no one would have dared lay hands upon him, but like many others he lost the opportunity of a life time by fearing to trust God. Notwithstanding the fact that the Lord's prophet told him plainly that if he failed to obey he would cause Jerusalem to be burned with fire, still he was afraid to obey the word of the Lord.

Zedekiah was a stranger to the faith that enabled Shadrach, Meshach, and Abed-nego to enter the fiery furnace rather than dishonor their Lord.

The trial on the plains of Dura was the crowning act in the lives of the three Hebrews. We are told that they were advanced to higher positions [54] in the province of Babylon, but we hear nothing further of them. In the testing time they

---

Have faith in God. Verily I say unto you, That whosoever shall say unto this mountain, Be thou removed, and be thou cast into the sea; and shall not doubt in his heart, but shall believe that those things which he saith shall come to pass; he shall have whatsoever he saith. Therefore I say unto you, What things soever ye desire, when ye pray, believe that ye receive them, and ye shall have them.　　　　　　　　　　　Mar 11:22-24.

Be still, and know that I am God: I will be exalted among the heathen, I will be exalted in the earth.
　　　　　　　　　　　　　　　　　Ps 46:10.
Dan. 3:19-30.

And there I will meet with thee, and I will commune with thee from above the mercy seat, from between the two cherubims which are upon the ark of the testimony, of all things which I will give thee in commandment unto the children of Israel.
　　　　　　　　　　　　　　　　　Exo 25:22.

Jer. 38:20.

Trust ye in the Lord for ever: for in the Lord Jehovah is everlasting strength.
　　　　　　　　　　　　　　　　　Isa 26:4.

Jer. 39:5-20.

When a man's ways please the LORD, he maketh even his enemies to be at peace with him.
　　　　　　　　　　　　　　　　　Prov 16:7.

We can do nothing against the truth, but for the truth.　　　　　　　　　　　　2 Cor. 13:8.
Jer. 38:23.

I say, Have they not heard? Yes verily, their sound went into all the earth, and their words unto the ends of the world.
　　　　　　　　　　　　　　　　　Rom 10:18.

Ps. 19:3, 4.

Then the king promoted Shadrach, Meshach, and Abednego, in the province of Babylon.
　　　　　　　　　　　　　　　　　Dan 3:30.

Trust in the LORD, and do good; so shalt thou dwell in the land, and verily thou shalt be fed.

Ps 37:3.

Shew thy marvellous lovingkindness, O thou that savest by thy right hand them which put their trust in thee from those that rise up against them.

Ps 17:7.

Mark 6:51, 52.

For the eyes of the LORD run to and fro throughout the whole earth, to shew himself strong in the behalf of them whose heart is perfect toward him. Herein thou hast done foolishly: therefore from henceforth thou shalt have wars.

2 Chron. 16:9.

Our God whom we serve is able to deliver us.

Dan 3:17:.

Jer. 31:19.
Isa. 59:1.

The eyes of the Lord are upon the righteous, and his ears are open unto their cry.

Ps 34:15.

I will make a man more precious than fine gold; even a man than the golden wedge of Ophir.

Isa 13:12.

James 5:17.

Whatsoever thy hand findeth to do, do it with thy might; for there is no work, nor device, nor knowledge, nor wisdom, in the grave, whither thou goest."

Eccl 9:10.

Whatsoever things were written aforetime were written for our learning.

Rom 15:4.

Thus saith the high and lofty One that inhabiteth eternity, whose name is Holy; I dwell in the high and holy place, with him also that is of a contrite and humble spirit, to revive the spirit of the humble, and to revive the heart of the contrite ones.

Isa 57:15.

My son, attend to my words; incline thine ear unto my sayings. Let them not depart from thine eyes; keep them in the midst of thine heart. For they are life unto those that find them, and health to all their flesh.

Prov 4:20-22.

Be not wise in thine own eyes: fear the LORD, and depart from evil. It shall be health to thy navel, and marrow to thy bones.

Prov 3:7-8.

did not know that the Lord would deliver them from the furnace, but they had faith to believe that He had power to do it if it were His will to do so. In such times it takes more faith to trust that God will bring about His purposes in His own way than it does to believe in our own way. It is the absence of this faith and trust in critical times, which brings perplexity, distress, fear, and surmising of evil. God is ever ready to do great things for His people when they put their trust in Him. "Godliness with contentment is great gain."

Seldom are we placed in the same circumstances twice. Abraham, Moses, Elijah, Daniel, and others were sorely tried, even unto death, yet each test came in a different way. Every individual has an experience peculiar to his own character and circumstances. God has a work to accomplish in the life of each individual. Every act, however small, has its place in our life experience. God is more than willing to guide us in the right way. He has not closed the windows of heaven to prayer, but his ears are ever open to the cries of His children, and His eye watches every movement of Satan to counteract His work.

Shadrach, Meshach, and Abed-nego were men of like passions with ourselves. Their lives are given to show what man may become even in this life, if he will make God his strength and wisely improve the opportunities within his reach. Among the captives of the king who had similar advantages, only Daniel and his three companions bent all their energies to seek wisdom [55] and knowledge from God as revealed in His Word and works. Although they afterward held high positions of trust, they were neither proud nor self-sufficient. They had a living connection with God, loving, fearing, and obeying Him. They allowed their light to shine in undimmed luster, while occupying positions of responsibility. Amid all the temptations and fascinations of the court, they stood firm as a rock in adherence to principle.

A direct compliance with Bible requirements, and a faith in God, will bring strength to both the will and the body. The fruit of the Spirit is not only love, joy, and peace, but temperance also. If these youth had compromised with the heathen officers at first, and yielded to the pressure of the occasion by eating and drinking according to the custom of the Babylonians, contrary to God's requirements, that one wrong step would undoubtedly have led to others, until their consciences would have been seared, and they would have been turned into wrong paths. Faithfulness in this one point prepared them to withstand greater temptation, until finally they stood firm in this crucial test on the plain of Dura.

The third chapter of Daniel may be studied with profit in connection with the message referred to in the thirteenth chapter of Revelation. The principles are the same in both. All the world was called to worship the image set up in the province of Babylon; refusing, they would suffer death. In Revelation there is brought to view an image to the beast,—governments on earth which will frame laws contrary to the requirements of God. Life and power will be [56] given to this image, and it shall both speak and decree that as many as will not worship it shall be put to death. All, small and great, rich and poor, free and bond, will be required to receive a mark in the right hand or in the forehead. Men will be disfranchised for not worshiping this image; for no one will be allowed to buy or sell who has not the mark, or the name of the beast, or the number of his name.

Who will be able to stand the test when this decree to worship the image to the beast is enforced? Who will choose rather to "suffer affliction with the people of God than to enjoy the pleasures of sin for a season"? What children are now being trained and educated in these principles of integrity to God? From what homes will come the Daniels and Meshachs? This will be the final test brought upon the servants of God. The scenes portrayed in the third chapter of Daniel are but a miniature representation of those trials into which the people of God are coming as the end approaches. [57]

Gal. 6:22, 23.
Prov. 23:20, 21.
1 Tim. 4:2.

And shall begin to smite his fellowservants, and to eat and drink with the drunken; The lord of that servant shall come in a day when he looketh not for him, and in an hour that he is not aware of, And shall cut him asunder, and appoint him his portion with the hypocrites.
Matt 24:49-51.

And the third angel followed them, saying with a loud voice, If any man worship the beast and his image, and receive his mark in his forehead, or in his hand. Rev 14:9.

And deceiveth them that dwell on the earth by the means of those miracles which he had power to do in the sight of the beast; saying to them that dwell on the earth, that they should make an image to the beast, which had the wound by a sword, and did live. And he had power to give life unto the image of the beast, that the image of the beast should both speak, and cause that as many as would not worship the image of the beast should be killed. And he causeth all, both small and great, rich and poor, free and bond, to receive a mark in their right hand, or in their foreheads: And that no man might buy or sell, save he that had the mark, or the name of the beast, or the number of his name. Rev 13:14-17.

Who art thou that judgest another man's servant? to his own master he standeth or falleth. Yea, he shall be holden up: for God is able to make him stand. Rom 14:4.

Choosing rather to suffer affliction with the people of God, than to enjoy the pleasures of sin for a season; Esteeming the reproach of Christ greater riches than the treasures in Egypt: for he had respect unto the recompence of the reward. By faith he forsook Egypt, not fearing the wrath of the king: for he endured, as seeing him who is invisible. Heb 11:25-27.

Train up a child in the way he should go: and when he is old, he will not depart from it. Prov 22:6.
There shall be a time of trouble, such as never was since there was a nation even to that same time: and at that time thy people shall be delivered, every one that shall be found written in the book. Dan 12:1.

THE MOST HIGH RULETH

THE fourth chapter of Daniel is, in some respects, the most wonderful chapter in the Bible. It is a public document written by Nebuchadnezzar, king of Babylon, after his humiliation by the God of heaven. It was sent "unto all people, nations, and languages, that dwell in all the earth." It therefore comes to us with as much freshness and vitality as though it were issued to the generation in which we live. The object was, says Nebuchadnezzar, "to show the signs and wonders that the high God hath wrought towards me." Contemplating what had been done, he exclaimed in language similar to that of the apostle Paul, "How great are His signs! His kingdom is an everlasting kingdom, and His dominion is from generation to generation."

Nebuchadnezzar's reign had been one long scene of warfare. He was a man of war. This characteristic was so prominent in the life of the great king that prophecy calls him "the terrible [58] of the nations," and the "hammer of the whole earth." He had met foes on every side and had been successful, because God had put His "sword into the hand of the king of Babylon," and had made use of this monarch to punish other nations which had refused the light of truth. To illustrate: For thirteen years the city of Tyre resisted every effort made by Nebuchadnezzar. Finally he was successful, but gained no spoils, for Tyre, captured on the seacoast, removed to an island. Although Nebuchadnezzar knew it not, he was fulfilling prophecy in the destruction of Tyre. The Lord rewarded him for this work by sending word to him through the prophet Ezekiel that he could have the spoil of Egypt as wages for his army while destroying Tyre,

1. Nebuchadnezzar the king, unto all people, nations, and languages, that dwell in all the earth; Peace be multiplied unto you.
2. I thought it good to shew the signs and wonders that the high God hath wrought toward me.
3. How great are his signs! and how mighty are his wonders! his kingdom is an everlasting kingdom, and his dominion is from generation to generation.
Dan 4:1-3.

Now all these things happened unto them for ensamples: and they are written for our admonition, upon whom the ends of the world are come.
1 Cor. 10:11.

Dan. 2:44, 45.
2 Peter 1:11.

Eze. 30:10, 11.

Jer. 50:23.
Eze. 32:12.
Eze. 30:25.

And it came to pass in the seven and twentieth year, in the first month, in the first day of the month, the word of the Lord came unto me, saying, Son of man, Nebuchadnezzar king of Babylon caused his army to serve a great service against Tyrus: yet had he no wages, nor his army. Therefore thus saith the Lord God; Behold, I will give the land of Egypt unto Nebuchadnezzar king of Babylon; and he shall take her multitude, and take her spoil, and take her prey; and it shall be the wages for his army. Ezek 29:17-21.

for Egypt as well as Tyre had rejected the knowledge of the true God. Then Nebuchadnezzar turned his arms against Egypt, and that nation, which years before had held Israel in bondage, now became a slave to the Babylonian power.

The prophet Ezekiel, one of the Hebrew captives, was given a view of the capture of Egypt by Nebuchadnezzar, and was told to send the testimony to Pharaoh, king of Egypt. In this prophecy Egypt is represented as a mighty tree towering above all the trees of the earth. Even the trees of Eden envied the splendor of this tree. All the fowls of heaven nested in its boughs; the hosts of earth dwelt beneath its branches. But this tree of Egypt was lifted up because of its greatness, and God sent Babylon to hew it to the ground. The crash of its fall shook the earth.

This prophecy must have been known to [59] Nebuchadnezzar, if not before, at least after his victory over Egypt, for it was familiar to the Jews, and there were Jews in the Babylonian court. This throws light on the fourth chapter of Daniel.

Having conquered the world, Nebuchadnezzar was at rest in his house, when one night he dreamed a dream. Success had followed him wherever he turned. At his feet bowed the representatives of all nations. Into his coffers flowed the wealth of the east and the west, the north and the south. About him was clustered the wit and learning of the age. Libraries were at his command, and art flourished. Why should not king Nebuchadnezzar flourish in his kingdom? But he had dreamed a dream which troubled him, and he called upon his wise men for an interpretation. They listened, but strange to say, could give no explanation. God always permitted the wise men of the earth to have the first trial. When these wise men failed, Daniel was called.

Daniel's name had been changed when he first entered the Babylonian court, and to the king and his associates he was known as Belteshazzar, a son of the heathen god Bel, but Daniel himself always retained his own Hebrew name. Years before this, however, the God of Daniel had said, "Bel boweth and Nebo stoopeth; . . . they could not deliver the burden, but themselves are gone into captivity."

Eze. 30:9-11.

The word of the Lord came unto me, saying, Son of man, speak unto Pharaoh king of Egypt, and to his multitude; Whom art thou like in the greatness? Behold, the Assyrian was a cedar in Lebanon with fair branches, and with a shadowing shroud, and of an high stature; and his top was among the thick boughs. Eze. 31:1-8.

4. I Nebuchadnezzar was at rest in mine house, and flourishing in my palace:
5. I saw a dream which made me afraid, and the thoughts upon my bed and the visions of my head troubled me.
6. Therefore made I a decree to bring in all the wise men of Babylon before me, that they might make known unto me the interpretation of the dream.
7. Then came in the magicians, the astrologers, the Chaldeans, and the soothsayers: and I told the dream before them; but they did not make known unto me the interpretation thereof.
8. But at the last Daniel came in before me, whose name was Belteshazzar, according to the name of my god, and in whom is the spirit of the holy gods: and before him I told the dream, saying, Dan 4:4-8.

The wise men are ashamed, they are dismayed and taken: lo, they have rejected the word of the Lord; and what wisdom is in them? Jer. 8:9.

9. O Belteshazzar, master of the magicians, because I know that the spirit of the holy gods is in thee, and no secret troubleth thee, tell me the visions of my dream that I have seen, and the interpretation thereof. Dan. 4:9.

Bel boweth down, Nebo stoopeth, their idols were upon the beasts, and upon the cattle: your carriages were heavy loaden; they are a burden to the weary beast. They stoop, they bow down together; they could not deliver the burden, but themselves are gone into captivity. Isa. 46:1-2.

Daniel again had an opportunity of proving the wisdom of his God and the weakness of Babylonian deities.

The dream, as repeated by the king in Daniel's hearing, is wonderful to contemplate. The tree [60] was a familiar object and a striking symbol. The most magnificent specimens that the world afforded had been transplanted into the Babylonian gardens. The story of Eden and its trees had been handed down by tradition, and the people knew of the tree of life, and also of the tree of the knowledge of good and evil. The tree seen in the dream was planted in the midst of the earth, and as he watched, the king saw it grow until the top reached heaven, and its boughs stretched to the ends of the earth. Strange that this tree, which grew toward heaven in spite of everything, which was watered by the dews of heaven and fed by God's own sunshine, knew only of the earth and earthly kingdoms!

As it had been with the Egyptian tree, so with this: fowls rested in the branches and beasts dwelt in its shadow. The king in his dream saw only the upper part of the tree, the branches, leaves, and fruit, but the roots of any tree are as numerous and widespread as its branches; hence this mighty tree, whose top reached heaven, and whose branches spread forth to the ends of the earth, was supported by roots which, though hidden, ran through all the earth. Deep-rooted, it was drawing nourishment from hidden springs. In fact, the fair leaves and abundant fruit were dependent upon the condition of the roots.

As Nebuchadnezzar gazed upon the tree, he saw a "watcher, even an holy one,"—a messenger from heaven, whose appearance was similar to the One who walked in the midst of the fiery furnace with the Hebrew children. At the command of this divine messenger, the tree was [61] hewn down, the stump alone remaining. Hewing down the tree did not kill the stump nor the roots. The life remained, and it was ready to send forth new shoots more numerous than before.

It is doubtful whether man ever received a message freighted with greater importance than this one given to Nebuchadnezzar. In his former dream he was shown the

They were no gods, but the work of men's hands, wood and stone. Isa. 37:19.

10. Thus were the visions of mine head in my bed; I saw, and behold a tree in the midst of the earth, and the height thereof was great.
11. The tree grew, and was strong, and the height thereof reached unto heaven, and the sight thereof to the end of all the earth:
12. The leaves thereof were fair, and the fruit thereof much, and in it was meat for all: the beasts of the field had shadow under it, and the fowls of the heaven dwelt in the boughs thereof, and all flesh was fed of it. Dan. 4:10-12.

This wisdom descendeth not from above, but is earthly, sensual, devilish. Jam 3:15.

I have seen the wicked in great power, and spreading himself like a green tree that groweth in his own soil. Ps. 37:35 [margin].

Boast not against the branches. But if thou boast, thou bearest not the root, but the root thee. Rom 11:18.

Are they not all ministering spirits, sent forth to minister for them who shall be heirs of salvation? Heb 1:14.

For there is hope of a tree, if it be cut down, that it will sprout again, and that the tender branch thereof will not cease. Though the root thereof wax old in the earth, and the stock thereof die in the ground; Yet through the scent of water it will bud, and bring forth boughs like a plant. Job 14:7-9.

"Hew down the tree, and cut off his branches, shake off his leaves and scatter his fruit."

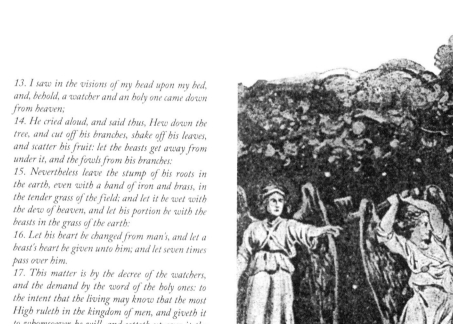

13. I saw in the visions of my head upon my bed, and, behold, a watcher and an holy one came down from heaven;

14. He cried aloud, and said thus, Hew down the tree, and cut off his branches, shake off his leaves, and scatter his fruit: let the beasts get away from under it, and the fowls from his branches:

15. Nevertheless leave the stump of his roots in the earth, even with a band of iron and brass, in the tender grass of the field; and let it be wet with the dew of heaven, and let his portion be with the beasts in the grass of the earth:

16. Let his heart be changed from man's, and let a beast's heart be given unto him; and let seven times pass over him.

17. This matter is by the decree of the watchers, and the demand by the word of the holy ones: to the intent that the living may know that the most High ruleth in the kingdom of men, and giveth it to whomsoever he will, and setteth up over it the basest of men.

18. This dream I king Nebuchadnezzar have seen. Now thou, O Belteshazzar, declare the interpretation thereof, forasmuch as all the wise men of my kingdom are not able to make known unto me the interpretation: but thou art able; for the spirit of the holy gods is in thee.

Dan. 4:13-18.

shortness of his kingdom and given proof [62] of the decline of the empire. Had he lived in harmony with what was then revealed to him, the experience about to come would have been avoided. The parting words of the angel as he left Nebuchadnezzar were, "This matter is by the decree of the watchers. . . to the intent that the living may know that the Most High ruleth in the kingdom of men, and giveth it to whomsoever He will." More than that, "He setteth up over it the basest of men." Because a man holds a position, it does not signify that he is better than others.

When Daniel realized the true significance of the dream, and foresaw the humiliation of the king of Babylon, "his thoughts troubled him." He was encouraged by the king not to be troubled, but to give the true interpretation. He did so, plainly telling the king that the tree seen in the vision was emblematic of Nebuchadnezzar himself, and his dominion. "It is thou, O king, that art grown and become strong; for thy greatness is grown and reacheth unto heaven, and thy dominion to the end of the earth." Great as was Nebuchadnezzar's kingdom, it had grown from a small beginning. Gradually the principles upon which it was founded—principles much older than the king, for they originated with Lucifer, and were a perversion of heavenly truths—had taken root. In government it was the most rigid monarchy; the king held the lives of his subjects in his hands. Slaves bowed before him in abject subjugation; exorbitant taxes were forced from subject provinces; crowned heads were laid low and men enslaved that the king of Babylon might revel in the wealth of the world. The seeds of that [63] form of government were sown wherever Babylon established her power, and as she sowed, so she, as well as others, have reaped. When Babylon fell, the principles by which she had controlled others were in turn applied to her. Wherever there is tyranny in government in any nation of the earth to-day, it is an offshoot of that root which filled the earth, the stump of which was allowed to remain until the end of time.

Wherever Babylon laid her hand in conquest, the principles of her religion were implanted. The vilest forms

As for man, his days are as grass: as a flower of the field, so he flourisheth. For the wind passeth over it, and it is gone; and the place thereof shall know it no more. Ps. 103:15-16

The Lord hath prepared his throne in the heavens; and his kingdom ruleth over all. Ps. 103:19.

19. Then Daniel, whose name was Belteshazzar, was astonied for one hour, and his thoughts troubled him. The king spake, and said, Belteshazzar, let not the dream, or the interpretation thereof, trouble thee. Belteshazzar answered and said, My lord, the dream be to them that hate thee, and the interpretation thereof to thine enemies.
20. The tree that thou sawest, which grew, and was strong, whose height reached unto the heaven, and the sight thereof to all the earth;
21. Whose leaves were fair, and the fruit thereof much, and in it was meat for all; under which the beasts of the field dwelt, and upon whose branches the fowls of the heaven had their habitation:
22. It is thou, O king, that art grown and become strong: for thy greatness is grown, and reacheth unto heaven, and thy dominion to the end of the earth.
23. And whereas the king saw a watcher and an holy one coming down from heaven, and saying, Hew the tree down, and destroy it; yet leave the stump of the roots thereof in the earth, even with a band of iron and brass, in the tender grass of the field; and let it be wet with the dew of heaven, and let his portion be with the beasts of the field, till seven times pass over him.
Dan. 4:19-23.

Shout against her round about: she hath given her hand: her foundations are fallen, her walls are thrown down: for it is the vengeance of the Lord: take vengeance upon her; as she hath done, do unto her. Call together the archers against Babylon: all ye that bend the bow, camp against it round about; let none thereof escape: recompense her according to her work; according to all that she hath done, do unto her: for she hath been proud against the Lord, against the Holy One of Israel. Jer. 50:15-16, 29.

Gal. 6:7.

of worship were practiced in that kingdom with all its outward glory. The heart was rotten. The mystery of iniquity held full sway, hidden by the outward glitter of gold. The mysteries of Greece in a later day were but a repetition of the Babylonian mysteries. From the golden cup which she held in her hand, and which was a familiar symbol in Babylonian secret societies, she made all nations drunk with the wine of her fornication.

Nations and peoples to-day, unconscious of their origin, are perpetuating Babylonian religious customs when they celebrate Christmas with feasting, lighted candles, holly, and mistletoe. It is in commemoration of Babylonian heathen gods that they eat eggs on Easter; and even the wild capers of Hallowe'en repeat the mysteries of Babylon. The root was not destroyed; her religious principles have sprung up afresh in every generation and borne fruit in every country.

The influence of Babylon in educational lines was no less marked than her influence in government and religion, and the educational root of [64] the tree was as vigorous as the others. We are in the habit of tracing the educational system of the world to Greece or Egypt; its principles are older than Greece. They belong to Babylon. The prominence given this phase of Babylonian life by the Spirit of God in the book of Daniel, and the fact that the leading educators and educational institutions of the world were brought in direct contact with the more simple principles of true education every time the Hebrews met the Chaldeans and wise men, shows the place which education occupies both in the false kingdoms of which Babylon is a type, and in the true, which the Hebrew government represented. The co-called "higher education" of to-day, which exalts the science of the world above the science of salvation; which sends forth stu-

They have sown the wind, and they shall reap the whirlwind. Hosea 8:7.

I will punish the world for their evil, and the wicked for their iniquity; and I will cause the arrogancy of the proud to cease, and will lay low the haughtiness of the terrible. Isa. 13:11.

All nations have drunk of the wine of the wrath of her fornication, and the kings of the earth have committed fornication with her, and the merchants of the earth are waxed rich through the abundance of her delicacies. Rev. 18:3.

But now, after that ye have known God, or rather are known of God, how turn ye again to the weak and beggarly elements, whereunto ye desire again to be in bondage? Ye observe days, and months, and times, and years. I am afraid of you, lest I have bestowed upon you labor in vain. Gal. 4:9-11.

The thing that hath been, it is that which shall be; and that which is done is that which shall be done: and there is no new thing under the sun. Is there any thing whereof it may be said, See, this is new? it hath been already of old time, which was before us. Eccl. 1:9-10.

That which hath been is now; and that which is to be hath already been; and God requireth that which is past. Eccl. 3:15.

"Leave the stump of his roots in the earth, even with a band of iron and brass."

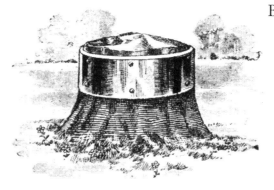

dents bearing worldly credentials, but not recognized in the books of heaven, students who love display, who are filled with pride, selfishness, and self-esteem,—this education is a plant which has sprung from that broad root which supported the tree representing the Babylonian dominion.

Seeds of truth had been planted in Babylon. The Holy Watcher sought constantly for the growth of a tree which would bring life. All nations were gathered under the influence of Babylon in hopes that they might there be fed with fruit which would prove to be the bread of life; but instead, it was a mixture of good and evil, which poisoned the consumer.

The leaves of the tree were fair to look upon, [65] and might have been for the healing of the nations; but the very odor they exhaled, intoxicated and led to excess. So with the plant which has sprung from those hidden roots. It may be fair to look upon, its fruit may be so sweet that the eater can not be persuaded that it is not truth, but the wisdom of God will stand long after that of the world has been destroyed. We should watch and guard against the evils which spring from the Babylonian root.

Aside from the general application to the entire kingdom, a part of the dream pictures the experience of Nebuchadnezzar personally. Because of his pride of heart, he would lose his reason, forsake the abodes of men, find his home with the beasts of the field, and remain in this condition for seven years—until he had learned "that the Most High ruleth in the kingdom of men, and giveth it to whomsoever he will." Daniel exhorted the king, "Let my counsel be acceptable unto thee, and break off thy sins by righteousness, and thine iniquities by showing mercy to the poor." There was yet time for repentance, and had the king heeded this counsel, it would have saved him from the great humiliation which came upon him. But when men's hearts are set, the message to change, 'though given by an angel from heaven, remains unheeded. Consequently, "all this came upon the king Nebuchadnezzar."

A year of probation was granted the king after this solemn warning had been given. At the end of this time the

Dan. 1:20.
Dan. 2:27, 19.
Dan. 3:18.
Dan. 3:18.
Dan. 5:8, 13, 14.

All that is in the world, the lust of the flesh, and the lust of the eyes, and the pride of life, is not of the Father, but is of the world.
1 John 2:16.

We would have healed Babylon, but she is not healed: forsake her, and let us go every one into his own country: for her judgment reacheth unto heaven, and is lifted up even to the skies.
Jer. 51:9.

Gen. 2:17.

There is hope of a tree, if it be cut down, that it will sprout again, and that the tender branch thereof will not cease. Though the root thereof wax old in the earth, and the stock thereof die in the ground; Yet through the scent of water it will bud, and bring forth boughs like a plant.
Job 14:7-9.

2 Cor. 11:3.

24. This is the interpretation, O king, and this is the decree of the most High, which is come upon my lord the king:
25. That they shall drive thee from men, and thy dwelling shall be with the beasts of the field, and they shall make thee to eat grass as oxen, and they shall wet thee with the dew of heaven, and seven times shall pass over thee, till thou know that the most High ruleth in the kingdom of men, and giveth it to whomsoever he will.
26. And whereas they commanded to leave the stump of the tree roots; thy kingdom shall be sure unto thee, after that thou shalt have known that the heavens do rule.
Dan. 4:24-26.

Dan. 11:13 [margin].
Isa. 1:16-20.
Isa. 58:7-11.
Matt. 23:12.
Luke 16:31.

Every man of the house of Israel that setteth up his idols in his heart, and putteth the stumblingblock of his iniquity before his face, and cometh to the prophet: I the Lord will answer him that cometh according to the multitude of his idols; and I will set my face against that man, and will make him a sign and a proverb.
Eze. 14:4-8.

27. Wherefore, O king, let my counsel be acceptable unto thee, and break off thy sins by righteousness, and thine iniquities by shewing mercy to the poor; if it may be a lengthening of thy tranquillity.
28. All this came upon the king Nebuchadnezzar.

Dan. 4:27-28.

I will ascend above the heights of the clouds: I will be like the most High. Isa. 14:13, 14.

29. At the end of twelve months he walked in the palace of the kingdom of Babylon.
30. The king spake, and said, Is not this great Babylon, that I have built for the house of the kingdom by the might of my power, and for the honour of my majesty?
31. While the word was in the king's mouth, there fell a voice from heaven, saying, O king Nebuchadnezzar, to thee it is spoken; The kingdom is departed from thee.
32. And they shall drive thee from men, and thy dwelling shall be with the beasts of the field: they shall make thee to eat grass as oxen, and seven times shall pass over thee, until thou know that the most High ruleth in the kingdom of men, and giveth it to whomsoever he will.

Dan. 4:29-32.

Ps. 37: 35, 36.

Whom the Lord loveth he chasteneth, and scourgeth every son whom he receiveth. Heb. 12:4-11.

Blessed is the man whom thou chastenest, O Lord, and teachest him out of thy law; That thou mayest give him rest from the days of adversity, until the pit be digged for the wicked. Ps. 94:12-13

33. The same hour was the thing fulfilled upon Nebuchadnezzar: and he was driven from men, and did eat grass as oxen, and his body was wet with the dew of heaven, till his hairs were grown like eagles' feathers, and his nails like birds' claws.

Dan. 4:33.

I am the Lord: that is my name: and my glory will I not give to another, neither my praise to graven images. Isa. 42:8.

Humble yourselves therefore under the mighty hand of God, that he may exalt you in due time. 1Pet 5:6.
Base things of the world, and things which are despised, hath God chosen, yea, and things which are not, to bring to naught things that are: that no flesh should glory in his presence. But of him are ye in Christ Jesus, who of God is made unto us wisdom,

king, in his royal palace, thinking of his kingdom with pride and satisfaction, exclaimed, "Is not this great Babylon, that *I* have built for the house of the kingdom [66] by the might of *my* power, and for the honor of *my* majesty?" He was repeating the thoughts, almost the exact words, of Satan, when he thought to exalt his throne above God. When proud thoughts were entertained, and these words were uttered, the sentence was pronounced which blasted the tree, and degraded the monarch whom the tree symbolized. It was God who had given the king his reason and ability to establish a kingdom like this. The same God could take away the judgment and wisdom upon which the king prided himself. And God did so. It is the mind which elevates man above the beast. When the power of the mind is removed, man sinks to the lowest level. Nebuchadnezzar became as the beasts. David says, "I have seen the wicked in great power, and spreading himself like a green bay tree. Yet he passed away, and, lo, he was not: yea, I sought him, but he could not be found."

When God can not save men in prosperity, he brings upon them adversity. If in all this they reject God, then they bring upon themselves destruction. Let the results be as they may, God is clear from all censure. This is illustrated by Nebuchadnezzar's case. The proud and powerful monarch no longer swayed the scepter. He became a maniac, and for seven years he was found with cattle, the companion of beasts, feeding as they fed. His reason dethroned, he was no longer regarded even as a man. The mandate had gone forth, "Hew down the tree, and cut off his branches, shake off his leaves, and scatter his fruit."

It is necessary in the cause of God and in the world, that men bear responsibility. But [67] when men are lifted up in pride and depend upon worldly wisdom, God can no longer sustain them, and they fall. Nations and individuals alike have this experience. Even the professed Church of Christ, when it departs from the humility of the Master, -loses its power, and will certainly be brought low. The people who glory in wealth, or intellect, or knowledge, or in anything save Jesus Christ, will be brought to confusion. In Christ alone "are hid all the treasures of wisdom and knowl-

"Is not this great Babylon that I have built for the house of the kingdom by the might of my power, and for the honor of my majesty?"

edge." Every brilliant thought, every intellectual idea, which in any way brings greatness, originates with our Lord. It is God who is dealing with humanity. He rules.

It should be remembered that in all of His dealings with the king Nebuchadnezzar, God was working for the salvation of the ruler and those affected by his influence. God allowed him to [68] suffer seven years of deplorable degradation, and then removed His chastening hand. After passing through this terrible humiliation, he was brought to see his own weakness; he confessed his guilt, and acknowledged the God of heaven. He sent to all the world the description of this experience as recorded in the fourth chapter of Daniel. He had learned that those who walk in pride, God is able to abase. In comparison with God and His universe, the inhabitants of the earth sink into insignificance, and are reputed as nothing. "He doeth according to His will in the army of heaven, and among the inhabitants of the earth: and none can stay His hand, or say unto Him, What doest Thou?" [69]

and righteousness, and sanctification, and redemption. 1 Cor. 1:28-30.

Col. 2:3.

34. And at the end of the days I Nebuchadnezzar lifted up mine eyes unto heaven, and mine understanding returned unto me, and I blessed the most High, and I praised and honoured him that liveth for ever, whose dominion is an everlasting dominion, and his kingdom is from generation to generation:
35. And all the inhabitants of the earth are reputed as nothing: and he doeth according to his will in the army of heaven, and among the inhabitants of the earth: and none can stay his hand, or say unto him, What doest thou?
36. At the same time my reason returned unto me; and for the glory of my kingdom, mine honour and brightness returned unto me; and my counsellors and my lords sought unto me; and I was established in my kingdom, and excellent majesty was added unto me.
37. Now I Nebuchadnezzar praise and extol and honour the King of heaven, all whose works are truth, and his ways judgment: and those that walk in pride he is able to abase.

Dan. 4:34-37.

CHAPTER 5

THE LAST YEARS OF THE BABYLONIAN KINGDOM

THE history of the Babylonian nation reveals to one who searches for hidden principles, all that is necessary in order to understand the relation of earthly governments to God, the dealings of God with all the nations of the earth, and the attitude which men should assume toward God and toward earthly governments. These four principles can be learned from a study of the history of Babylon as recorded in the book of Daniel, and by the prophets who wrote concerning this kingdom. This is true, because in Babylon is seen in some respects the most complete development of the plans of Satan. Here were counterfeited the principles of the heavenly kingdom, and so much of the true metal was mingled with the alloy that an unusual strength was developed. In other words, the kingdom of Babylon was built and developed in accordance with laws which were in themselves divine; but since the greatest evil lies near to and is a perversion of the greatest good, [70] so the perversion of the principles of the government of heaven made the strongest of earthly- kingdoms. Built so that it was difficult for beings who were watching the progress of events to detect error, God, who never deals arbitrarily with men or angels, not even with Satan himself, allowed the Babylonian kingdom to run its natural course, that the world

When the most High divided to the nations their inheritance, when he separated the sons of Adam, he set the bounds of the people according to the number of the children of Israel.
Deut 32:8.

Ps. 75:4-7.
Acts 17:26, 27.
Matt. 22:18-22.

Let every soul be subject unto the higher powers. For there is no power but of God: the powers that be are ordainded of God.
Rom. 13:1-7.

1 Sam. 22:9.
1 Sam. 14:6.

In every nation he that feareth him, and worketh righteousness, is accepted with him.
Acts 10:34, 35.

Upon her forehead was a name written, MYSTERY, BABYLON THE GREAT, THE MOTHER OF HARLOTS AND ABOMINATIONS OF THE EARTH.   Rev. 17:5.

Hab. 1:5-13.
Isa. 10:1-16.
Ps. 33:15-17.

Behold, all souls are mine; as the soul of the father, so also the soul of the son is mine: the soul that sinneth, it shall die.   Eze. 18:4.

The wages of sin is death; but the gift of God is eternal life through Jesus Christ our Lord.
Rom. 6:23.

Dan. 4:17.

Yet had he no wages, nor his army, for Tyrus, for the service that he had served against it: Therefore thus saith the Lord GOD; Behold, I will give the land of Egypt unto Nebuchadrezzar king of Babylon; and he shall take her multitude, and take her spoil, and take her prey; and it shall be the wages for his army. I have given him the land of Egypt for his labour wherewith he served against it, because they wrought for me, saith the Lord God.
Eze. 29:18-20.

In whose hand is the soul of every living thing, and the breath of all mankind. Job 12:10.

What could have been done more to my vineyard, that I have not done in it? wherefore, when I looked that it should bring forth grapes, brought it forth wild grapes? Isa. 5:4.

Isa. 14:4-6.

We would have healed Babylon, but she is not healed. Jer. 51:9.

Jer. 18:7, 8.
Eze. 11:14-16.
Isa. 13:1-15.
Amos 3:7.

Now all these things happened unto them for ensamples: and they are written for our admonition, upon whom the ends of the world are come.
1Cor. 10:11.

Eccl. 1:9.
Jer. 51:63, 64.
Rev. 18:21.

The Lord said, Because the cry of Sodom and Gomorrah is great, and because their sin is very grievous; I will go down now, and see whether they have done altogether according to the cry of it, which is come unto me; and if not, I will know.
Gen. 18:20-21.

Up, get you out of this place; for the LORD will destroy this city. Gen 19:14

Dan. 10:20.

Thou art my battle ax and weapons of war: for with thee will I break in pieces the nations, and with thee will I destroy kingdoms; And with thee will I break in pieces the horse and his rider; and with thee will I break in pieces the chariot and his rider. Jer. 51:20-23.

might have an objectlesson, and know forever after that truth brings life, but that the least perversion of truth, no matter how slight, brings death.

In order to vindicate Himself before the universe, God bestowed all manner of blessings upon this earthly kingdom which Satan boastingly claimed as his own. Wisdom was given to the people of Babylon, the Holy Watcher protected the king on his throne, and God gave power to the ruler in battle, making him a conqueror. It was God who caused the tree to reach unto heaven, and gave strength and beauty to its branches. Everything by way of warning and entreaty was used by Infinite Wisdom to cause the Babylonians to see the difference between the true and the false, and lead them to choose the true. It is one of the most forcible commentaries in earth's history on the care of God for all, even the veriest sinner.

Had Babylon taken the proffered help, she would, in spite of all the power of Satan as prince of this world, have linked her throne with the throne of God, and would have been an everlasting kingdom. How easily might the history of the world have been changed!

People living in these, last days, whether they be Christians or not, need not remain ignorant concerning their duty toward the civil government. [71] Nations can not plead ignorance concerning their duty toward Christians, toward other nations, nor toward God, for the prophecies of Daniel explain it all. It is a book for rulers as well as for the common people. Babylon is an object-lesson to the nations which are in existence to-day. Her growth was according to the laws of the growth of nations; her failures describe the failures which are made to-day, and her destruction is a description of the end of all earthly kingdoms.

Nations have a time of probation, as do individuals. A record is kept of national events, and when the cup of iniquity is full, destruction comes, and another power, more vigorous, because less corrupt, takes its place. "The Most High ruleth in the kingdom of men," whether He is recognized or not, and things which, to human eyes, appear to have happened by chance, are directly under the control of the *Holy Watcher.*

The study of the book of Daniel demands, therefore, that we take time to trace the history of Babylon as a nation.

A period of about twenty-five years intervenes between the close of the fourth and the opening of the fifth chapter. The reign of Nebuchadnezzar closed shortly after the restoration of his reason, as related in the fourth chapter. From a worldly point of view, his had been a long and prosperous reign, and at its close there were no signs of weakening in the empire. Nebuchadnezzar had a son of age to fill the place of his father. No one questioned his right to the throne, and while they mourned the death of [72] Nebuchadnezzar, apparently the subjects had much reason to rejoice over the succession of the son. In the eyes of Heaven this history was a checkered one. There had been periods when a desire to know the right and rule justly were written opposite the name of the king. But these were followed by still longer periods when the voice of the Divine One was altogether unheeded. There was a record of wonderful providences, rich blessings, and bitter trials, all having one object,—to turn the minds of the world to the only Source of life and power. If Heaven ever grows weary watching the struggles of nations, what must have been the burden as they saw this kingdom repeatedly choose the course which was leading to inevitable ruin.

Evil-merodach, the son of Nebuchadnezzar, is mentioned but twice in

Jehoiachin in prison.

the Scriptures, and in each case reference is made to one act of his life. It seems strange that such a father should be followed by a son of whom so little is recorded, but it is gratifying to notice that when the silence is broken, *it is to relate a deed of kindness.* In the first year of his reign he took from prison Jehoiachin, the former king of Jerusalem, a man now

Dan. 4:36, 37.
Jer. 28:14.

It shall come to pass, that the nation and kingdom which will not serve the same Nebuchadnezzar the king of Babylon, and that will not put their neck under the yoke of the king of Babylon, that nation will I punish, saith the LORD, with the sword, and with the famine, and with the pestilence, until I have consumed them by his hand.
Jer. 27:5-8.

Dan. 2: 47.
Dan. 3:28.
Dan. 4:37.
Jer. 39:11-14.
Jer. 44:30.

Before I was afflicted I went astray: but now have I kept thy word.   Ps. 119:67.

Though he were a Son, yet learned he obedience by the things which he suffered.   Heb. 5:8.

It is good for me that I have been afflicted; that I might learn thy statutes.   Ps. 119:71.

It is the land of graven images, and they are mad upon their idols.   Jer. 50:38.

Ephraim is joined to idols: let him alone.
Hosea 4:17.

It came to pass in the seven and thirtieth year of the captivity of Jehoiachin king of Judah, in the twelfth month, on the seven and twentieth day of the month, that Evilmerodach king of Babylon in the year that he began to reign did lift up the head of Jehoiachin king of Judah out of prison; And he spake kindly to him, and set his throne above the throne of the kings that were with him in Babylon; And changed his prison garments:

and he did eat bread continually before him all the days of his life. And his allowance was a continual allowance given him of the king, a daily rate for every day, all the days of his life.

2 Kin. 25:27-30.

Blessed are the merciful: for they shall obtain mercy.   Matt. 5:7.

Then the king made Daniel a great man, and gave him many great gifts, and made him ruler over the whole province of Babylon, and chief of the governors over all the wise men of Babylon.

Dan. 2:48.

Blessed is he that considereth the poor: the Lord will deliver him in time of trouble. The Lord will preserve him, and keep him alive; and he shall be blessed upon the earth: and thou wilt not deliver him unto the will of his enemies. The Lord will strengthen him upon the bed of languishing: thou wilt make all his bed in his sickness. I said, Lord, be merciful unto me: heal my soul; for I have sinned against thee. But thou, O LORD, be merciful unto me, and raise me up, that I may requite them. By this I know that thou favorest me, because mine enemy doth not triumph over me.

Ps. 41:1-11.

All nations shall serve him, and his son, and his son's son, until the very time of his land come: and then many nations and great kings shall serve themselves of him.

Jer. 27:7.

Beshazzar, whiles he tasted the wines, commanded to bring the golden and silver vessels which his grandfather Nebuchadnezzar had taken.

Dan. 5:2 [margin].

Dan. 5:1.
Jer. 51:60-64.

fifty years of age, who had languished in bonds since a boy of eighteen. The Jewish ex-ruler was given clothing and a king's provisions, and exalted above other kings in Babylon all the remainder of his days.

Evil-merodach had been raised in the Babylonian court, and had known of the Jews and their history from his youth up. It would not be an [73] impossible thing that Daniel, made chief of the Chaldean wise men by Nebuchadnezzar, had been the instructor of the prince. While details are omitted, true it is that for some reason the destruction of Babylon was delayed beyond the reign of Evil-merodach. His brief reign- of two years was followed by an unsettled period, a most dangerous experience in a monarchy.

Finally Nabonadius, the son-in-law of Nebuchadnezzar, was seated on the throne, and about the year 541 he associated with him his son

Jehoiachin at the king's table.

Belshazzar. The two reigned conjointly until the destruction of the kingdom in 538 B. C. This youth, the grandson of the great Nebuchadnezzar, soon proved himself to be headstrong, wayward, cruel, and dissolute.

Daniel was no longer retained in the court. The time of his dismissal is not stated, but in the third year of Belshazzar's reign, he was living at Shushan, the capital of Elam, some distance east of Babylon, and it was at that place that he saw the vision which the eighth chapter of the book of Daniel relates.

During the reign of Nabonadius and Belshazzar, events of the greatest importance occurred. To the Jews who accepted the words of the prophets whom God sent, rising up early and sending, the downfall of the kingdom in the near future was well known. In spite of their own oppression, there was a world to be warned, and as the host of the redeemed gather about the throne of God, made up, as it will be, of representatives of every nation, kindred, tongue, and people, there will be some souls from ancient Babylon, who, having heard the proclamation of the message, separated from her sins, and were saved.

As the knowledge of God was lost by the ruling monarchs, and God-fearing men were no longer among the counselors, the oppression of the Jews became almost unbearable.

On going into Babylon, they had been instructed by the Lord to build houses and plant vineyards, to marry and increase in numbers, and to pray for the peace and prosperity of Babylon, for their captivity would last seventy years. The people of God had the observance of the Sabbath of the fourth commandment to preserve their peculiarity and keep them from mingling with the heathen. The time came when the Babylonians, who were sun-worshipers, mocked the Jews because of the Sabbath. They were forbidden to celebrate their feasts; priests and rulers were degraded and persecuted. The Babylonians often demanded songs from the Jews. "They that wasted us required of us mirth, saying, Sing us one of the songs of Zion;" but their hearts were mournful. "Israel is a scattered sheep," wrote Jeremiah; "the lions have [75] driven him away; ... Nebuchadnezzar king of Babylon hath broken his bones." The Babylonians boasted that it was no sin to oppress the Jews, reasoning that God had placed the Hebrews in bondage because of their sins.

It is little wonder that the yoke was hard to bear and that the king was unrelenting. It was a time of trouble, a foretaste of the great time of trouble through which the people of God will pass before the second coming of the

---

In the third year of the reign of king Belshazzar a vision appeared unto me, even unto me Daniel, after that which appeared unto me at the first.
Dan. 8:1.

Flee out of the midst of Babylon, and deliver every man his soul: be not cut off in her iniquity; for this is the time of the Lord's vengeance; he will render unto her a recompence.
Jer. 51:6.

After this I beheld, and, lo, a great multitude, which no man could number, of all nations, and kindreds, and people, and tongues, stood before the throne, and before the Lamb, clothed with white robes, and palms in their hands.
Rev. 7:9.

Rev. 18:4.
Ex. 1:18.
Lam. 4:16, 18, 19.
Jer. 29:4-7.
Jer. 25:11, 12.
Jer. 29:10.
2 Chron. 36:21.

Moreover also I gave them my sabbaths, to be a sign between me and them, that they might know that I am the Lord that sanctify them. And hallow my sabbaths; and they shall be a sign between me and you, that ye may know that I am the Lord your God.
Eze. 20:12, 16, 20.

The ways of Zion do mourn, because none come to the solemn feasts: all her gates are desolate: her priests sigh, her virgins are afflicted, and she is in bitterness. Her princes are become like harts that find no pasture, and they gone without strength before the pursuer.
Lam. 1:2-6.

Ps. 137:1-6.
Jer. 50:17.

Their adversaries said, We offend not, because they have sinned against the Lord, the habitation of justice, even the Lord, the hope of their fathers.
Jer. 50:7.

Dan. 9:16.
Jer. 2:3.

For thus saith the Lord; We have heard a voice of trembling, of fear, and not of peace. Ask ye now, and see whether a man doth travail with child? wherefore do I see every man with his hands on his loins, as a woman in travail, and all faces are turned into paleness? Alas! for that day is great, so that none is like it: it is even the time of Jacob's trouble; but he shall be saved out of it. Jer. 30:3-9.

Their Redeemer is strong; the Lord of hosts is his name: he shall thoroughly plead their cause. Jer. 50:33, 34.

Behold, the days come, saith the LORD, that I will raise unto David a righteous Branch, and a King shall reign and prosper, and shall execute judgment and justice in the earth. In his days Judah shall be saved, and Israel shall dwell safely: and this is his name whereby he shall be called, THE LORD OUR RIGHTEOUSNESS. Jer. 23:5-6.

He shall destroy the sinners thereof out of it. Every one that is found shall be thrust through; and every one that is joined unto them shall fall by the sword. Isa. 13:6-22.

Then I spake unto them of the captivity all the things that the Lord had showed me. Eze. 11:24, 25.

Isa. 21:9.
Jer. 51:8, 6, 35, 49.
Dan. 2:36.
Dan. 4:24.
Dan. 7:1.
Eze. 27:1, 2.
Eze. 29:2, 3.
Eze. 25:2, 3.
Jer. 25:15-28.
Isa. 44:28.
Isa. 45:1, 2.
Isa. 14:13.

Go up, O Elam: besiege, O Media; all the sighing thereof have I made to cease. Isa. 21:2.

Moab hath been at ease from his youth, and he hath settled on his lees, and hath not been emptied from vessel to vessel, neither hath he gone into captivity: therefore his taste remained in him, and his scent is not changed. Therefore, behold, the days come, saith the LORD, that I will send unto him wanderers, that shall cause him to wander, and shall empty his vessels, and break their bottles. Jer. 48:11-12.

2 Kings 5:2-4.
Dan. 2:49.

Lest your heart faint, and ye fear for the rumour that shall be heard in the land; a rumour shall both come one year, and after that in another year shall come a rumour, and violence in the land, ruler against ruler. Jer. 51:46.

Saviour. Both periods are called by the same name,—the time of *Jacob's trouble,*—by the prophet Jeremiah. Under these trying circumstances the Jews were obliged to preach the gospel which they once had the opportunity to give with power from Jerusalem.

Groaning beneath oppression, they taught of the coming Messiah, the deliverer; they taught righteousness by faith, and the everlasting gospel, the hour of God's judgment, the fall of Babylon, and the destruction of those upon whom was found the mark of the Babylonian worship. The spirit of prophecy, as belonging to the Jews, was known to the Babylonians throughout the period of captivity. Daniel, in the presence of the king, had more than once received divine enlightenment. Ezekiel was sending messages broadcast from the Lord, and Jeremiah had received word from God with the command to make it known to all the nations round about. There was no hiding the fact that the God of the Jews had prophets among His people. It was in this way that not only the Jews, but Moab, Edom, Tyre and Sidon, Ammon, Egypt, Arabia, and even Media and Persia knew that the fall of Babylon was [76] decreed. Many of these nations, and the Persians among the number, knew just what kingdom would be used to destroy Babylon, and the name of the man whom God had chosen to accomplish the overthrow.

Such are the messages which God sent, and thus it was that He made use of His people. Those whom He could not use when granted peace and prosperity and a city of their own, He used when slaves under the iron heel of Babylon. Babylon was like a city on the edge of a volcanic crater, but she believed it not. In the year 539 B. C., the combined forces of the Medes and Persians started toward Babylon. The news reached the city that the enemy was on the march. Then it was that the message came to flee from the city and be as goats upon the mountainside. Jews who heeded the word of the Lord, then withdrew from Babylon. But the Persian army did not come. History says that Cyrus was stopped by the death of a sacred white horse, which was drowned in crossing a river.

"The gates were closed and the seige began."

Cyrus set his men to dig-ging [77] chan-nels for the river, spending one year in this way. Prophecy says, "The walls of Babylon shall fall. My people, *go* ye out of the midst of her, and deliver ye every man his soul. . . . And lest your heart faint, and ye fear for the rumor that shall be heard in the land; a rumor shall both come one year, and after that in another year, shall come a rumor, and violence in the land, ruler against ruler."

And so it was; one spring the rumor came, but the army failed to appear. The careless and unbelieving scoffed, but to the believing this was the opportune time. The next spring the rumor came again, but there was no time then to sell or pre-pare to leave, for the army came also, and the Babylonian and Medo-Persian forces met in open battle. The Babylonians were defeated, and retired within the fortifications of the city.

The gates were closed and the siege began. Those who were now in Babylon must live or die with the Babylonians, except God stay the hand of the destroyer.

At the noise of the taking of Babylon the earth is moved, and the cry is heard among the nations.
Jer. 50:46.

I will render unto Babylon and to all the inhabit-ants of Chaldea all their evil that they have done in Zion in your sight, saith the Lord.
Jer. 51:24.

Knowing this first, that there shall come in the last days scoffers, walking after their own lusts.
2 Pet. 3:3.

The king of Babylon hath heard the report of them, and his hands waxed feeble: anguish took hold of him, and pangs as of a woman in travail.
Jer. 50:43.

The land shall tremble and sorrow: for every pur-pose of the LORD shall be performed against Babylon, to make the land of Babylon a desolation without an inhabitant.
Jer. 51:29.

Thou carriest them away as with a flood; they are as a sleep: in the morning they are like grass which groweth up.   Ps. 90:5.

The climax was reached by the greatest of earthly governments. All heaven was alive with anxiety. Only man was asleep to his impending destruction. [78]

CHAPTER 6

THE HANDWRITING ON THE WALL

DANIEL 5

IT was the last night of a nation's existence, but the people knew it not. Some slept in unconscious peace; some reveled and whirled away in thoughtless dance. In the dens of Babylon, men steeped in vice continued their wild orgies; in the palace halls Belshazzar feasted with a thousand of his lords. Music resounded through the brilliantly lighted rooms. The nobles lounged about the tables sumptuously spread. Court women and concubines of the king entered those halls. It was a feast of Bacchus, and they drank to the health of the king on his throne. He ordered that the sacred vessels be brought from the temple to show that no being, human or divine, could raise a hand against him, the king of Babylon. The golden cup filled with wine was raised and the blessing of Bel invoked, but [79] it never reached the lips of the half-intoxicated king. His hand was stayed. Those vessels had been moulded by hands divinely skilled, and after heavenly models. Angels had watched them as they were taken from the temple at Jerusalem and carried to Babylon. Messengers

1. Belshazzar the king made a great feast to a thousand of his lords, and drank wine before the thousand.
2. Belshazzar, whiles he tasted the wine, commanded to bring the golden and silver vessels which his father Nebuchadnezzar had taken out of the temple which was in Jerusalem; that the king, and his princes, his wives, and his concubines, might drink therein.
3. Then they brought the golden vessels that were taken out of the temple of the house of God which was at Jerusalem; and the king, and his princes, his wives, and his concubines, drank in them.
4. They drank wine, and praised the gods of gold, and of silver, of brass, of iron, of wood, and of stone.
Dan. 5:1–4.

All the vessels of gold and of silver were five thousand and four hundred. All these did Sheshbazzar bring up with them of the captivity that were brought up from Babylon unto Jerusalem.
Ezra 1:11.

A thousand charges of silver.
Ezra 1:9.

And look that thou make them after their pattern, which thou wast caused to see in the mount.
Ex. 25:40 [margin].

Ex. 31:2-7.
Ex 25:9, 40.

The voice of them that flee and escape out of the land of Babylon, to declare in Zion the vengeance of the LORD our God, the vengeance of his temple.   Jer. 50:28.
Jer. 50:24-28.
Jer. 51:11.

5. In the same hour came forth fingers of a man's hand, and wrote over against the candlestick upon the plaister of the wall of the king's palace: and the king saw the part of the hand that wrote.
6. Then the king's countenance was changed, and his thoughts troubled him, so that the joints of his loins were loosed, and his knees smote one against another.
                                    Dan. 5:5-6.

Isa. 21:3-5.

7. The king cried aloud to bring in the astrologers, the Chaldeans, and the soothsayers. And the king spake, and said to the wise men of Babylon, Whosoever shall read this writing, and shew me the interpretation thereof, shall be clothed with scarlet, and have a chain of gold about his neck, and shall be the third ruler in the kingdom.
8. Then came in all the king's wise men: but they could not read the writing, nor make known to the king the interpretation thereof.
9. Then was king Belshazzar greatly troubled, and his countenance was changed in him, and his lords were astonied.
                                    Dan. 5:7-9.
Jer. 45:1-3.
Jer. 51:53.

Except the LORD build the house, they labour in vain that build it: except the LORD keep the city, the watchman waketh but in vain.
                                    Ps. 127:1.

For, behold, I will shake mine hand upon them, and they shall be a spoil to their servants: and ye shall know that the LORD of hosts hath sent me.
                                    Zech. 2:9.

Lift not up the horn: Lift not up your horn on high: speak not with a stiff neck. For promotion cometh neither from the east, nor from the west, nor from the south. But God is the judge: he putteth down one, and setteth up another.
                                    Ps. 75:4-7.

We are made a spectacle unto the world, and to angels, and to men.   1 Cor. 4:9.
Gen. 7:7-9.

The LORD hath opened his armoury, and hath brought forth the weapons of his indignation: for this is the work of the Lord GOD of hosts in the land of the Chaldeans.   Jer. 50:25.

divinely appointed had guarded them, and their very presence in the heathen temple was a witness of the God of the Jews. Some day the silence would be broken. The desecration of His temple would not always remain unpunished.

That time came when the king lifted the goblet filled with sparkling wine. His hand grew stiff, for on the opposite wall, over against the lights, was a bloodless hand, writing words of an unknown language. The winecup fell to the floor; the king's countenance grew pale; he trembled violently, and his knees smote together until the gorgeous girdle of his loins loosened and fell aside. The loud laughter ceased, and the music died away. Terror-stricken, a thousand guests looked from the face of the king to the writing on the wall.

The Chaldean astrologers and soothsayers were called, but the writing was meaningless to them. They who taught all earthly languages failed to recognize the language of heaven. The four strange characters remained as at first seen, emblazoned in letters of fire on the wall.

For days the siege of Babylon had been on. The gates were closed and her walls were considered impregnable, while within the city were provisions for twenty years. But however strong she might seem, God had said, "Though Babylon should mount up to heaven, and though [80] she should fortify the height of her strength, yet from me shall spoilers come unto her."

The strongest strongholds which man can build are crushed like a dying leaf when the hand of God is laid upon them. But this was a lesson which the rulers of Babylon had not yet learned. The father of iniquity, who was urging these rulers forward into deeper sin, had not yet owned the weakness of his cause. Heaven and unfallen worlds' watched the progress of affairs in this great city, for it was the battleground of the two mighty forces of good and evil. Christ and Satan here contended.

Angels, unseen by human eyes, as when they gathered the animals into the ark before the flood, had mustered forces against Babylon. God was using men who knew Him not as God, but who were true to principle and wished to do right. To Cyrus, the leader of the Persian army, which was now outside the city walls, God had said that He held his hand to make him strong. Before you "I will loose the loins of kings." I will open those two-leaved gates, and the gates shall not be shut; "I will go before thee and make the crooked places straight: I will break in pieces the gates of brass and cut in sunder the bars of iron."

While Belshazzar and his lords drank and feasted, the army of Cyrus was lowering the waters in the bed of the Euphrates, preparatory to entering the city.

As the Chaldeans were unable to read the writing on the wall, the king's terror increased. He knew that this was a rebuke of his sacrilegious feast, and yet he could not learn the exact meaning. Then the queen-mother remembered [81] Daniel, who had "the Spirit of the holy gods," and who had been made master of the wise men in the days of Nebuchadnezzar as the result of interpreting the king's dream.

Daniel, the prophet of God, was called to the banquet room. As he came before Belshazzar, the monarch promised to make him third ruler in the kingdom if he would interpret the writing. The prophet, with the quiet dignity of a servant of the most high God, stood before the gorgeous, terror-stricken throng that bore evidence of intemperate feasting and wicked revelry.

In Israel, children were named under the inspiration of the Spirit of God, and the name was an expression of character. When God changed a name, as in the case of Abraham, Jacob, or Peter, it was because of a change of character in the individual. True to the name given him by his mother, Daniel—God's judge—again appears to vindicate the truth. Nebuchadnezzar had called him Belteshazzar, in honor of the Babylonian god Bel, but to the last this Hebrew, who knew the Lord, remained true to his God-given name, as shown in the twelfth verse of this chapter. He did not speak with flattering words, as the professedly wise men of the kingdom had done, but he spoke the truth of God. It was a moment of intensity, for there was but a single hour in which to make known the future. Daniel was now an old man, but he sternly disclaimed all desire

Jer. 51:25.
Isa. 13:1-5.
Isa. 45:1-4.
Isa. 43:1-3.

Set ye up a standard in the land, blow the trumpet among the nations, prepare the nations against her, . . . prepare against her the nations with the kings of the Medes, the captains thereof, and all the rulers thereof, and all the land of his dominion. Jer. 51:27-28.

That saith to the deep, Be dry, and I will dry up thy rivers. Isa. 44:27.

A drought is upon her waters; and they shall be dried up. Jer. 50:38.

10. Now the queen, by reason of the words of the king and his lords, came into the banquet house: and the queen spake and said, O king, live for ever: let not thy thoughts trouble thee, nor let thy countenance be changed:

11. There is a man in thy kingdom, in whom is the spirit of the holy gods; and in the days of thy father light and understanding and wisdom, like the wisdom of the gods, was found in him; whom the king Nebuchadnezzar thy father, the king, I say, thy father, made master of the magicians, astrologers, Chaldeans, and soothsayers;

12. Forasmuch as an excellent spirit, and knowledge, and understanding, interpreting of dreams, and shewing of hard sentences, and dissolving of doubts, were found in the same Daniel, whom the king named Belteshazzar: now let Daniel be called, and he will shew the interpretation.

13. Then was Daniel brought in before the king. And the king spake and said unto Daniel, Art thou that Daniel, which art of the children of the captivity of Judah, whom the king my father brought out of Jewry?
Dan. 5:10-13.

Gen. 17:5.
Gen. 32:28.
John 1:42.
Acts 4:36.

14. I have even heard of thee, that the spirit of the gods is in thee, and that light and understanding and excellent wisdom is found in thee.

15. And now the wise men, the astrologers, have been brought in before me, that they should read this writing, and make known unto me the interpretation thereof: but they could not shew the interpretation of the thing:

16. And I have heard of thee, that thou canst make interpretations, and dissolve doubts: now if thou canst read the writing, and make known to me the interpretation thereof, thou shalt be clothed with scarlet, and have a chain of gold about thy neck, and shalt be the third ruler in the kingdom.

17. Then Daniel answered and said before the king, Let thy gifts be to thyself, and give thy rewards to another; yet I will read the writing unto the king, and make known to him the interpretation.

18. O thou king, the most high God gave Nebuchadnezzar thy father a kingdom, and majesty, and glory, and honor:

19. And for the majesty that he gave him, all people, nations, and languages, trembled and feared before him: whom he would he slew; and whom he would he kept alive; and whom he would he set up; and whom he would he put down.

20. But when his heart was lifted up, and his mind hardened in pride, he was deposed from his kingly throne, and they took his glory from him:

21. And he was driven from the sons of men; and his heart was made like the beasts, and his dwelling was with the wild asses: they fed him with grass like oxen, and his body was wet with the dew of heaven; till he knew that the most high God ruled in the kingdom of men, and that he appointeth over it whomsoever he will.

Dan. 5:14–21.

For in him we live, and move, and have our being.
Acts 17:28.

22. And thou his son, O Belshazzar, hast not humbled thine heart, though thou knewest all this;

23. But hast lifted up thyself against the Lord of heaven; and they have brought the vessels of his house before thee, and thou, and thy lords, thy wives, and thy concubines, have drunk wine in them; and thou hast praised the gods of silver, and gold, of brass, iron, wood, and stone, which see not, nor hear, nor know: and the God in whose hand thy breath is, and whose are all thy ways, hast thou not glorified:

Dan. 5:22–23.

Job 31:16.

Then was the part of the hand sent from him; and this writing was written.

Dan. 5:24.

Ps. 62:9.

25. And this is the writing that was written, MENE, MENE, TEKEL, UPHARSIN.

26. This is the interpretation of the thing: MENE; God hath numbered thy kingdom, and finished it."

Dan. 5:25, 26.

Prov. 6:2,11.

TEKEL; Thou art weighed in the balances, and art found wanting.

Dan. 5:27.

for rewards or honor, and proceeded to review the history of Nebuchadnezzar, and the Lord's dealings with that ruler,—his dominion and glory, his punishment for pride of heart, and his subsequent [82] acknowledgment of the mercy and power of the God who created the heavens and the earth. He rebuked Belshazzar for his departure from true principles, and for his great wickedness and pride.

"And thou, his son, O Belshazzar, hast not humbled thine heart, though thou knewest all this; but hast lifted up thyself against the Lord of heaven; . . . and the God in whose hand thy breath is, and whose are all thy ways, hast thou not glorified." Straightforward and strong were the words of Daniel. Belshazzar had trodden on sacred ground; he had laid unholy hands on holy things; he had severed the ties which bind heaven and earth together; and there was no way for that life-giving Spirit of God to reach him or his followers. Day by day his breath had been given him, a symbol of the spiritual breath, but he praised and thanked the gods of wood and stone. His every motion had been by virtue of the power of the God of heaven, but he had prostituted that power to an unholy cause. "Then was the part of the hand sent from Him; and this writting was written." What he could not see written in his own breath and muscles, what he could not read in his own heart-beats, God wrote in mystic characters on the palace wall, over, against the candlestick.

The people waited with bated breath as Daniel turned to the writing on the wall, and read the message traced by the angel hand. The hand had been withdrawn, but four terrible words remained. The prophet announced their meaning to be: "Mene, Mene, Tekel, Upharsin: . . . God hath numbered thy kingdom, and finished it: . . . thou art weighed in the balances, [83] and art found wanting: . . . thy kingdom is divided, and given to the Medes and Persians."

In dealing with men God always uses a language which appeals forcibly to their understanding. This is illustrated in the handwriting on the wall. It is a common belief among idolaters that the gods weigh deeds in balances, and that if the good deeds outweigh the evil, the individual enters into his reward; if the opposite result is obtained, punishment follows. The language, therefore, was familiar to King Belshazzar. "God hath numbered thy kingdom; . . . thou art weighed in the balances, and art found wanting."

Say unto them, As I live, saith the Lord God, I have no pleasure in the death of the wicked; but that the wicked turn from his way and live: turn ye, turn ye from your evil ways; for why will ye die, O house of Israel? . . . When I shall say to the righteous, that he shall surely live; if he trust to

The handwriting on the wall.

his own righteousness, and commit iniquity, all his righteousnesses shall not be remembered; but for his iniquity that he hath committed, he shall die for it. Again, when I say unto the wicked, Thou shalt surely die; if he turn from his sin, and do that which is lawful and right; . . . none of his sins that he hath committed shall be mentioned unto him: he hath done that which is lawful and right; he shall surely live. Eze. 33:10-16.

They received not the love of the truth, that they might be saved. 2 Thess. 2:10.

Wherefore I say unto thee, Her sins, which are many, are forgiven; for she loved much: but to whom little is forgiven, the same loveth little. Luke 7:47.

Where sin abounded, grace did much more abounded. Rom. 5:20.

1 John 1:9.

I acknowledged my sin unto thee, and mine iniquity have I not hid. I said, I will confess my transgressions unto the LORD; and thou forgavest the iniquity of my sin. Selah. Ps. 32:5.

He that covereth his sins shall not prosper: but whoso confesseth and forsaketh them shall have mercy. Prov. 28:13.

At what instant I shall speak concerning a nation, and concerning a kingdom, to pluck up, and to pull down, and to destroy it; If that nation, against whom I have pronounced, turn from their evil, I will repent of the evil that I thought to do unto them. And at what instant I shall speak concerning a nation, and concerning a kingdom, to build and to plant it; If it do evil in my sight, that it obey not my voice, then I will repent of the good, wherewith I said I would benefit them. Jer. 18:7-10.

28. PERES; Thy kingdom is divided, and given to the Medes and Persians.
29. Then commanded Belshazzar, and they clothed Daniel with scarlet, and put a chain of gold about his neck, and made a proclamation concerning him, that he should be the third ruler in the kingdom.
Dan. 5:28-29.

To the magicians who stood within hearing, as Daniel gave the interpretation, the words came with peculiar force because of their familiarity with religious customs.

To the one who knows God, the attitude of the Lord toward the sinner is very different, and still the symbol of the weights and balances is applicable. That this subject might be understood, God had sent an explanation by the prophet Ezekiel. When a man sins and dies without repentance, he is cut off from God, because his iniquities separate between him and God, and he cannot be saved. If a man loves Christ and accepts Him and His righteousness, Christ's character is written opposite the name of that man in the books of heaven, and so long as a love of the truth is cherished, the man hides in Christ and is known by the character of Christ. God deals with men in the present. We may have been the worst of sinners, but if *to-day* we are hidden in Christ, heaven takes into account only our present position.

So it was that God dealt with the nations, [84] and this answers the question why Nebuchadnezzar might one day be in favor with God and the next day be in condemnation; why Zedekiah's course of action was condemned once, and then again he was told that it lay in his power to save Jerusalem.

God gave the Babylonian monarchs, and through them the entire kingdom, an abundance of time to accept Him. He waited long. The Holy Watcher hovered long near the center of earthly governments; every blessing which Heaven could bestow was given to woo the kingdom to the side of right. But at last the slender cord which connected earth with heaven snapped; there was no channel for the flow of the Holy Spirit; death and death only could result. That there might be no misunderstanding, the last word read, "Thy kingdom is divided, and given to the Medes and Persians."

Scarcely had the scarlet robe been placed on Daniel and the golden chain hung about his neck, when the shouts of the invading army rang through the palace.

In the midst of their feasting and rioting, none had noticed that the waters in the Euphrates were steadily diminishing. The besieging army of Cyrus, which had long been held at bay by the massive walls, was eagerly watching the river. The river had been turned from its course, and as soon as the water had sufficiently subsided to allow the men a passage in the bed of the river, they entered from opposite sides of the city. In their reckless feeling of security, the Babylonians had left open the gates in the walls which lined the river-banks inside the city. So the Persians, once in the river-bed, [85] easily entered the city through" the open gates.

Soon one post was running to "meet another, and one messenger to meet another," to show the king of Babylon that his city is taken at one end." But the news was received too late to save the king. God had numbered and finished his kingdom. The enemy made a rush for the palace. The pen of Inspiration describes the overthrow of the kingdom more vividly than any human historian. Of those guests at the banquet of Belshazzar it is said, "I will make them drunken, that they may rejoice, and sleep a perpetual sleep, and not awake. ... I will bring them down like lambs to the slaughter." Then as if the eye of the prophet failed to separate Satan from the kingdom which he had so long controlled, he exclaims, "How is Sheshach taken! and how is the praise of the whole earth surprised! How is Babylon become an astonishment among the nations!" Fire raged through the streets, and as the people realized that destruction was upon them, their cry reached heaven. It was a hand-to-hand fight with fire and sword until men grew weary and gave up the struggle.

"In that night was Belshazzar slain," and the [86] kingdom was given to Darius, the aged king of the Medes. Thus came to an end one of the proudest monarchies that has ever been upon the earth. When an individual or a nation fills up the cup of iniquity and passes the limit of God's mercy, it is quickly humbled in the dust.

The question naturally arises, Why did not the conquering army destroy Daniel, who was the third ruler in the kingdom, at this critical moment? The answer is simple and natural. When the kingdom was taken and Belshazzar slain, Nabonadius, the first ruler, at the head of an army, was sur-

A sword is upon the Chaldeans, saith the Lord, and upon the inhabitants of Babylon, and upon her princes, and upon her wise men. A sword is upon the liars; and they shall dote: a sword is upon her mighty men; and they shall be dismayed. A sword is upon their horses, and upon their chariots, and upon all the mingled people that are in the midst of her; at the noise of the taking of Babylon the earth is moved, and the cry is heard among the nations.   Jer. 50:35-46.

Thus saith the LORD of hosts, the God of Israel; The daughter of Babylon is like a threshingfloor, it is time to thresh her: yet a little while, and the time of her harvest shall come.   Jer. 51:33.

God giveth to a man that is good in his sight wisdom, and knowledge, and joy: but to the sinner he giveth travail, to gather and to heap up, that he may give to him that is good before God.   Eccl. 2:26.

Though Babylon should mount up to heaven, and though she should fortify the height of her strength, yet from me shall spoilers come unto her, saith the LORD. A sound of a cry cometh from Babylon, and great destruction from the land of the Chaldeans. . . . Thus saith the LORD of hosts; The broad walls of Babylon shall be utterly broken, and her high gates shall be burned with fire; and the people shall labour in vain, and the folk in the fire, and they shall be weary.   Jer. 51:53-58.

Isa. 51:57.
I will bring them down like lambs to the slaughter, like rams with he goats.   Jer. 51:40.
Jer. 51:41.
I have laid a snare for thee, and thou art also taken, O Babylon, and thou wast not aware: thou art found, and also caught, because thou hast striven against the LORD.   Jer. 50:24.

30. In that night was Belshazzar the king of the Chaldeans slain.
31. And Darius the Median took the kingdom, being about threescore and two years old.
    Dan. 5:30-31.

Whoso walketh uprightly shall be saved: but he that is perverse in his ways shall fall at once.   Prov. 28:18.
LORD, thou wilt ordain peace for us: for thou also hast wrought all our works in us.   Isa. 26:12.

Isa. 45:1-3.
That saith of Cyrus, He is my shepherd, and shall perform all my pleasure: even saying to Jerusalem, Thou shalt be built; and to the temple, Thy foundation shall be laid.   Isa. 44:28.

Dan. 8:2.
Jer. 49:39.
Isa. 21:2.

rounded by the enemy in another part of the kingdom. This left Daniel sole ruler in Babylon. He, knowing that over one hundred years before, Isaiah had prophesied that Cyrus should take the kingdom, was ready to welcome him whom God had said should build the house of the Lord at Jerusalem.

There is also good reason to believe that Daniel and Cyrus were not strangers. When excluded from the council of Belshazzar, Daniel had spent a portion of his time at Shushan, the capital of Elam. Elam had revolted from Babylon, in fulfillment of the prophecy of Jeremiah.

I will dry up the rivers.   Isa. 44:27.

Isa. 45:1, 2.
Jer. 50:38.
Jer. 51:36.

Daniel may have formed an acquaintance with Cyrus, and showed to him, as the high priest did to Alexander on a certain occasion, the prophecy that pertained to himself, and also revealed to him the way God had said he should enter Babylon. It is evident from the wording of the decree given in the first chapter of Ezra, that Cyrus was familiar with these prophecies.

The Lord God of heaven. . . hath charged me to build him an house at Jerusalem.
                              Ezra 1:1-5.
Ps. 119:105.
Rom. 13:11.
For there is nothing hid, which shall not be manifested; neither was any thing kept secret, but that it should come abroad.   Mar. 4:22.

Ps. 139:1-16.

I say unto you, That every idle word that men shall speak, they shall give account thereof in the day of judgment. For by thy words thou shalt be justified, and by thy words thou shalt be condemned.   Mat. 12:36-37.

God gives continual opportunities for His people to prepare the way for blessings to come [87] to them, when they are walking in the light. God is never taken by surprise, but His Word is a lamp to the feet and a guide to the life. This illustrates the importance of God's people "knowing the time" in which they live from the light of prophecy. There is a Witness in every scene of sacrilegious mirth, and the recording angel writes, "Thou art weighed in the balances, and art found wanting." This same Witness is with us wherever we are. Although we may feel that we have liberty to follow the promptings of the natural heart, and indulge in lightness and trifling, yet an account must be rendered for these things. As we sow, so shall we reap.

Who raised up the righteous man from the east, called him to his foot, gave the nations before him, and made him rule over kings? he gave them as the dust to his sword, and as driven stubble to his bow. He pursued them, and passed safely.
                              Isa. 41:1-5.

Nations to-day are repeating the history of the last years of the kingdom of Babylon. Medo-Persia was the instrument in the Lord's hands to punish Babylon. The next great overthrow of governments will usher in the kingdom of our Lord. For the final battle, nations are now mustering their forces. The cry has gone forth, "Flee out of the midst of Babylon, and deliver every man his soul; be not cut off in her iniquity; for this is the time of the Lord's vengeance." [88]

Jer. 51:16.
Rev. 18:4.

CHAPTER 7

DANIEL IN THE LIONS' DEN

DANIEL 6

THE first five chapters of the book of Daniel relate the history of the kingdom of Babylon. With the close of the fifth chapter, the government is transferred to the Medes, of whom Darius, known in history as Darius the Mede, a man of sixty-two years, is king. With him is associated Cyrus, the Persian, the leader of the army, and heir to the throne. The time represented by the golden head of the image has passed, and a baser metal represents the rising power. The Medes were not, however, a new or unknown power, for they are mentioned in chronology as descendants of Japheth, and as early as the eighth century B. C., when [89] Israel was taken captive by the Assyrians, they were scattered through the cities of the Medes. This had brought the Medes into contact with the Jews two centuries before the

And Darius the Median took the kingdom, being about threescore and two years old.

Dan. 5:31.

This image's head was of fine gold, his breast and his arms of silver. . . . And after thee shall arise another kingdom inferior to thee.   Dan. 2:32-39.

In the ninth year of Hoshea the king of Assyria took Samaria, and carried Israel away into Assyria, and placed them in Halah and in Habor by the river of Gozan, and in the cities of the Medes.

2 Kings 17:6.

Isa. 43:1-13.

Who changed the truth of God into a lie, and worshiped and serverd the creature more than the Creator, who is blessed forever. Amen.

Rom. 1:19, 20, 25.

fall of Babylon. To their knowledge of the God of the Jews may be attributed the purity of their worship, for while they were heathens, they had never fallen into the gross forms of idolatry which were practiced by most of the nations of Western Asia.

The habits of both the Medes and the Persians, but more particularly of the Persians, brought them in close touch with nature, and in their worship they took the elements,—fire, earth, water, and air—as the highest manifestations of the Deity. They therefore sought a hill country, and kept a perpetual fire burning. They believed in the struggle between good and evil as represented by light and darkness, and doubtless the words of Isaiah, which are addressed to Cyrus, had this belief in mind, for the Lord says, I form the light and create darkness: I make peace, and create evil; I the Lord do all these things" In these words He places Himself above the gods of the Persians, and explains why He called Cyrus to his strange work.

The Persians at the time of the overthrow of Babylon were physically strong and rugged, due in great measure to the simplicity of their habits and their temperance in eating. Such were the conditions which made it possible for the Medes and Persians to be the rod in the Lord's hand for the punishment of Babylon. The organization of the kingdom as effected by the Babylonian monarchs is given in the first [90] verse of the sixth chapter, for Darius immediately placed one hundred and twenty princes over the one hundred and twenty provinces. This change in the administration of the government of the provinces is highly important, since the strength of the ruling monarch is in proportion to the sympathy and co-operation of the subject princes. It was impossible to maintain a representative government where there were conquered provinces, and peace depended much upon the strength of the central organization. Over the one hundred and twenty princes were the three presidents, of whom Daniel was the first.

It was not after the order of the world that Daniel, belonging to a race held in bondage, should at once be given one of the highest positions in the newly organized govern-

---

The people still sacrificed and burnt incense in the high places.　　　　2 Kings 12:3.

Ye shall utterly destroy all the places, wherein the nations which ye shall possess served their gods, upon the high mountains, and upon the hills, and under every green tree.　　　Deut. 12:2.
Isa. 45:7.

Lo, I will raise and cause to come up against Babylon an assembly of great nations from the north country: and they shall set themselves in array against her; from thence she shall be taken: their arrows shall be as of a mighty expert man; none shall return in vain.　　　Jer. 50:9.

Make bright the arrows; gather the shields: the LORD hath raised up the spirit of the kings of the Medes.　　　Jer. 51:11.

Lift ye up a banner upon the high mountain, exalt the voice unto them, shake the hand, that they may go into the gates of the nobles. I have commanded my sanctified ones, I have also called my mighty ones for mine anger, even them that rejoice in my highness.　　　Isa. 13:1-5.

In multitude of consellors there is safety.
　　　　Prov. 24:6.

Prov. 15:22.

In the multitude of people is the king's honour: but in the want of people is the destruction of the prince.　　　Prov. 14:28.

1. It pleased Darius to set over the kingdom an hundred and twenty princes, which should be over the whole kingdom.
2. And over these three presidents; of whom Daniel was first: that the princes might give accounts unto them, and the king should have no damage.
3. Then this Daniel was preferred above the presidents and princes, because an excellent spirit was in him; and the king thought to set him over the whole realm.
　　　　　　　Dan. 6:1-3.

ment. It will appear still more unusual when it is remembered that Daniel had been made third ruler of the Babylonian kingdom under Belshazzar. Reference to the first and second verses of the eighth chapter of Daniel shows that Daniel was not a stranger to the new government, for before the death of Belshazzar, he had lived at Shushan, in the province of Elam. To the fact of acquaintanceship it may be added that the excellent spirit and unsurpassed business ability of Daniel brought him into prominence.

He brought me forth also into a large place; he delivered me, because he delighted in me. The LORD rewarded me according to my righteousness; according to the cleanness of my hands hath he recompensed me. Ps. 18:19-20.

When a man's ways please the LORD, he maketh even his enemies to be at peace with him. Prov. 16:7.

I was at Shushan in the palace, which is in the province of Elam. Dan. 8:2.

Here is recorded the case of a man who was a devout follower of God, one whose honesty, accuracy, and skill in every particular were a wonder to the world. It is a powerful witness to the duties and privileges of every Christian business man. He was a noble statesman, an [91] example for all office-holders, but not a politician. He fulfilled his duties under the Medes just as faithfully as under the Babylonians. He served the God of heaven, and not a man-made party. A business man does not necessarily have to be a sharp, policy man, but may be instructed by God at every step. When prime minister of Babylon, Daniel, as a prophet of God, was receiving the light of heavenly inspiration. The usual type of statesman,—worldly, ambitious, scheming,—is compared in the Scriptures to the grass of the field, and to the fading flower. The Lord is pleased to have men of intelligence in His work if they remain true to Him. Through the grace of Christ, man may preserve the integrity of his character when surrounded by adverse circumstances. Daniel made God his strength, and was not forsaken in his time of greatest need.

The king's favour is toward a wise servant. Prov. 14:35.

A man of understanding is of an excellent spirit. Prov. 17:27.

Seest thou a man diligent in his business? he shall stand before kings; he shall not stand before mean men. Prov 22:29.

Blessed is the man that walketh not in the counsel of the ungodly, nor standeth in the way of sinners, nor sitteth in the seat of the scornful. But his delight is in the law of the LORD; and in his law doth he meditate day and night. And he shall be like a tree planted by the rivers of water, that bringeth forth his fruit in his season; his leaf also shall not wither; and whatsoever he doeth shall prosper. Ps. 1:1-3.

Enter not into the path of the wicked, and go not in the way of evil men. Avoid it, pass not by it, turn from it, and pass away. Prov. 4:14-15.

The very position which he occupied put Daniel to the severest test. As chairman or chief of the presidents over the princes, Daniel was obliged to deal with all the under-rulers of the empire. One by one they were required to render an account to him. This was that the king might receive no damage. The king, then, was in danger; not in danger of losing his life, but these officials were scheming politicians who were robbing the government in every possible way. If they had taxes to gather, they turned a large per cent, to their own account. There

And whatsoever ye do in word or deed, do all in the name of the Lord Jesus, giving thanks to God and the Father by him. Col. 3:17.

Prov. 23:17-19.

But now ye rejoices in yur boastings; all such rejoicing is evil. James 4:11-16.

These things I have spoken unto you, that in me ye might have peace. In the world ye shall have tribulation: but be of good cheer; I have overcome the world. John 16:33.

For man also knoweth not his time: as the fishes that are taken in an evil net, and as the birds that are caught in the snare; so are the sons of men snared in an evil time, when it falleth suddenly upon them. Eccl. 9:12.

And over these three presidents; of whom Daniel was first: that the princes might give accounts unto them, and the king should have no damage. Dan. 6:2.

The king by judgment establisheth the land: but he that receiveth gifts overthroweth it. Prov. 29:4.

Thou shalt not wrest judgment; thou shalt not respect persons, neither take a gift: for a gift doth blind the eyes of the wise, and pervert the words of the righteous. Deut. 16:19.

The good man is perished out of the earth: and there is none upright among men: they all lie in wait for blood; they hunt every man his brother with a net. That they may do evil with both hands earnestly, the prince asketh, and the judge asketh for a reward; and the great man, he uttereth his mischievous desire: so they wrap it up. The best of them is as a brier: the most upright is sharper than a thorn hedge: the day of thy watchmen and thy visitation cometh; now shall be their perplexity. Micah 7:2-4.

Is there any thing whereof it may be said, See, this is new? it hath been already of old time, which was before us. Eccl. 1:10.

Thy princes are rebellious, and companions of thieves: every one loveth gifts, and followeth after rewards: they judge not the fatherless, neither doth the cause of the widow come unto them. Isa. 1:23.

Micah 3:11.
1 Sam. 8:1-5.

For from the least of them even unto the greatest of them every one is given to covetousness; and from the prophet even unto the priest every one dealeth falsely. Jer. 6:13.

There is a sore evil which I have seen under the sun, namely, riches kept for the owners thereof to their hurt. Eccl. 5:13.

So I returned, and considered all the oppressions that are done under the sun: and behold the tears of such as were oppressed, and they had no comforter; and on the side of their oppressors there was power; but they had no comforter. Eccl. 4:1.

was bribery, cheating, wire pulling, and buying of positions in the Babylonian government, as there is in the world to-day. Dishonesty was found everywhere.

Inspiration does not describe the iniquity in [92] detail, but it does say, "The godly is perished out of the earth; . . . they hunt every man his brother with a net. That they may do evil with both hands earnestly, the prince asketh, and the judge asketh for a reward; and the great man, he uttereth his mischievous desire: so they wrap it up." The princes and men in power not only work mischievously, but they work with *both hands earnestly.* If details are wanted, study the governments of to-day. They are the off-shoots from that same root of Babylon, and by studying the iniquity of to-day, we can know 'the sins against which Daniel had tp stand. Even in the best of earthly governments, hundreds of thousands of dollars are used annually in an unlawful manner. When $3,500 is paid for a single vote, and the individual returns the money because he has an offer of $3,700 from the other party; when the mayor of a city can afford to spend three or four times his salary to obtain an office, it must be known that money comes from some unlawful source.

Roman history, with its stories of trusts, monopolies, and corporations, its bribery in the senate and outside the senate, is the history of Babylon, for Rome was one of the governments which were built upon Babylonian principles. French history during the period of the Revolution repeats the story. The history of England, the continental countries, and the United States to-day repeat the same story. So in current history may be read in detail what had to be met by the prime minister in the city of Babylon. The sixth chapter of Daniel is left on record to show how a man of God, when [93] elevated to such a position, can remain uncontaminated. It shows that attitude which any man of God must assume toward popular vice and corruption, and more than that, it shows what treatment a man who is true to principle must expect to receive from the hands of those who are corrupt.

Because Daniel did guard the king's interests, Darius was about to set him over the whole realm. But the honesty of one man is like a thorn in the flesh of the unjust, and in their political meetings the princes and presidents sought to destroy the man who made accurate reports, and who was faultless in his dealings. "Render unto Caesar the things that are Caesar's," is a principle of divine government, and from this principle Daniel could not be swerved.

One can imagine the language of the princes as they discussed the matter. Every scheme they had tried had been checked, and yet it was generally acknowledged that it would be useless to bring a complaint concerning the work of Daniel. There was but one possible way to condemn him, and that must be concerning his religion. Even on that point they dared not make open accusation, but must accomplish their end without revealing their object. Their contemptible, under-handed method of procedure brought them in conflict with the God of Daniel, not with Daniel as an individual.

With manifest respect for the king, and with words which flattered him, a committee of the princes waited upon Darius. The first words they spoke revealed that there was a plan on foot, for they said, "All the presidents of the [94] kingdom, the governors," and other officers had consulted together, when in truth they had held secret meetings, and the chief of the presidents was kept in ignorance of the matter.

The king placed great confidence in his prime minister, and anything purporting to have his approval was accepted without further investigation. The form of a decree was presented to the king. It exalted Darius above all earthly monarchs, and attempted to place him above God. King Darius placed his seal upon the document, making it a law of the land, that for thirty days no man should bow down or worship or ask any petition, save of the king.

The heart of God was drawn toward Babylon. Heaven was bound very close to earth, notwithstanding the iniquity, for God's chosen people were there, and the time of their deliverance drew near. While the Medes and the Persians knew *about* God, they did not know Him. An actual experience was needed, and God would manifest His power

James 5:1-5.

Eccl. 1:9, 10, 15.

Isa. 8:9-12.

Jer. 10:2, 3.

Enter not into the path of the wicked, and go not in the way of evil men. Avoid it, pass not by it, turn from it, and pass away. Prov. 4:14-15.

The wicked plotteth against the just, and gnasheth upon him with his teeth. Ps. 37:12.

Prov. 22:4.

They hate him that rebuketh in the gate, and they abhor him that speaketh uprightly Amos 5:10, 12.

4. Then the presidents and princes sought to find occasion against Daniel concerning the kingdom; but they could find none occasion nor fault; forasmuch as he was faithful, neither was there any error or fault found in him. Dan. 6:4.
5. Then said these men, We shall not find any occasion against this Daniel, except we find it against him concerning the law of his God. Dan. 6:5.

Thus saith the LORD of hosts; After the glory hath he sent me unto the nations which spoiled you: for he that toucheth you toucheth the apple of his eye. Zech. 2:8.

6. Then these presidents and princes assembled together to the king, and said thus unto him, King Darius, live for ever.
7. All the presidents of the kingdom, the governors, and the princes, the counsellors, and the captains, have consulted together to establish a royal statute, and to make a firm decree, that whosoever shall ask a petition of any God or man for thirty days, save of thee, O king, he shall be cast into the den of lions.
8. Now, O king, establish the decree, and sign the writing, that it be not changed, according to the law of the Medes and Persians, which altereth not.

Prov. 24:5.

Wherefore king Darius signed the writing and the decree. Dan 6:6-9.

For the LORD'S portion is his people; Jacob is the lot of his inheritance. Deut. 32:9.

I girded thee, though thou hast not known me: Isa. 45:5.

Even to your old age I am he; and even to hoar hairs will I carry you: I have made, and I will bear; even I will carry, and will deliver you. Isa. 46:4.

Job 5:26.

Mark the perfect man, and behold the upright: for the end of that man is peace. Ps. 37:37.

The law of his God is in his heart; none of his steps shall slide. Ps. 37:31.

They are life unto those that find them, and health to all their flesh. Prov. 4:22.

10. Now when Daniel knew that the writing was signed, he went into his house; and his windows being open in his chamber toward Jerusalem, he kneeled upon his knees three times a day, and prayed, and gave thanks before his God, as he did aforetime. Dan. 6:10.

As for me, I will call upon God; and the LORD shall save me. Evening, and morning, and at noon, will I pray, and cry aloud: and he shall hear my voice. Ps. 55:16-17.

2. Chron. 6:36-39.

On the sabbath we went out of the city by a river side, where prayer was wont to be made; and we sat down, and spake unto the women which resorted thither. Acts 16:13.

I am crucified with Christ: nevertheless I live; yet not I, but Christ liveth in me: and the life which I now live in the flesh I live by the faith of the Son of God, who loved me, and gave himself for me. Gal. 2:20.

1 Cor. 2:14.

through that same faithful servant who had witnessed for Him sixty-eight years.

Daniel was true, noble, and generous. He was anxious to be at peace with all men, but would not permit any power to turn him aside from the path of duty. He was willing to obey those who had rule over him; but kings and decrees could not make him swerve from his allegiance to the King of kings. He realized that compliance with Bible requirements was a blessing to both soul and body.

Daniel was aware of the purpose of his enemies to destroy his influence and his life; he [95] knew of the decree, but it made no difference in his daily life. He did nothing unusual to provoke wrath, but in a straight-forward manner performed his accustomed duties, and three times a day, at his usual times for prayer, he went into his room, and with

King Darius placed his seal upon the document, making it a law of the land, that for thirty days no man should bow down or worship or ask any petition, save of the king.

his windows open toward Jerusalem, earnestly [96] pleaded with the God of heaven to give him strength to be faithful.

Daniel had a special meeting-place, and an appointed hour when he met the Lord, and these appointments were kept. There is a beauty in the thought of the soul connection between Daniel and Heaven. His spiritual life was an actual thing, a life which he lived as real and true as the physical life. The only life which his enemies knew or could comprehend was the physical life. To sever the intercourse with God would be as painful to Daniel as to deprive him of natural life; and as Christ withdrew to the mountains after days of soul-harrowing labor in order to be refilled with that life which He constantly imparted to the hungering multitudes, so Daniel sought God in prayer. It was only by these frequent times of spirit filling, as it were, that he had strength to meet the nervous strain of his official duties. When the outward pressure was greatest, then he had the greatest need of being filled, that the equilibrium might be maintained. Fifteen pounds to every square inch of surface on the body is the pressure under which we live physically. Why does it not crush us? Because the pressure is equal on all sides, and thus we are unconscious of it. It is but a type of the spiritual life. He who balances the clouds will so balance outward pressure with inward power, if we but let Him, that we never need be disturbed. If trials are great, open the soul to Heaven, and equalize the pressure by being filled from above.

Daniel did not and could not deny his Saviour by concealing himself in some corner of his [97] room to pray. He knelt by the open window, toward Jerusalem. He did not pray in his heart, silently, he prayed aloud, as had been his custom before the decree was issued. Noble arid true is the one who has God ruling in his heart. Underhanded and mean are the actions of those who yield to the influence of Satan. All that is noble in man is lost forever when such a leader is chosen. Satan was in the councils of those officials as they plotted against Daniel, and after the decree was signed, they set spies to catch him. They saw him kneel in his usual place of prayer; three times each day they

And it came to pass in those days, that he went out into a mountain to pray, and continued all night in prayer to God.   Luke 6:12.

And when he had sent the multitudes away, he went up into a mountain apart to pray: and when the evening was come, he was there alone.   Matt. 14:23.

That he would grant you, according to the riches of his glory, to be strengthened with might by his Spirit in the inner man; That Christ may dwell in your hearts by faith; that ye, being rooted and grounded in love, May be able to comprehend with all saints what is the breadth, and length, and depth, and height; And to know the love of Christ, which passeth knowledge, that ye might be filled with all the fulness of God.   Eph. 3:16-19.

Job 37:19.

There hath no temptation taken you but such as is common to man: but God is faithful, who will not suffer you to be tempted above that ye are able; but will with the temptation also make a way to escape, that ye may be able to bear it.   1 Cor. 10:13.

Be filled with the Spirit.   Eph. 5:18.

Eph. 2:22

11. Then these men assembled, and found Daniel praying and making supplication before his God.
12. Then they came near, and spake before the king concerning the king's decree; Hast thou not signed a decree, that every man that shall ask a petition of any God or man within thirty days, save of thee, O king, shall be cast into the den of lions? The king answered and said, The thing is true, according to the law of the Medes and Persians, which altereth not.
13. Then answered they and said before the king, That Daniel, which is of the children of the captivity of Judah, regardeth not thee, O king, nor the decree that thou hast signed, but maketh his petition three times a day.   *Dan 6:11-13.*

Prov. 6:17-19.
Prov. 1:11.
Jer. 5:26.

14. Then the king, when he heard these words, was sore displeased with himself, and set his heart on Daniel to deliver him: and he laboured till the going down of the sun to deliver him.
16. Then these men assembled unto the king, and said unto the king, Know, O king, that the law of the Medes and Persians is, That no decree nor statute which the king establisheth may be changed.   *Dan. 6:14-15.*
16. Then the king commanded, and they brought Daniel, and cast him into the den of lions. Now the king spake and said unto Daniel, Thy God whom thou servest continually, he will deliver thee.
17. And a stone was brought, and laid upon the mouth of the den; and the king sealed it with his own

To sever the intercourse with God would be as painful to Daniel as to deprive him of natural life.

signet, and with the signet of his lords; that the pur-
pose might not be changed concerning Daniel.
                                        Dan. 6:16-17.

heard his voice raised in earnest supplication. It was enough; the accusation was made against *"that* Daniel which is of the children of the captivity of Judah."

For the first time the design of the counselors flashed across the mind of Darius. A decree signed by the king's seal was unalterable in the kingdom of the Medes and Persians, yet the king spent the entire day pleading with those high in authority, [98] and searching for some way of esescape; but with Satanic smiles those princes met every argument with the words, "Know, O king, that the law of the Medes and Persians is, That no decree or statute which the king establisheth may be changed."

When the hands of men are tied, when there is no power on earth to help, then is God's opportunity. And Daniel's prayer still ascended: "It is time for Thee, Lord, to work. Keep me in perfect harmony with Thee" While his own heart was in sympathy with Heaven, there was no power on earth that could deprive him of his life, if God desired him to live.

Daniel and Darius met at the mouth of the lions' den, but there was not another man in the realm so fitted to go inside as this same Daniel. Pressing the hand of his esteemed minister, Darius said, "Thy God whom thou servest continually, He will deliver thee." Daniel passed into the midst of the wild beasts of the forest, and a stone was brought and laid upon the mouth of the den. Probably some feared that friends and sympathizers of Daniel might come to the rescue, so the seal of the king was placed upon the stone, that the purpose might not be changed.

Satan exulted as he did years later when he saw the Son of God in the sepulcher, with a stone before the door, and the stone sealed with the Roman seal. But there was no more power to hold Daniel in the den of lions than to keep Christ in the grave. The angel came, not to the stone, but into the den, and one of the most precious times for Daniel was when he sat in the center of the cave, and those lions [99] couched at his feet or fondly licked his hands.

There was a time when the lion and the lamb played together, and man was given dominion over the beasts of the earth. It was only after sin entered, and man took the life of the beasts, that they in turn sought to destroy man. Harmony with God will finally restore man to his God-given place as king over the beasts. Daniel's heart was beating with the heart of God, and when he entered the den, the beasts were at peace with him. The unity of feeling is shown in the fact that an angel was visible, and Daniel talked face to face with the heavenly visitor.

But the king's heart was sad, and he spent the night in fasting and prayer. Hastening to the den in the early hours of the morning, he called: "O Daniel, servant of the living God, is thy God, whom thou servest continually, able to deliver thee from the lions?" And from the recesses of the den came the words of cheer, "My God hath sent His angel, and hath shut the lions' mouths."

"He is not here, but risen." "Why seek ye the living among the dead?" said the angel, as the women came to the sepulcher of Christ. So no manner of hurt was found upon Daniel, the representative of Christ, "because he believed in his God;" because innocency was found in him.

When Daniel's accusers were cast into the lions' den, they were crushed and devoured at once. Again the nations of the world saw the power of Israel's God to preserve His faithful people. Darius had his belief in God confirmed; and Cyrus had received a lesson he could not

Ps. 57:1-5.
Matt. 27:63-66.
Acts 2:24.
Daniel at this time was about eighty-five years of age.

Mark 1:13.
Gen. 1:28.
Gen. 2:19, 20.

At destruction and famine thou shalt laugh: neither shalt thou be afraid of the beasts of the earth. For thou shalt ne in league with the stones of the fiels: and the beasts of the field shall be at peace with thee.   Job 5:22-27.

And in that day will I make a covenant for them with the beasts of the field, and with the fowls of heaven, and with the creeping things of the ground: and I will break the bow and the sword and the battle out of the earth, and will make them to lie down safely.   Hos. 2:18.

The angel of the LORD encampeth round about them that fear him, and delivereth them.
   Ps. 34:7.

18. Then the king went to his palace, and passed the night fasting: neither were instruments of musick brought before him: and his sleep went from him.
19. Then the king arose very early in the morning, and went in haste unto the den of lions.
20. And when he came to the den, he cried with a lamentable voice unto Daniel: and the king spake and said to Daniel, O Daniel, servant of the living God, is thy God, whom thou servest continually, able to deliver thee from the lions?
21. Then said Daniel unto the king, O king, live forever.
22. My God hath sent his angel, and hath shut the lions' mouths, that they have not hurt me: forasmuch as before him innocency was found in me; and also before thee, O king, have I done no hurt.
23. Then was the king exceeding glad for him, and commanded that they should take Daniel up out of the den. So Daniel was taken up out of the den, and no manner of hurt was found upon him, because he believed in his God.
24. And the king commanded, and they brought those men which had accused Daniel, and they cast them into the den of lions, them, their children, and their wives; and the lions had the mastery of them, and brake all their bones in pieces or ever they came at the bottom of the den.   Dan. 6:18-24.

Blessed is the man that endureth temptation: for when he is tried, he shall receive the crown of life, which the Lord hath promised to them that love him.   Jam. 1:12.

25. Then king Darius wrote unto all people, nations, and languages, that dwell in all the earth; Peace be multiplied unto you.

"Is thy God... able to deliver thee from the lions?"

soon forget. It was a fresh token to the Israelites that God was in their midst to bless them. To Daniel came the voice of God promising patience and strength to perform his duties as a servant of God. Greater light came to Daniel, for it was after this experience that a large portion of the prophecies were given to him.

Darius published to "all people, nations, and languages, that dwell in all the earth," "that in every dominion of my kingdom men tremble and fear before the God of Daniel." Thus God not only honored Daniel by a most miraculous deliverance, but his integrity was the means of publishing the truth throughout the world. From this time Daniel prospered—during the reign of Darius, and in the reign of Cyrus, who issued the wonderful decree for the deliverance of the Jews.

If sick at heart because of the seeming prosperity of the wicked and the increase of wickedness among men in high places, learn their fate from the sixth chapter of Daniel.

If oppressed because of adherence to the Word of God, remember that Daniel represents all such, and what was done for him will be done for all whom Heaven favors to-day. Though death claim the body, the promise of God is a speedy resurrection; and whether in death, in prison, or in a den of lions, Satan has no power over Christ. "I am come that ye might have life, and that ye might have it more abundantly." [101]

26. I make a decree, That in every dominion of my kingdom men tremble and fear before the God of Daniel: for he is the living God, and stedfast for ever, and his kingdom that which shall not be destroyed, and his dominion shall be even unto the end.
27. He delivereth and rescueth, and he worketh signs and wonders in heaven and in earth, who hath delivered Daniel from the power of the lions.
28. So this Daniel prospered in the reign of Darius, and in the reign of Cyrus the Persian.

Dan 6:25-28.

But evil men and seducers shall wax worse and worse, deceiving, and being deceived.

2 Tim. 3:13.

I will ransom them from the power of the grave; I will redeem them from death: O death, I will be thy plagues; O grave, I will be thy destruction: repentance shall be hid from mine eyes.

Hos 13:14.

Isa. 26:19.
John 10:10.

Chapter 8

The Seventh Chapter of Daniel

The Judgment Scene

THE first half of the book of Daniel deals with questions pertaining particularly to the kingdom of Babylon as it existed in the days of the prophet. The last six chapters are devoted entirely to the history of the world as a whole, and in visions given at various times, the prophet is shown the great events until the end of time. Looking into the future, he sees, as it were, the mountain peaks lighted with the glory of God, and these striking features are noted with unerring accuracy to serve as guideposts, not to the Jews only, but to all people, that they may understand the times in which they live, and know what is about to come on the earth.

To the student of prophecy, the seventh chapter of Daniel is a most important record. By a continuous chain of events, the prophet gives [102] the history from the days of Babylon to the great investigative judgment, which is the central theme of the chapter.

The fact that God could open the future to a heathen king was remarkable. To Nebuchadnezzar the future of earthly governments only was shown, because he himself was earthly, and was incapable of grasping higher things; but to Daniel God opened scenes in heaven. Although the prophet was shown the history of nations, the angel of revelation touched briefly on those subjects, but lingered on the soul-thrilling description of the investigative judgment.

The seventh chapter of Daniel reveals the future of God's people, not only of the Hebrew nation, but the true,

Babylon, the glory of kingdoms, the beauty of the Chaldees' excellency. Isa. 13:19.

Surely the Lord GOD will do nothing, but he revealeth his secret unto his servants the prophets. Amos 3:7.

I will show thee that which is noted in the scripture of truth. Dan. 10:21.

Counsel is mine, and sound wisdom: I am understanding; I have strength. By me kings reign, and princes decree justice. By me princes rule, and nobles, even all the judges of the earth. Prov. 8:14-16.

When ye therefore shall see the abomination of desolation, spoken of by Daniel the prophet, stand in the holy place, (whoso readeth, let him understand). Matt. 24:15.

But there is a God in heaven that revealeth secrets, and maketh known to the king Nebuchadnezzar what shall be in the latter days. Dan. 2:28.

Dan. 2:31-35.
Dan. 7:9-14.

God shall judge the righteous and the wicked: for there is a time there for every purpose and for every work. Eccl. 3:17.

The secret things belong unto the LORD our God: but those things which are revealed belong unto us and to our children for ever, that we may do all the words of this law. Deut 29:29.

In the first year of Belshazzar king of Babylon Daniel had a dream and visions of his head upon his bed: then he wrote the dream, and told the sum of the matters. Dan. 7:1.

The four beasts.

the spiritual Israel. This vision was given to Daniel in the first year of the reign of Belshazzar, about 540 B. C. The mere giving of this view bears the strongest testimony to the results of Daniel's education when a youth, to his steadfastness of purpose, and his growth in spiritual things. At the age of eighty-five, after sixty-seven years of court life, with all its allurements, and the natural tendency of human nature to sink to a purely physical existence, his eye of faith was so undimmed that at the bidding of Michael, Gabriel could carry Daniel into heaven itself, there to behold the Father and the Son in the final work of the sanctuary above. Moses once saw these things from the top of Mount Horeb when the tabernacle was to be built, and so great was the glory that he had to veil his face before common people could behold him. Daniel's heart was with God, hence things which eye [103] hath not seen nor ear heard, could be revealed to him by the Spirit.

God said by the prophet Hosea, "I have spoken by the prophets, and I have multiplied visions, and used similitudes, by the ministry of the prophets." The kingdoms which have ruled the world were represented before Daniel as beasts of prey, which arose when the "four winds of the heaven strove upon the great sea." Winds are, in prophecy, a symbol of war and strife. The after-scenes of war and revolution, by which kingdoms come into power, are represented in the seventh chapter of Daniel by the four winds of heaven which strove upon the great sea. Sea or waters denote "people, and multitudes, and nations, and tongues." The beasts referred to represent kings or kingdoms.

Four great beasts came up from the sea; that is, they arose into prominence from the midst of the multitudes of earth. In other words, there was war among the nations, and four kingdoms arose, diverse from one another. Babylon, the first of these kingdoms, was represented to Nebuchadnezzar as the golden head of the great image. To Daniel the same power appeared as a lion, having eagles' wings. The strength of the monarch of the forest, to which is added the swiftness of the king of birds, is taken to represent the kingdom of

Righteousness keepeth him that is upright in the way: but wickedness overthroweth the sinner.
Prov. 13:6.

Look that thou make them after their pattern, which thou wast caused to see.
Ex. 25:40 [margin].

Till Moses had done speaking with them, he put a vail on his face.
Ex. 34:29-33.

It is written, Eye hath not seen, nor ear heard, neither have entered into the heart of man, the things which God hath prepared for them that love him. But God hath revealed them unto us by his Spirit: for the Spirit searcheth all things, yea, the deep things of God.
1 Cor. 2:9-10.

Hosea 12:10.

Daniel spake and said, I saw in my vision by night, and, behold, the four winds of the heaven strove upon the great sea.
Dan. 7:2.

I scattered them with a whirlwind among all the nations whom they knew not.
Zech. 7:14.

Jer. 25:32, 33.
Isa. 8:7.

He saith unto me, The waters which thou sawest, where the whore sitteth, are peoples, and multitudes, and nations, and tongues.
Rev. 17:15.

Dan. 7:17, 23.

And four great beasts came up from the sea, diverse one from another.
Dan. 7:3:

Thou art this head of gold.
Dan. 2:38.

Dan. 2:32, 38.

The first was like a lion, and had eagle's wings: I beheld till the wings thereof were plucked, and it was lifted up from the earth, and made stand upon the feet as a man, and a man's heart was given to it.
Dan. 7:4.

Behold the land of the Chaldeans; this people was not, till the Assyrian founded it for them that dwell in the wilderness: they set up the towers thereof, they raised up the palaces thereof.
Isa. 23:13.

Hab. 1:6-10.

I was wroth with my people, I have polluted mine inheriance, and given them into thine hand: thou didst show them no mercy; upon the ancient hast thou very heavily laid thy yoke.
Isa. 47:6.

What time she lifteth up herself on high, she scorneth the horse and his rider.
Job 39:18.

Thou hast trusted in thy wickedness: thou hast said, None seeth me. Thy wisdom and thy knowledge, it hath perverted thee; and thou hast said in thine heart, I am, and none else beside me.
Isa. 47:10.

Thy terribleness hath deceived thee, and the pride of thine heart, O thou that dwellest in the clefts of the rock, that holdest the height of the hill: though thou shouldest make thy nest as high as the eagle, I will bring thee down from thence, saith the LORD.
Jer. 49:16.

The mighty men of Babylon have forborn to fight, they have remained in their holds: their might hath failed; they became as women: they have burned her dwellingplaces; her bars are broken.
Jer. 51:30.
Jer. 17:9.

These two things shall come to thee in a moment in one day, the loss of children, and widowhood: they shall come upon thee in their perfection for the multitude of thy sorceries, and for the great abundance of thine enchantments.
Isa. 47:9.

Hab. 1:11.
Dan. 5:1-4.

It is the land of graven images, and they are mad upon their idols.
Jer. 50:38.

They clothed Daniel with scarlet, and put a chain of gold about his neck, and made a proclamation concerning him, that he should be the third ruler in the kingdom. In that night was Belshazzar the king of the Chaldeans slain. And Darius the Median took the kingdom, being about threescore and two years old.
Dan. 5:29-31.

which the city of Babylon was the capital. Over fifty years before, Jeremiah had spoken of the Babylonian power as a lion.

Before Babylon was known as an independent kingdom, while it was still a subject province of Assyria, Habakkuk, a prophet of Israel, had [104] been given a view of its work which shows the force of the symbol of a lion with eagles' wings. Speaking to Israel, he tells them of a work so wonderful that they will not believe it when told. "Lo, I raise up the Chaldeans, that *bitter* and *hasty* nation, which shall march through the breadth of the land, to possess the dwelling places that are not theirs. They are terrible and dreadful. . . . Their horses also are swifter than the leopards, and are more fierce than the evening wolves. . . . They shall fly as the eagle that hasteth to eat. They shall come all for violence; . . . they shall gather the captivity as the sand. And they shall scoff at the kings, and the princes shall be a scorn unto them; they shall deride every stronghold."

This is Babylon as Habakkuk saw it. While Daniel watched the same kingdom in his vision, the noble lion with its wings, denoting power and rapidity of conquest, had been lifted up from the earth into an unnatural position, and made to stand upon its feet as a man, and a man's heart was given to it. Man's heart without Christ is simply sin. The wings were shorn, and then Babylon was represented as it existed at the time of the vision, bereft of its strength, abandoned by God, with Belshazzar standing at the head of the government.

The prophet Habakkuk gives the reason for this sudden weakening of the mighty power of Babylon. He says, "Then shall his mind change, and he shall pass over, and offend, *imputing his power unto his god.*" The history of the kingdom as given in previous chapters shows how and when this was done. Babylon committed the unpardonable sin by imputing [105] the power and Spirit of God to the gods of the heathen. In this act the lion was shorn of its strength, the wings were plucked, and a man's heart was given to it. A few years after this vision, in the year 538 B.C., Daniel was a witness to the complete overthrow of the kingdom.

The Medo-Persian kingdom was bloodthirsty and cruel in its nature, and is represented by a bear. Darius was a Mede; and Cyrus, the leading general, a Persian. Darius the Mede took the Babylonian kingdom, and ruled for a short time. Cyrus the Persian was the leading spirit in the government after Darius had passed away. The bear, as well as the other beasts which followed the lion, represented kingdoms yet in the future at the time Daniel saw the vision. The bear of the seventh chapter of Daniel symbolizes the same power as the ram of the eighth chapter which the angel there tells the prophet represented the Medo-Persian empire. The history of this empire, given in the eleventh chapter of the book of Daniel, and the study of that chapter together with the thirteenth and twenty-first chapters of Isaiah and the book of Esther, will reveal the bearlike character of the nation which arose and devoured much flesh. The history of the second great kingdom covers the years from 538 to 331 B. C.

After the Medo-Persian.kingdom arose and fell, there came forth another kingdom of an entirely diferent nature from that represented by the bear. In the explanation of the vision of the eighth chapter of Daniel, the angel plainly states that the nation following Media [106] and Persia is Grecia. The Grecian kingdom, which followed Media and Persian, is compared to the sprightliness of a leopard in its natural state. This not being sufficient to represent the rapidity of the conquests of Alexander, the first king, the leopard had on its back four wings of a fowl. It also had four heads, which symbolized the division of Alexander's empire after his death, when four of his generals took his kingdom and dominion was given to them. Alexander's power is represented by the goat with the notable horn, which stamped all beneath its feet, as described in the eighth chapter of Daniel.

The history of the first three kingdoms is but lightly touched upon in this chapter, but when the fourth beast, "dreadful and terrible, and strong exceedingly," appeared, Daniel "would know the truth," and the angel explained that power minutely.

Behold, I will stir up the Medes against them, which shall not regard silver; and as for gold, they shall not delight in it. Their bows also shall dash the young men to pieces; and they shall have no pity on the fruit of the womb; their eye shall not spare children. Isa. 13:17-18.

And behold another beast, a second, like to a bear, and it raised up itself on one side, and it had three ribs in the mouth of it between the teeth of it: and they said thus unto it, Arise, devour much flesh.

Dan. 7:5.

The ram which thou sawest having two horns are the kings of Media and Persia.

Dan. 8:20.

And the letters were sent by posts into all the king's provinces, to destroy, to kill, and to cause to perish, all Jews, both young and old, little children and women, in one day, even upon the thirteenth day of the twelfth month, which is the month Adar, and to take the spoil of them for a prey. Esther 3:13.

A grievous vision is declared unto me; the treacherous dealer dealeth treacherously, and the spoiler spoileth. Go up, O Elam: besiege, O Media. Isa. 21:2.

6. After this I beheld, and lo another, like a leopard, which had upon the back of it four wings of a fowl; the beast had also four heads; and dominion was given to it.

Dan. 7:6.

When he shall stand up, his kingdom shall be broken, and shall be divided toward the four winds of heaven; and not to his posterity, nor according to his dominion which he ruled: for his kingdom shall be plucked up, even for others beside those. Dan. 11:4.

The rough goat is the king of Grecia: and the great horn that is between his eyes is the first king. Now that being broken, whereas four stood up for it, four kingdoms shall stand up out of the nation, but not in his power.

Dan. 8:21-22.

Everyone that asketh receiveth; and he that seeketh findeth; and to him that knocketh it shall be opened. Luke 11:10.

7. After this I saw in the night visions, and behold a fourth beast, dreadful and terrible, and strong exceedingly; and it had great iron teeth: it devoured and brake in pieces, and stamped the residue with the feet of it: and it was diverse from all the beasts that were before it; and it had ten horns.

8. I considered the horns, and, behold, there came up among them another little horn, before whom there were three of the first horns plucked up by the roots: and, behold, in this horn were eyes like the eyes of man, and a mouth speaking great things.

Dan. 7:7-8.

Hew the tree down, and destroy it; yet leave the stump of the roots thereof in the earth.

Dan. 4:23

Rom. 11:18.

I beheld till the thrones were cast down, and the Ancient of days did sit, whose garment was white as snow, and the hair of his head like the pure wool: his throne was like the fiery flame, and his wheels as burning fire.

Dan. 7:9.

There is hope of a tree, if it be cut down, that it will sprout again, and that the tender branch thereof will not cease. Though the root thereof wax old in the earth, and the stock thereof die in the ground; Yet through the scent of water it will bud, and bring forth boughs like a plant.

Job 14:7-9.

10. A fiery stream issued and came forth from before him: thousand thousands ministered unto him, and ten thousand times ten thousand stood before him: the judgment was set, and the books were opened.

11. I beheld then because of the voice of the great words which the horn spake: I beheld even till the beast was slain, and his body destroyed, and given to the burning flame.

12. As concerning the rest of the beasts, they had their dominion taken away: yet their lives were prolonged for a season and time.

13. I saw in the night visions, and, behold, one like the Son of man came with the clouds of heaven, and came to the Ancient of days, and they brought him near before him.

Dan. 7:10-13.

Dan. 2:40-42.

And there was given him dominion, and glory, and a kingdom, that all people, nations, and languages, should serve him: his dominion is an everlasting dominion, which shall not pass away, and his kingdom that which shall not be destroyed.

Dan. 7:14.

Rev. 8:7-13.

Luke 2:1-4.

The three preceding powers were symbolized by three of the mightiest beasts of the earth, but when the fourth beast was considered, there was no animal with a character to represent its terrible nature; so a beast without name having iron teeth, brass nails, and ten horns, was presented to the prophet.

The angel said to Daniel, "As concerning the rest of the beasts, they had their dominion taken away; yet their lives were prolonged." Each one, before being destroyed, was merged into the succeeding one, and its characteristic principles are represented in succession until the end of time. This is clearly shown in the second chapter of Daniel, where the gold, silver, brass, iron, and clay are broken to pieces together [107] and blown away like the chaff, when all earthly nations are destroyed. The same truth was represented in the fourth chapter, when the tree representing Babylon was cut down, but the roots remained in the ground. The roots represented the foundation principles upon which Babylon was built, and they have remained in the earth ever since. When Medo-Persia fell, she left her principles of government, education, and religion still alive, transmitting them to her posterity, the nations of earth. Greece did likewise, and with each succeeding empire those foundation principles, so clearly portrayed in Babylon, which were placed there by the prince of the power of the air, instead of appearing in a weakened state, sprang into life with renewed vigor. So it was that when the fourth kingdom appeared, those same principles of government, which were the counterfeit of heaven's underlying principles, were so strong that no natural beast could symbolize even pagan Rome.

Rome in religion renewed all the religious errors of Babylon, and in education she perpetuated the errors of Greece, while in cruelty she followed in the footsteps of Media and Persia. But as the prophet watched, things still more wonderful appeared. The fourth beast, representing Rome, which succeeded Greece in 161 B. C., had ten horns, which, said the angel, "are ten kings that shall arise." This fourth beast is identical with the legs of iron in the image shown to Nebuchadnezzar, and the ten horns correspond to the mixture of iron and clay in the feet of that image. Each of the preceding kingdoms had [108] fallen into the hands of some strong general who took the rule, but with Rome the case was different. The details of this history are given in the eighth chapter of Revelation under the symbol of the seven trumpets. Barbarian hordes from the north of Europe and Asia swept over the Roman empire between the years 351 and 483 A. D., crushing the government into ten parts. The ten kingdoms which arose as the result of the breaking up of the old Roman kingdom are: the Huns, the Ostrogoths, the Visigoths, the Franks, the Vandals, the Heruli, the Burgundians, the Suevi, the Anglo-Saxons, and the Lombards. The connection between these and the nations of modern Europe, can readily be traced in the names, as France, England, Lombardy, Burgundy, etc.

There was a time when the Roman empire had a most wonderful opportunity to accept the true God. Rome was the universal kingdom during the life of Christ. To Babylon God sent His people, the Jews, to scatter the truths of His kingdom, and lead men to repentance. The Medes and the Persians received the gospel from this same people, and representatives from Greece went to Jerusalem, into the very temple, in touch with the priests, in order that there might be no excuse for their refusing Christ. But to the Roman kingdom heaven itself was poured out in the person of the Saviour, and it was Rome that nailed Him to the cross. It was a Roman seal on His tomb, and a Roman guard at His grave. The early church suffered persecution at the hands of this same power. Judgment came on Rome when these barbarians overran the empire with fire and sword, [109] and the kingdom was divided into ten parts.

But Roman history did not end with the division. Daniel watched, "and, behold, there came up among them another little horn, before which there were three of the first horns plucked up by the roots." A new power, one outside the empire, is here represented by the little horn. The three divisions which were plucked up were the Heruli in 493, the Vandals in 534, and the Ostrogoths in 538 A. D. Justin-

15. I Daniel was grieved in my spirit in the midst of my body, and the visions of my head troubled me.

16. I came near unto one of them that stood by, and asked him the truth of all this. So he told me, and made me know the interpretation of the things.

17. These great beasts, which are four, are four kings, which shall arise out of the earth.

18. But the saints of the most High shall take the kingdom, and possess the kingdom for ever, even for ever and ever.

19. Then I would know the truth of the fourth beast, which was diverse from all the others, exceeding dreadful, whose teeth were of iron, and his nails of brass; which devoured, brake in pieces, and stamped the residue with his feet;

20. And of the ten horns that were in his head, and of the other which came up, and before whom three fell; even of that horn that had eyes, and a mouth that spake very great things, whose look was more stout than his fellows.

21. I beheld, and the same horn made war with the saints, and prevailed against them;

22. Until the Ancient of days came, and judgment was given to the saints of the most High; and the time came that the saints possessed the kingdom.

23. Thus he said, The fourth beast shall be the fourth kingdom upon earth, which shall be diverse from all kingdoms, and shall devour the whole earth, and shall tread it down, and break it in pieces.

Dan. 7:15-23.

There were certain Greeks among them that came up to worship at the feast: The same came therefore to Philip, which was of Bethsaida of Galilee, and desired him, saying, Sir, we would see Jesus.

John 12:20-21.

Acts 4:26, 27.

Pilate said unto them, Ye have a watch: go your way, make it as sure as ye can. So they went and made the sepulcher sure, sealing the stone, and setting a watch. Matt. 27:62-66.

24. And the ten horns out of this kingdom are ten kings that shall arise: and another shall rise after them; and he shall be diverse from the first, and he shall subdue three kings.

Dan. 7:24.

He leadeth princes away spoiled, and overthroweth the mighty. Job 12:19.

He shall speak great words against the most High, and shall wear out the saints of the most High, and think to change times and laws: and they shall be given into his hand until a time and times and the dividing of time.

Dan. 7:25.

25. And he shall speak great words against the most High, and shall wear out the saints of the most High, and think to change times and laws: and they shall be given into his hand until a time and times and the dividing of time.

26. But the judgment shall sit, and they shall take away his dominion, to consume and to destroy it unto the end.

Dan. 7:25-26.

The great God that formed all things both rewardeth the fool, and rewardeth transgressors.

Prov. 26:10.

I saw a woman sit upon a scarlet coloured beast, full of names of blasphemy, having seven heads and ten horns. Rev. 17:3.

And I saw the woman drunken with the blood of the saints, and with the blood of the martyrs of Jesus: and when I saw her, I wondered with great admiration. Rev. 17:6.

Through his policy also he shall cause craft to prosper in his hand; and he shall magnify himself in his heart, and by peace shall destroy many: he shall also stand up against the Prince of princes; but he shall be broken without hand.

Dan. 8:25.

Acts 28:16, 30.

Your obedience is come abroad unto all men.

Rom. 16:19.

Your faith is spoken of throughout the whole world. Rom. 1:8.

The mistery of iniquity doth already work: only he who now letteth will let, until he be taken out of the way. 2 Thess. 2:7.

He increaseth the nations, and destroyeth them: he enlargeth the nations, and straiteneth them again. Job 12:23.

The husband is the head of the wife, even as Christ is the head of the church: and he is the saviour of the body. Eph. 5:23.

ian, the emperor, whose seat was at Constantinople, working through his general Belisarius, was the power that overthrew the three kingdoms represented by the three horns, and the reason for their overthrow was their adherence to Arianism in opposition to the orthodox Catholic faith. The details of the overthrow, and the religious controversy which was the root of the trouble, are fully given by Gibbon in the "Decline and Fall of the Roman Empire," by [110] Mosheim in his church history, and by others.

The little horn which gained power by plucking up three horns, was diverse from all the others. It had eyes "like the eyes of a man, and a mouth speaking great things;" his look also was more stout than his fellows.

Rome was dropping into ruin; her cities had been sacked, her government broken. As from the decaying log of the marsh the mushroom springs up in a night, gaining its life from the decay, so there arose in the Roman empire a power which was nourished by this national decay. This power was the little horn known as the papacy.

It is written that Babylon, the mother of harlots, fell because of imputing her power unto the gods of the heathen Pagan Rome fell because she presumed to hold authority over the person of Christ and His followers. Then arose the little horn, and it "made war with the saints, and prevailed against them." "He shall speak great words against the Most High, and shall wear out the saints of the Most High, and think to change times and laws."

Rome in the days of Christ was the center of the world. Paul and others preached the gospel in that city. A church was organized there and for years this church of Rome ranked with the churches of Jerusalem, Constantinople, and others. Gradually but surely, worldliness took the place of the Spirit of Christ, and Roman bishops became exalted. The mystery of iniquity of which Paul wrote in his letter to the Thessalonians, was at work in Rome. At the time of the division of the empire the bishops were greedy for civil power, and in the time of [111] national distress the church grasped the reins of government; the little horn had received power. This was in A. D. 538, when the last of the three horns was plucked up, and the decree made by Justinian in 533, recognizing the bishop of Rome as head over all the churches, went into effect. (See Gibbon, chapter 41.) Paganism on the throne had been cruel enough, but when those pagan principles which had lived since the days of Babylon took the name and outward form of Christianity, the power which bore sway was still more cruel. Not only would the little horn speak stout words against the Most High, but it would "presume to change the appointed times and the law." (Spurrell's trans.)

Unholy hands had been laid in years past upon the temple of God and the consecrated vessels in the temple, and upon God's people, but the little horn laid hands upon the very law of God, attempting to change the Sabbath of the fourth commandment. The little horn had all the power of Babylon. In government it was an absolute monarchy, holding authority over all the thrones of Europe. Kings rose and fell at the dictates of Rome. From a religious viewpoint, it was the ruling power, dictating to the consciences of men, bringing them before its tribunal and peering into their very thoughts. The rack and the inquisition were its instruments, and no man escaped the scrutiny of the man's eyes in the little horn The means by which this power was maintained was its system of education, which kept Europe in darkness for over one thousand years. [112]

This was a long-lived kingdom. "They [the saints, the times, and the law] would be given into his hands for a *time and times* and the dividing of time." [The reader is referred to Dan. 11:13, margin; also Dan. 12:7, and to Rev. 12:6; 13:5, and Num. 14:34 for different expressions giving the same time and referring to the same power.] This time,—three and one-half years, or forty-two months, or twelve hundred and sixty days, as it is variously designated,—began in 538, when three horns were plucked up to make way for the establishment of this one power, the little horn. It continued until 1798, when its dominion was taken away. Its power, however, is not yet destroyed.

Thou shalt have no other gods before me.

Ex. 20:3.

Then shall be great tribulation, such as was not since the beginning of the world to this time, no nor ever shall be. And except those days should be shortened, there should no flesh be saved: but for the elect's sake those days shall be shortened.

Matt. 24:21, 22.

Therefore he brought upon them the king of the Chaldees, who slew their young men with the sword in the house of their sanctuary, and had no compassion upon young man or maiden, old man, or him that stooped for age: he gave them all into his hand. And all the vessels of the house of God, great and small, and the treasures of the house of the LORD, and the treasures of the king, and of his princes; all these he brought to Babylon. And they burnt the house of God, and brake down the wall of Jerusalem, and burnt all the palaces thereof with fire, and destroyed all the goodly vessels thereof.

2 Chron. 36:17-19.

As a roaring lion, and a ranging bear; so is a wicked ruler over the poor people.

Prov. 28:15.

There shall be false teachers among you, who privily shall bring in damnable heresies.

2 Peter 2:1-3.

2 Thess. 2:5-7.

The same horn made war with the saints, and prevailed against them; until the Ancient of days came, and judgement was given to the saints of the most High; and the time came that the saints possessed the kingdom.   Dan. 7:21, 22.

Rev. 11: 2, 3.
Eze. 4:6.

3 ½ years=1260 days.
42 months=1260 days.
1 prophetic day=1 literal year.
1260 prophetic days=1260 literal years.

I beheld till the thrones were cast down, and the Ancient of days did sit, whose garment was white as snow, and the hair of his head like the pure wool: his throne was like the fiery flame, and his wheels as burning fire. A fiery stream issued and came forth from before him: thousand thousands ministered unto him, and ten thousand times ten thousand stood before him: the judgment was set, and the books were opened.

Dan. 7:9-10.

Christ is not entered into the holy places made with hands, which are the figures of the true; but into heaven itself, now to appear in the presence of God for us. Heb. 9:24.

It was therefore necessary that the patterns of things in the heavens should be purified with these; but the heavenly things themselves with better sacrifices than these. Heb. 9:23.

O that one might plead for a man with God, as a man pleadeth for his neighbour! Job 16:21.

Thou that dwellest between the cherubims, shine forth. Ps. 80:1.

The Lord hath prepared his throne in the heavens; and his kingdom ruleth over all. Bless the Lord, ye his angels, that excel in strength, that do his commandments, hearkening unto the voice of his word. Ps. 103:19-21.

Their appearance and their work was as it were a wheel in the middle of a wheel. Eze. 1:16.

His brightness was as the light: he had bright beams out of his side, and there was the hiding of his power. Hab. 3:4 [margin].

He is before all things, and in him all things hold together. Col. 1:17, R. V. [margin].

Dost thou know the balancings of the clouds, the wondrous works of him which is perfect in knowledge? Job 37:16.

Daniel in his vision was shown not only earthly kingdoms and powers, but after listening to the voice of the little horn, which spake great words against the Most High, his attention was called to scenes in the heavenly court which would transpire simultaneously with the fulfillment of the prophecy concerning the nations of the earth.

It was during the time when the fourth beast had dominion and power that the Saviour was crucified. He was the Lamb slain in the outer court, and on His ascension He entered the holy place of the heavenly sanctuary. There He was seen by John as described in the fourth and fifth chapters of Revelation. But this work in the holy place was only a part of the Saviour's ministry for mankind. The time came when He must perform in heaven that service of which the day of atonement in the earthly sanctuary was the type. Spurrell renders the ninth verse: "I beheld until the thrones were [113] *pitched* [Revised Version, *placed*], when the Ancient of days was enthroned [or did sit] in judgment. His raiment was white as snow, the hair of His head like pure wool, His throne was flames of fire, His rolling wheels the ardent flame."

Here within the holy of holies is the abiding place of the King of kings, God the Father, where thousands and tens of thousands of angels minister before Him. This, the throne of God, is the center of all creation; about it revolve the solar systems throughout the whole extent of space. Worlds circle about their suns, and suns with their attendant planets in turn circle about the throne of God. It is the wheel within a wheel which Ezekiel describes. Daniel said, "A fiery stream issued and came forth from before Him," for there all is life, a living, constantly moving throne.

God's power pervades space in every direction. Like beams of light, there radiates from Him a force which holds worlds in their orbits. The power man calls gravity is but a portion of the drawing power of God. It holds the orbs of heaven in their places, it balances the clouds, weighs the mountains, and measures the waters of the sea. The same power notes the fall of every leaf on earth, the death of the tiniest sparrow, and the pulse beats of

The Law of God

I

Thou shalt have no other gods before me.

II

Thou shalt not make unto thee any graven image, or any likeness of anything that is in heaven above, or that is in the earth beneath, or that is in the water under the earth; thou shalt not bow down thyself to them, nor serve them: for I the Lord thy God am a jealous God, visiting the iniquity of the fathers upon the children unto the third and fourth generation of them that hate me, and showing mercy unto thousands of them that love me, and keep my commandments.

III

Thou shalt not take the name of the Lord thy God in vain: for the Lord will not hold him guiltless that taketh his name in vain.

IV

Remember the Sabbath day to keep it holy. Six days shalt thou labor, and do all thy work: but the seventh day is the Sabbath of the Lord thy God: in it thou shalt not do any work, thou, nor thy son, nor thy daughter, thy manservant, nor thy maid-servant, nor thy cattle, nor thy stranger that is within thy gates: for in six days the Lord made heaven and earth, the sea, and all that in them is, and rested the seventh day; wherefore the Lord blessed the Sabbath day, and hallowed it.

V

Honor thy father and thy mother, that thy days may be long upon the land which the Lord thy God giveth thee.

VI

Thou shalt not kill.

VII

Thou shalt not commit adultery.

VIII

Thou shalt not steal.

IX

Thou shalt not bear false witness against thy neighbor.

X

Thou shalt not covet thy neighbor's house, thou shalt not covet thy neighbor's wife, nor his man-servant, nor his maid-servant, nor his ox, nor his ass, nor any thing that is thy neighbor's.

The Law as Changed by the Papacy

I

I am the Lord thy God: thou shalt not have strange gods before me.

II

Thou shalt not take the name of the Lord thy God in vain.

III

Remember that thou keep holy the Sabbath day.

IV

Honor thy father and thy mother.

V

Thou shalt not kill.

VI

Thou shalt not commit adultery.

VII

Thou shalt not steal.

VIII

Thou shalt not bear false witness against thy neighbor.

IX

Thou shalt not covet thy neighbor's wife.

X

Thou shalt not covet thy neighbor's goods.

Job 28:24-27.
Isa. 40:12-17.
Matt. 10:29.
Acts 17:28.
Matt. 5:14.

And now, O Father, glorify thou me with thine own self with the glory which I had with thee before the world was. John 17:5.
Lamb slain from the foundation of the world. Rev. 13:8.

God so loved the world, that he gave his only begotten Son, that whosoever believeth in him should not perish, but have everlasting life. John 3:16.
Ps. 57:17.
Isa. 49:16.

One shall say unto him, What are these wounds in thine hands? Then he shall answer, Those with which I was wounded in the house of my friends. Zech. 13:6.
Eph. 3:9, 10.

And there was given him dominion, and glory, and a kingdom, that all people, nations, and languages, should serve him: his dominion is an everlasting dominion, which shall not pass away, and his kingdom that which shall not be destroyed. Dan. 7:14.

Eze. 28:14.
Job 37:19-23.

Then the moon shall be confounded, and the sun ashamed, when the Lord of hosts shall reign in mount Zion, and in Jerusalem, and before his ancients gloriously. Isa. 24:23.
Behold, I have set before thee an open door, and no man can shut it. Rev. 3:8.

I saw in the night visions, and, behold, one like the Son of man came with the clouds of heaven, and came to the Ancient of days, and they brought him near before him. Dan. 7:13.

And I saw another angel fly in the midst of heaven, having the everlasting gospel to preach unto them that dwell on the earth, and to every nation, and kindred, and tongue, and people, Saying with a loud voice, Fear God, and give glory to him; for the hour of his judgment is come: and worship him that made heaven, and earth, and the sea, and the fountains of waters. Rev. 14:6-7.

every man. From Him comes all life: "in Him we live and move and have our being."

The Son was one with the Father, and it was from this glory that He stepped when He offered Himself at the foundation of the world. He was the Lamb slain, and the heart of God was broken in that offering. Every time the [114] knife was plunged into a victim at the altar of the earthly sanctuary, the flowing blood touched afresh the heart of the eternal Father. Every time a broken-hearted man or woman approaches the throne in penitence, the Father's heart is touched. "The broken and the contrite heart Thou wilt not despise, O God." Never, never, throughout all eternity, will that Son resume His former condition. What He assumed for fallen man He will retain forever. He is a man still in the heavenly court, touched by every human woe. The universe beheld the gift, and bowed in adoration. The temple is filled with the glory. There seraphim and cherubim with their shining glory, as guardians, stretch their wings above His throne, veil their faces in adoration, and bow before Him.

"Oh, instruct us what we shall say of Him; we can not do justice because of our ignorance. . . . If a man venture to speak, surely he shall be overwhelmed.

"We can not even now gaze upon the light of the sun when it shineth forth in the heavens; and the wind passing along hath cleared the sky. But what splendor from the holy of holies shall appear! With God is insufferable majesty! The Almighty! we can not comprehend Him!"—*Spurrell's Translation.*

The door into the holy of holies was opened in 1844, and "behold, one like the Son of Man came with the clouds of heaven, and came to the Ancient of days, and they brought Him near before Him."

No words could be framed that would give a more vivid view of the opening of the judgment, which occurred at the time of the announcement, [115] "The hour of His judgment is come." In the seventh chapter of Daniel is the only description found in the Bible of the judgment scene announced by the first angel of the fourteenth chapter of

Revelation. The message itself is the only announcement in the Bible that the time had arrived; and the fourteenth verse of the eighth chapter of Daniel is the only prophetic period given in the Bible which marks the time of the beginning of God's judgment. That period is the twenty-three hundred days, or literal years, which began in the year 457 B. C., with the decree to build and restore Jerusalem, and expired in 1844, A. D. It was at this latter date that the first angel of the fourteenth chapter of Revelation proclaimed the hour of God's judgment. The message went to all lands, and the islands of the sea heard it.

When God had taken His position over His law in the most holy place in the heavenly sanctuary, then Christ came in to plead before Him for His people. This coming could not have been when He ascended up on high; for then He ascended to the Father, and the judgment was in the future. It can not refer to His second coming to this earth; for then He comes *from* the Father. It was His coming before the Father when He took His position in the judgment at the end of the twenty-three hundred days. He came before the Father surrounded by the clouds of heaven; that is, with thousands of angels who, as ministering spirits, have watched the lives of men, recording their every word and deed and thought. Characters have been formed, and whether they are good or bad, [116] they have been mirrored in the books of heaven. When Christ came before the Father, the books were opened and the cases of the dead began to be investigated. The deeds may have been committed in the light of day, or in the darkness of night, yet they are all open and manifest before Him with whom we have to do. Heavenly intelligences have witnessed each sin, and have faithfully recorded the same. Sin may be concealed from friends, relatives, and our most intimate associates. None but the guilty actors may have the least knowledge of wrong deeds, but these things are all laid bare before the angels and the inhabitants of other worlds. The darkest of all dark nights, the deepest-laid plot of individuals or nations, can not hide even one thought from the heavenly in-

Unto two thousand and three hundred days; then shall the sanctuary be cleansed.

Dan. 8:14.

I said in mine heart, God shall judge the righteous and the wicked: for there is a time there for every purpose and for every work.

Eccl. 3:17.

Righteousness and judgment are the establishment of this throne. Ps. 98:2 [margin].

He reasoned of righteousness, temperance, and judgment to come. Acts 24:25.

He that overcometh, the same shall be clothed in white raiment; and I will not blot out his name out of the book of life, but I will confess his name before my Father, and before his angel.

Rev. 3:5.

Who maketh his angels spirits; his ministers a flaming fire. Ps. 104:4.

Ps. 34:7.

The books were opened: and another book was opened, which is the book of life: and the dead were judged out of those things which were written in the books, according to their works.

Rev. 20:12.

Therefore judge nothing before the time, until the Lord come, who both will bring to light the hidden things of darkness, and will make manifest the counsels of the hearts: and then shall every man have praise of God. 1 Cor. 4:5.

Thine iniquity is marked before me, saith the Lord God. Jer 2:22.

Neither is there any creature that is not manifest in his sight: but all things are naked and opened unto the eyes of him with whom we have to do.

Heb. 4:13.

Yea, the darkness hideth not from thee.

Ps. 139:7-12.

"The dead were judged out of those things which were written in the books, according to their works."

Counting one by one, to find out the account.
Eccl. 7:27.

The blood of Jesus Christ his Son cleanseth us from all sin. 1 John 1:7.

There was a rainbow round about the throne, in sight like unto an emerald. Rev. 4:3.

If we confess our sins, he is faithful and just to forgive us our sins, and to cleanse us from all unrighteousness. 1 John 1:9.

He that is unjust, let him be unjust still: and he which is filthy, let him be filthy still: and he that is righteous, let him be righteous still: and he that is holy, let him be holy still. Rev. 22:11.

My witness is in heaven, and my record is on high. Job 16:19.

But I say unto you, That every idle word that men shall speak, they shall give account thereof in the day of judgment. For by thy words thou shalt be justified, and by thy words thou shalt be condemned. Matt 12:36-37.
Heb. 3:7, 8.

I beheld then because of the voice of the great words which the horn spake: I beheld even till the beast was slain, and his body destroyed, and given to the burning flame. Dan 7:11.
2 Thess. 2:4.

Wherefore he is able also to save them to the uttermost that come unto God by him, seeing he ever liveth to make intercession for them. Heb. 7:25.

He shall offend, imputing this his power unto his god. Hab. 1:11.

telligences. God has a faithful record of every crooked dealing, of every sin and unjust practice. If the inward heart is full of hypocrisy, an outward appearance of uprightness can not deceive Him.

As one by one these names are read, the Saviour holds up His hands, still bearing the imprints of the nails of Calvary, and cries, "My blood, Father, my blood, my blood." Above His throne is the rainbow; mercy and justice mingle there. God's heart is touched by [117] the pleadings of His Son, and pardon is written opposite the name. Then through the arches of heaven, a shout of triumph resounds. The angels cast their crowns before the throne, crying, "Holy, holy, holy!"

For over sixty years the work of the investigative judgment has been in progress. It is fast drawing to a close. Before it closes, it will settle the case of every living man and woman. Day by day we are making the record which will determine our future for weal or woe. How solemn the thought that words once uttered, actions once performed, can never be changed. The atoning blood of Christ is offered to-day. "To-day if ye will hear His voice, harden not your hearts."

The life of the fourth beast, especially of the little horn, was prolonged beyond the time of the investigative judgment. Even after the thrones were set and the work in the holy of holies was begun, The great words of the little horn attracted the attention of the prophet. The greatest word ever spoken against God was the decree of infallibility issued by the ecumenical council in 1870. This was the attempt to seat a man on the throne beside the Son of God. While Christ stood as a slain Lamb before the Father, pleading for the salvation of the world, poor, frail man was exalting his throne above the stars of God.

Babylon fell because she imputed her power unto the gods. Of the fourth beast Daniel says, "I beheld till the beast was slain, and his body destroyed, and given to the burning flame." Thus at the end, instead of being conquered by some other power arising on [118] earth, this power goes into the lake of fire. The other beasts which represent kingdoms, had their dominion taken away, yet their lives were prolonged for a time and a season; that is, each was merged into the succeeding kingdom, But not so with the fourth kingdom; its destruction will be complete.

The fifth kingdom, which is the heavenly, the kingdom of God, is not in human hands. God Himself will establish it under the whole heaven, and it will exist forever and ever. "The kingdom and dominion, and the greatness of the kingdom under the whole heaven, shall be given to the people of the saints of the Most High." Those who are accounted worthy in the investigative judgment will come forth in the first resurrection, or will be translated without seeing death, and will reign with Christ forever and ever. Sin, with all who have clung to it, will be forever destroyed. The pride and arrogance of Babylon of old, her iniquity of every form which has been repeated by all the nations of the earth, together with the instigator of all evil, will at last be blotted out. The end of the controversy is reached. The triumph of truth is witnessed by all created beings. The scar which sin has made is gone forever. The discord which for six thousand years has marred the universe, is forgotten. The music of the spheres is taken up anew, and man reigns with his Creator. "Hitherto is the end of the matter." What wonder that the vision troubled Daniel, and that his countenance changed! The matchless love of Christ, who can understand? [119]

Dan. 7:11.

And the beast was taken, and with him the false prophet that wrought miracles before him, with which he deceived them that had received the mark of the beast, and them that worshipped his image. These both were cast alive into a lake of fire burning with brimstone.
Rev. 19:20.

Thou sawest till that a stone was cut out which was not in hands: which smote the image upon his feet that were of iron and clay, and brake them in pieces. Dan. 2:34 [margin].

27. And the kingdom and dominion, and the greatness of the kingdom under the whole heaven, shall be given to the people of the saints of the most High, whose kingdom is an everlasting kingdom, and all dominions shall serve and obey him.
Dan. 7:27.

Rev. 20:4, 6.

For this purpose the Son of God was manifested, that he might destroy the works of the devil.
1 John 3:8.

That through death he might destroy him that had the power of death, that is, the devil.
Heb. 2:14.

And there shall be no more curse: but the throne of God and of the Lamb shall be in it; and his servants shall serve him. Rev. 22:3.

28. Hitherto is the end of the matter. As for me Daniel, my cogitations much troubled me, and my countenance changed in me: but I kept the matter in my heart. Dan. 7:28.

CHAPTER 9

THE EIGHTH CHAPTER OF DANIEL

A PERIOD of two years had passed since the vision recorded in the seventh chapter of Daniel. The prophet's mind had dwelt often upon the scenes which his eye then beheld, and the subject of the judgment had been pondered again and again. He kept the matter in his heart, he himself says, for in the days of Daniel, as at the present time, only the few could comprehend and appreciate spiritual topics. Many changes of a material nature had taken place during those two years. Wickedness had increased in the kingdom of Babylon, and no reverence whatever was shown for God or His people. This saddened the heart of Daniel. [120] He who for years had been the chief counselor in the empire, now no longer dwelt in the capital, but had his residence in the palace at Shushan. Shushan was the capital of Elam, which was formerly a subject province of the kingdom of Babylon, but as that empire began to weaken, and the strength of Cyrus, the Persian general, was recognized, Elam, under Abra- dates, the viceroy or prince, had revolted from Babylon, and joined the forces of the Persians. Years before this, the prophet Isaiah had said that Elam and Media would join forces in the conquest of Babylon. As Daniel lived in the palace of Shushan, he saw the way opening for the fulfillment of this prophecy. If Babylon was not already undergoing a siege at the hands of Cyrus and Darius, her downfall was so imminent that in this vision the history of nations begins with the rising kingdom of the Medes and Persians.

Daniel was transported to the river Ulai, by the side of which stood a ram having two horns, one higher than

1. In the third year of the reign of king Belshazzar a vision appeared unto me, even unto me Daniel, after that which appeared unto me at the first.
Dan. 8:1.

As for me Daniel, my cogitations much troubled me, and my countenance changed in me: but I kept the matter in my heart.
Dan. 7:28.

But the natural man receiveth not the things of the Spirit of God: for they are foolishness unto him: neither can he know them, because they are spiritually discerned. 1 Cor. 2:14.

2. And I saw in a vision; and it came to pass, when I saw, that I was at Shushan in the palace, which is in the province of Elam; and I saw in a vision, and I was by the river of Ulai.
Dan. 8:2.

But it shall come to pass in the latter days, that I will bring again the captivity of Elam, saith the LORD. Jer. 49:39.

Behold, I will stir up the Medes against them, which shall not regard silver; and as for gold, they shall not delight in it. Isa. 13:17.

A grievous vision is declared unto me; the treacherous dealer dealeth treacherously, and the spoiler spoileth. Go up, O Elam: besiege, O Media; all the sighing thereof have I made to cease. Isa. 21:1-3.

3. Then I lifted up mine eyes, and saw, and, behold, there stood before the river a ram which had two horns: and the two horns were high; but one was higher than the other, and the higher came up last. Dan. 8:3.

And behold another beast, a second, like to a bear, and it raised up itself on one side, and it had three ribs in the mouth of it between the teeth of it: and they said thus unto it, Arise, devour much flesh.
Dan. 7:5.

Thus saith the Lord to his anointed, to Cyrus, whose right hand I have holden, to subdue nations before him.   Isa. 41:1-5.

4. I saw the ram pushing westward, and northward, and southward; so that no beasts might stand before him, neither was there any that could deliver out of his hand; but he did according to his will, and became great.   Dan 8:4.

Dan. 6:11.

Now it came to pass in the days of Ahasuerus, (this is Ahasuerus which reigned, from India even unto Ethiopia, over an hundred and seven and twenty provinces).   Esther 1:1.

When he shewed the riches of his glorious kingdom and the honour of his excellent majesty many days, even an hundred and fourscore days.   Esther 1:4.

And a mighty king shall stand up, that shall rule with great dominion, and do according to his will.   Dan. 11:3.

5. And as I was considering, behold, an he goat came from the west on the face of the whole earth, and touched not the ground: and the goat had a notable horn between his eyes.
6. And he came to the ram that had two horns, which I had seen standing before the river, and ran unto him in the fury of his power.   Dan. 8:5-6.

The rough goat is the king of Grecia: and the great horn that is between his eyes is the first king.   Dan. 8:21.

Now will I shew thee the truth. Behold, there shall stand up yet three kings in Persia; and the fourth shall be far richer than they all: and by his strength through his riches he shall stir up all against the realm of Grecia.   Dan 11:2.

the other, and the higher came up last. In his previous vision the second kingdom had been represented by a bear which raised itself on one side and had three ribs in its mouth. Both symbols apply to the double nature of the kingdom of the Medes and Persians, but the uneven horns of the ram give a more specific description; for while the Median kingdom was the older of the two, the Persian excelled it in strength, and its position in history must be attributed to the line of Persian kings which began with Cyrus the Great. The definiteness with which this symbol is interpreted is an illustration of the fact that the [121] Scriptures are their own best commentaries. Said the angel, "The ram which thou sawest having two horns are the kings of Media and Persia."

As the ram pushed westward, northward, and southward, and no beast could stand before it, so the Medo-Persian empire extended its dominion in these directions. At the fall of Babylon one hundred and twenty provinces recognized the authority of Cyrus and Darius. These were held in subjection, and others added, so that in the time of the Ahasuerus of Esther, the kingdom controlled one hundred and twenty-seven provinces, extending from India on the east to the Mediterranean on the west, and from the Caspian Sea to Ethiopia. It was then called a glorious kingdom, and the monarch was spoken of as "his excellent majesty." The same facts are made prominent in the eleventh chapter of Daniel, where Xerxes, the fourth from Cyrus, stirs up all the Eastern nations to war with Greece: "He did according to his will, and became great."

Nevertheless, the greatness of the second kingdom did not insure length of life, and the prophet was shown a he goat coming from the west, and, as Spurrell's translation gives it, "rushing over the face of the whole earth, without touching the ground." The goat had a notable horn between his eyes. In the interpretation the angel said, "The rough goat is the king [or kingdom] of Grecia, and the great horn... is the first king." The kingdom of Greece was described in the previous vision (Dan. 7:6), but at the time now under consideration, the details of its rise are given. [122] The eleventh chapter states that the fourth kingdom after Cyrus should stir up the nations against Greece. This was done when Xerxes crossed the Hellespont with a large army in 480 B. c. His army is said by Herodotus to have numbered over a million and a half. It was a gathering of nations, and so vast was the army that seven days were required to pass from Asia to Greek soil. But in spite of all preparations, the Persian army was defeated at Thermopylae, at Salamis, and at Plataea, and Xerxes, discouraged and disheartened, gave over the attempt to invade Greece. Prophecy had foretold that when Medo-Persia and Greece should contend, Greece would be the aggressive power.

Later, the he goat, Greece, came toward the ram, Medo-Persia, "and rushed upon him in the heat of his strength. And I saw him coming up close to the ram, and he was exceedingly embittered against him, and smote the ram, and brake his two horns, so that there was no strength in the ram to stand before him, for he threw him down to the ground, and trampled on him; neither could any one deliver the ram from his grasp."—*Spurrell.*

No historian has ever given a more graphic account of the contest between the Greeks under Alexander the Great and the Persians under Darius. That kingdom which before had shown such wonderful strength, crumbled and fell, and there was none to help. She had passed her probation and filled the cup of her iniquity. Michael, the Lord of heaven, had stood at the right hand of the Persian monarch on the throne to persuade him, and yet he had [123] resisted the divine influence, and that kingdom which had been a rod in the hand of God to overthrow Babylon in its wickedness, repeated her sins, and in turn met the same fate. Although the Persians restored the Jews to Jerusalem, that could not save them. It is only as nations or individuals continue in a love of the truth, only as they partake constantly of the leaves of the tree of life, that their existence is prolonged.

The ram and the goat met on a river. The first successful battle fought by the Grecians against the Medes was on the banks of the Granicus, a stream of Asia Minor. This

The noise of a whip, and the noise of the rattling of the wheels, and of the pransing horses, and of the jumping chariots. The horseman lifteth up both the bright sword and the glittering spear: and there is a multitude of slain, and a great number of carcases. Nahum 3:2-3.

Put not your trust in princes. Ps. 146:3.

Isa. 17:12, 13.

7. *And I saw him come close unto the ram, and he was moved with choler against him, and smote the ram, and brake his two horns: and there was no power in the ram to stand before him, but he cast him down to the ground, and stamped upon him: and there was none that could deliver the ram out of his hand.* Dan. 8:7.

Reprobate silver shall men call them, because the LORD hath rejected them. Jer. 6:30.

The iniquity of the Amonites is not yet full. Gen. 15:16.

And he did very abominably in following idols, according to all things as did the Amorites, whom the LORD cast out before the children of Israel. 1 Kings 21:26.

Also I in the first year of Darius the Mede, even I, stood to confirm and to strengthen him. Dan 11:1.

Thou art my battle axe and weapons of war: for with thee will I break in pieces the nations. Jer 51:20.

Deut. 30:19, 20.
Prov. 3:13, 18.

He came to the ram that had two horns, which I had seen standing before the river, and ran unto him in the fury of his power. Dan. 8:6.
Known unto God are all his works from the beginning of the world. Acts 15:18.

The ram and the goat.

was in the year 334 B. C. Already the victory of Greece was recorded in the books of heaven. The battle at Granicus was soon followed by the defeat of the Medo-Persian forces at the pass of Issus, and the third and overwhelming defeat was on the plains of Arbela, 331 B. C. None could deliver the sinking cause of the Medo-Persian empire from the hands of the victorious Alexander.

Alexander stands without a rival for the rapidity of his conquests. He was but a young man of twenty when, by the death of his father, Philip of Macedon, he fell heir to a small dominion. He united the Greek states, placed himself at the head of affairs, and led her armies in a series of wonderful victories. In the space of a few short years he was the recognized master of the world. He who rose to the highest position the world could offer, fell equally as suddenly. He had conquered kingdoms, but was not master of his own passions. His love of praise led him to have himself proclaimed [124] Son of Jupiter-Ammon in Egypt, and his love of drink caused his death at the age of thirty-two years, after a universal reign of only two years. Such was the fate of one who feared neither God nor man. "The Most High ruleth in the kingdom of men."

"Promotion cometh neither from the east, nor from the west, nor from the south, but God is judge. He putteth down one and setteth up another."

"By strength shall no man prevail." There is no restraint of the Lord to save by many or by few.

"There is no king saved by the multitude of an host: a mighty man is not delivered by much strength. A horse is a vain thing for safety: neither shall he deliver any by his great strength. Behold, the eye of the Lord is upon them that fear Him, upon them that hope in His mercy; to deliver their souls from death, and to keep them alive in famine."

Truly the Lord "increaseth the nations, and destroyeth them; He enlargeth the nations, and straighteneth them again. He taketh away the heart of the people of the earth, and causeth them to wander in a wilderness where there is

He leadeth counsellors away spoiled, and maketh the judges fools. He looseth the bond of kings, and girdeth their loins with a girdle. He leadeth princes away spoiled, and overthroweth the mighty.
Job 12:17-19.

After this I beheld, and lo another, like a leopard, which had upon the back of it four wings of a fowl; the beast had also four heads; and dominion was given to it. Dan 7:6.

In prosperity the destroyer shall come upon him.
Job 15:21.

8. Therefore the he goat waxed very great: and when he was strong, the great horn was broken; and for it came up four notable ones toward the four winds of heaven.
Dan. 8:8.

Ps. 107:40.

He that is slow to anger is better than the mighty; and he that ruleth his spirit than he that taketh a city.
Prov. 16:32.

Dan. 4:17.
Ps. 75:6, 7.

The LORD maketh poor, and maketh rich: he bringeth low, and lifteth up.
1 Sam. 2:7.

1 Sam. 2:9.

Lord, it is nothing with thee to help, whether with many, or with them that have no power.
2 Chron. 14:11.

1 Sam. 14:6.
Ps. 33:16-18.
For I will not trust in my bow, neither shall my sword save me. Ps. 44:6.
Some trust in chariots, and some in horses: but we will remember the name of the LORD our God. Ps. 20:7.
Job 12:23-25.
Isa. 26:15.
Isa. 9:3.

The most High ruleth in the kingdom of men, and giveth it to whomsoever he will, and setteth up over it the basest of men.
Dan. 4:17-25.

Dan. 2:21.
Dan. 5:21.

8. Therefore the he goat waxed very great: and when he was strong, the great horn was broken; and for it came up four notable ones toward the four winds of heaven.
Dan 8:8.

Dan. 11:4.

Now that being broken, whereas four stood up for it, four kingdoms shall stand up out of the nation, but not in his power.
Dan. 8:22.

9. And out of one of them came forth a little horn, which waxed exceeding great, toward the south, and toward the east, and toward the pleasant land.
10. And it waxed great, even to the host of heaven; and it cast down some of the host and of the stars to the ground, and stamped upon them.
Dan. 8:9-10.

"Out of one of them came forth a little horn which waxed exceeding great."

Then I would know the truth of the fourth beast, which was diverse from all the others, exceeding dreadful, whose teeth were of iron, and his nails of brass; which devoured, brake in pieces, and stamped the residue with his feet.
Dan. 7:19.

Visiting the iniquity of the fathers upon the children, and upon the children's children, unto the third and to the fourth generation.
Ex. 34:7.

2 Thess. 2:4.
John 3:16.

And said, O full of all subtilty and all mischief, thou child of the devil, thou enemy of all righteousness, wilt thou not cease to pervert the right ways of the Lord?
Acts 13:10.

no way. They grope in the dark without light, and He maketh them to stagger like a drunken man."

"When he was strong, the great horn was broken, and for it came up four notable ones toward the four winds of heaven." Alexander left no heir capable of ruling the kingdom, and in less than twenty years of strife, his four leading generals succeeded in dividing the empire among themselves. [125]

Ptolemy took Egypt and the southern territory; Seleucus took Syria and the eastern division; Lysimachus took Asia Minor and territory to the north; while Cassander took possession of Greece, the western division. These four men had not the power of Alexander. The prophetic history of these four divisions is given in the eleventh chapter of Daniel.

In the division under consideration, the prophet sees a little horn coming forth from one of these four divisions. Here is brought to view the power symbolized by the fourth beast of the seventh chapter of Daniel. In his first vision the fourth beast was so terrible and had such a strange appearance that Daniel asked for a clearer explanation of its work. In his second vision the little horn is not named, but its work as a kingdom is still further portrayed. One feels while reading both the vision and the interpretation of the little horn, that he is coming into the presence of a power greater and more terrible than any which had hitherto existed. The accumulated forces of the evil of past ages is concentrated in this rising power, which waxed exceeding great. It was in truth the masterpiece from Satan's workshop. Four thousand years of trial had not passed in vain. As heaven was about to be emptied in the gift [126] of the Saviour, so all the fiendishness of the lower world was brought into play to counteract the love of God and destroy the effect of the sacrifice. There is a world of meaning in the words of the angel.

Said Gabriel, "His power shall be mighty, but not by his own power." No merely human power could do what this kingdom did. As light and love and power come from above to those whose eyes are directed heavenward, so a power from beneath takes possession of individuals and nations which resist the love of God. This kingdom "waxed exceeding great, toward the south, and toward the east, and toward the pleasant land." Rome extended her territory around the Mediterranean; there was no place where her arms were not victorious. Some of the greatest battles which history records were fought by the Roman armies. The pen of Inspiration says, "He [the little horn] shall destroy *wonderfully*." Cities which dared resist the power of Rome were blotted out of existence. In describing the government, the angel said, "He shall prosper and practice," and "through his policy also he shall cause craft to prosper in his hand."

But aside from the strong central government which was built up by Rome; which brought every other nation to her feet, and made slaves of the noblest of races; which was robbing men of God-given rights, and violating every principle of equity and justice,—aside from all this, the great arrogance of Rome was displayed when the nation magnified itself against the host (church) of heaven. "Yea, he magnified himself even against [mar.] the Prince of the [127] host." "He shall also stand up against the Prince of princes."

God's people are precious in His sight, and he who touches them touches the apple of His eye. Rome first deprived the Jews of the right to worship, grinding that nation beneath the heel of oppression. Then Christ came, when the oppression was the most severe, that Rome might see God in human flesh. He came to identify Himself with that downtrodden people, and to show to men that God is always on the side of the oppressed and enslaved. He came to illustrate the workings of the Spirit in the human heart, and

His power shall be mighty, but not by his own power: and he shall destroy wonderfully, and shall prosper, and practise, and shall destroy the mighty and the holy people. Dan. 8:24.

John 3:7 [margin].

The dragon gave him his power, and his seat, and great authority. Rev. 13:2.

Wherein in time past ye walked according to the course of this world, according to the prince of the power of the air, the spirit that now worketh in the children of disobedience. Eph. 2:2.

Which devoured, brake in pieces, and stamped the residue with his feet. Dan. 7:19.

In the latter time of their kingdom, when the transgressors are come to the full, a king of fierce countenance, and understanding dark sentences, shall stand up. And his power shall be mighty, but not by his own power: and he shall destroy wonderfully, and shall prosper, and practise, and shall destroy the mighty and the holy people. And through his policy also he shall cause craft to prosper in his hand; and he shall magnify himself in his heart, and by peace shall destroy many: he shall also stand up against the Prince of princes; but he shall be broken without hand. Dan. 8:23-25.

Yea, he magnified himself even to the prince of the host, and by him the daily sacrifice was taken away, and the place of his sanctuary was cast down.
Dan. 8:11.

He that toucheth you toucheth the apple of his eye. Zech. 2:8.

The Lord's portion in his people: Jacob is the lot of his inheritance. He found him in a desert land, and in the waste howling wilderness; he led him about, he instructed him, he kept him as the apple of his eye. Deut. 32:9-12.

These things I have spoken unto you, that in me ye might have peace. In the world ye shall have tribulation: but be of good cheer; I have overcome the world. John 16:33.

Acts 3:13-16.
Acts 4:26, 27.
Acts 7:52.

And the dragon was wroth with the woman, and went to make war with the remnant of her seed, which keep the commandments of God, and have the testimony of Jesus Christ.   Rev. 12:17.

Gen. 3:15.
Rev. 12:9, 12.

Through his policy also he shall cause craft to prosper in his hand; and he shall magnify himself in his heart, and by peace shall destroy many.
                                                  Dan. 8:25.

Matt. 7:15.

Also of your own selves shall men arise, speaking perverse things, to draw away disciples after them.
                                                  Acts 20:30.

Zech. 3:6, 7.

And that from a child thou hast known the holy scriptures, which are able to make thee wise unto salvation through faith which is in Christ Jesus.
                                                  2 Tim. 3:15.

2 Tim. 1:5.
Acts 15:20, 28, 29.
Acts 21:25.
Rev. 2:14.

If any man see thee which hast knowledge sit at meat in the idol's temple, shall not the conscience of him which is weak be emboldened to eat those things which are offered to idols; And through thy knowledge shall the weak brother perish, for whom Christ died? But when ye sin so against the brethren, and wound their weak conscience, ye sin against Christ.   1 Cor. 8:9-13.

1 Cor. 10:19, 20.
Rom. 1:8.
Col. 1:6.
Gen. 3:1.
Eph. 4:14.
Rom. 16:17, 18.
1 Cor. 1:11.
Phil. 1:15, 16.
Titus 3:9.
Mark 10:35-37.
Isa. 8:12.
James 5:1-6.

And an host was given him against the daily sacrifice by reason of transgression, and it cast down the truth to the ground; and it practised, and prospered.
                                                  Dan. 8:12.

to prove that it is possible to have a heaven within, although outward circumstances are to the contrary.

But Rome crucified Him whom Heaven sent. The dragon was wroth, and made war with the seed of the woman—Christ—who had been promised when sin entered the world. This was paganism in its greatest strength. It was in its dying throes, but even in the agony of death it smote the truth.

What Satan could not accomplish through open opposition, he sought to accomplish by policy and strategy. Silently, stealthily, the principles of evil crept into the church of Christ, which had grown up in spite of the pagan opposition. The humility of the Son of God at first characterized the body of Christians, and therein lay the power of the early church. Christian mothers gathered their children about them as the Jewish mothers had done in the days of their prosperity. From infancy the truths of God's Word were implanted in their hearts; sacred songs were on their lips; the Word of [128] God was the text-book from which all lessons were learned. Parents dared not allow their children to remain in the pagan schools, for the very atmosphere breathed of the heathen worship; the air was heavy with the odor of sacrifices to idols. They dared not sit at the table with those with whom they had once been familiar, for the food had been consecrated to idols. In the most careful way the rising generation was educated, and Christianity took the place of paganism.

But Satan could not see his power overthrown without making a desperate struggle, and by stealth he insinuated his principles into the new church. Wrangles, disputes, theological controversies drove out the spirit of life. Selfexaltation put men in power; the equal rights of all fell before the rising power of a hierarchy. The principle of trusts and monopolies, of unions and leagues, which had always characterized pagan society, twined its tendrils about the new organization of Christians, and choked its life. Paganism—the "*daily*" of Dan. 8:12—was taken away, it is true, and Rome became nominally a Christian empire. Her emperor professed the name of Christ, and carried before his army the banner of the cross.

Decrees were issued causing men to worship according to the dictates of Rome. Then it was that man—the emperor—and the empire attempted to exalt themselves above the God of heaven. The principles of Lucifer himself had crowded out the truth of Christ, and, as was shown to Daniel, the truth was cast down to the ground.

To John this transfer from paganism to the [129] papacy is represented as a transfer of power from the dragon to the beast. Rev. 13:7. The eleventh and twelfth verses of the eighth chapter of Daniel are parallel with the twenty-first and twenty-fifth verses of the seventh chapter, where the little horn makes war with the saints, and speaks great words against the Most High, attempting to change His times and law. Twice Daniel had been shown the twofold history of Rome: first as a pagan power, when it was more cruel than any pagan government before it; and later as a professedly Christian power, when its cruelty far surpassed all the workings of paganism.

The prophet was heart-sick as he beheld these scenes and the deep sufferings of the people of God. He was unable to grasp the idea of the time when these events, should occur, and thought that his own people, perhaps the very ones who were at that time in bondage to Babylon, would be called to suffer these things. The investigative judgment had been revealed to him, when the cases of men would be tried and the oppressor condemned. The end also of this oppressive power he had been shown was the lake of fire, when Roman authority should be broken without hands. In Nebuchadnezzar's dream the end would come when the stone cut out without hands should smite the image and finally fill the whole earth. As these scenes passed like a panorama before the eye of the prophet, angels also watched, for they are interested in all that affects God's people on earth.

The universe has waited now six thousand years for the final issue between truth and [130] error. It is not strange that angelic hosts wonder when the struggle will end, and when the song of songs can be taken up by the choir of heaven. These times are hidden with the Father, but man may un-

I know this, that after my departing shall grievous wolves enter in among you, rot sparing the flock. Acts 20:29, 30.

Yea, he magnified himself even to the prince of the host. . . . It cast fown the truth to the ground; and it practiced and prospered. Dan. 8:11, 12.

I beheld, and the same horn made war with the saints, and prevailed against them. Dan. 7:21.

Dan. 7:25.
Dan. 7:7, 8.
Dan. 8:23-25.

O Lord, hear; O Lord, forgive; O Lord, hearken and do; defer not, for thine own sake, O my God: for thy city and thy people are called by thy name. Dan. 9:19.

The judgement was set, and the books were opened. Dan. 7:9, 10.
1 Peter 4:17.

I beheld then because of the voice of the great words which the horn spake: I beheld even till the beast was slain, and his body destroyed, and given to the burning flame. Dan 7:11.

Thow sawest till that a stone was cut out, which was not in hands, which smote the image upon his feet that were of iron and clay, and brake them to pieces. Dan. 2:34 [margin].

The stone that smote the image became a great mountain, and filled the whole earth. Dan 2:35.

Which things the angels desire to look into. 1 Peter 1:12.

13. Then I heard one saint speaking, and another saint said unto that certain saint which spake, How long shall be the vision concerning the daily sacrifice, and the transgression of desolation, to give both the sanctuary and the host to be trodden under foot?
14. And he said unto me, Unto two thousand and three hundred days; then shall the sanctuary be cleansed.
15. And it came to pass, when I, even I Daniel, had seen the vision, and sought for the meaning, then, behold, there stood before me as the appearance of a man.

16. And I heard a man's voice between the banks of Ulai, which called, and said, Gabriel, make this man to understand the vision.

17. So he came near where I stood: and when he came, I was afraid, and fell upon my face: but he said unto me, Understand, O son of man: for at the time of the end shall be the vision.

18. Now as he was speaking with me, I was in a deep sleep on my face toward the ground: but he touched me, and set me upright.

19. And he said, Behold, I will make thee know what shall be in the last end of the indignation: for at the time appointed the end shall be.

20. The ram which thou sawest having two horns are the kings of Media and Persia.

21. And the rough goat is the king of Grecia: and the great horn that is between his eyes is the first king.

22. Now that being broken, whereas four stood up for it, four kingdoms shall stand up out of the nation, but not in his power.

23. And in the latter time of their kingdom, when the transgressors are come to the full, a king of fierce countenance, and understanding dark sentences, shall stand up.

24. And his power shall be mighty, but not by his own power: and he shall destroy wonderfully, and shall prosper, and practise, and shall destroy the mighty and the holy people.

25. And through his policy also he shall cause craft to prosper in his hand; and he shall magnify himself in his heart, and by peace shall destroy many: he shall also stand up against the Prince of princes; but he shall be broken without hand.

26. And the vision of the evening and the morning which was told is true: wherefore shut thou up the vision; for it shall be for many days.

27. And I Daniel fainted, and was sick certain days; afterward I rose up, and did the king's business; and I was astonished at the vision, but none understood it.
                                                    Dan. 8:13-27.

Follow after charity, and desire spiritual gifts, but rather that ye may prophesy.   1 Cor. 14:1.

1 Cor. 12:28, 29.

And he gave some, apostles; and some, prophets; and some, evangelists; and some, pastors and teachers.   Eph. 4:11.

Blessed are the pure in heart: for they shall see God.   Matt. 5:8.

I am Gabriel, that stand in the presence of God; and am sent to speak unto thee, and to shew thee these glad tidings.   Luke 1:19.

But I will shew thee that which is noted in the scripture of truth: and there is none that holdeth with me in these things, but Michael your prince.
                                               Dan. 10:21.

derstand some of the secrets of the Almighty. The interest Heaven manifests in these scenes of earth is shown by the thirteenth verse. One angel called to Gabriel, asking, "How long shall be the vision concerning the daily sacrifice [pagan Rome], and the transgression of desolation [the papacy], to give both the sanctuary and he host to be trodden under foot?" And Gabriel answered, "Unto two thousand and three hundred days; then shall the sanctuary be cleansed."

Daniel longed for an understanding of what he had seen, and the close connection between human longing and Christ's heart is shown here; for Christ, appearing as a man, stood before the prophet, and to Gabriel He said, "Make this man to understand the vision." Gabriel drew near, and before his exceeding brightness Daniel fell upon the ground with his face to the earth. Then, as if to lift the strain from the mind of him who carried Israel [131] on his heart, he said, "Understand, O son of man: for *at the time of the end* shall be the vision. ... I will make thee know what shall be in the last end of the indignation; for at the time appointed the end shall be."

Gabriel took up the history of the kingdoms one by one, and when he came to the two thousand three hundred days, he said, "The vision of the evening and the morning [Dan. 8:14, margin, same as the two thousand three hundred days] which was told is true. Wherefore shut thou up the vision; for it shall be for many days." Daniel fainted, for the crucifixion of the Saviour had just been revealed to him, and the view was more than he could endure. Further explanation was delayed until a later vision. The events which would take place during that period are noted in the following chapter of the book of Daniel.

In addition to the truth taught by the prophecy itself, there are connected with the eighth chapter of Daniel some underlying principles of wonderful beauty.

The spirit of prophecy is a gift to be coveted. God never leaves Himself without some representatives on earth, and among His people certain ones are prophets. The study of Daniel's life reveals the character which makes it possible for man to understand the language of God. A clean, pure soul is necessary. Gabriel is the angel of prophecy, the messenger who bears the light of truth to men. To the father of John the Baptist he said, "I am Gabriel, that stand in the presence of God." To Daniel he said, "There is none that holdeth with me in these things, but Michael your Prince"— [132] Christ Himself. Gabriel is, then, the personal attendant of the Son of God, holding the position as light bearer which Satan occupied before his fall. It was Gabriel who announced the birth of the Saviour to Mary in Nazareth. It was he who led the angel choir on the plains of Bethlehem; he with others, as the star, guided the wise men to the Babe of Bethlehem.

It was Gabriel who brought strength to the Saviour at the close of the forty days' conflict in the wilderness of temptation, and he who lifted the prostrate form of the Son of Man in Gethsemane, and pillowed that aching head, wet with bloody sweat, upon his own bosom. Before Gabriel, the Roman guard fell like dead men, and his voice shook the earth as the Saviour came from the tomb. Taking his seat on the empty sepulcher, he met the disciples and the women, and bade them seek their Lord among the living.

The Saviour ascended to heaven, leaving His disciples alone, but not alone, for "behold, two men stood by them in white apparel." While heaven rang with songs of welcome to the returning Son of God, two angels stood on earth to comfort the lonely ones. One of these was Gabriel, Christ's attendant angel. Of all the angels of heaven none have been more closely connected with man than has Gabriel. Yet to John, who fell before him to worship, he said, "See thou do it not; for I am thy fellow-servant." Gabriel was only an angel, upheld by the same Power that sustained John, and he would not for one moment allow John to be deceived by thinking he was a part of the great Trinity of heaven, and worthy of the worship of man-kind. [133] He assured John that he was only one of the hosts of "ministering spirits sent forth to minister for them who should be heirs of salvation," by saying, "I am thy fellow-servant." So bound up in the affairs of man is this mighty angel that he counts himself one

Isa. 14:12-14.
Luke 1:26, 27.
Luke 2:13, 14.

There shall come a Star out of Jacob.
Num 24:17.

When they had heard the king, they departed; and, lo, the star, which they saw in the east, went before them, till it came and stood over where the young child was. Matt. 2:9.

Then the devil leaveth him, and, behold, angels came and ministered unto him.
Matt. 4:11.

There appeared an angel unto him from heaven, strengthening him. Luke 22:43.

For fear of him the keepers did shake, and became as dead men. Matt. 28:4.

Matt. 28:2.
Ye seek Jesus of Nazareth, which was crucified: he is risen; he is not here: behold the place where they laid him. Mark 16:6.
Why seek ye the living among the dead?
Luke 24:5.

Acts 1:9-11.
Lift up your heads, O ye gates; even lift them up, ye everlasting doors; and the King of glory shall come in. Who is this King of glory? The LORD of hosts, he is the King of glory. Selah.
Psa. 24:9-10.

Dan. 10:21.
Rev. 19:10.
Rev. 22:9.

For there are three that bear record in heaven, the Father, the Word, and the Holy Ghost: and these three are one. 1 John 5:7.

Why should we tremble to convey
The Christian to the tomb?
There once the flesh of Jesus lay,
And left a long perfume.

The graves of all His saints He blest,
And softened every bed;
Where should the dying members rest,
But with their dying Head?

Thence He arose, ascending high,
And showed our feet the way:
Up to the Lord we all shall fly
At the great rising day.

—*Isaac Watts.*

with us. This [134] is the one whom Christ has used to convey the light of future events to men upon earth. To every prophet, from Moses to John, the same angel came, and

"The angel answered and said unto the women, Fear not ye: for I know that ye seek Jesus."

to the remnant church it is still Gabriel who reveals truth through the person of the prophet.

Before his fall, Lucifer was the light bearer. Since that time he has used his power in bearing darkness to the sons of men. There always have been, and will be to the end of time, false prophets and seers. Men who might be used by God, were their hearts given to Him, often yield themselves to the influence of the counterfeit power. Herein lies the explanation of spirit manifestations. So great will be this power that before the end Satan himself, personifying an angel of light, will appear on the earth, deceiving, if possible, the very elect. The safety of God's people will lie in heeding the voice of Gabriel as he speaks through some chosen instrument. Christ speaks through Gabriel to His prophet.

Daniel, though living in the palace of Shushan, was carried by the angel to the river Ulai. On the banks of the river he witnessed the contest between the ram and the goat—between the Medo-Persian empire and the Greeks. Ulai represents the river of time, which has its source in eternity. Time with which we have to deal is but an infinitely small fraction of eternity, as a drop in the bucket, as the stream to the ocean. But on the banks of this river all nations are located; there they rise and there they fall. Christ presides over the waters, and His voice was heard from between the banks of the river calling to Gabriel, "Make [135] this man to understand the vision." Nation may contend with nation on its banks, but the "Holy Watcher" is ever near. This river contains the water of life for all who will drink, but all nations have built river walls exceeding the height of those of Babylon, to keep men away from the water, and to break the influence of Him who calls from between the banks. [136]

The Revelation of Jesus Christ, which God gave unto him, to shew unto his servants things which must shortly come to pass; and he sent and signified it by his angel unto his servant John.   Rev. 1:1.

John 8:44.
Deut. 13:1-3.
For there shall arise false Christs, and false prophets, and shall shew great signs and wonders; insomuch that, if it were possible, they shall deceive the very elect.
                                   Matt. 24:24.

Acts 16:16.
Acts 13:6-10.
Rev. 16-18.

No marvel: for Satan himself is trransformed into an angel of light.   2 Cor. 11:14.

2 Chron. 20:20.
Num. 12:6.
I saw in a vision, and I was by the river of Ulai.
                                   Dan. 8:2.
I saw him come close unto the ram, and he was moved with choler against him, and smote the ram, and brake his two horns: and there was no power in the ram to stand before him, but he cast him down to the ground, and stamped upon him: and there was none that could deliver the ram out of his hand.
                                   Dan. 8:7.
Then I Daniel looked, and, behold, there stood other two, the one on this side of the bank of the river, and the other on that side of the bank of the river. And one said to the man clothed in linen, which was upon the waters of the river, How long shall it be to the end of these wonders?
                                   Dan. 12:5-6.
Dan. 8:16.
He shall drink of the brook in the way: therefore shall he lift up the head.   Ps. 110:7.

But your iniquities have separated between you and your God, and your sins have hid his face from you, that he will not hear.   Isa. 59:2.

CHAPTER 10

THE HISTORY OF THE JEWS

DANIEL 9

A FEW months only elapsed between the vision of the eighth chapter and the events which the first part of the ninth chapter records. The parting words of Gabriel had been that the things seen concerning the two thousand three hundred days were true. Daniel was unable to hear the explanation at this time; and while he went about the king's business, he thought often upon the vision. In the meantime he had been called from Shushan into Babylon, into the king's court, to interpret the strange writing on the wall. The fate of the nation had been read, and [137] the words had scarcely died away before the slaughter of the Babylonians began. That same night Belshazzar was slain, and the king of the Medes was proclaimed monarch of the world. By Darius, Daniel had been made chief president, and occupied a position in Babylon next to Cyrus, the associate of Darius the king.

During the turmoil and bustle of all the change in affairs, while Daniel's hands were filled with court duties and business cares, he yet had time for prayer and study.

The vision of the evening and the morning which was told is true. Dan. 8:26.

TEKEL; Thou art weighed in the balances, and art found wanting. PERES. Thy kingdom is divided, and given to the Medes and Persians. Dan. 5:27. 28.

In that night was Belshazzar the king of the Chaldeans slain. And Darius the Median took the kingdom, being about threescore and two years old. Dan. 5:30-31.

Over these three presidents; of whom Daniel was first: that the princes might give accounts unto them, and the king should have no damage. Dan. 6:2.

1. In the first year of Darius the son of Ahasuerus, of the seed of the Medes, which was made king over the realm of the Chaldeans;
2. In the first year of his reign I Daniel understood by books the number of the years, whereof the word of the LORD came to Jeremiah the prophet, that he would accomplish seventy years in the desolations of Jerusalem. Dan. 9:1-2.

For thus saith the LORD, That after seventy years be accomplished at Babylon I will visit you, and perform my good word toward you, in causing you to return to this place.   Jer. 29:10.

Jer. 25:11, 12.
2 Chron. 36:21.

3. And I set my face unto the Lord God, to seek by prayer and supplications, with fasting, and sack-cloth, and ashes:
4. And I prayed unto the LORD my God, and made my confession, and said, O Lord, the great and dreadful God, keeping the covenant and mercy to them that love him, and to them that keep his commandments;
5. We have sinned, and have committed iniquity, and have done wickedly, and have rebelled, even by departing from thy precepts and from thy judgments:
6. Neither have we hearkened unto thy servants the prophets, which spake in thy name to our kings, our princes, and our fathers, and to all the people of the land.
7. O Lord, righteousness belongeth unto thee, but unto us confusion of faces, as at this day; to the men of Judah, and to the inhabitants of Jerusalem, and unto all Israel, that are near, and that are far off, through all the countries whither thou hast driven them, because of their trespass that they have trespassed against thee.
8. O Lord, to us belongeth confusion of face, to our kings, to our princes, and to our fathers, because we have sinned against thee.
9. To the Lord our God belong mercies and forgivenesses, though we have rebelled against him;
Dan. 9:3-9.

Ezra 8:21-23.
Neh. 2:19.

10. Neither have we obeyed the voice of the LORD our God, to walk in his laws, which he set before us by his servants the prophets.

Gen. 19:12-16.

11. Yea, all Israel have transgressed thy law, even by departing, that they might not obey thy voice; therefore the curse is poured upon us, and the oath that is written in the law of Moses the servant of God, because we have sinned against him.

Zech. 7:11.

12. And he hath confirmed his words, which he spake against us, and against our judges that judged us, by bringing upon us a great evil: for under the whole heaven hath not been done as hath been done upon Jerusalem.
13. As it is written in the law of Moses, all this evil is come upon us: yet made we not our prayer before the LORD our God, that we might turn from our iniquities, and understand thy truth.

'Prophecy had foretold that Cyrus would restore to the Jews their freedom; the time of their deliverance drew near, and Daniel searched carefully for an understanding of the time. The prophecies of Jeremiah were the only ones which told plainly the length of the captivity. Doubtless the mind of Daniel was perplexed over the two thousand three hundred days, of which Gabriel had spoken, for to the Hebrews the temple in Jerusalem was God's sanctuary, and the cleansing, to them, meant the removal of unholy hands from Mount Zion.

Twice in the book of Jeremiah the length of the captivity is stated. "These nations shall serve the king of Babylon seventy years. And it shall come to pass, when the seventy years are accomplished, that I will punish the king of Babylon." Again the prophet had said, "After seventy years be accomplished, at Babylon I will visit you, and perform my good word toward you, in causing you to return to this place." Babylon had fallen, and Jerusalem had been desolate nearly seventy years. A crisis was near for God's people, and Daniel sought by prayer and fasting to understand the matter. [138]

This is one of the instances in the Scriptures when a prayer is recorded. This one is given as an example of the fervent, effectual prayer of a righteous man, which availeth much. Daniel realized that sin had darkened the vision of many of God's professed people. Some who were in Babylon were careless and indifferent concerning the truths of God. Many had gotten them homes, and rested secure in the assurance that, when the captivity began, they were told to buy land and build homes. Some were content with present surroundings, and dreaded the difficulties which must attend the journey to Jerusalem, which was in the hands of hostile tribes, and where there were no pleasant homes. Jerusalem should be built, they agreed, but others should do it, not they.

A love of Babylon was strong in the hearts of many. Seventy years after the decree of Cyrus had given all the Jews liberty to return to Palestine, there were still thousands of them in Babylon. In fact, but a small per cent of the Jews ever returned. The youth, who had been educated in the city, had, many of them, like the daughters of Lot in Sodom, partaken so largely of its customs, that they lingered among the heathen, though angels bade them hurry out. The spirit of prophecy was passed by with a few remarks, or fell upon ears entirely deaf; although in bondage, present conditions were preferable to freedom with the effort necessary to obtain it. Daniel knew of this condition, and he confessed the sins of the people before God. He identified himself with his people. His is one of the most wonderful prayers on record. [139]

This man, whom heaven called "greatly beloved," in whom no fault could be found, even by his bitterest enemies, placed himself beneath the load of sin which was oppressing Israel. Bowed before God, he met the Father with the words, "*We* have sinned, and committed iniquity, and have done wickedly, and have rebelled;" "neither have *we* hearkened unto Thy servants the prophets." "O Lord, righteousness belongeth unto Thee, but unto *us* confusion of face, to *our* kings, to *our* princes, and to *our* fathers, because *we* have sinned;" "*we* have rebelled against Him; neither have *we* obeyed;" "the curse is poured upon *us* "all this evil is come upon *us*, yet made *we* not *our* prayer before the Lord *our* God, that *we* might turn from *our* iniquities;" "*we* obeyed not His voice;" "*we* have sinned, *we* have done wickedly;" "because for *our* sins and for the iniquities of *our* fathers," "behold *our* desolations;" "*we* do not present *our* supplications before Thee for *our* righteousnesses."

Before the Father we have One, even Christ, who "hath borne our griefs and carried our sorrows," "who His own self bare our sins in His own body." Daniel was a representative of Christ, and he had lived so close to God, and knew Him so intimately, that the spirit which distinguished Christ from all others was manifested in Daniel also. He was a true shepherd in Israel, and his prayer is a rebuke to all selfrighteousness; a cutting rebuke to those who say by word or act, "I am more holy than thou."

"O Lord, hear; O Lord, forgive; O Lord, hearken and do; defer not for Thine own sake, O my God, for Thy city and Thy people are [140] called by Thy name." Such was the entreaty

---

14. Therefore hath the LORD watched upon the evil, and brought it upon us: for the LORD our God is righteous in all his works which he doeth: for we obeyed not his voice.

15. And now, O Lord our God, that hast brought thy people forth out of the land of Egypt with a mighty hand, and hast gotten thee renown, as at this day; we have sinned, we have done wickedly.

16. O Lord, according to all thy righteousness, I beseech thee, let thine anger and thy fury be turned away from thy city Jerusalem, thy holy mountain: because for our sins, and for the iniquities of our fathers, Jerusalem and thy people are become a reproach to all that are about us.

17. Now therefore, O our God, hear the prayer of thy servant, and his supplications, and cause thy face to shine upon thy sanctuary that is desolate, for the Lord's sake.

18. O my God, incline thine ear, and hear; open thine eyes, and behold our desolations, and the city which is called by thy name: for we do not present our supplications before thee for our righteousnesses, but for thy great mercies.

Dan. 9:12-18.

Isa. 53:4.
1 Peter 2:24.

2 Cor. 3:18.
2 Cor. 5:20.

Isa. 60:2.
John 10:11-17.

Isa. 65:5.
O Lord, hear; O Lord, forgive; O Lord, hearken and do; defer not, for thine own sake, O my God: for thy city and thy people are called by thy name.

Dan. 9:19.

A broken and a contrite heart, O God, thou wilt not despise. Ps. 51:17.

Acquaint now thyself with him, and be at peace: thereby good shall come unto thee. Job. 22:21

20. And whiles I was speaking, and praying, and confessing my sin and the sin of my people Israel, and presenting my supplication before the LORD my God for the holy mountain of my God;
21. Yea, whiles I was speaking in prayer, even the man Gabriel, whom I had seen in the vision at the beginning, being caused to fly swiftly, touched me about the time of the evening oblation.
Dan. 9:20-21.
22. And he informed me, and talked with me, and said, O Daniel, I am now come forth to give thee skill and understanding.
23. At the beginning of thy supplications the commandment came forth, and I am come to shew thee; for thou art greatly beloved: therefore understand the matter, and consider the vision.
Dan. 9:22-23.

of a burdened heart. Such were the words with which Daniel approached his God. He was acquainted with the Father, and knew that his words reached the throne of heaven. Faith and prayer are the two arms which mortal man may entwine around the neck of Infinite Love. Christ stooped to listen, and bade Gabriel speed earthward. We let go of the arm of the Lord too soon in our prayers. We should press our petitions higher and still higher. God sometimes tests the strength of our desires by delaying an immediate answer.

"Yea, whiles I was speaking in prayer, even the man Gabriel, whom I had seen in the vision at the beginning, being caused to fly swiftly, touched me about the time of the evening oblation."

The very thing for which Daniel had asked, was first mentioned as Gabriel laid his hands upon the prophet. "O Daniel, I am now come forth to give thee skill and understanding. At the beginning of thy supplication the word [margin] came forth, and I am come to show thee." Heaven was more interested than man could be [141] in the very thing for which Daniel prayed, and as soon as the channel was open, the Spirit flowed in. In the spiritual as in the natural world, a vacuum is abhorred. As the air

"O Daniel, I am now come forth to give thee skill and understanding."

Behold, I stand at the door, and knock: if any man hear my voice, and open the door, I will come in to him, and will sup with him, and he with me.
Rev. 3:20.

Them that honor me I will honor.
1 Sam. 2:30.

rushes into a vessel when a liquid is poured out, so the Holy Spirit fills the heart when it is emptied of self. If there was more room made for Christ in our hearts, the pentecostal experience would often be repeated.

God has many favorites among the sons of men. Indeed, every man is a special favorite, and highly honored by the King of heaven, but there are very few to whom angels have spoken the word, "Thou art greatly beloved." The marginal reading of the twenty-third verse gives the Hebrew rendering as "a man of desires." That man whose desires are heavenward, who longs for spiritual food as the hart panteth after the water brook, is greatly beloved of God, for God is in search of such to fulfill His will on earth. To such Gabriel can speak.

Beginning with the twenty-fourth verse the angel explains the period of time, the two thousand three hundred days of Daniel 8:14. There are no preliminaries. Gabriel knows the thoughts of the prophet, and hence he says, "Seventy weeks are determined [or cut off] upon thy people and upon thy holy city, to finish the transgression, and to make an end of sins, and to make reconciliation for iniquity, and to bring in everlasting righteousness, and to seal up the vision and prophecy, and to anoint the most holy." The entire future history of the Jews as a nation is contained in this one verse. No other history ever crowded so much into so few words. Here is given the exact date for [142] the beginning of the work of Christ; the time allotted Israel as a nation for repentance, the time when type would meet antitype in all sacrificial offerings; the period when probation would end for the Hebrew race, and everlasting righteousness would be preached to the world at large. In this interview with Gabriel only that part of the two thousand three hundred days which applied to the Hebrew nation was mentioned. To Daniel had already been revealed the history of the nations of the world; the two thousand three hundred day's has to do more especially with God's people, independently of national governments.

The period of seventy weeks, or four hundred and ninety days [70 x 7 = 490], of prophetic time, covers a period of four hundred and ninety years, during which Jewish history as such would continue. This four hundred and ninety years

Because he hath set his love upon me, therefore will I deliver him: I will set him on high, because he hath known my name. Ps. 91:14.

Thou art a men of desires, therefore understand the matter, and consider the vision.
Dan. 9:23 [margin].

I have esteemed the words of his mouth more than my necessary food. Job 23:12.

As the hart panteth after the water brooks, so panteth my soul after thee, O God. Ps. 42:1.

The LORD said unto Satan, Hast thou considered my servant Job, that there is none like him in the earth, a perfect and an upright man, one that feareth God, and escheweth evil? Job 1:8.

Seventy weeks are determined upon thy people and upon thy holy city, to finish the transgression, and to make an end of sins, and to make reconciliation for iniquity, and to bring in everlasting righteousness, and to seal up the vision and prophecy, and to anoint the most Holy.
Dan. 9:24.

And thou shalt take the anointing oil, and anoint the tabernacle, and all that is therein, and shalt hallow it, and all the vessels thereof: and it shall be holy. Exo. 40:9.

Mark 1:15.

Then Paul and Barnabas waxed bold, and said, It was necessary that the word of God should first have been spoken to you: but seeing ye put it from you, and judge yourselves unworthy of everlasting life, lo, we turn to the Gentiles.
Acts 13:46.

For the time is come that judgment must begin at the house of God: and if it first begin at us, what shall the end be of them that obey not the gospel of God? 1 Peter 4:17.

I have not spoken in secret, in a dark place of the earth: I said not unto the seed of Jacob, Seek ye me in vain: I the LORD speak righteousness, I declare things that are right. Isa 45:19.

25. Know therefore and understand, that from the going forth of the commandment to restore and to build Jerusalem unto the Messiah the Prince shall be seven weeks, and threescore and two weeks: the street shall be built again, and the wall, even in troublous times.
26. And after threescore and two weeks shall Messiah be cut off, but not for himself: and the people of the prince

that shall come shall destroy the city and the sanctuary; and the end thereof shall be with a flood, and unto the end of the war desolations are determined.

Dan. 9:25-26.

Heb. 2:3.

Search the scriptures; for in them ye think ye have eternal life: and they are they which testify of me.
John 5:39.

That saith of Cyrus, He is my shepherd, and shall perform all my pleasure: even saying to Jerusalem, Thou shalt be built; and to the temple, Thy foundation shall be laid. Isa. 44:28.

2 Chron. 36:23.

I have raised him up in righteousness, and I will direct all his ways: he shall build my city, and he shall let go my captives, not for price nor reward, saith the Lord of hosts. Isa 45:13.

Who is there among you of all his people? his God be with him, and let him go up to Jerusalem, which is in Judah, and build the house of the LORD God of Israel, (he is the God,) which is in Jerusalem. Ezra 1:3.

They shall bring all your brethren for an offering unto the LORD out of all nations upon horses, and in chariots, and in litters, and upon mules, and upon swift beasts, to my holy mountain Jerusalem Isa. 66:20.

Shake thyself from the dust; arise, and sit down, O Jerusalem: loose thyself from the bands of thy neck, O captive daughter of Zion. Isa. 52:2.

Therefore, behold, the days come, saith the LORD, that it shall no more be said, The LORD liveth, that brought up the children of Israel out of the land of Egypt; But, The LORD liveth, that brought up the children of Israel from the land of the north, and from all the lands whither he had driven them: and I will bring them again into their land that I gave unto their fathers.
Jer. 16:14-15.

did not begin at once, for the angel said they should begin to reckon from the going forth of the commandment to restore and build Jerusalem. The period of seventy weeks of Jewish history is thus divided by the angel: Seven weeks for building the walls and streets of Jerusalem; threescore and two (62) weeks till the work of the Messiah; and one week, which would cover the period of His ministry and the time following until the gospel should go forth to the Gentiles. This last week is devoted to the confirmation of the covenant.

For an understanding of the first division, the seven weeks or forty-nine years, we have the history as recorded in Ezra, Nehemiah, Haggai, and Zechariah. God raised up Cyrus and placed [143] him on the throne, that he might restore the Jews to their native city. Long before the Babylonish captivity began, the prophet Isaiah (44: 28) wrote of Cyrus, "He is My shepherd, and shall perform all My pleasure; even saying to Jerusalem, Thou shalt be built; and to the temple, thy foundation shall be laid."

In the first chapter of the book of Ezra is recorded the decree of Cyrus. The fulfillment by Cyrus of the prophecy of Isaiah is striking: "In the first year of Cyrus king of Persia. . . the Lord stirred up the spirit of Cyrus, the king of Persia, that he made a proclamation throughout all his kingdom, and put it in writing, saying, Thus saith Cyrus king of Persia, The Lord God of heaven. . . hath charged me to build him a house at Jerusalem."

Then it was that every Jew in Babylon was at liberty to return to Palestine. If necessary, the expenses of going would be borne by the government of Cyrus. There was ample provision for all the poor and the sick. Such a decree had never before been issued. Israel should have arisen *en masse*, taking with them all those of other nationalities, who, having heard the gospel, were willing to cast in their lot with the people of God. The land should have rung with shouts of praise and with the songs of the ransomed. The exodus from Babylon should have been a mighty witness to the nations of the earth of the power of the God of Israel. The exodus from Egypt, and the wonders attending the crossing of the Red Sea and the Jordan, and the feeding of the thousands in the wilderness, would have dwindled into insignificance had Israel taken advantage [144] of the way which God had prepared.

What was the result of the decree? Daniel watched with anxiety the preparations which were made to depart, and at the end of the first year scarcely fifty thousand had journeyed from Babylon to Jerusalem.

Cyrus was discouraged and disgusted because of the feeble response, and relapsed into indifference. Later the angel of God with Michael's help pleaded with him for *three* weeks in order to touch his heart again.

The vessels taken from the temple to Babylon by Nebuchadnezzar were returned to the leaders of the Jews, who carried them back to Jerusalem. In the second year of their coming into Palestine, the work of restoring the temple was begun. The site of Solomon's temple, which had been burned by Nebuchadnezzar, was hidden by rubbish, the accumulation of nearly seventy years. The work of restoration was soon stopped by the Samaritans living in the country, and further progress was impossible until the issuing of a second decree by Darius, king of Persia, in 520 B. C. Work on the house of God stopped for fifteen years. Then the prophets Haggai and Zechariah rebuked the people for their inactivity.

It would seem that the Jews while professing to be God's people, yet built their own houses, and delayed work on the temple, because there was no direct command from the king to proceed. But God wanted them to go forward, exercising faith, and when, in response to the word of the Lord by the prophet Haggai, they did go to work, the Lord stirred up the heart of the Persian king to help them. This will be further [145] seen in chapter twelve. Men of the world, enemies of the Jews, openly complained to the king, but this, instead of hindering the work, occasioned a searching of the royal records, which revealed the decree of Cyrus. Then Darius, instead of rebuking the Jews, issued a decree that the work should go forward, and further commanded that the work of building be helped forward by money from the royal treasury.

The whole congregation together was forty and two thousand three hundred and threescore.
Ezra 2:64-67.

The prince of the kingdom of Persia withstood me one and twenty days: but, lo, Michael, one of the chief princes, came to help me; and I remained there with the kings of Persia.
Dan. 10:13.
Ezra 1:7-11.
And when the builders laid the foundation of the temple of the LORD, they set the priests in their apparel with trumpets, and the Levites the sons of Asaph with cymbals, to praise the LORD, after the ordinance of David king of Israel. And they sang together by course in praising and giving thanks unto the LORD; because he is good, for his mercy endureth for ever toward Israel. And all the people shouted with a great shout, when they praised the LORD, because the foundation of the house of the LORD was laid.
Ezra 3:10-11.
Then ceased the work of the house of God which is at Jerusalem. So it ceased unto the second year of the reign of Darius king of Persia.
Ezra 4:24.

Ezra 5:1, 2.
Haggai, 1st and 2nd chapters.
Is it time for you, O ye, to dwell in your ceiled houses, and this house lie waste? Haggai 1:4.

Consider now from this day and upward, from the four and twentieth day of the ninth month, even from the day that the foundation of the Lord's temple was laid in the barn? yea, as yet the vine and the fig tree, and the pomegranite, and the olive tree, hath not brought forth: from this day will I bless you. Haggai 2:18, 19.
Ezra 5:1-17.
Now this is the copy of the letter that the king Artaxerxes gave unto Ezra the priest, the scribe, even a scribe of the words of the commandments of the LORD, and of his statutes to Israel. Artaxerxes, king of kings, unto Ezra the priest, a scribe of the law of the God of heaven, perfect peace, and at such a time. I make a decree, that all they of the people of Israel, and of his priests and Levites, in my realm, which are minded of their own freewill to go up to Jerusalem, go with thee. Forasmuch as thou art sent of the king, and of his seven counsellors, to enquire concerning Judah and Jerusalem, according to

the law of thy God which is in thine hand; And to carry the silver and gold, which the king and his counsellors have freely offered unto the God of Israel, whose habitation is in Jerusalem, And all the silver and gold that thou canst find in all the province of Babylon, with the freewill offering of the people, and of the priests, offering willingly for the house of their God which is in Jerusalem: That thou mayest buy speedily with this money bullocks, rams, lambs, with their meat offerings and their drink offerings, and offer them upon the altar of the house of your God which is in Jerusalem. And whatsoever shall seem good to thee, and to thy brethren, to do with the rest of the silver and the gold, that do after the will of your God. The vessels also that are given thee for the service of the house of thy God, those deliver thou before the

Jerusalem was subject to the Persian government until the days of Ezra in the reign of Artaxerxes. In the seventh year of the reign of that king, 457 B. C., was issued the third decree concerning the rebuilding of Jerusalem. This decree (1) permitted all Jews who so desired to return to Jerusalem; (2) it allowed the taking of a free-will offering from all Babylon for the cause at Jerusalem; (3) it proclaimed perfect freedom to follow the commands of God in all the territory west of the Jordan; (4) it relieved all Levites and ministers from paying toll or tribute; (5) it directed that the walls [146] of, Jerusalem be rebuilt; (6) it arranged for the appointment of magistrates arid judges tn Palestine from among the Jews themselves, thus organizing a government of the people, a thing wholly foreign to the policy of an Oriental monarchy.

This was in the year 457 B. C., and is the time from which the period of seventy weeks should be reckoned, according to the words of Gabriel to Daniel. That it required the *three decrees* to constitute the commandment of Dan. 9:25, is evident from the words of Inspiration in Ezra 6:14: "They builded, and finished it, . . . according *to the commandment of Cyrus, and*

The Jewish Leaders receiving the Sacred vessels.

Darius, and *Artaxerxes,* king of Persia." The three decrees are thus connected.

The "troublous times," during which the building should be carried forward are described by the prophet Nehemiah. Full thirteen long weary years after the decree of Artaxerxes was issued, Nehemiah, who was a cupbearer for the king in Babylon, was mourning over the troubles in Jerusalem, and in answer to his petition he was permitted to go up to the city in behalf of the work. Under the direction of Nehemiah the people worked on the wall of Jerusalem with weapons fastened to their sides. "They which builded on the wall, and they that bare burdens, with those that laded, every one with one of his hands wrought in the work, and with the other hand held a weapon.... So we labored in the work; and half of them held the spears from the rising of the morning till the stars appeared."

Nehemiah in these times of trouble was a wonderful leader for Israel. His lessons to the [147] people on the taking of usury, wages, and rent should be followed by Christians to-day. The rebuilding of Jerusalem in troublous times is a fit symbol of carrying the gospel to all nations in the last days. Israel brought this trouble upon herself by her sins and lack of faith; and what she should have done by way of warning the world in peace and quietude, had to be done in great distress. Furthermore, it will be noticed that a few years of rest always found sin and iniquity abounding in Israel. The nation was scarcely from under the hands of Babylon till the people held their own brethren as slaves because of debt. A proclamation of freedom must come from within their own borders before there could be peace and help from without. When it should come from within, God's Word pledged the support of even their enemies. These principles are true in the body of Christians to-day. The spread of the gospel will be an easy work, and it will be as the voice of a mighty angel enlightening the world, when God's people proclaim liberty among themselves.

"From the going forth of the commandment to restore and to build Jerusalem unto the Messiah the Prince shall be seven weeks and threescore and two weeks" (7 + 62 = 69 weeks,

God of Jerusalem. And whatsoever more shall be needful for the house of thy God, which thou shalt have occasion to bestow, bestow it out of the king's treasure house. And I, even I Artaxerxes the king, do make a decree to all the treasurers which are beyond the river, that whatsoever Ezra the priest, the scribe of the law of the God of heaven, shall require of you, it be done speedily, Unto an hundred talents of silver, and to an hundred measures of wheat, and to an hundred baths of wine, and to an hundred baths of oil, and salt without prescribing how much. Whatsoever is commanded by the God of heaven, let it be diligently done for the house of the God of heaven: for why should there be wrath against the realm of the king and his sons? Also we certify you, that touching any of the priests and Levites, singers, porters, Nethinims, or ministers of this house of God, it shall not be lawful to impose toll, tribute, or custom, upon them. And thou, Ezra, after the wisdom of thy God, that is in thine hand, set magistrates and judges, which may judge all the people that are beyond the river, all such as know the laws of thy God; and teach ye them that know them not. And whosoever will not do the law of thy God, and the law of the king, let judgment be executed speedily upon him, whether it be unto death, or to banishment, or to confiscation of goods, or to imprisonment. Ezra 7:11-26.

I pray you, let us leave off this usury. Restore, I pray you, to them, even this day, their lands, their vineyards, their oliveyards, and their houses, also the hundreth part of the money, and of the corn, the wine, and the oil, that ye exact of them. Neh. 5:1-13.

Neh. 5:14, 15.
Neh. 9:28.

Some of our daughters are brought unto bondage already: neither is it in our power to redeem them; for other men have our lands and vineyards. Neh. 5:5-8.

Zech. 9:9-11.
Haggai 2:15-19.
If the Son therefore shall make you free, ye shall be free indeed. John 8:36.
Ye shall know the truth, and the truth shall make you free. John 8:32.
After these things I saw another angel come down from heaven, having great power: and the earth eas lightened with his glory. Rev. 18:1.
Dan. 9:35.
We have found the Messisas, which is, being interpreted, the anointed. John 1:41 [margin].

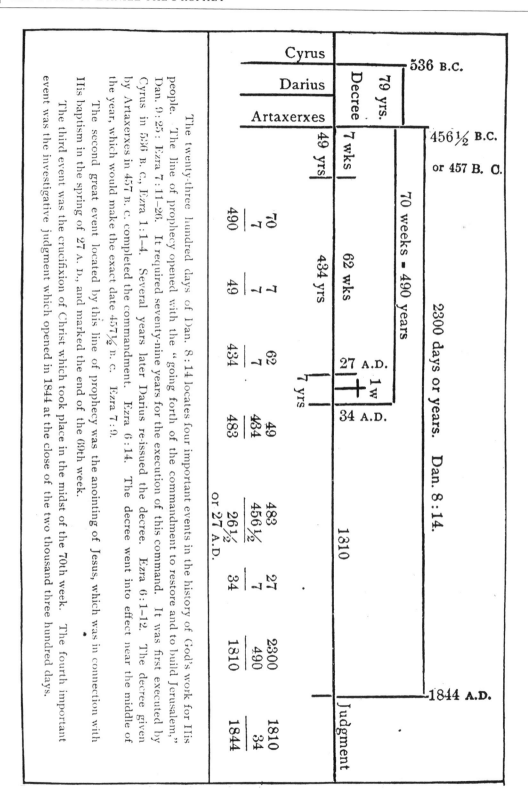

The twenty-three hundred days of Dan. 8:14 locates four important events in the history of God's work for His people. The line of prophecy opened with the "going forth of the commandment to restore and to build Jerusalem," Dan. 9:25; Ezra 7:11-26. It required seventy-nine years for the execution of this command. It was first executed by Cyrus in 536 B.C., Ezra 1:1-4. Several years later Darius re-issued the decree. Ezra 6:1-12. The decree given by Artaxerxes in 457 B.C. completed the commandment. Ezra 6:14. The decree went into effect near the middle of the year, which would make the exact date 457½ B.C. Ezra 7:9.

The second great event located by this line of prophecy was the anointing of Jesus, which was in connection with His baptism in the spring of 27 A.D., and marked the end of the 69th week.

The third event was the crucifixion of Christ which took place in the midst of the 70th week. The fourth important event was the investigative judgment which opened in 1844 at the close of the two thousand three hundred days.

or 483 prophetic days, or literal years). *Messiah,* in the Hebrew, and *Christ,* in the Greek, are the same as anointed" in English. God anointed Jesus of Nazareth with the Holy Ghost. This anointing took place at the time of His baptism. The sixty-nine weeks, or four hundred and eighty-three years, reached to the baptism of Christ by- John in the River Jordan. [148]

From the decree of Artaxerxes, four hundred and fifty-seven years reach into the year 1 A. D., in the present dispensation. But twenty-six years remained of the sixty-nine weeks (483 — 457 = 26), which terminated with the baptism of Christ. Twenty-six years added to the year 1 A. D. bring us to 27 A. D., in the fall of which year Christ was baptized. (See Mark 1:10, margin; Luke 3:21-23, margin).

For years the Jewish nation had had the promise of a Deliverer. The close of the sixty-nine weeks found the Jews under the control of the fourth kingdom, the dreadful and terrible beast which Daniel had before described. The desire of every Jewish woman who was true to her God was to be the mother of the Saviour. Whenever a babe was presented to the Lord, it was with the hope that he might be the accepted One. The birthplace of the Messiah had been foretold. Malachi had prophesied concerning John, the forerunner of the Saviour, and for six months the voice of this witness had been heard throughout the land of Israel. The time of the preaching of John is established by six historical facts. (See Luke 3:1, 2). Israel and Judah flocked to the banks of the Jordan, and among them came Jesus of Nazareth. John recognized Him by a sign from heaven; and as He came out of the water, the heavens opened, and he saw the heavenly dove resting on His head, and heard the voice proclaiming Him the Son of God.

The sixty-nine weeks had closed. Those who were at that time studying the prophecies of [149] Daniel were looking for the Messiah, and believed the words of John when he said, "Behold the Lamb of God, which taketh away the sin of the world." Christ also said, "The time is fulfilled," referring to the period of sixty-nine weeks of Daniel. But the nation as a whole was blind. "He came unto His own,

How God anointed Jesus of Nazareth with the Holy Ghost and with power: who went about doing good, and healing all that were oppressed of the devil; for God was with him.

Acts 10:38.

Luke 3:21, 22.
And straightway coming up out of the water, he saw the heavens opened, and the Spirit like a dove descending upon him.

Mark 1:10.

The kingdom is the LORD'S: and he is the governor among the nations.

Ps. 22:28.

But John forbad him, saying, I have need to be baptized of thee, and comest thou to me? And Jesus answering said unto him, Suffer it to be so now: for thus it becometh us to fulfil all righteousness.

Matt. 3:14-15.

It came to pass in those days, that there went out a decree from Caesar Augustus, that all the world should be taxed. And this taxing was first made when Cyrenius was governor of Syria.)

Luke 2:1-2.

But thou, Bethlehem Ephratah, though thou be little among the thousands of Judah, yet out of thee shall he come forth unto me that is to be ruler in Israel; whose goings forth have been from of old, from everlasting.

Micah 5:2.

Mal. 3:1.
Mal. 4:5, 6.

Luke 3:1-3.
Matt. 3:5, 13.
John 1:31-34.
Matt. 3:17.

Again the next day after John stood, and two of his disciples; And looking upon Jesus as he walked, he saith, Behold the Lamb of God! And the two disciples heard him speak, and they followed Jesus.

John 1:35-37.

Mark 1:15.
Luke 19:41-45.

John 1:11.
Matt. 24:15.
Dan. 7:9, 10.
Dan. 8:14.
Rev. 14:6-12.
Luke 21:35.

And after threescore and two weeks shall Messiah be cut off, but not for himself: . . . in the midst of the week he shall cause the sacrifice and the oblation to cease, and for the overspreading of abominations he shall make it desolate, even until the consummation, and that determined shall be poured upon the desolate.
Dan. 9:26-27.

He hath sent me to heal the brokenhearted, to preach deliverance to the captives, and recovering of sight to the blind, to set at liberty them that are bruised. Luke 4:18-19.

And he shall confirm the covenant with many for one week: and in the midst of the week he shall cause the sacrifice and the oblation to cease, and for the overspreading of abominations he shall make it desolate, even until the consummation, and that determined shall be poured upon the desolate.
Dan. 9:27.

Behold, your house is left unto you desolate.
Matt. 23:38.

For the law having a shadow of good things to come, and not the very image of the things.
Heb. 10:1.

Which are a shadow of things to come: but the nody is of Christ. Col. 2:17.

And that repentance and remission of sins should be preached in his name among all nations, begining at Jerusalem. Luke 23:47.

How shall we escape, if we neglect so great salvation; which at the first began to be spoken by the Lord, and was confirmed unto us by them that heard him? Heb. 2:3.

And after threescore and two weeks shall Messiah be cut off, but not for himself: and the people of the prince that shall come shall destroy the city and the sanctuary; and the end thereof shall be with a flood, and unto the end of the war desolations are determined. Dan 9:26.

Ezra 7:11-26.
Mark 1:10 [margin].
Acts 8:1-4.

and His own received Him not." They might have known. The book of Daniel was for them to study. The same book, together with the book of Revelation, proclaims the hour of God's judgment, and His second coming, but men will be taken unawares because they heed not the prophecies.

As the baptism of Christ was one sign given by Gabriel by which the Jews might have known the Messiah, so His death was a second token. One week—seven years—remained of the allotted time for the Jewish nation. During one half of that time—three and one-half years—the Son of God walked among the people. The sick were healed; he comforted the broken-hearted, and preached the gospel to the poor. High and low, rich and poor, alike came within the circle of His influence.

"In the midst of the week," said the angel to Daniel, "He shall cause the sacrifice and the oblation to cease," At the time of the passover feast, in the spring of 31 A. D., three and one-half years after His baptism, Christ was crucified by the very people He had tried to save. As His life went out, the inner veil of the temple was rent from the top to the bottom. The mercy seat, seen only by the high priest once each year, was laid open to the gaze of the multitudes. The knife fell from the hand of the [150] priest, and the sacrificial lamb escaped. God had withdrawn His presence from the temple. The Lamb of God Himself had been slain, and sacrifice and oblation were forever done away. Those ceremonies which had shadowed forth the death of the Saviour, ceased at the cross. This was in the midst of the last week of the prophetic seventy weeks.

Mercy still lingered over the Jewish people; there was yet a little time in which to repent. What was not accomplished in the person of Christ, God, sending His Holy Spirit, sought to accomplish through His disciples. Humble fishermen imbued with the power of God taught the people concerning a crucified and risen Saviour. In one day three thousand accepted the message. When many believed, the enmity of Satan was again aroused. In 34 A. D., Stephen was stoned, 'and as the result of the severe persecution which followed, the believers were driven from Jerusalem and "went *everywhere* preaching the word." Israel had withdrawn from

God, and His spirit could no longer protect them. In less than forty years the city was captured by the army of Titus; the temple was burned, and the Jews were scattered to the ends of the earth, there to remain until the consumation of all things at the time determined. [151]

There can be no question as to the accuracy of the date 457 B. c., as the beginning of the seventy weeks, for it is established by four events: the decree of Artaxerxes; the Baptism of Christ; the crucifixion; and the spread of the gospel among the Gentiles. History establishes the date 457 B. c. as the seventh year of Artaxerxes by more than twenty eclipses. The four hundred and ninety years can be reckoned backward from the New Testament history, or forward from the decree to restore and build Jerusalem.

The angel has given the events during the first four hundred and-ninety years of the two thousand three hundred days of Dan. 8:14. Eighteen hundred and ten years remains, 2300 - 490 = 1810. The four hundred and ninety years ended in the year 34 A. D. To this add eighteen hundred and ten years, and we have the year 1844 A. D. Daniel had been shown the events which would mark this year. It was the investigative judgment, and the giving of the message of the first angel of the fourteenth chapter of Revelation.

This message was given within the memory of many who are still living, and is known as the advent message. About twenty years before the expiration of the prophetic period of the two thousand three hundred days, the attention of some men were called to the study of the prophecies. Foremost among these students was William Miller, who became thoroughly convinced that the prophetic period of Dan. 8:14 would close

Stoning of Stephen.

And God said, Let there be lights in the firmament of the heaven to divide the day from the night; and let them be for signs, and for seasons, and for days, and years: Gen. 1:14.

Thou shalt bear the iniquity of the house of Judah forty days: I have appointed thee each day for a year. Eze. 4:6.

After the number of the days in which ye searched the land, even forty days, each day for a year, shall ye bear your iniquities, even forty years, and ye shall know my breach of promise. Num. 14:34.

Dan. 8:14.

Fear God, and give glory to him; for the hour of his judgment is come: and worship him that made heaven, and earth, and the sea, and the fountains of waters. Rev. 14:7.

Knowing this first, that no prophecy of the scripture is of any private interpretation. 2 Peter 1:20.

Thy words were found, and I did eat them; and thy word was unto me the joy and rejoicing of mine heart.   Jer. 15:16.

I saw another mighty angel come down from heaven, clothed with a cloud: and a rainbow was upon his head, and his face was as it were the sun, and his feet as pillars of fire: And he had in his hand a little book open: and he set his right foot upon the sea, and his left foot on the earth.
                                             Rev. 10:1-2.
Rev. 14:6, 7.

I went unto the angel, and said unto him, Give me the little book. And he said unto me, Take it, and eat it up; and it shall make thy belly bitter, but it shall be in thy mouth sweet as honey.
                                             Rev. 10:9.

Heb. 10:32-36.

The temple of God was opened in heaven, and there was seen in his temple the ark of his testament.   Rev. 11:19.

There are priests that offer gifts according to the law: Who serve unto the example and shadow of heavenly things, as Moses was admonished of God when he was about to make the tabernacle: for, See, saith he, that thou make all things according to the pattern shewed to thee in the mount.
                                             Heb. 8:1-5.

Dan. 7:9, 10.

Behold, I come quickly; and my reward is with me, to give every man according as his work shall be.
                                             Rev. 22:12.

Dan. 11:1-45.

And all men shall fear, and shall declare the work of God; for they shall wisely consider of his doing.   Ps 64:9.

in 1844. The expression "unto two thousand and three hundred days then shall the sanctuary be cleansed," was interpreted to [152] mean that at the end of that stated period the earth would be destroyed by fire at the second coming of Christ. Consequently between 1833 and 1844 the personal coming of the Saviour was preached throughout the world. Men were warned according to the wording of the first angel's message of the fourteenth chapter of Revelation, that the judgment was at hand, and thousands prepared to meet the Lord.

When the year 1844 passed, and Christ did not appear, many lost faith in the prophecies; but others, knowing that the word of God abideth sure, were led to search more diligently for the events which did take place at the close of the prophetic period. Further study corroborated the truth of the interpretation of the time, and revealed also the light on the sanctuary question.

For the first time men saw that the "sanctuary" spoken of in Daniel's vision referred to the work in heaven rather than upon earth. An investigation of the typical service instituted in the wilderness revealed the work of cleansing the sanctuary on the day of atonement. It was seen that the work of the high priest in the earthly tabernacle was but a figure of the service upon which Christ, the great High Priest, entered in 1844. At that time He entered into the presence of the Ancient of Days, as seen in the vision of the seventh chapter of Daniel, and began the work of the investigative judgment in the heavenly sanctuary, at the end of which work He will appear in the clouds of heaven. William Miller and others who preached the second advent in 1844 were mistaken in the event, but not [153] in the reckoning of the prophetic time of Dan. 8:14.

The events which took place between 34 a. d. and 1844 a. d. are described in the next vision, which was given to Daniel, four or five years later than the vision of the ninth chapter.

Since Gabriel explained with such care and minuteness the history of the Jews, and as a nation they were without excuse in the rejection of the Son God, we may expect that this same angel of prophecy will set the waymarks high and clear, that men in the last days may know the time of Christ's appearing in judgment, and of His second coming in the clouds of heaven.

Let us watch and be ready.

And that, knowing the time, that now it is high time to awake out of sleep: for now is our salvation nearer than when we believed. The night is far spent, the day is at hand: let us therefore cast off the works of darkness, and let us put on the armour of light.   Rom. 13:11-12.

Watch and be ready.

THE SANCTUARY

SINCE a misunderstanding of the sanctuaryquestion led to the disappointment in 1844, it seems proper to devote one chapter to the consideration of this all-important subject.

Three sanctuaries, or temples, are brought to view in the Bible. The first is the heavenly sanctuary, where God reigns upon His throne, surrounded by ten thousand times ten thousands of angels. This temple was opened to the wondering, gaze of the lonely seer on the Isle of Patmos, and also to Moses on Mount Sinai. The second, or earthly, sanctuary was a miniature model of the heavenly one, in which the priests served unto the example and shadow of [155] the service in the heavenly temple. For more than fourteen hundred years; God designed that the service should be in the shadowy sanctuary. The time came when those following the shadow reached the substance.

Two days before the crucifixion, Christ slowly and regretfully left the temple for the last time. The priests and rulers were struck with terror as they heard His mournful words: "Behold, your house is left unto you desolate." The beautiful structure remained until A. D. 70, but it had ceased to be the temple of God. The Father showed by an unmis-

For he hath looked down from the height of his sanctuary; from heaven did the LORD behold the earth.   Ps. 102:19.

The LORD is in his holy temple, the LORD'S throne is in heaven: his eyes behold, his eyelids try, the children of men.   Ps. 11:4.

I beheld till the thrones were cast down, and the Ancient of days did sit: thousand thousands miistered unto him, and ten thousand times ten thousand stood before him.
                                    Dan. 7:9, 10. R. V.

The temple of God was opened in heaven.
                                    Rev. 11:19.

Look that thou make them after their pattern, which thou wast caused to see in the mount.
                                    Ex. 24:40 [margin].

Who serve unto the example and shadow of heavenly things, as Moses was admonished of God when he was about to make the tabernacle: for, See, saith he, that thou make all things according to the pattern shewed to thee in the mount.
                                    Heb. 8:5.

Heb. 9:8, 9, 11, 23, 24.

Ye know that after two days is the feast of the passover, and the Son of man is betrayed to be crucified.   Matt. 26:2.

Behold, your house is left unto you desolate.
                                    Matt. 23:38.

Behold, the veil of the temple was rent in twain from the top to the bottom.   Matt. 27:51.

For there is one God, and one mediator between God and men, the man Christ Jesus.
1 Tim. 2:5-6.

The blood of Jesus Christ his Son cleanseth us from all sin.
1 John 1:7.

The way into the holiest of all was not yet made manifest, while as the first tabernacle was yet standing.
Heb. 9:8-9.

Heb. 9:24.
Heb. 6:19, 20.

What? know ye not that your body is the temple of the Holy Ghost which is in you?
1 Cor. 6:19, 20.

Jesus answered and said unto them, Destroy this temple, and in three days I will raise it up. Then said the Jews, Forty and six years was this temple in building, and wilt thou rear it up in three days? But he spake of the temple of his body.
John 2:19-2.

Give ear, O Shepherd of Israel, thou that leadest Joseph like a flock; thou that dwellest between the cherubims, shine forth.
Ps. 80:1.

God hath made man upright.
Eccl. 7:29.

Rom. 6:6-8.

All that dwell upon the earth shall worship him, whose names are not written in the book of life of the Lamb slain from the foundation of the world.
Rev. 13:8.

I am crucified with Christ: nevertheless I live; yet not I, but Christ liveth in me: and the life which I now live in the flesh I live by the faith of the Son of God, who loved me, and gave himself for me.
Gal. 2:20.

I will put enmity between thee and the woman, and between thy seed and her seed; it shall bruise thy head, and thou shalt bruise his heel.
Gen. 3:15.

To him that overcometh will I give to eat of the tree of life, which is in the midst of the paradise of God.
Rev 2:7:

takable sign that the glory had departed. When the words, "It is finished," were pronounced by the Sufferer upon the cross, the veil of the temple was rent from the top to the bottom by unseen hands. Terror and confusion prevailed. The knife raised to slay the sacrifice fell from the nerveless hand of the priest, and the lamb escaped.

Henceforth the sinner need no longer wait for a priest to offer his sacrifice. The great Sacrifice had been made. Every child of Adam could accept His atoning blood. The way into the heavenly temple was now made manifest. The heavenly had taken the place of the earthly sanctuary. Hereafter' man's faith was to enter within the veil, where Christ officiated.

The third temple brought to view in the Bible is the temple of the human body. The Jews had lost sight of the fact that their bodies were to be the temples of the Spirit of God; and when the Saviour said, "Destroy this temple, and in three days I will raise it up," they thought only of the massive structure of marble and stone, and replied that it had taken [156] forty-six years to build the temple, not perceiving that "He spake of the temple of His body."

Glorious rays of light shine from the heavenly sanctuary upon those who study the typical work in the earthly sanctuary. These rays, when gathered into the temple of the body, reflect the character of our great High Priest in the heavenly courts.

In the beginning the body of man was created to be a dwelling place for the Holy Spirit; but Satan gained possession, and man partook of an evil nature. Before the body can again become a temple for the Spirit of God, the evil nature must die. Christ offered His life for the sinner; before the foundation of the world He was counted as a "Lamb slain."

That man in his fallen condition might comprehend this gift, and understand the work of redemption, the sinner that longed to crucify "the old man," the evil nature, was directed to bring an innocent animal, and take its life, as an object lesson of the Lamb of God, and also to illustrate the fact that the evil nature of the sinner must die, in order that the Holy Spirit may dwell within.

The three temples.

He shewed me a pure river of water of life, clear as crystal, proceeding out of the throne of God and of the Lamb. In the midst of the street of it, and on either side of the river, was there the tree of life, which bare twelve manner of fruits, and yielded her fruit every month: and the leaves of the tree were for the healing of the nations.
Rev. 22:1-2.

Eze. 47:12.
Zech. 14:8.

And there came a fire out from before the LORD, and consumed upon the altar the burnt offering and the fat: which when all the people saw, they shouted, and fell on their faces.   Lev. 9:24.

Then the fire of the Lord fell, and consuumed the burnt sacrifice.   1 Kings 18:38.

Judges 6:21.

In process of time it came to pass, that Cain brought of the fruit of the ground an offering unto the LORD. And Abel, he also brought of the firstlings of his flock and of the fat thereof. And the LORD had respect unto Abel and to his offering.   Gen. 4:3-4.

Heb. 11:4.

He placed at the east of the garden of Eden Cherubims, and a flaming sword which turned every way, to keep the way of the tree of life.
Gen. 3:24.

But unto Cain and to his offering he had not re-spect. And Cain was very wroth, and his counte-nance fell.   Gen. 4:5.

For the life of the flesh is in the blood: and I have given it to you upon the altar to make an atonement for your souls: for it is the blood that maketh an atonement for the soul.   Lev. 17:11.

Now all these things happened unto them for en-samples: and they are written for our admonition, upon whom the ends of the world are come.
1 Cor. 10:11.

And he removed from thence unto a mountain on the east of Bethel, and pitched his tent, having Bethel on the west, and Hai on the east: and there he builded an altar unto the LORD, and called upon the name of the LORD.   Gen. 12:8.

Before the gates of the garden of Eden, Adam and his family presented their offerings. Their clear minds grasped by faith the promise of the Redeemer, who would again open to them the joys of the garden. Adam by faith looked forward to the time when the Saviour would lead him once more to the Tree of Life, and bid him pluck and eat of its life-giving fruit. As he took the life of the innocent lamb, and saw by faith the "one sinless Man" suffering death for him, his heart went out in love and gratitude [157] to God for His wonderful love, and for a time he forgot the terrible sorrow that weighed upon his soul. Every falling leaf, while it taught the death of Christ, was also a constant reminder to him that sin had brought death into the hitherto perfect earth.

While men lived near God, the altars were lighted by fire from heaven. But this perfect worship was marred. Cain's mind became so blinded by sin that he failed to grasp the infinite sacrifice. Satan convinced him that God was an austere judge, demanding service. The love and sacrifice of the Saviour was overlooked. Cain and Abel each brought an offering to the gate of the garden; but the desires of the two hearts were greatly different. Abel brought a lamb, and as he took its life, his faith laid hold of the Lamb of God. The lamb was laid upon the altar, and fire flashed from the shining sword of the cherubim guarding the way to the Tree of Life, and the sacrifice was consumed.

Cain brought an offering of fruits. There was nothing in his offering that typified the dying Lamb of Calvary. No innocent life was taken in exchange for his forfeited life. He waited for the fire to consume it, but there was nothing to call forth the fire from the heavenly Watcher. There was no sweet love, no longing for deliverance from the thralldom of sin and death.

Cain and Able are types of all worshipers from that time to the present. The followers of Cain multiplied cere-monies, and made offerings to the sun and various other ob-jects. In it they overlooked the all-important principle that self must die, and that Christ [158] must live im the temple of the human body.

Anciently each family erected its own altars. The father was priest of the household, and was succeeded by the eldest son. At times-sin separated the eldest from the family, and character, instead of age, decided who should act as priest.

Jacob knew the character of the one great High Priest; and as he lay with his head upon the stone in Bethel, and watched the angels ascending and descending upon that glorious ladder, he also saw the Lord above it. He beheld His glorious vestments, and in imitation of those garments he made Joseph a "coat of many colors." The other sons of Jacob could not comprehend these beautiful truths. Even the coat was an object of hatred to them. When the brothers sold Joseph, they dipped the coat in blood, and its beauty was marred. The future revealed that Jacob had read aright the character of Joseph, for in the midst of Egyptian darkness he reflected the light of heaven. He was a temple for the indwelling of the Spirit of God.

When Israel came out of Egypt, their minds were so beclouded by sin that they no longer saw the promised Saviour in the simple offerings. God then said: "Let them make me a sanctuary, that I may dwell among them." Six days were spent by Moses on the mountain side in deep searching of heart; then the thick cloud of glory covering Mount Sinai broke forth like devouring fire in the eyes of all Israel, and Moses was ushered into the presence of Deity. Before his wondering gaze was spread out the beauties of the heavenly sanctuary. Forty days the Lord communed with him, giving minute [159] directions in regard to building a shadow of that heavenly structure upon the earth. In the midst of the idolatry of Egypt, Israel had lost the spiritual truth that the body is the dwelling place for the Holy Spirit. Neither could they form any conception of the work done in heaven for sinful man.

To reach man in his fallen condition, God directed the building of the earthly tabernacle, that humanity might become acquainted with the nature of the work in the heavenly sanctuary. In this building, men divinely appointed were to perform in the sight of the people a shadow of the work that would be done in the heavenly

Let us arise and go up to Bethel; and I will make there an altar unto God.　　　　Gen. 35:3.

Behold a ladder set up on the earth, and the top of it reached to heaven: and behold the angels of God ascending and descending on it. And, behold, the LORD stood above it.
　　　　Gen. 28:12-13.

Now Israel loved Joseph more than all his children, because he was the son of his old age: and he made him a coat of many colours.
　　　　Gen. 37:3.
And they took Joseph's coat, and killed a kid of the goats, and dipped the coat in the blood.
　　　　Gen. 37:31.

How then can I do this great wickedness, and sin against God?　　　　Gen. 39:9.

And let them make me a sanctuary; that I may dwell among them. According to all that I shew thee, after the pattern of the tabernacle, and the pattern of all the instruments thereof, even so shall ye make it.　　　　Exo. 25:8-9.

The glory of the LORD abode upon mount Sinai, and the cloud covered it six days: and the seventh day he called unto Moses out of the midst of the cloud. And the sight of the glory of the LORD was like devouring fire on the top of the mount in the eyes of the children of Israel. And Moses went into the midst of the cloud, and gat him up into the mount: and Moses was in the mount forty days and forty nights.　　　　Ex. 24:16-18.

But the natural man receiveth not the things of the Spirit of God: for they are foolishness unto him: neither can he know them, because they are spiritually discerned.　　　　1 Cor. 2:14.

Which was a figure for the time then present, in which were offered both gifts and sacrifices.
　　　　Heb. 9:9.
For Aaron's sons thou shalt make coats, and thou shalt make for them girdles, and bonnets shalt thou make for them, for glory and for beauty. And thou shalt put them upon Aaron thy brother, and his sons with him; and shalt anoint them, and consecrate them, and sanctify

them, that they may minister unto me in the priest's office. *Ex. 28:40-41.*

And the scripture, foreseeing that God would justify the heathen through faith, preached before the gospel unto Abraham, saying, In thee shall all nations be blessed. *Gal. 3:8.*

Do not think that I will accuse you to the Father: there is one that accuseth you, even Moses, in whom ye trust. For had ye believed Moses, ye would have believed me: for he wrote of me. But if ye believe not his writings, how shall ye believe my words? *John 5:45-47.*

The governor answered and said unto them, Whether of the twain will ye that I release unto you? They said, Barabbas. Pilate saith unto them, What shall I do then with Jesus which is called Christ? They all say unto him, Let him be crucified. *Matt. 27:21-22.*

Lev. 4:27-35.

Speak unto the children of Israel, When a man or woman shall commit any sin, . . . Then they shall confess their sin which they have done. *Num. 5:6-7.*

It came to pass, as she continued praying before the LORD, that Eli marked her mouth. Now Hannah, she spake in her heart; only her lips moved, but her voice was not heard: therefore Eli thought she had been drunken. *1 Sam. 1:12-13.*

The priest that is anointed shall take of the bullock's blood, and bring it to the tabernacle of the congregation. *Lev. 4:5.*

After the second veil, the tabernacle which is called the Holiest of all; Which had the golden censer, and the ark of the covenant overlaid round about with gold, wherein was the golden pot that had manna, and Aaron's rod that budded, and the tables of the covenant; And over it the cherubims of glory shadowing the mercyseat; of which we cannot now speak particularly. *Heb. 9:1-6.*

Ex. 29:42, 43.

Bake twelve cakes thereof: two tenth deals shall be in one cake. And thou shalt set them in two rows, six on a row, upon the pure table before the LORD. And thou shalt put pure frankincense upon each row. *Lev. 24:5-7.*

sanctuary by the Saviour of mankind, when He should officiate as our High Priest.

The whole Jewish economy was a compacted prophecy of the gospel. Every act of the priest in the shadowy service, as he went in and out, was a prophecy of the Saviour's work when He entered heaven as our High Priest. "It was the gospel in figures," the Lord's object lesson or kindergarten for the "children" of Israel. They had become children in understanding, and in order to reach them God taught the gospel in a way that the senses could grasp.

Man finally became so depraved that he failed to see light flashing from the Levitical laws and sacrificial offerings, and when the Antitype of all their offerings came, they rejected Him.

Let us in imagination go back to the wilderness tabernacle, and see if we can discern the glorious gospel of Christ shining from the Jewish economy. A man enters the outer court with a lamb, which he brings to the door of the [160] tabernacle. With solemn awe, and eyes raised to heaven, he lays his hand upon its head, while his moving lips, like Hannah's of old, betray the burden of his heart. Then he lifts the knife, and takes the life of the sacrifice. His faith lays hold of the bleeding Lamb of Calvary, and his sin rolls from off his burdened heart on to the great Sacrifice. The blood is carefully caught; every drop is precious, for by faith he views the *real* sacrifice. The priest meets him, takes the blood of the sacrificed life, and passes from sight within the first veil, while the worshiper awaits with anxiety his return.

In childhood his father had told him of the "ark of the covenant overlaid round about with gold, wherein was the golden pot that had manna, and Aaron's rod that budded, and the tables of the covenant; and over it the cherubim of glory shadowing the mercy seat;" that at times the bright glory of the shekinah above the mercy seat shone out and filled the sanctuary.

He had been told of that mystical table, with its twelve loaves covered with frankincense; also of the beautiful candlestick, whose seven lamps were ever burning; how the golden-plated walls on either side reflected the light, and like great mirrors reproduced again and again the brilliant hues of the richly embroidered curtains with their shining angels. Before the second veil, which concealed the sacred ark, he pictured the altar, from which the fragrant incense constantly ascended.

By faith he sees the priest place the blood of the atoning sacrifice upon the horns of the altar. His faith looks past the shadowy service [161] to the time when Christ shall plead His blood in the heavenly sanctuary. It is the gospel of a crucified and risen Saviour that he beholds in the object lesson he himself is helping to carry out.

Soon the veil is lifted, and the priest returns. The offering has been accepted. The priest has made atonement for him, and he is forgiven. In the joy and freedom of forgiveness he prays: "O that the *influence* of all my sins might be forever wiped away!" when lo, he sees the priest go to the brazen altar in the court, and "pour out all the blood at the bottom of the altar." As he sees that blood, precious to him, because it represents his own ransomed life as well as the sacrificed life of the Saviour, poured out upon the ground, his heart bounds with joy. [162] He grasps the fact that the decree, "Cursed is the ground for thy sake," is met in Christ, and that the promised Saviour will finally cleanse the earth from all the effects of his sins.

The body of the lamb still lies near the door of the sanctuary, where the life was taken. He next turns to it, and with a sharp knife separates from the flesh every particle of fat—"all the fat that covereth the inwards," etc. "All the fat is taken away, and the priest bums it upon the altar of burnt offering for a sweet savor unto the Lord." The fat is burned as a type of the final destruction, when "the wicked shall perish, and the enemies of the Lord shall be as the fat of lambs; they shall consume; into smoke shall they consume away." Ps. 37:20. Every sinner that clings to sin will be destroyed with the sin. God has made provision for every one to separate from sin, that He may destroy the sin and save the sinner. The burning fat upon the altar came up as a sweet savor before God, for it represented sin that had been sepa-

Cause the lamp to burn always.
Ex. 27:20, 21.
Thou shall overlay the boards with gold.
Ex. 26:29.
Ex. 26:31, 32.
Aaron shall burn thereon sweet incense every morning: when he dresseth the lamps, he shall burn incense upon it. And when Aaron lighteth the lamps at even, he shall burn incense upon it, a perpetual incense before the LORD throughout your generations. Ex. 30:7-8.

But Christ being come an high priest of good things to come, by a greater and more perfect tabernacle, not made with hands, that is to say, not of this building; Neither by the blood of goats and calves, but by his own blood he entered in once into the holy place, having obtained eternal redemption for us. Heb 9:11-12.

Heb. 9:9.

The priest shall make an atonement for him as concerning his sin, and it shall be forgiven him. Lev. 4:26.

The priest shall take of the blood of the sin offering with his finger, and put it upon the horns of the altar of burnt offering, and shall pour out his blood at the bottom of the altar of burnt offering. Lev. 4:7, 18, 25, 30.

Gen. 3:17.
Lev. 4:8-10.

He shall take away all the fat thereof, as the fat is taken away from off the sacrifice of peace offerings; and the priest shall burn it upon the altar for a sweet savour unto the LORD. Lev. 4:31.

But the wicked shall perish, and the enemies of the LORD shall be as the fat of lambs: they shall consume; into smoke shall they consume away. Ps. 37:20.

Now thanks be unto God, which always causeth us to triumph in Christ, and maketh manifest the savour of his knowledge by us in every place. For we are unto God a sweet savour of Christ, in them that are saved, and in them that perish: To the one we are the savour of death unto death; and to the other the savour of life unto life. And who is sufficient for these things? 2 Cor. 2:14-16.

Let them make me a sanctuary, that I may dwell among them. Ex. 25:8.

Lev. 7:30.
Lev. 4:27-31.

I can do all things through Christ which strengtheneth me.   Phil. 4:13.
That he would grant you, according to the riches of his glory, to be strengthened with might by his Spirit in the inner man; That Christ may dwell in your hearts by faith; that ye, being rooted and grounded in love.   Eph. 3:16-17.
John 6:63.
The word of God is quick, and powerful, and sharper than any twoedged sword, piercing even to the dividing asunder of soul and spirit, and of the joints and marrow, and is a discerner of the thoughts and intents of the heart.   Heb. 4:12.
Then he saith, I will return into my house from whence I came out: and when he is come, he findeth it empty, swept, and garnished.
     Matt. 12:43-45.

rated from the sinner and destroyed, while the sinner lived a new life through Christ.

The sinner separated the fat from the sacrifice; the priest received it and burned it, illustrating the truth that we must co-operate with the Lord; and through. Christ who strengthens us we can do all things.

As the man carefully searched for the fat, he realized more fully than before that his body was to be a temple of the Holy Spirit, and that when his past sin is forgiven and he is accepted, it is that he may become a dwelling place for the Spirit of God. When that spirit enters a man, it, like [163] a sharp knife, reveals one sin after another, and separates them from the sinner until the soul temple is cleansed. His faith grasps the promise of the "One" who dwells in the hearts of His people by faith. As he goes from the shadowy temple court, he realizes that he is a temple, not *"empty,* swept, and garnished," ready to be again entered by the power of evil, but a temple in which the Spirit of God rules and reigns.

Another man brings an offering; and as the priest takes the blood, instead of entering within the veil, he pours it at the base of the altar of burnt offering. Then a portion of the flesh, which represents sin, is prepared and eaten by the priest in the holy place. In this act the priest taught the children of Israel the wonderful truth that Christ bore our sins *in his own body on the tree.*

Each separate offering presented some different phase of the work of Christ. The incense constantly ascending from the altar was an object lesson of the inexhaustible fund of perfect obedience accruing from the sinless life of our Saviour, which, added to the prayers of all saints as they are offered upon the golden altar in heaven, makes them acceptable before God. The perfume of the incense filled the air far beyond the temple court. Likewise the sweet influence of Christians who live a life of faith in God, is felt by all who come in contact with them.

The fire was replenished morning and evening, representing the morning and evening worship in the family. "The whole multitude of the people were praying without at the time of incense." The lamps were a type of the seven [164] lamps of fire before the throne of God in heaven, which are the seven spirits of God. These "are the eyes of the Lord, which run to and fro through the whole earth." Seven denotes the complete Spirit of God that enlighteneth every man that cometh into the world. Its life-giving rays lead the Christian to the celestial city.

The golden table held the "bread of His presence," which represented man's dependence upon God for both temporal and spiritual help and strength.

The ark was the center of all worship; it was the first article mentioned in describing the sanctuary. The law hidden in it was the great standard of judgment, and a perfect copy of that heavenly law before which the character of every child of Adam will be tried in the tribunal on high. If that law witnesses to a character cleansed from sin by the

Wherefore have ye not eaten the sin offering in the holy place, seeing it is most holy, and God hath given it you to bear the iniquity of the congregation, to make atonement for them before the LORD? Behold, the blood of it was not brought in within the holy place: ye should indeed have eaten it in the holy place, as I commanded. Lev. 10:16-18.

Lev. 6:30.
1 Peter 2:24.

Christ also hath loved us, and hath given himself for us an offering, and a sacrifice to God for a sweet-smelling savor. Eph. 5:2.

Another angel came and stood at the altar, having a golden censer; and there was given unto him much incense, that he should add it to the prayers of all saints upon the golden altar which was before the throne. Rev. 8:3, 4 [margin].

The house was filled with the odor of the ointment. John 12:3.

Matt. 26:13.
Ex. 30:7, 8.
Jer. 10:25.

The whole multitude of the people were praying without at the time of incense. Luke 1:9, 10.

There were seven lamps of fire burning before the throne, which are the seven Spirits of God. Rev. 4:5.

Isa. 11:2, 3.
Ex. 35:31-35.
Zech 4:10.

That was the true Light, which lighteth every man that cometh into the world. John 1:9.

Prov. 4:18.
Ex. 25:8-10.

He wrote on the tables, according to the first writing, the ten commandments. And I turned myself and came down from the mount, and put the tables in the ark which I had made; and there they be, as the LORD commanded me. Deut. 10:4-5.

For as many as have sinned without law shall also perish without law: and as many as have sinned in the law shall be judged by the law. Rom. 2:12, 13.

Being witnessed by the law and the prophets.
Rom. 3:21.

And whosoever was not found written in the book of life was cast into the lake of fire. And fire came down from God out of heaven, and devoured them. Rev. 20:15.

Take up the ashes which the fire hath consumed with the burnt offering on the altar, and he shall put them beside the altar. And he shall put off his garments, and put on other garments, and carry forth the ashes without the camp unto a clean place. Lev. 6:10-11.

Without the camp unto a clean place, where the ashes are poured out. Lev. 4:12.

Ps. 17:9, 10.
Mal. 4:1-3.
Obadiah 1:16.
Prov. 11:31.

Therefore will I bring forth a fire from the midst of thee, it shall devour thee, and I will bring thee to ashes upon the earth in the sight of all them that behold thee. Ezek. 28:18.

Ye shall teach them your children, speaking of them when thou sittest in thine house, and when thou walkest by the way, when thou liest down, and when thou risest up. Deut. 11:19.

He will comfort all her waste places; and he will make her wilderness like Eden, and her desert like the garden of the LORD; joy and gladness shall be found therein, thanksgiving, and the voice of melody. Isa. 51:3.

If any man defile the temple of God, him shall God destroy; for the temple of God is holy, which temple ye are. 1 Cor. 3:17.

When your children shall ask their fathers in time to come, saying, What mean these stones? Then ye shall let your children know, saying, Israel came over this Jordan on dry land. Joshua 4:21-22.

And it shall come to pass, when your children shall say unto you, What mean ye by this service? That ye shall say, It is the sacrifice of the LORD'S passover, who passed over the houses of the children of Israel in Egypt, when he smote

blood of the atoning sacrifice, then the name will be confessed before the Father and the holy angels.

The continual burning of that which typified sin pointed forward to the time when sin and sinners would be consumed in the fire of the last day. As the ashes accumulated upon the altar of burnt offering, they were carefully collected by the side of the altar; and at a certain time the priest laid aside his priestly robes, carried the ashes without the court, and deposited them in a "clean place." They were not thrown carelessly to one side, but put in a *clean place*. These ashes represented all that will be left of sin and sinners after the fires of the last day. "For behold, the day cometh that shall burn as an oven; and all the proud, yea, and all that do wickedly, shall be stubble; and the day that [165] cometh shall burn them up, saith the Lord of hosts, that it shall leave them neither root nor branch. But to you that fear my name shall the Suri of righteousness arise, with healing in His wings, and ye shall go forth and grow up as calves of the stall. And ye shall tread down the wicked, for they shall be ashes under the soles of your feet in the day that I shall do this, saith the Lord of hosts." Mal. 4 : 1-3. In that day the real ashes of the wicked will be left upon a "clean earth."

As the Jewish father walked to the sanctuary with his child, the mind of the child would be attracted by the ashes in the clean place. He would ask, "Why are *those* ashes put in a clean place, when you throw the ashes from our fire upon the dunghill?" The father's answer would explain the beauties of the new earth, when it shall be made like Eden, and sin and sorrow shall be forever removed. With it would come the gentle admonition to separate from sin, and keep the body temple pure, that in the great burning day the sin may be consumed without the sinner, and he be among the ransomed of the Lord.

Much of the service and many of the customs of ancient Israel were designed to call out questions from the children, that the spiritually minded parents might instruct them in the ways of God.

After speaking of the peculiar manner in which the passover should be eaten, God adds, "Your children shall say

The live bird was let loose in the open field.

unto you, What mean ye by this service?" showing that He intended that it should call forth questions from children of all ages, and thus the children become acquainted [166] with the saving blood of the great Passover Lamb.

The sight of the pile of stones by the Jordan was to arouse inquiries in the minds of the children of future generations, which, if answered properly, would acquaint them with the mighty power of God. The same was true of the whole Jewish service.

the Egyptians, and delivered our houses. And the people bowed the head and worshipped.
Exo. 12:26-27.

Then shall the priest command to take for him that is to be cleansed two birds alive and clean, and cedar wood, and scarlet, and hyssop: And the priest shall command that one of the birds be killed in an earthen vessel over running water: As for the living bird, he shall take it, and the cedar wood, and the scarlet, and the hyssop, and shall dip them and the living bird in the blood of the bird that was killed over the running water: And he shall sprinkle upon him that is to be cleansed from the leprosy seven times, and shall pronounce him clean, and shall

let the living bird loose into the open field.
Lev. 14:4-7.

Death is come up into our windows, and is entered into our palaces, to cut off the children from without, and the young men from the streets.
Jer. 9:21.

Cursed is the ground for thy sake: in sorrow shalt thou eat of it all the days of thy life.   Gen. 3:17.

The earth also is defiled under the inhabitants thereof: therefore hath the curse devoured the earth.   Isa. 24:5, 6.

And he spake of trees, from the cedar tree that is in Lebanon even unto the hyssop that springeth out of the wall.   1 Kings 4:33.

Isa. 35:1, 2.

There shall be no more curse.
Rev. 22:3.

Though your sins be as scarlet, they shall be as white as snow; though they be red like crimson, they shall be as wool.   Isa. 1:18.

I saw a new heaven and a new earth.
Rev. 22:1.

Which he hath purchased with his own blood.
Acts 20:28.

Until the redemption of the purchased possession, unto the praise of his glory.   Eph. 1:14.

And being in an agony he prayed more earnestly: and his sweat was as it were great drops of blood falling down to the ground.   Luke 22:44.

But one of the soldiers with a spear pierced his side, and forthwith came there out blood and water.   John 19:34.

Now there was set a vessel full of vinegar: and they filled a spunge with vinegar, and put it upon hyssop, and put it to his mouth.   John 19:29.

The leper that sought cleansing was to bring two birds alive and clean, and cedar wood and scarlet and hyssop. The priest commanded that one of the birds be killed in an earthen vessel, over running water. The live bird, cedar wood, scarlet, and hyssop were all dipped in the blood, and the leper was sprinkled with the blood; then the live bird was let loose in the open field. [167] It flew through the air, bearing on its feathers the blood, which was a type of Christ's blood that will purify the air, and remove from it all the germs of sin and death. Now death comes in at our windows, but the blood of Christ will give us a new atmosphere.

Earth, air, and water are elements which compose our planet. All are tainted by sin. The earthen dish containing the blood held over the running water typified the time when earth, air, and water would be freed from the curse of sin by the blood of Christ. The cedar wood and hyssop represented the two extremes in vegetation, from the giant of the forest to the hyssop on the wall. They were dipped in the blood, thus teaching Israel that Christ's blood would free the entire vegetable world from the curse, and again clothe the earth in Eden beauty.

It might seem to man that the curse was so deeply marked upon the earth, air, and sea that it could never be removed; but the little piece of scarlet wool, dipped in the blood with the live bird, the cedar, and the hyssop, was a pledge that the blood of Christ would remove the deepest marks from the sin-cursed earth.

We have the real sacrifice to study as well as the shadow. Type met antitype. The blood of Christ has been shed; the price has been paid that will restore the purity of the earth, air, and sea. The sin-cursed earth received the blood of Christ as He prayed in the garden. "From His hands and feet the blood fell drop by drop upon the rock drilled for the foot of the cross." Thus through the air passed the precious blood. From the wound in His side "there flowed two copious and distinct streams, one of blood and [168] the other of water." The blood of Christ was brought in contact with the earth, air, and water. The two extremes in vegetation also met at Calvary. The cross was made of wood taken from the trees of the forest; "and they filled a sponge with vinegar, and put it upon hyssop, and put it to His mouth."

Was there an antitype of the scarlet while His blood was trickling from those cruel wounds?—Yes. In Jesus as He hung upon the cross, bruised, mocked, and bleeding, the thief beheld the Lamb of God that taketh away the sins of the world. Hope kindled in his soul, and he cast himself upon a dying Saviour. With full faith that Christ would possess the kingdom, he cried, "Lord, remember me, when Thou comest into Thy kingdom." In a soft, melodious tone, full of love, the answer was quickly given: "Verily I say unto thee to-day, Shalt thou be with me in paradise." As these words were spoken, the darkness around the cross was pierced with living light. The thief felt the peace and joy of sins forgiven. Christ was glorified. While all thought they beheld Him conquered, He was the conqueror. They could not rob Him of His power to forgive sins.

Type has fully met antitype; the price has been paid; the blood of the world's Redeemer has been *poured upon the ground*. It has dropped *through the air* from the cruel cross. It *has flowed* with water from the wound of the cruel spear. - The extremes of vegetation also came in contact with it, and he whose sins were as scarlet, experienced the peace of having them made white as snow by the precious blood, even while it was flowing from the open wounds. [169]

The various feasts throughout the year typified different phases of the gospel. The passover was a type of Christ in an especial sense. Christ is our Passover. The first fruits offered the third day after the passover lamb was slain, taught the resurrection of Christ. Type met antitype, and was fulfilled when Christ, the first fruits of them that slept, came forth on the third day, and presented Himself before the Father.

Throughout the varied services of the year, everything pointed forward to the Lamb of God, while it also taught the lesson of cleansing the body, and keeping the temple pure for the Spirit of God.

The next day John seeth Jesus coming unto him, and saith, Behold the Lamb of God, which taketh away the sin of the world. John 1:29.

He said unto Jesus, Lord, remember me when thou comest into thy kingdom. And Jesus said unto him, Verily I say unto thee, To day shalt thou be with me in paradise. Luke 23:42-43.

Who his own self bare our sins in his own body on the tree, that we, being dead to sins, should live unto righteousness: by whose stripes ye were healed. 1 Peter 2:24.

Ought not Christ to have suffered these things, and to enter into his glory? And beginning at Moses and all the prophets, he expounded unto them in all the scriptures the things concerning himself. Luke 24:26-27.

Behold the Lamb of God, which beareth away the sin of the world. John 1:29 [margin].

He said unto them, These are the words which I spake unto you, while I was yet with you, that all things must be fulfilled, which were written in the law of Moses, and in the prophets, and in the psalms, concerning me. Luk. 24:44.

These are they which came out of great tribulation, and have washed their robes, and made them white in the blood of the Lamb. Rev. 7:14.

Christ our passover is sacrificed for us. 1 Cor. 5:7.

These are the feasts of the LORD, even holy convocations, which ye shall proclaim in their seasons. In the fourteenth day of the first month at even is the LORD'S passover. And on the fifteenth day of the same month is the feast of unleavened bread unto the LORD: seven days ye must eat unleavened bread. In the first day ye shall have an holy convocation: ye shall do no servile work therein. . . . Then ye shall bring a sheaf of the firstfruits of your harvest unto the priest: And he shall wave the sheaf before the LORD, to be accepted for you: on the morrow after the sabbath the priest shall wave it. Lev. 23:4-11.

Who serve unto the example and shadow of heavenly things, as Moses was admonished of God when he was about to make the tabernacle: for, See, saith he, that thou make all things according to the pattern shewed to thee in the mount.   Heb. 8:5.

He said unto me, Unto two thousand and three hundred days; then shall the sanctuary be cleansed.   Dan. 8:14.

Remember the sabbath day, to keep it holy. Six days shalt thou labour, and do all thy work: But the seventh day is the sabbath of the LORD thy God: in it thou shalt not do any work, thou, nor thy son, nor thy daughter, thy manservant, nor thy maidservant, nor thy cattle, nor thy stranger that is within thy gates: For in six days the LORD made heaven and earth, the sea, and all that in them is, and rested the seventh day: wherefore the LORD blessed the sabbath day, and hallowed it.   Exo. 20:8-11.

If thou turn away thy foot from the sabbath, from doing thy pleasure on my holy day; and call the sabbath a delight, the holy of the LORD, honourable; and shalt honour him, not doing thine own ways, nor finding thine own pleasure, nor speaking thine own words.   Isa. 58:13.

Ps. 119:59, 60.

So speak ye, and so do, as they that shall be judged by the law of liberty.   James 2:12.

Rev. 14:8-12.
Rev. 11:1.

Then shalt thou cause the trumpet of the jubile to sound on the tenth day of the seventh month, in the day of atonement shall ye make the trumpet sound throughout all your land.   Lev. 25:9.

In the autumn, on the tenth day of the seventh month, came the crowning service of the year. All other services were a preparation for this. Day by day the sins of the people had been transferred in type and shadow to the priest and the sanctuary, and once each year these were to be cleansed, and the sins forever removed.

Gabriel revealed to Daniel the antitype of the time of cleansing the earthly sanctuary, "Unto two thousand three hundred days, then shall the sanctuary be cleansed." This period of cleansing, we have found in the study of the ninth chapter of Daniel, began in 1844. The cover of the ark in the heavenly sanctuary was then lifted, and the law of God was seen by the people, not broken, but entire. In the midst of the law they traced the words, "The seventh day is the Sabbath of the Lord thy God: in it thou shalt not do any work." They awoke to the fact that they had been resting upon the first day of the week instead of the seventh. As they gazed at the law, a halo of light seemed to [170] encircle the fourth commandment, which for so many years had been trampled underfoot. Reverently they listened to the words, "If thou turn away thy foot from the Sabbath, from doing thy pleasure on My holy day; and call the Sabbath a delight, the holy of the Lord, honorable; and shalt honor Him, not doing thine own ways, nor finding thine own pleasure, nor speaking thine own words: then shalt thou delight thyself in the Lord." Isa. 58:13, 14.

They thought on their ways, and made haste, and delayed not to keep the commandments. The period of the investigative judgment opened in 1844, when every character was to be measured by the standard of God's law. As the work opened in heaven, it was the will of God that on earth His people should test their lives by the law of God, and come into harmony with His holy precepts. The day of atonement was the type of the judgment. This was the most solemn day of the year to ancient Israel.

When the sun gilded the western hills of the land of Judea, on the ninth day of the seventh month, the trumpet was blown throughout Israel. The solemn warning of the

Remember the Sabbath day to keep it holy. Six days shalt thou labor, and do all thy work: but the seventh day is the Sabbath of the Lord thy God: in it thou shalt not do any work, thou, nor thy son, nor thy daughter, thy man-servant, nor thy maid-servant, nor thy cattle, nor thy stranger that is within thy gates: for in six days the Lord made heaven and earth, the sea, and all that in them is, and rested the seventh day: wherefore the Lord blessed the Sabbath day, and hallowed it.

This is that which the LORD hath said, To morrow is the rest of the holy sabbath unto the LORD: bake that which ye will bake to day, and seethe that ye will seethe.   Exo. 16:23.

Ye shall do no manner of work: it shall be a statute for ever throughout your generations in all your dwellings. It shall be unto you a sabbath of rest, and ye shall afflict your souls: in the ninth day of the month at even, from even unto even, shall ye celebrate your sabbath.   Lev. 23:31-32.

Wherefore have we fasted, say they, and thou seest not? wherefore have we afflicted our soul, and thou takest no knowledge? Behold, in the day of your fast ye find pleasure, and exact all your labours.   Isa. 58:3.

Lev. 23:29.

And in that day did the Lord GOD of hosts call to weeping, and to mourning, and to baldness, and to girding with sackcloth: And behold joy and gladness, slaying oxen, and killing sheep, eating flesh, and drinking wine: let us eat and drink; for to morrow we shall die. And it was revealed in mine ears by the LORD of hosts, Surely this iniquity shall not be purged from you till ye die, saith the Lord GOD of hosts.   Isa. 22:12-14.

Lev. 16:11-14.

He shall take of the blood of the bullock, and sprinkle it with his finger upon the mercy seat eastward.   Lev. 16:14.

Thou shalt see greater abominations than these. . . . About five and twenty men, with their backs toward the temple of the LORD, and their faces toward the east; and they worshipped the sun toward the east.   Eze. 8:15-16.

And the goat shall bear upon him all their iniquities unto a land not inhabited: and he shall let go the goat in the wilderness.   Lev. 16:22.

Aaron shall lay both his hands upon the head of the live goat, and confess over him all the iniquities of the children of Israel, and all their transgressions in all their sins, putting them upon the head of the goat, and shall send him away by the hand of a fit man into the wilderness.   Lev. 16:21.

trumpet produced a marked effect in every home. All work was laid aside, and quiet reigned. It was not the ordinary rest of the weekly Sabbath, for no evening meal was spread. There was not the usual baking and seething customary on the preparation for the Sabbath. No food was prepared, for this was not a feast, but a fast day. The father of the household gathered his family about him, and read from the Sacred Scroll: "Ye shall do no manner of work: it shall be a statute forever throughout your generations in. [171] all your dwellings. It shall be unto you a sabbath of rest, and ye shall afflict your souls." With prayer, fasting, and deep searching of heart the day was spent by the Israel of God. With solemn awe they repeated, "Whatsoever soul shall not be afflicted in that same day, he shall be cut off from among His people."

In the Gentile homes around them were eating and drinking and all the busy activities of daily life, but quiet reigned in the homes of Israel. In the temple court all was activity. The bullock without blemish was brought, and the high priest laid his hands on its head, confessing his sins and the sins of his household. Then it was slain, and with the blood he made an atonement for himself and his household, that he might be prepared to perform the solemn service of the day.

When he came out, after presenting the blood of the bullock before the Lord, two goats were brought, lots were cast, and one was chosen for the Lord's goat, while the other, Azazel, the scapegoat, represented the evil one. The Lord's goat was slain. With its blood and the golden censer, the priest entered within the second veil of the sanctuary. As he neared the mercy seat with the glorious light of the shekinah shining above it, he sprinkled "much incense" upon the coals in the censer, "that the cloud of the incense may cover the mercy seat that he die not." Then with his back toward the sun rising, he sprinkled the atoning blood seven times above and before that broken law within the ark. He paused in the holy place, and made atonement for it, and for the tabernacle of the congregation. The golden altar, that had so often [172] during the year witnessed to the sins of Israel by the scarlet spots upon its horns, was now cleansed from all defilement by the blood of the Lord's goat. The people without listened attentively to the sound of the bells on his robes, as he moved about within the sanctuary.

"When he hath made an end of reconciling the holy place, and the tabernacle of the congregation, and the altar, he shall bring the live goat." The work of reconciliation ended, God and man were one. The at-one-ment had been made in figure. The separating sins had been removed. The people rejoiced in God that He had accepted them, and that their sins were all removed from before the Lord.

As they beheld the high priest lay his hands on the head of the scapegoat, and confess over him all the iniquities of the children of Israel, and all their

The high priest confessing the sins of the people on the head of the scapegoat.

transgressions in all their sins, putting them upon the head of the goat, and sending "him away by the hand of a fit man into the wilderness," their hearts filled with the peace that passeth understanding. They praised [173] God for the wonderful gift of His love in giving His Son to die for sinful man, delivering him from sin and death. It was not until the goat was sent away into the barren wilderness that this peace filled the hearts of the people, and they felt that they were forever free from their sins.

That was the type. What does the antitype mean to us? Since 1844 the world has been living in the great antitypical day of atonement. The investigative judgment has been in session in heaven. In the type the people were to control their appetites, and to hold their own business interests secondary to the worship of God. This was shown by the day of atonement in the type being a rest and a fast day.

God commendeth his love toward us, in that, while we were yet sinners, Christ died for us.
Rom. 5:8.

Unto two thousand and three hundred days; then shall the sanctuary be cleansed.
Dan. 8:14.

But into the second went the high priest alone once every year, not without blood, which he offered for himself, and for the errors of the people.
Heb. 9:7.

Lev. 16:20.

He is our peace, who hath made both one, and hath broken down the middle wall of partition between us; Having abolished in his flesh the enmity, even the law of commandments contained in ordinances; for to make in himself of twain one new man, so making peace; And that he might reconcile both unto God in one body by the cross, having slain the enmity thereby.

Eph. 2:14-16.

Repent ye therefore, and be converted, that your sins may be blotted out, when the times of refreshing shall come from the presence of the Lord; And he shall send Jesus Christ, which before was preached unto you: Whom the heaven must receive until the times of restitution of all things, which God hath spoken by the mouth of all his holy prophets since the world began.

Acts 3:19-21.

I saw an angel come down from heaven, having the key of the bottomless pit and a great chain in his hand. And he laid hold on the dragon, that old serpent, which is the Devil, and Satan, and bound him a thousand years, And cast him into the bottomless pit, and shut him up, and set a seal upon him, that he should deceive the nations no more, till the thousand years should be fulfilled: and after that he must be loosed a little season. Rev. 20:1-3.

Rev. 20:10.

And ye shall tread down the wicked; for they shall be ashes under the soles of your feet in the day that I shall do this, saith the LORD of hosts. Mal. 4:3.

2 Sam. 22:43.

Now shall she be trodden down as the mire of the streets. Micah 7:10.

Ps. 7:16.

In those days, and in that time, saith the LORD, the iniquity of Israel shall be sought for, and there shall be none; and the sins of Judah, and they shall not be found: for I will pardon them whom I reserve. Jer. 50:20.

Jer. 31:34.
Isa. 65:17.
Nahum 1:19.

He ever liveth to make intercession for them.
Heb. 7:25.
Seeing then that we have a great high priest, that is passed into the heaven, Jesus the Son of God, let us hold fast our profession. Heb. 4:14-16

We are living in the time when our great High Priest is cleansing the heavenly sanctuary, removing the sin records. We are admonished to repent and be converted, that our sins may be blotted out "when the times of refreshing shall come from the presence of the Lord." When the reconciling is completed, and the last case is decided in the final judgment of heaven, the Saviour will pronounce the decree: "He that is unjust, let him be unjust still; and he which is filthy, let him be filthy still; and he that is righteous, let him be righteous still; and he that is holy, let him be holy still." Every case will be decided for eternity. Satan, the great instigator of all evil, the antitypical scapegoat, will then come in for his part of the service.

In the type the sins were laid upon the scapegoat in the presence of the congregation; in the antitype, the Saviour, in the presence of the Father, the angels of God, and all the redeemed [174] host, will lay the sins of the righteous upon the head of Satan, and a mighty angel will lead him away to the desolate earth, where he will remain a thousand years. At the end of the thousand years, he will go into the fire which destroys the earth. Type will fully meet antitype when all the sins of the righteous are burned up with Satan, and nothing remains but the ashes in a "clean place." It will then be seen that "Satan bore not only the weight and punishment of his own sins, but also the sins of the redeemed host, which had been placed upon him; and he must also suffer for the ruin of souls which he has caused."

The sins of Israel will never again be found. The former things will not be remembered nor come into mind. Throughout eternity, joy and peace will forever reign. The prophet says, "He will make an utter end; affliction shall not rise up the second time."

Type must meet antitype. The great High Priest in heaven is now performing His service. Are you performing your part? In homes scattered all over the earth faithful children of God *will* carry out the antitype in the way God directed the Israelites to spend the typical day of atonement.

The priest might have performed his part of the service perfectly in, the temple; but unless the people in their homes fasted, rested, and prayed, the work was of no avail for them. Every Israelite who ate and conducted himself like the Gentiles around him on the day of atonement was cut off from among the people of God.

Is your home a place where the appetite is controlled? Do you hold your business interests [175] secondary to the work of God? Are you heeding the Saviour's words, "Take heed lest at any time your hearts be overcharged with surfeiting [eating to excess], and drunkenness [partaking of improper food], and cares of this life, and so that day come upon you unawares?" There will be one hundred and forty-four thousand who will heed the warning, and in the fear of God will fulfill the antitype. While Christ in heaven is faithfully interceding for them, they will present their bodies a living sacrifice, holy, acceptable unto God, that God may be glorified. [176]

Lev. 23:29, 30.

For the wages of sin is death; but the gift of God is eternal life through Jesus Christ our Lord.
Rom 6:23.

Take heed to yourselves, lest at any time your hearts be overcharged with surfeiting, and drunkenness, and cares of this life, and so that day come upon you unawares.
Luke 21:34.

And they sung as it were a new song before the throne, and before the four beasts, and the elders: and no man could learn that song but the hundred and forty and four thousand, which were redeemed from the earth. These are they which were not defiled with women; for they are virgins. These are they which follow the Lamb whithersoever he goeth. These were redeemed from among men, being the firstfruits unto God and to the Lamb. And in their mouth was found no guile: for they are without fault before the throne of God.
Rev. 14:3-5.

Rom. 12:1, 2.

Chapter 12

Introduction to the Last Vision

Daniel 10

The last three chapters of the book of Daniel are inseparable, for they relate to the last recorded vision of the prophet. The tenth chapter is preliminary to a detailed history of the world, and is valuable because of the important spiritual lessons which it contains. Daniel was an old man, and nearing the end of a long and eventful career, but his last days were full of anxiety for his race; he still carried the burden of their captivity on his heart. Since the events recorded in the ninth chapter, he had been in the lions' den, thrust there because of the cruel hatred of men in high positions. His godly life was a constant rebuke to the corruption of men in office, and they sought to destroy him, but God put these men to confusion, and [177] witnessed to the purity of Daniel's life. The prophet had been held in high esteem by Darius the Mede, and on his death and the accession of Cyrus. Daniel had remained in the court, a counselor of the king.

Cyrus, in the first year of his reign, had issued an emancipation proclamation to the Jews. The Spirit of God had pleaded with the heart of the king, and he felt that he was brought into power for that purpose. When, after every provision had been made for the return, but a small fraction of the Jews took advantage of it, Cyrus began to doubt the wisdom of the decree. It was with the Jews as with sinners to-day. Pardon is granted and freedom offered, but they choose to remain in sin until they receive the penalty—death. The sins of Babylon dazzled the eyes of the Jews who beheld them, and the voice of their God was but faintly heard. (Comp. Eze. 33 : 30-32.)

The righteous shall flourish like the palm tree: he shall grow like a cedar in Lebanon. Those that be planted in the house of the LORD shall flourish in the courts of our God. They shall still bring forth fruit in old age; they shall be fat and flourishing. Ps. 92:12-14.

Daniel must have been about ninety of age at this time.

Dan. 6:4-22.

Then this Daniel was preferred above the presidents and princes, because an excellent spirit was in him; and the king thought to set him over the whole realm. Dan. 6:3.

The LORD stirred up the spirit of Cyrus king of Persia, that he made a proclamation throughout all his kingdom, and put it also in writing, saying, Thus saith Cyrus king of Persia, The LORD God of heaven hath given me all the kingdoms of the earth; and he hath charged me to build him an house at Jerusalem, which is in Judah. Ezr. 1:1-2.

Let favour be shewed to the wicked, yet will he not learn righteousness: in the land of uprightness will he deal unjustly, and will not behold the majesty of the LORD. Isa. 26:10.
Eze. 23:14-16.
Lam. 4:1, 2.

Thou art greatly beloved: therefore understand the matter, and consider the vision.

Dan. 9:23.

1. *In the third year of Cyrus king of Persia a thing was revealed unto Daniel, whose name was called Belteshazzar; and the thing was true, but the time appointed was long: and he understood the thing, and had understanding of the vision.*
2. *In those days I Daniel was mourning three full weeks.*
3. *I ate no pleasant bread, neither came flesh nor wine in my mouth, neither did I anoint myself at all, till three whole weeks were fulfilled.*

Dan. 10:1-3.

I therefore so run, not as uncertainly; so fight I, not as one that beateth the air: But I keep under my body, and bring it into subjection: lest that by any means, when I have preached to others, I myself should be a castaway.

1 Cor. 9:26-27.

For which cause we faint not; but though our outward man perish, yet the inward man is renewed day by day.   2 Cor. 4:16.

4. *And in the four and twentieth day of the first month, as I was by the side of the great river, which is Hiddekel;*
5. *Then I lifted up mine eyes, and looked, and behold a certain man clothed in linen, whose loins were girded with fine gold of Uphaz:*
6. *His body also was like the beryl, and his face as the appearance of lightning, and his eyes as lamps of fire, and his arms and his feet like in colour to polished brass, and the voice of his words like the voice of a multitude*

Rev. 1:15-18.

7. *And I Daniel alone saw the vision: for the men that were with me saw not the vision; but a great quaking fell upon them, so that they fled to hide themselves.*
8. *Therefore I was left alone, and saw this great vision, and there remained no strength in me: for my comeliness was turned in me into corruption, and I retained no strength.*

Dan. 10:4-8.

That the trial of your faith, being much more precious than of gold that perisheth, though it be tried with fire, might be found unto praise and honour and glory at the appearing of Jesus Christ.

1 Peter 1:7.

Daniel could not understand the situation. The spiritual condition of his own people weighed heavily upon him, and the changing attitude of the king worried him. He thought upon the previous vision, and wondered if it could be that his people—the Jews—would cling to the sins of Babylon until they were overtaken by the persecutions described as belonging to the latter days. He could not understand the times, although the words spoken by Gabriel seemed clear of comprehension.

Two years after the decree of Cyrus, Daniel determined to humble his heart before God by prayer and fasting until he should understand the matter. He did not practice total abstinence from food, for this fast was not the fast [178] of a day. But he withdrew from the king's table and partook of the plainest kinds of food, spending much time in prayer and study. It was his purpose to have his appetite so in subjection that physical wants would not crowd out his desire for spiritual insight. The spiritual life of man too often partakes of the earthly mold of his body by over-indulgence of appetite. The soul should control the body, and not be burdened by the body. This condition Daniel sought to attain. He sought also to strengthen the mind by retiring to a quiet spot on the banks of the river Tigris. He took with him a few men as companions. Doubtless these were Jews who also felt a burden for Israel. The solitude of the spot, the swiftly flowing waters of the river, the lofty trees, and the clear sky above, led the prophet's mind out after his God.

For three weeks he thus sought for light and truth. Then it was that he looked up and beheld the Son of God by his side, the same who appeared to John on the Isle of Patmos. The brightness which shone round about Michael was too great for the eyes of the companions of Daniel, and they hastened to hide themselves. The countenance of Christ was like lightning, and as He gazed upon the prostrate form of Daniel, the other men fled for their lives. But what would have been death to those who harbored sin, was life to the one whose character was pure. The dross had been consumed before, and the light shone upon the prophet as sunlight on a mirror.

So full of life is the Son of God that His eyes appeared as lamps of fire, flashing light. [179] He it is who says, "I will guide thee with Mine eye." Daniel could bear the gaze, but his companions felt that those eyes burned into their very souls, and they hid from His gaze.

To the ears of Daniel, accustomed by long experience to heavenly sounds, the voice of the "One Man" was as the voice of the multitude, or as the sound of many waters, clear and beautiful. To human ears, dull of hearing, it is like thunder. The Jews, at the time that the Greeks came to Christ, had a similar experience to that of the companions of Daniel. As Christ sat in the temple court, the lightning played about His head and the voice which to Him was the voice of God, to them sounded like the crash of a thunder bolt.

Daniel was left alone in the presence of the Son of God, and as he compared his own condition to that of Christ, he seemed to be a lump of clay, a broken vessel, uncomely and useless. "My vigor was turned in me into corruption, and I retained no strength." He clung close to the cold earth, his face to the ground in a deep sleep, helpless in the hands of God. "What is man that Thou art mindful of him, or the son of man that Thou visitest him?"

Then Gabriel, the angel who had so often talked with Daniel, touched him with his hand, and lifted his prostrate form. He said, "O Daniel, a man greatly beloved, understand the words that I speak unto thee, and stand upright; for unto thee am I now sent." There was power in the touch of the angel's hand. There was power in the touch of the Saviour's hand. When on earth, virtue, life, the healing power of God, constantly radiated from Him. He [180] could touch the leper, arid a life-current flowed from Him to the diseased one.

So it was with Gabriel's touch. He who stood in the presence of God was so filled with life that as he laid his hand on man, a thrill of life was felt in every nerve. It may be so with beings to-day. The follower of Christ should have the life-current so strong within him that sin is rebuked, and disease driven from him. "A thousand shall fall at thy side and ten thousand at thy right hand, but it shall not

In him was life; and the life was the light of men. John 1:4.

Ps. 32:8.

And thine ears shall hear a word behind thee, saying, This is the way, walk ye in it, when ye turn to the right hand, and when ye turn to the left. Isa. 30:21.

Blessed is the people that know the joyful sound: they shall walk, O LORD, in the light of thy countenance. Ps. 89:15.

Father, glorify thy name. Then came there a voice from haeven, saying, I have both glorified it, and will glorify it again. The people therefore, that stood by, and heard it, said that it thundered: others said, An angel spake to him. John 12:20-30.

9. Yet heard I the voice of his words: and when I heard the voice of his words, then was I in a deep sleep on my face, and my face toward the ground. Dan. 10:9.

Behold now, I have taken upon me to speak unto the Lord, which am but dust and ashes: Gen. 18:27.

Ps. 8:3-5.

10. And, behold, an hand touched me, which set me upon my knees and upon the palms of my hands. 11. And he said unto me, O Daniel, a man greatly beloved, understand the words that I speak unto thee, and stand upright: for unto thee am I now sent. And when he had spoken this word unto me, I stood trembling. Dan. 10:10-11.

Mark 1:31.

And the whole multitude sought to touch him: for there went virtue out of him, and healed them all. Luke 6:19.

Jesus put forth his hand, and touched him, saying, I will; be thou clean. And immediately his leprosy was cleansed. Matt. 8:2-3.

I am Gabriel that stand in the presence of God. Luke 1:19.

These signs shall follow them that believe; In my name shall they cast out devils; they shall speak with new tongues; They shall take up serpents; and if they drink any deadly thing, it shall not hurt them; they shall lay hands on the sick, and they shall recover. Mark 16:17-18.

Ps. 91:7.

But is now made manifest by the appearing of our Saviour Jesus Christ, who hath abolished death, and hath brought life and immortality to light through the gospel.   2 Tim. 1:10. John 10:10.

12. Then said he unto me, Fear not, Daniel: for from the first day that thou didst set thine heart to understand, and to chasten thyself before thy God, thy words were heard, and I am come for thy words.

13. But the prince of the kingdom of Persia withstood me one and twenty days: but, lo, Michael, one of the chief princes, came to help me; and I remained there with the kings of Persia.

Dan. 10:12-13.

Are they not all ministering spirits, sent forth to minister for them who shall be heirs of salvation?
Heb. 1:14.

By me kings reign, and princes decree justice. By me princes rule, and nobles, even all the judges of the earth.   Prov. 8:15-16.

Every good gift and every perfect gift is from above, and cometh down from the Father of lights, with whom is no variableness, neither shadow of turning.   James 1:17.

The effectual fervent prayer of a righteous man availeth much.   James 5:16:

They that wait upon the LORD shall renew their strength; they shall mount up with wings as eagles; they shall run, and not be weary; and they shall walk, and not faint.   Isa. 40:31.
Isa. 65:24.

For since the beginning of the world men have not heard, nor perceived by the ear, neither hath the eye seen, O God, beside thee, what he hath prepared for him that waiteth for him.   Isa 64:4.

Peace be unto thee, be strong, yea be strong.
Dan. 10:19

14. Now I am come to make thee understand what shall befall thy people in the latter days: for yet the vision is for many days.
15. And when he had spoken such words unto me, I set my face toward the ground, and I became dumb.
Dan. 10:14-15.
O Lord, open thou my lips; and my mouth shall show forth thy praise.   Ps. 51:15.

16. And, behold, one like the similitude of the sons of men touched my lips: then I opened my mouth, and spake, and said unto him that stood before me, O my lord, by the vision my sorrows are turned upon me, and I have retained no strength.
17. For how can the servant of this my lord talk with this my lord? for as for me, straightway there remained no strength in me, neither is there breath left in me.
Dan. 10:16-17.

come nigh thee," is the promise. Christ came that we might have an abundance of life, the cup full to overflowing. We do not half realize our privilege.

It was three full weeks since Daniel had begun to pray, and Gabriel explained the cause of the delay. From the first day of the fast his words had been heard, but their answer required the co-operation of Cyrus, the Persian king. So while Daniel waited, ignorant of the work of Heaven in his behalf, and little dreaming of the strivings in the heart of the king, Gabriel had been at the Persian court pleading with Cyrus.

One may wonder how Gabriel worked. Details are not given, but one thing is sure: until the moment of a nation's rejection, angels are always in the midst of their councils. Men will be led to take positions for the truth, not knowing the real reason for their own decisions. The Holy Watcher is a constant witness in legislative halls to-day, and every just decree is the result of an impulse from the throne of God. This influence was at work in the heart of Cyrus, and so pressing were the petitions offered by Daniel that Christ Himself came in person to [181] help Gabriel, To Daniel doubtless it seemed that his prayer was unheard, but God was working out the answer in a way unknown to the prophet. Had he ceased to make intercession at the end of one week, or at the end of two weeks, the history of an entire people would have been changed. The promise is, "Before they call I will answer, and while they are yet speaking I will hear." God is often testing the strength of our desires when He withholds an immediate answer to our prayer.

"Knowest thou wherefore I am come unto thee?" asked Gabriel. "I am come to make thee understand what shall befall thy people in the latter days: for yet the vision is for many days." Daniel fell to the ground, and the breath went from his body. This was his condition when in vision. He was unable to speak until Christ touched his lips. Then He spoke to Gabriel, who stood by Daniel's side to strengthen him, and to explain to him the history of the latter days.

God has had many prophets. The effect of the Spirit upon a human being when in vision is [182] unexplainable. There is an overpowering presence which so pervades the physical being that it has no strength to act of itself. The breath leaves the body, and the voice of God speaks through the human instrument. The eyes remain open, as Balaam described his condition, but the person sees things outside the world. He is often taken far beyond the bounds of earth, as in the case of Ezekiel, John, and Paul. Earth's attraction is broken, and with an angel guide the prophet visits other places, or beholds the future, reading there the history of men and nations. When the living coal from the altar is laid upon those lips, they speak words of heavenly wisdom. Isaiah had this experience.

For the third time Gabriel expressed the love of God for Daniel, adding, "Peace be unto thee; be strong, yea, be strong." By word and by touch, Gabriel strengthened the gray-haired prophet. Then he was ready for the revelation, and said, "Let my Lord speak; for thou hast strengthened me."

The things which are noted in the history of truth were related by this great revealer. Man sees not as God sees, and in his shortsightedness he often emphasizes the unimportant, and passes lightly over events of universal interest. But when history is given in God's Word, it is a chronicler of those things Which are "noted in the Scripture of truth." This fact is noticeable in the history of the Persian kings, which is contained in the next few verses. In the most abbreviated manner, Gabriel touches the events of hundreds of years, but he brings into prominence things which are noted elsewhere in the Word of God, and which can be understood [183] only by a careful study of other books of the Bible.

For an understanding of the history of Persia, it is necessary to study carefully Ezra, Esther, Nehemiah, Haggai, and Zechariah. These books carry the history to the time of Persia's greatest strength, and through the time when that nation worked for God and His people. Then, and not till then, is the record silent. [184]

Num. 24:15, 16.
The heavens were opened, and I saw visions of God. Eze. 1:1.

Rev. 4:1.

How that he was caught up into paradise. 2 Cor. 12:4.

18. Then there came again and touched me one like the appearance of a man, and he strengthened me, 19. And said, O man greatly beloved, fear not: peace be unto thee, be strong, yea, be strong. And when he had spoken unto me, I was strengthened, and said, Let my lord speak; for thou hast strengthened me. 20. Then said he, Knowest thou wherefore I come unto thee? and now will I return to fight with the prince of Persia: and when I am gone forth, lo, the prince of Grecia shall come. 21. But I will shew thee that which is noted in the scripture of truth: and there is none that holdeth with me in these things, but Michael your prince. Dan. 10:18-21.

Which things also we speak, not in the words which man's wisdom teacheth, but which the Holy Ghost teacheth; comparing spiritual things with spiritual. But the natural man receiveth not the things of the Spirit of God: for they are foolishness unto him: neither can he know them, because they are spiritually discerned. 1 Cor. 2:13-14.

Ezra, Nehemiah, Haggai, Zechariah, and Esther record events connected with the return of the Jews form the Babylonian captivity.

Chapter 13

The History of the Decrees

Daniel 11:1, 2

THE angel began with the history of the Persian king-dom, for at the time of the vision the Babylonian mon-archy was entirely gone. It was the third year of the sole reign of Cyrus, and the fifth year since Darius the Mede had taken Babylon. It will be remembered that Daniel had seen the various nations, as they rose one after another on the stream of time. God is the only perfect, authentic his-torian; the only unbiased record of national events is found in the Scriptures. Men record acts, but only God can give those acts their proper setting in the great drama of life. There is one unbroken chain of events, a silken thread in the web of life, a perpetual spring in the tide of human af-fairs. This is the record of God's dealings with His chosen people. Egyptian history is noted in the Inspired Record of the world, but [185] only as it played some part in connection with Jehovah's people. Likewise Assyria, Babylon, Greece, and Rome; whatever the nation and whatever its place in time, its history is noted by the divine historian only during the time when it has been an instrument in God's hand to spread His truth or to protect His people.

It was for such a purpose that the Medo-Persian kingdom came into existence, and when it had fulfilled that work, and the Spirit of God was withdrawn, it passed from the stage of action.

The Medo-Persian empire was born when the time was ripe for Israel's deliverance from the bondage of Bab-ylon. The first king of the united empire was Darius the Mede. He was a man well advanced in life when he came to

In the third year of Cyrus king of Persia a thing was revealed unto Daniel, whose name was called Belteshazzar; and the thing was true, but the time appointed was long: and he understood the thing, and had understanding of the vision.
Dan. 10:1.

Dan. 2:31-35.
Dan. 7:1-8.
Dan. 8:1-8.

Thy word is truth.   John 17:17

The Lord is a God of knowledge, and by him actions are weighed.   1 Sam. 2:3.

Ps. 105:13, 14.

O thou daughter dwelling in Egypt, furnish thyself to go into captivity: for Noph shall be waste and desolate without an inhabitant. Egypt is like a very fair heifer, but destruction cometh; it cometh out of the north.   Jer. 46:19-20.

Mercy and truth presefve the king: and his throne is upholden by mercy   Prov. 20:28.

Thou rulest the raging of the sea: when the waves thereof arise, thou stillest them. Thou hast bro-ken Egypt in pieces, as one that is slain: thou hast scattered thine enemies with thy strong arm. The heavens are thine, the earth also is thine: as for the world and the fullness thereof, thou hast founded them.   Ps. 89:9-11 [margin].

Jer. 10:7.
Dan. 9:1, 2.
B. C. 538.

Dan. 5:30, 31.

1. Also I in the first year of Darius the Mede, even I, stood to confirm and to strengthen him.
Dan. 11:1.

Dan. 6:23.
So this Daniel prospered in the reign of Darius, and in the reign of Cyrus the Persian.   Dan 6:28.

Then the king went to his palace, and passed the night fasting: neither were instruments of musick brought before him: and his sleep went from him.
Dan. 6:18.

If God be for us, who can be against us?
Rom. 8:31.

Dan. 10:20.
Dan. 8:7.

There is no king saved by the multitude of a host: a mighty man is not delivered by much strength.
Ps. 33:16-19.

Dan. 10:1.

Thus saith Cyrus king of Persia, The LORD God of heaven hath given me all the kingdoms of the earth; and he hath charged me to build him an house at Jerusalem, which is in Judah. Who is there among you of all his people? his God be with him, and let him go up to Jerusalem, which is in Judah, and build the house of the LORD God of Israel, (he is the God,) which is in Jerusalem.
Ezra 1:1-6.

Isa. 5:3, 4.

Hear, O heavens, and give ear, O earth: for the LORD hath spoken, I have nourished and brought up children, and they have rebelled against me. The ox knoweth his owner, and the ass his master's crib: but Israel doth not know, my people doth not consider. Ah sinful nation, a people laden with iniquity, a seed of evildoers, children that are corrupters: they have forsaken the LORD, they have provoked the Holy One of Israel unto anger, they are gone away backward.
Isa. 1:2-4.

I drew them with cords of a man, with bands of love: and I was to them as they that take off the yoke on their jaws, and I laid meat unto them.
Hos. 11:4.
Because I have called, and ye refused; I have stretched out my hand, and no man regarded; But ye have set at nought all my counsel, and would none of my reproof.
Prov. 1:24-25.

the throne; threescore and two years old, the record states. But throughout his reign, Gabriel stood by him "to confirm and to strengthen him." To Darius was given the opportunity to liberate the Jews. The Spirit of God pleaded with him, and it brought Daniel into his favor, so that he placed the prophet in the third position in the kingdom. Darius knew of God and His power, for it was he who spent the sleepless night in prayer while Daniel was in the lions' den. Darius, however, did no great work for the Lord. He reigned but two years, then Cyrus took the kingdom.

From the accession of Cyrus to the end of the history of Medo-Persia, Gabriel worked with the kings. His first words to Daniel in this last vision are to this effect: "I will return to fight with the prince of Persia; *and when I am gone forth, lo, the prince of Grecia shall come.*" [186] When, therefore, the influence of God should be withdrawn from the king of Persia, no power on earth could help him. This thought was made emphatic when the rough goat was seen to meet the ram on the banks of the River Granicus. Wealth, arms, and influence were without avail.

Of the seven years of the reign of Cyrus, the third was already entered at the time of the vision. His first recorded act on taking the kingdom was to issue the proclamation of freedom to the Jews. Throughout the length and breadth of the land the tidings were heralded. It did not take over twelve months for the message to reach the most remote corners of the empire where the Jews might be found. Every inducement which monarch could offer was held out to that people. The slow movement on the part of a few, and the utter inactivity with the great majority, surprised Cyrus beyond measure. It is one of the saddest commentaries in the whole Bible on the perverseness of the human heart, and its desire to cling to sin.

When it is remembered that Babylon was the personification of all vileness; that injustice and oppression abounded, and that the decree of Cyrus was a call from God to liberty and purity of life, the effect of living long even in the sight of sin ought to appall one. This is a picture of the way the calls of God have been treated over and over again. Here is seen the exact counterpart of what people are doing to-day when asked of God to forsake modern Babylon.

One reason why the Jews were slow about withdrawing from ancient Babylon was because the children and youth had been neglected during [187] the seventy years' captivity. Jewish homes should have been schools, training these children for the city of Jerusalem. Instead, Jewish children attended Babylonian schools, mingled with Babylonian society, wore Babylonian apparel, talked, ate, and acted like the Babylonians; and consequently, when the time came to leave Babylon, they had no desire to leave.

Had the Hebrew race been true to its privileges, they might have established schools of the prophets, from which light would have radiated to all parts of the kingdom. This opportunity was offered in the first days of the captivity, when Nebuchadnezzar was witness to the fact that all the Chaldean learning was not worth one-tenth what God could teach. Daniel and his companions were brought into favor because of their knowledge of true educational principles; and had schools been established at that time, Chaldean youth would doubtless have been educated by the Jews, and in the religion of the Jews. God had always intended that Israel should be the teachers of the world; and even after sin had led them into slavery, He gave them an opportunity to teach their captors and their captors' children. Did Israel do so? The end of the seventy years and the response to the decree of Cyrus answer, No. They did not teach others; they failed to teach even their own children. As a result, thousands perished with Babylon.

Those who did go up to Jerusalem were half-hearted in their service, and ready to give up before the least opposition. When the foundation of the temple was laid, the old men wept because it did not equal in splendor the temple [188] of Solomon, and there was little influence exerted to bring others from Babylon. There is little wonder that after waiting two full years to see results, Cyrus was perplexed and astonished at the outcome. What wonder that Daniel

For all this his anger is not turned away, but his hand is stretched out still. Isa. 5:25.

How shall I pardon thee for this? thy children have forsaken me, and sworn by them that are no gods. Jer. 5:7.

For shame hath devoured the labour of our fathers from our youth; their flocks and their herds, their sons and their daughters. We lie down in our shame, and our confusion covereth us: for we have sinned against the LORD our God, we and our fathers, from our youth even unto this day, and have not obeyed the voice of the LORD our God. Jer. 3:24-25.

They that be teachers shall shine as the brightness of the firmament; and they that turn many to righteousness as the stars forever and ever. Dan. 12:3 [margin].

If God be for us, who can be against us. Rom. 8:31.

Go ye therefore, and teach all nations, baptizing them in the name of the Father, and of the Son, and of the Holy Ghost: Teaching them to observe all things whatsoever I have commanded you: and, lo, I am with you alway, even unto the end of the world. Amen. Matt. 28:19-20.

John 3:2.

The rod and reproof give wisdom: but a child left to himself bringeth his mother to shame. Prov. 29:15.

But many of the priests and Levites and chief of the fathers, who were ancient men, that had seen the first house, when the foundation of this house was laid before their eyes, wept with a loud voice; and many shouted aloud for joy: So that the people could not discern the noise of the shout of joy from the noise of the weeping of the people: for the people shouted with a loud shout, and the noise was heard afar off. Ezra 3:12-13.

But the prince of the kingdom of Persia withstood me one and twenty days: but, lo, Michael, one of the chief princes, came to help me; and I remained there with the kings of Persia.

Dan. 10:13.

Now when the adversaries of Judah and Benjamin heard that the children of the captivity builded the temple unto the LORD God of Israel; Then they came to Zerubbabel, and to the chief of the fathers, and said unto them, Let us build with you: for we seek your God, as ye do; and we do sacrifice unto him since the days of Esarhaddon king of Assur, which brought us up hither. But Zerubbabel, and Jeshua, and the rest of the chief of the fathers of Israel, said unto them, Ye have nothing to do with us to build an house unto our God; but we ourselves together will build unto the LORD God of Israel, as king Cyrus the king of Persia hath commanded us. Then the people of the land weakened the hands of the people of Judah, and troubled them in building, And hired counsellors against them, to frustrate their purpose, all the days of Cyrus king of Persia, even until the reign of Darius king of Persia. And in the reign of Ahasuerus, in the beginning of his reign, wrote they unto him an accusation against the inhabitants of Judah and Jerusalem.

Ezra 4:1-6.

Esther 3:6, 13-15.

And in the days of Artaxerxes wrote Bishlam, Mithredath, Tabeel, and the rest of their companions, unto Artaxerxes king of Persia; and the writing of the letter was written in the Syrian tongue, and interpreted in the Syrian tongue. ... The letter which ye sent unto us hath been plainly read before me. And I commanded, and search hath been made, and it is found that this city of old time hath made insurrection against kings, and that rebellion and sedition have been made therein. There have been mighty kings also over Jerusalem, which have ruled over all countries beyond the river; and toll, tribute, and custom, was paid unto them. Give ye now commandment to cause these men to cease, and that this city be not builded, until another commandment shall be given from me. Take heed now that ye fail not to do this: why should damage grow to the hurt of the kings? Now when the copy of king Artaxerxes' letter was read before Rehum, and Shimshai the scribe, and their companions, they went up in haste to Jerusalem unto the Jews, and made them to cease by force and power. Then ceased the work of the house of God which is at Jerusalem. So it ceased unto the second year of the reign of Darius king of Persia.

Ezra 4:7,18-24.

had to wait three weeks for an answer to his prayer, while Gabriel and Michael pleaded with the disheartened Cyrus! Cyrus was ready, had the Jews done their part, to make Jerusalem the glory of the whole earth. As it was, we do not find any record of further work by this king. He died, the work he might have done but partially accomplished because of neglect and inactivity on the part of God's chosen people.

Satan had witnessed the workings of the Spirit of God on the hearts of men at the very center of the government he claimed as his own. It was due to his influence that the Jews did not make a grand entry into Jerusalem. Cyrus struggled between two influences, but was restrained by Gabriel from doing any act of violence. Cambyses, his son, reigned nearly eight years, but most of his time was spent in useless and expensive warfare in Egypt and Ethiopia. Cambyses is the Ahasuerus of Ezra 4 : 6. To him the Samaritans wrote letters of complaint against the Jews at Jerusalem. But Cambyses was too busy with his foreign wars to give heed to this matter, and hence no action was taken either for or against the work at Jerusalem. The Jews were still at liberty to leave Babylon, but such a time of national quiet was not conducive to great activity on their part, and they remained where they were. The time came when they wished with all their hearts that they had gone out during those peaceful years. [189]

Cambyses was slain while in Egypt; and before the report was circulated throughout the Medo-Persian empire, an impostor took the throne which belonged to Smerdis, the son of Cambyses. The impostor, known in history as Pseudo-Smerdis (the false Smerdis), is the Artaxerxes of Ezra 4:7. He reigned only seven months, but that gave him time to consider complaints from the Samaritans and the tribes about Jerusalem, and to issue a commandment for the building of Jerusalem to cease until further word should come from the throne. This letter of the false Smerdis is found in Ezra 4: 18-22. This is the only act which the divine historian mentions in the life of this Persian monarch.

Although very little is said about him, God knew every move he made. This is seen as we follow the history of the decrees. As soon as the Jews at Jerusalem heard the reading of the letter from the false Smerdis, all work ceased. "For," reasoned they, "how can we go on?" After they ceased to build, God raised up two prophets, Haggai and Zechariah, and from these we gain a knowledge of the condition of affairs in Jerusalem.

The people ceased to build the temple, and turned to building houses for themselves. When urged to continue the Lord's work, they complained that money was scarce. They sowed seed, but the harvest was less than the amount sown; their trees bore little or no fruit; there was drought, and the cattle died; men could not pay their rent or taxes, and became slaves because of debt, and sold their children into bondage. Then they complained to God. But [190] all the time God was working for them, and they knew it not.

This is the way He worked: In the city of Babylon, six of the chief men of the empire suspected that the reigning king was not the rightful heir, and they banded themselves together to find out. Forcing their way into the presence of Smerdis, they recognized the impostor, and slew him, and Darius, the chief of the band, was made king. This is the man in history known as Darius Hystaspes, and is Darius the Persian spoken of in Ezra 4:24.

Gabriel still guarded the throne of the Persians, and while the weak-hearted Jews left off building the temple because of a little opposition, God was bringing a man to the throne who would carry forward the work of Cyrus. Haggai and Zechariah gathered the people together and urged them to resume the work of building, giving the word of the Lord that their poverty was the direct result of their own refusal to build in the face of difficulties. The Jews took up the burden, but presently Tatnai and others, governors of tribes in Palestine, came to Jerusalem and warned the Jews to cease. Haggai, Zechariah, Zerrubbabel, and Jeshua quoted the decree of Cyrus. Tatnai then wrote to Darius, expecting, of course, that he would put an end to the work. Darius, however, caused a search to be made, and found the decree of Cyrus, with all its particulars concerning the building,

Then the prophets, Haggai the prophet, and Zechariah the son of Iddo, prophesied unto the Jews that were in Judah and Jerusalem in the name of the God of Israel, even unto them.
Ezra 5:1.

In the second year of Darius the king, in the sixth month, in the first day of the month, came the word of the LORD by Haggai the prophet unto Zerubbabel the son of Shealtiel, governor of Judah, and to Joshua the son of Josedech, the high priest, saying, Thus speaketh the LORD of hosts, saying, This people say, The time is not come, the time that the LORD'S house should be built. Then came the word of the LORD by Haggai the prophet, saying, Is it time for you, O ye, to dwell in your cieled houses, and this house lie waste? Now therefore thus saith the LORD of hosts; Consider your ways. Ye have sown much, and bring in little; ye eat, but ye have not enough; ye drink, but ye are not filled with drink; ye clothe you, but there is none warm; and he that earneth wages earneth wages to put it into a bag with holes.
Haggai 1:1-6.

An evil man seeketh only rebellion: therefore a cruel messenger shall be sent against him.
Prov. 17:11.

They sent a letter unto him, wherein was written thus; Unto Darius the king, all peace. Be it known unto the king, that we went into the province of Judea, to the house of the great God, which is builded with great stones, and timber is laid in the walls, and this work goeth fast on, and prospereth in their hands. Then asked we those elders, and said unto them thus, Who commanded you to build this house, and to make up these walls? We asked their names also, to certify thee, that we might write the names of the men that were the chief of them. And thus they returned us answer, saying, We are the servants of the God of heaven and earth, and build the house that was builded these many years ago, which a great king of Israel builded and set up. . . . But in the first year of Cyrus the king of Babylon the same king Cyrus made a decree to build this house of God. . . . Now therefore, if it seem good to the king, let there be search made in the king's treasure house, which is there at Babylon, whether it be so, that a decree was made of Cyrus the king to build this house of God at Jerusalem, and let the king send his pleasure to us concerning this matter.
Ezra 5:7-17.

Then Darius the king made a decree, and search was made in the house of the rolls, where the treasures were laid up in Babylon. And there was found at Achmetha, in the palace that is in the province of the Medes, a roll, and therein was a record thus written: In the first year of Cyrus the king the same Cyrus the king made a decree concerning the house of God at Jerusalem, Let

the house be builded, the place where they offered sacrifices, and let the foundations thereof be
strongly laid; . . . Now therefore, Tatnai, governor
beyond the river, Shetharboznai, and your companions the Apharsachites, which are beyond the
river, be ye far from thence: Let the work of this
house of God alone; let the governor of the Jews
and the elders of the Jews build this house of God
in his place. Moreover I make a decree what ye
shall do to the elders of these Jews for the building of this house of God: that of the king's goods,
even of the tribute beyond the river, forthwith expenses be given unto these men, that they be not
hindered. Ezra 6:1-3.

The king's heart is in the hand of the Lord, as the
river of water: he turneth it withersoever he will.
Prov. 21:1.

Jer. 51:6, 9, 10.
Luke 24:35.

Then said I, Whither goest thou? And he said
unto me, To measure Jerusalem, to see what is the
breadth thereof, and what is the length thereof.
And, behold, the angel that talked with me went
forth, and another angel went out to meet him,
And said unto him, Run, speak to this young
man, saying, Jerusalem shall be inhabited as towns
without walls for the multitude of men and cattle
therein: For I, saith the LORD, will be unto her
a wall of fire round about, and will be the glory
in the midst of her. Ho, ho, come forth, and flee
from the land of the north, saith the LORD: for
I have spread you abroad as the four winds of the
heaven, saith the LORD. Deliver thyself, O Zion,
that dwellest with the daughter of Babylon. For
thus saith the LORD of hosts; After the glory
hath he sent me unto the nations which spoiled
you: for he that toucheth you toucheth the apple
of his eye. Zech. 2:2-8.

For, behold, I will shake mine hand upon them,
and they shall be a spoil to their servants: and ye
shall know that the LORD of hosts hath sent me.
Sing and rejoice, O daughter of Zion: for, lo, I
come, and I will dwell in the midst of thee, saith
the LORD. And many nations shall be joined to
the LORD in that day, and shall be my people:
and I will dwell in the midst of thee, and thou
shalt know that the LORD of hosts hath sent me
unto thee. And the LORD shall inherit Judah his
portion in the holy land, and shall choose Jerusalem again. Zech. 2:9-12.

Can a woman forget her sucking child, that she
should not have compassion on the son of her
womb? yea, they may forget, yet will I not forget
thee. Isa. 49:15.

the sacrifices, and the order for money for the same from the king's treasury.

Here is a manifestation of God's goodness and mercy. That which in the eyes of men looked like defeat was turned into a glorious [191] victory. Darius issued a decree which covered all that was contained in the decree of Cyrus, and more also. Tatnai and the men who had entered complaint were commanded to help forward the work at Jerusalem by giving their own money to bear the expense.

Watch those men, Tatnai, Shethar-boznai, and their companions, who raised such an outcry against God's work. When the decree of Darius was received, the accusers went with great speed to the Jewish leaders. Seeming defeat was turned into signal victory, because God was directing in the affairs of men. Bitter enemies became friends, or at least assistants, when the breath of Jehovah confounded their worldly policy. Again God especially favored Israel.

The warnings of Jeremiah were still heard: "Flee out of the midst of Babylon, and deliver every man his soul: be not cut off in her iniquity. . . . We would have healed Baby-lon, she is not healed: forsake her, and let us go every one into his own country. . . . The Lord hath brought forth our righteousness: come, and let us declare in Zion the work of the Lord our God."

"O fools, and slow of heart to believe all that the prophets have spoken." Israel heeded not. [192] For thirty-six years—think of it, over a quarter of a century—Darius reigned, and Gabriel stood at his right hand to keep his heart tender toward the chosen people.

The angels of heaven watched intently to see Israel return and build Jerusalem. To the prophet Zechariah, in the days of Darius, was given a wonderful view of the future history of the people of God. Jerusalem was given an oppor-tunity in those days to build so as to become an everlasting city. Said one angel to another in the hearing of Zecha-riah, "Run, speak to this young man, saying, Jerusalem shall be inhabited as towns without walls, for the multitude of men and cattle therein." Instead of walls of stone, such as

Jerusalem and the cities of the world had hitherto been accustomed to build, God promised to be a wall of fire round about it. "Ho, ho, come forth, and flee from the land of the north. . . . Deliver thyself, O Zion, that dwellest with the daughter of Babylon."

Abounding love, like the love of a mother for her firstborn, is heard in the words of Jehovah: "Sing and rejoice, O daughter of Zion! for lo, *I come*. I will dwell in the midst of thee." Christ's first and His second coming were both promised then, and would doubtless have followed in quick succession had Israel heeded.

Throughout all the world the glory of the Lord should be seen upon Zion, daughter of the living God. "I am returned unto Zion, and will dwell in the midst of Jerusalem: and JERUSALEM SHALL BE CALLED A CITY OF TRUTH !" "Rejoice greatly, O daughter of Zion: shout, O daughter of Jerusalem: [193] behold, thy King cometh unto thee."

To those who mourned because the new temple seemed less glorious than the former one, Christ, looking forward to the time when He Himself should enter there with the words of life for His people, said, by the prophet Haggai, "I will shake all nations, and the Desire of all nations shall come: and I will fill this house with glory." "The glory of this latter house shall be greater than of the former, . . . and in this place will I give peace." This He said referring to His personal visit in the form of humanity.

And again, by the same prophet, He asked them to witness to the fact that from the very day they began to build, the land yielded abundantly; the silver and the gold flowed in, and there was general prosperity.

By Zechariah the latter rain was promised to Jerusalem; great clouds of His glory should overshadow them. In Jerusalem the weak should be as David, and David as the angel of the Lord. All this He told them by the prophet Zechariah. Read the entire prophecy for its glorious promises. If we had lived in Babylon in the days of Darius, would we have hearkened? The prophet as he looks still farther into the future, sees the Lord coming and all His saints with

Beautiful for situation, the joy of the whole earth, is mount Zion, on the sides of the north, the city of the great King. God is known in her palaces for a refuge. Ps. 48:2-3.

Zech. 8:3.
Zech. 9:9.
Haggai 2:7-9.
Luke 12:28-30.
Matt. 21:12-16.

Consider now from this day and upward, from the four and twentieth day of the ninth month, even from the day that the foundation of the LORD'S temple was laid, consider it. Is the seed yet in the barn? yea, as yet the vine, and the fig tree, and the pomegranate, and the olive tree, hath not brought forth: from this day will I bless you. Haggai 2:18-19.

Deut 11:13, 14.
Lev. 26:3-12.
James 5:8.
Ps. 72:6.
Prov. 16:15.
Zech. 10:1.
Hosea 10:12.
Zech. 12:8.
Deut. 32:2.
Amos 4:7, 8.
Job 29:23.
Isa. 44:3-6.
Joel 2:23.

The Lord my God shall come, and all the saints with thee. . . . And the Lord shall be king over all the earth: in that day shall there be one Lord, and his name one. Zach. 14:4-9.

Then said he unto him, A certain man made a great supper, and bade many: And sent his servant at supper time to say to them that were bidden, Come; for all things are now ready. And they all with one consent began to make excuse. The first said unto him, I have bought a piece of ground, and I must needs go and see it: I pray thee have me excused. . . . So that servant came, and shewed his lord these things. Then the master of the house being angry said to his servant, Go out quickly into the streets and lanes of the city, and bring in hither the poor, and the maimed, and the halt, and the blind. And the servant said, Lord, it is done as thou hast commanded, and yet there is room. And the lord said unto the servant, Go out into the highways and hedges, and compel them to come in, that my house may be filled. For I say unto you, That none of those men which were bidden shall taste of my supper.   Luke 14:16-24.

He that overcometh shall inherit these things; and I will be his God, and he shall be my son.
                                Rev. 21:7.

And now will I shew thee the truth. Behold, there shall stand up yet three kings in Persia; and the fourth shall be far richer than they all: and by his strength through his riches he shall stir up all against the realm of Grecia.   Dan. 11:2.

He that loveth silver shall not be satisfied with silver; nor he that loveth abundance with increase: this is also vanity. When goods increase, they are increased that eat them: and what good is there to the owners thereof, saving the beholding of them with their eyes?   Eccl. 5:10-11.

Treasures of wickedness profit nothing.
                                Prov. 10:2.

Now it came to pass in the days of Ahasuerus, (this is Ahasuerus which reigned, from India even unto Ethiopia, over an hundred and seven and twenty provinces:).
                                Esther 1:1.
That in those days, when the king Ahasuerus sat on the trone of his kingdom, which was in Shushan the palace.
                                Esther 1:2.
In the third year of his reign, he made a feast unto all his princes and his servants; the power of Persia and Media, the nobles and princes of the provinces, being before him: When he shewed the

Him to crown Jerusalem, the city of our God, the bride of the Apocalypse. It should be an eternal city, with sin and iniquity blotted from the earth.

Zechariah saw these things in the days of Darius, king of Persia; and had the Jews come out of Babylon, and followed where God would have led, such would have been the history of [194] the world. They heeded not His voice, and after a lapse of nearly twenty-five hundred years, the people of to-day find themselves heirs to exactly the same promises under precisely the same conditions. If the church of to-day follows the instruction of the prophets, every promise of Zechariah shall be theirs. If not, the history of the Jews during the reign of the king who followed Darius, will be repeated.

In giving this history to Daniel, these details were omitted, and Daniel did not live to see them carried out. To him the angel said, speaking in the third year of the reign of Cyrus, "Behold, there shall stand up yet three kings in Persia; and the fourth shall be far richer than they all."

The three kings who followed Cyrus were Cambyses, Pseudo-Smerdis, and Darius. These, and their part in the history of the Jews, we have already considered. The fourth king of Persia after Cyrus the Great was noted for his wealth, and the great army he raised against the Greeks. This king was Xerxes, who came to the throne on the death of Darius. Our interest lies in the record of his dealings with the Jews, and to that history one entire book of the Bible is devoted. Xerxes is supposed to be the Ahasuerus of Esther, and the book of Esther is the record of the acts of this king with reference to the people of God who were still living in the kingdom of Babylon, over which Xerxes was sole monarch.

The Medo-Persian kingdom was at its height during the reign of this king. He held in subjection one hundred and twenty-seven provinces, extending from India to Ethiopia. His capital [195] was at Shushan, in the province of Elam. Some estimate of the wealth at the disposal of this ruler may be gained from the fact that for six months the princes, rulers, and governors of all the provinces, representing the power of the Persian king in all parts of the realm, were entertained at the royal palace; and that when this gathering was over, the palace of Shushan was thrown open for a full week, during which time all the people were feasted in the gardens. There was drinking of wine and reveling. It was similar to the time when Belshazzar feasted with a thousand of his lords. The furnishings of the palace, with its marble walls and floors, its rich curtains and draperies of many colors, hanging by silver rings to the lofty pillars, told of the gratification of pride. The beds and couches were of gold and silver, and they drank from wine cups of gold. Truly Medo-Persia was the daughter of Babylon.

The story of Vashti is a familiar one. Ahasuerus commanded her to appear before his half-drunken company, and she refused. Then she was set aside, and a Jewish maiden, her nationality being unknown, became queen of the Persian kingdom. This was Hadassah, known as Esther, an orphan of the house of Saul, whose parents had been among the royal captives in the days of Nebuchadnezzar. She had lived always with a cousin by the name of Mordecai, who treated her as his own daughter. Little did Mordecai and his wife think, when they took the helpless infant Hadassah, that she would one day stand for her people in the presence of the king. She was an obedient child, and consequently became an obedient woman. She [196] was simple-hearted and unassuming, requiring little and demanding nothing. She loved her own people, although to be true to them meant that she must look death in the face.

Daniel was no longer living, and there were few if any to represent the worship of the true God in the court of the godless king. Mordecai sat at the king's gate, it is true, and in time of a conspiracy he reported the matter to the king; but there were few occasions when he could mingle with those in authority. Wickedness and injustice abounded, and Mordecai refused to countenance such principles, and would not bow before the haughty Haman, one of the king's counselors. This was pretext enough for the enemies of the Jews to work upon, for they were now a hated race throughout the empire. They

riches of his glorious kingdom and the honour of his excellent majesty many days, even an hundred and fourscore days.   Esther 1:3-4.

And when these days were expired, the king made a feast unto all the people that were present in Shushan the palace, both unto great and small, seven days, in the court of the garden of the king's palace.   Esther 1:5.
Dan. 5:1, 2.

Where were white, green, and blue, hangings, fastened with cords of fine linen and purple to silver rings and pillars of marble: the beds were of gold and silver, upon a pavement of red, and blue, and white, and black, marble.   Esther 1:6.

And they gave them drink in vessels of gold, (the vessels being diverse one from another,) and royal wine in abundance, according to the state of the king.   Esther 1:7.

Esther 1:9-22.
Where the word of a king is, there is power: and who may say unto him, What doest thou?   Eccl. 8:4.

The king loved Esther above all the women, and she obtained grace and favour in his sight more than all the virgins; so that he set the royal crown upon her head, and made her queen instead of Vashti.   Esther 2:17.

Esther had not shewed her people nor her kindred: for Mordecai had charged her that she should not shew it.   Esther 2:10.

Now in Shushan the palace there was a certain Jew, whose name was Mordecai, the son of Jair, the son of Shimei, the son of Kish, a Benjamite.   Esther 2:5.

Esther had not yet shewed her kindred nor her people; as Mordecai had charged her: for Esther did the commandment of Mordecai, like as when she was brought up with him.   Esther 2:20.

She required nothing but what Hegai the king's chamberlain, the keeper of the women, appointed. And Esther obtained favour in the sight of all them that looked upon her.   Esther 2:15.

In those days, while Mordecai sat in the king's gate, two of the king's chamberlains, Bigthan and Teresh, of those which kept the door, were wroth, and sought to lay hand on the king Ahasuerus. And the thing was known to Mordecai, who told it unto Esther the queen; and Esther certified the king thereof in Mordecai's name. And when inquisition was made of the matter, it was found out; therefore they were both hanged on a tree: and it was written in the book of the chronicles before the king.   Esther 2:21-23.

And all the king's servants, that were in the king's gate, bowed, and reverenced Haman: for the king had so commanded concerning him. But Mordecai bowed not, nor did him reverence.

Esther 3:2.

They refused to hearken, and pulled away the shoulder, and stopped their ears, that they should not hear. Zech. 7:11.

Acts 7:23-30

Forty years long was I grieved with this generation, and said, It is a people that do err in their heart, and they have not known my ways.

Ps. 95:10.

Heb. 3:17.

(There are eleven days' journey form Horeb by the way of Mount Seir unto Kadesh-barnea.)

Deut. 1:2.

When he had fasted forty days and forty nights, he was afterward an hungered. And when the tempter came to him. Matt. 4:1-11.

And Haman said unto king Ahasuerus, There is a certain people scattered abroad and dispersed among the people in all the provinces of thy kingdom; and their laws are diverse from all people; neither keep they the king's laws: therefore it is not for the king's profit to suffer them. If it please the king, let it be written that they may be destroyed. . . . And the king took his ring from his hand, and gave it unto Haman the son of Hammedatha the Agagite, the Jews' enemy. . . . Every people of every province according to the writing thereof, and to every people after their language; in the name of king Ahasuerus was it written, and sealed with the king's ring. . . . Then were the king's scribes called on the thirteenth day of the first month, and there was written according to all that Haman had commanded.

Esther 3:8-12.

had failed to take advantage of the time of national favor, and Persia had turned against them.

For about forty years mercy had been extended to Israel, and that people had turned a deaf ear to all entreaty. Forty years has often been called the allotted time for a generation to settle its destiny either for or against the truth. Moses was forty years in the wilderness, unlearning the things of Egypt, and being taught in the things of God; Israel wandered forty years in the wilderness, when only eleven days were necessary to make the journey from the Red Sea to the border of Canaan; forty days Christ endured severe temptation; forty years sealed the fate of the Reformation in Germany; and it was forty years from the preaching of the sealing message until the time of the loud cry.

So Israel was given forty years in Babylon [197] while angels held the winds of strife. At the end of that time Xerxes yielded to the suggestion of Haman, and issued a decree against that "certain people scattered abroad and dispersed among the people in all the provinces." If entreaty would no longer attract the attention of the Jews, God would in His mercy let persecution come, that they might be compelled to flee to His side for protection. But when persecution and hardship are ap-

"Mordecai bowed not, nor did him reverence."

proaching, the love of God is so great that He prepares the deliverer beforehand.

The angel of God had guarded Hadassah, and directed in her education. He had brought her [198] to the kingdom "for such a time as this." When there was no man to represent His cause, Jehovah used a woman, and she, a young woman. Her very beauty was consecrated to the Lord, and He made use of that. God loves the young people, as the history of the Jews certifies.

Messengers were sent by post to carry the king's decree to every province in the vast empire. It was sealed with the king's signet, and the laws of the Medes and Persians were unchangeable. On a set day, every Jew in the kingdom was to be put to death by the sword; old, young, men, women, and little children—none were exempted. Satan triumphed in the thought that at last Israel was in his hand, and the cause of God should fall. "The king and Haman," two of Satan's servants, "sat down to drink."

The city of Shushan first heard the decree, and consternation filled the hearts of the Jews. There was distress in every home. "The city of Shushan was perplexed." Scarcely one year from the date of the decree, and death would be their lot. There was seemingly no way of escape. Years before they might have gone up to Jerusalem, but now it was forever too late. A bitter wail of agony reached heaven, and as those messengers of the king sped on, the cry grew louder. The voices of the Jews at Shushan were strengthened by sounds of mourning from thousands of Jews in all the provinces.

Esther, in the king's palace, was ignorant of the decree, but Mordecai made known to her the universal distress, and sent her a copy of the king's command. The crucial moment had [199] come to her. Should she, could she, be true to her God? The Hebrews of Shushan put on sackcloth, and for three days fasted for the queen. Then she came forth in the strength of her God. Queenly, beautiful, trusting, she stood in the inner court over against the king's house, awaiting the recognition of the monarch of earth, to cross whose will meant death. On one hand she saw death at the hand of

That our sons may be as plants grown up in their youth; that our daughters may be as corner stones, polished after the similitude of a palace.
Ps. 144:12.

The letters were sent by posts into all the king's provinces, to destroy, to kill, and to cause to perish, all Jews, both young and old, little children and women, in one day, even upon the thirteenth day of the twelfth month. . . . The copy of the writing for a commandment to be given in every province was published unto all people, that they should be ready against that day. The posts went out, being hastened by the king's commandment, and the decree was given in Shushan the palace. And the king and Haman sat down to drink; but the city Shushan was perplexed.
Esther 3:13-15.

Mordecai rent his clothes, and put on sackcloth with ashes, and went out into the midst of the city, and cried with a loud and a bitter cry; . . . And in every province, whithersoever the king's commandment and his decree came, there was great mourning.
Esther 4:1.

Esther 4:1-17.

Also he gave him the copy of the writing of the decree that was given at Shushan to destroy them, to shew it unto Esther, and to declare it unto her, and to charge her that she should go in unto the king, to make supplication unto him, and to make request before him for her people.
Esther 4:8.

Then Esther bade them return Mordecai this answer, Go, gather together all the Jews that are present in Shushan, and fast ye for me, and neither eat nor drink three days, night or day: I also and my maidens will fast likewise; and so will I go in unto the king, which is not according to the law: and if I perish, I perish.
Esther 4:15-16.

Now it came to pass on the third day, that Esther put on her royal apparel, and stood in the inner court of the king's house, over against the king's house: and the king sat upon his royal throne in the royal house, over against the gate of the house.
Esther 5:1.

The proclamation of Haman's decree.

Xerxes; on the other, the approval of her God. "If I perish, I perish," she said, and God accepted her sacrifice.

God had prepared from afar for her deliverance. The very act of kindness done years before by Mordecai wrought in the deliverance of his people. Who says there is no record kept of man's acts, or that man performs any deed of kindness unprompted by heavenly beings? God used Esther to save His people; He also used Mordecai.

Haman, the one who proposed the decree, was hung on a gallows built for Mordecai; Mordecai was promoted to the position of chief counselor of Xerxes; and a decree was issued that on the day appointed for the slaughter of the Jews, every Jew should bear arms and defend himself against the Persians. And the fear of the Jews fell upon all the people. Again God defeated the schemes, not of men only, but of the arch-enemy. Truth triumphed in spite of the waywardness of His people. This decree of Ahasuerus, or Xerxes, is the counterpart of the decree which will soon be issued by the beast of the thirteenth chapter of Revelation against the followers of God. It will find a people situated as were the Jews in Babylon; it will find [200] others who have withdrawn from Babylon, and as the enemy rushes upon this latter class to slay them, the swords will fall like broken straws, for angels of God will fight for His people.

This record, given in the book of Esther, is preserved in Bible history that men may know the future. God's dealings with the Jews reveal the principles of His government, and in this history is a graphic description of the sins and deliverance of spiritual Israel.

Xerxes was a cruel, arrogant man, and his character is shown not only in his dealings with the Hebrew race, but with other peoples as well. Not content with the extent of territory under his control, he mustered an immense army—over five million, historians state—and crossed the Hellespont to subdue Grecia. Defeat and disaster accompanied the effort, however, and he returned unto his own kingdom.

The Spirit of God was not yet withdrawn from the Medo-Persian court, and although Xerxes is the last king men-

In those days, while Mordecai sat in the king's gate, two of the king's chamberlains, Bigthan and Teresh, of those which kept the door, were wroth, and sought to lay hand on the king Ahasuerus. And the thing was known to Mordecai, who told it unto Esther the queen; and Esther certified the king thereof in Mordecai's name.
Esther 2:21-23.

Wherein the king granted the Jews which were in every city to gather themselves together, and to stand for their life, to destroy, to slay, and to cause to perish, all the power of the people and province that would assault them, both little ones and women, and to take the spoil of them for a prey, Upon one day in all the provinces of king Ahasuerus, namely, upon the thirteenth day of the twelfth month, which is the month Adar. The copy of the writing for a commandment to be given in every province was published unto all people, and that the Jews should be ready against that day to avenge themselves on their enemies. So the posts that rode upon mules and camels went out, being hastened and pressed on by the king's commandment. And the decree was given at Shushan the palace. Esther 8:11-14.

The above diagram shows the period of time covererd by the books of Ezra, Haggai, Zecharia, Esther, and Nehemiah, and the Persians kings that reigned at that time.

And he causeth all, both small and great, rich and poor, free and bond, to receive a mark in their right hand, or in their foreheads: And that no man might buy or sell, save he that had the mark, or the name of the beast, or the number of his name.
Rev. 13:16-17.

That which hath been is now; and that which is to be hath already been; and God requireth that which is past.
Eccl. 3:15.

Ezra 7:11-16.
Rev. 15:2, 3.

This Ezra went up from Babylon; and he was a ready scribe in the law of Moses, which the LORD God of Israel had given: and the king granted him all his request, according to the hand of the LORD his God upon him.
Ezra 7:6.

Now when these things were done, the princes came to me, saying, The people of Israel, and the priests, and the Levites, have not separated themselves from the people of the lands, doing according to their abominations,

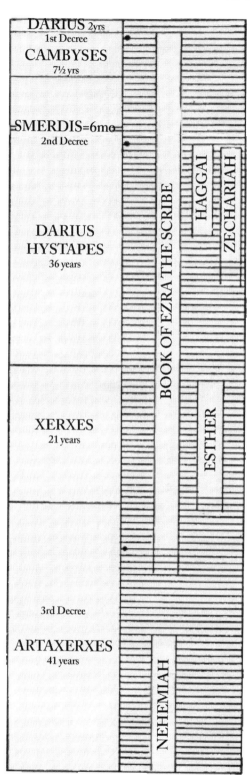

tioned in the vision which Daniel saw, yet God was still holding out mercy to the Israelites; and it was during the reign of Artaxerxes Longimanus, the successor of Xerxes, that the final decree for the return of the Jews was issued. In like manner the grand jubilee will immediately follow Satan's last effort to destroy the people of God.

In the seventh year of the reign of Artaxerxes, the heart of Ezra was stirred by the Spirit of God, and he appealed to the king for assistance. In response to the appeal Artaxerxes issued the commandment recorded in the seventh chapter of Ezra. This is the decree [201] of the year 457 B. C., mentioned in chapter ten, page 145, and is the date from which to reckon the beginning of the two thousand three hundred days of Daniel 8:14, and the seventy weeks of Daniel 9:24. The decree of Artaxerxes included all that was contained in the decrees of Cyrus and Darius, and gave further commandment to build the wall and establish a government.

Eighty years had passed since the decree of Cyrus—eighty years of forbearance; but even after the experience of the days of Esther and Xerxes there was little interest manifested in the rebuilding of Zion, and the company who went with Ezra was small compared with what it should have been. The condition in Jerusalem was discouraging, for there the Jews had intermarried with the Canaanites, bringing in iniquity and confusion. The Sabbath was desecrated, and the services of the Lord's house were neglected. It was not until the twentieth year of Artaxerxes, after Ezra had labored for Israel thirteen years, that Nehemiah came from Babylon and stirred the people into activity. Then, and not till then, were the walls rebuilt. Even then it was fighting with one hand and building with the other, because of a multitude of enemies. It was only then that they began to pay tithe, and to cease from ordinary traffic on the Sabbath; it was then that they put away their heathen wives; but they did it only because threatened with God's wrath.

Truly, Israel was stiffnecked and rebellious. A remnant was saved from Babylon, but it was only a remnant; and that remnant, after years [202] of struggling and much halting, was as a brand snatched from the burning.

Jerusalem, which might have been the glory of the earth, fell a prey to each succeeding kingdom. Daniel's mind turned to the rising power of the kingdom of Grecia, and Gabriel next spoke of the mighty one who should rule with great dominion. Medo-Persia sank into a state of weakness, and the angel withdrew his sheltering wings; probation was passed for another nation. It, too, had been numbered and found wanting; and its name is dropped by the inspired penman.

The history of the Persian empire, until it passed its zenith, is the history of the decrees; and when that nation ceased to help forward the people upon whom God was still bestowing light, it is lost sight of by the divine historian

Time waits for neither man nor nation. The life of each individual may be read in the history of the years of Medo-Persian supremacy. Let us hasten our steps toward the New Jerusalem.

even of the Canaanites, the Hittites, the Perizzites, the Jebusites, the Ammonites, the Moabites, the Egyptians, and the Amorites. For they have taken of their daughters for themselves, and for their sons: so that the holy seed have mingled themselves with the people of those lands: yea, the hand of the princes and rulers hath been chief in this trespass. Ezra 9:1-2.

Then I contended with the nobles of Judah, and said unto them, What evil thing is this that ye do, and profane the sabbath day? And it came to pass, that when the gates of Jerusalem began to be dark before the sabbath, I commanded that the gates should be shut, and charged that they should not be opened till after the sabbath. Neh. 13:1520.

And I perceived that the portions of the Levites had not been given them; then brought all Judah the tithe of the corn and the new wine and the oil unto the treasuries. Neh. 13:10,12.

Neh. 13:23, 24.

Neh. 2:1-6.

Neh. 4:13-21.

And they covet fields, and take them by violence; and houses, and take them away: so they oppress a man and his house, even a man and his heritage. Therefore thus saith the LORD; Behold, against this family do I devise an evil, from which ye shall not remove your necks; neither shall ye go haughtily: for this time is evil. Micah 2:2-3.

Who is a God like unto thee, that pardoneth iniquity, and passeth by the transgression of the remnant of his heritage? he retaineth not his anger for ever, because he delighteth in mercy. Micah 7:18.

Thus saith the Lord GOD; Remove the diadem, and take off the crown: this shall not be the same: exalt him that is low, and abase him that is high. I will overturn, overturn, overturn, it: and it shall be no more, until he come whose right it is; and I will give it him. Eze. 21:26-27.

When I am gone forth, lo, the prince of Grecia shall come. Dan. 10:20.

Dan. 5:26.

Why are thy valiant men swept away? they stood not, because the LORD did drive them. Jer. 46:15.

They did cry there, Pharaoh king of Egypt is but a noise; he hath passed the time appointed. Jer. 46:17.

CHAPTER 14

THE HISTORY OF GREECE

DANIEL 11:3-13

THE first two verses of the eleventh chapter of Daniel outline the history of the second kingdom, Medo-Persia. That portion of the chapter included in verses three to thirteen records the history of the third kingdom, Greece. Those things which are "noted in the Scripture of truth" concerning Greece are the things which Gabriel made known to Daniel. The prophet had found it difficult to grasp the full significance of the symbols used in previous visions to represent the kingdoms of the world, and so in this last interview between the servant of God and the angel of prophecy, symbols are laid aside, and the history is repeated in plain language. [203]

Notwithstanding the fact that Gabriel gives the prophecy in a plain narrative, the very words he uses, and the facts which he selects from the multitude of events which actually took place, have a significance. In reading God's Word in any of its parts there is first to be found the story which lies on the surface; and secondly, the deeper meaning, which is just as truly there, but which must be sought for as with a lighted candle. It is hoped that the reader may at least catch a glimpse of the deep spiritual lessons while reading the plain narrative of events.

God had a purpose when He gave the history of the four kingdoms, Babylon, Medo-Persia, Greece, and Rome. There is an incentive to understand these prophecies in the very fact that each nation is represented in a variety of ways, revealing different characteristics. And since, Daniel is a prophet for the latter days, there is an increased desire to read

And in those times there shall many stand up against the king of the south: also the robbers of thy people shall exalt themselves to establish the vision; but they shall fall. Dan. 11:14.

And the LORD answered me, and said, Write the vision, and make it plain upon tables, that he may run that readeth it. For the vision is yet for an appointed time, but at the end it shall speak, and not lie: though it tarry, wait for it; because it will surely come, it will not tarry. Hab. 2:2-3.

Isa. 8:1.
Isa. 30:8.

Every word of God is ppure: he is a shield unto them that put their trust him. Prov. 30:5.

Yea, if thou criest after knowledge, and liftest up thy voice for understanding; if thou seekest her as silver, and searchest for her as for hid treasures; then shalt thou understand the fear of the Lord, and find the knowledge of God. Prov. 2:1-5..

Look unto me, and be ye saved, all the ends of the earth: for I am god, and there is none else. Isa. 45:22.

For the prophecy came not in old time by the will of man: but holy men of God spake as they were moved by the Holy Ghost. 2 Peter 1:21.

Thou, O Daniel, shut up the words, and seal the book, even to the time of the end. Dan. 12:4.

Thou shalt rest, and stand in thy lot at the end of the days. Dan. 12:13.

And upon her forehead was a name written, MYSTERY, BABYLON THE GREAT, THE MOTHER OF HARLOTS AND ABOMINATIONS OF THE EARTH.   Rev. 17:5.
Rev. 18:2.
Eze. 23:17.

For all nations have drunk of the wine of the wrath of her fornication, and the kings of the earth have committed fornication with her, and the merchants of the earth are waxed rich through the abundance of her delicacies.
                                         Rev. 18:3.

And thou wentest to the king with ointment, and didst increase thy perfumes, and didst send thy messengers far off, and didst debase thyself even unto hell.   Isa. 57:9.

Michael, one of the chief princes, came to help me; and I remained there with the kings of Persia.
                                         Dan. 10:13.

And the letters were sent by posts into all the king's provinces, to destroy, to kill, and to cause to perish, all Jews, both young and old, little children and women, in one day, even upon the thirteenth day of the twelfth month, which is the month Adar, and to take the spoil of them for a prey.   Esther 3:13.

Ah sinful nation, a people laden with iniquity, a seed of evildoers, children that are corrupters: they have forsaken the LORD, they have provoked the Holy One of Israel unto anger, they are gone away backward.   Isa. 1:4.

But draw near hither, ye sons of the sorceress, the seed of the adulterer and the whore. Against whom do ye sport yourselves? against whom make ye a wide mouth, and draw out the tongue? are ye not children of transgression, a seed of falsehood.   Isa. 57:3-4.

Her gates are sunk into the ground; he hath destroyed and broken her bars: her king and her princes are among the Gentiles: the law is no more; her prophets also find no vision from the LORD.   Lam. 2:9.

The history of God's people during this period is given in the two books of Maccabees in the Apocrapha, and marginal references will be made in some instances from the Apocrapha.
Gen. 10:2, 4.

At that time Merodach-baladan, the son of Baladan, king of Babylon, sent letters and a present to Hezekiah.   Isa. 39:1.

not only the history, but God's purpose in tracing the history with such unerring accuracy. Babylon, as a nation, as has been seen from the study of Daniel in connection with Revelation, represents a condition of things which will exist in the church of the last days. Great was the splendor of that kingdom, but she was a harlot, and the mother of harlots. Above the city Heaven saw the words, "Mystery of iniquity," for she made all nations drunk with the wine of her fornication.

Medo-Persia was a daughter of Babylon, and she played, the harlot also; that is, she partook of the sins of Babylon, and departed from the living God. The principles of the religion of Babylon were carried out by the daughter, [205] though the wickedness was in a measure checked by the constant presence of angels in the court, who labored in behalf of the chosen people of God; but the constant tendency toward tyranny and oppression in the government is revealed in the decree of Ahasuerus in the days of Esther.

As Medo-Persia had an important part to play in connection with God's people, and while her part differed from the dealings of Babylon with that same people, so the Greek nation was called of God to do a work—a specific work. She, two, was a daughter of Babylon, partaking of her sins; but these sins, while the same, led to different outward manifestations than in Medo-Persia. Like children of the same family, each reproducing the character of the parents, yet differing widely from one another, so Greece, Medo-Persia, and Rome are three sisters, daughters of the same mother, but each endowed with special features and strong peculiarities.

Greece spans the gulf between the Old and the New Testament. Its principal work as a nation was done during the time when there was no prophet in Israel, the period between Malachi and Christ, hence the book of Daniel is the only portion of the Bible which deals with this nation. The history of Greece can be traced to Javan of the family of Japheth, who, with his sons, settled in the islands of the Mediterranean. The natural division of the country by the bays and mountains developed many independent or semi-independent tribes, but they had one common language and one religion.

It would seem that the principles of the worship [206] of Jehovah, as known to the sons of Noah, were carried into the isles of Greece, for throughout the entire system is traceable a close resemblance to the ceremonial law with its types and shadows, as carried on in Jerusalem in the days of Solomon. Again, when it is remembered that the kingdom of the Jews, in the days of its prosperity, was visited by representatives from all nations, it is easy to understand how the forms and ceremonies of the worship of Jehovah were adopted by the Greeks. Even the architecture of Palestine, especially the temple of Solomon, became a model to the Greeks, who were lovers of the beautiful. Everything that is good and beautiful in the world has its origin in the mind of God.

The gross idolatry of Babylon and Egypt was replaced in Greece by a more refined worship, if there can be said to be degrees of refinement in licentiousness. At any, rate Greek customs were less revolting on the surface, and hence more subtle and ensnaring. The aesthetic taste of the Greeks was developed by being in close contact with nature. They studied nature, and not having God's Word as an interpreter, they worshiped the forms instead of the Creator. They recognized the power of life, but not knowing the source of life, they were led into licentious practices, known as "the mysteries," where things which are sacred were defiled with drinking and passionate indulgence.

There is a pathetic strain throughout their history. They came so close to the God of nature, and yet, not knowing Him, they wandered in such utter darkness. Theirs is a constant [207] reminder of the fate of those students of to-day who seek to understand natural phenomena, but do not interpret nature by the word of its Creator. They, too, worship Zeus and Demeter, Pluto, or Poseidon, instead of the Christ. The fact is, that the children of to-day are fed upon the myths and traditions of this very people, who were groping in darkness, worshiping the gods of Olympus, and ignorant of the God whose voice shook the mountains in every storm, whose smile was in every sunbeam, and whose rivers watered the fields.

When the queen of Sheba heard of the fame of Solomon, she came to prove Solomon with hard questions at Jerusalem. 2 Chron. 9:1.

Every good gift and every perfect gift is from above, and cometh down from the Father of lights, with whom is no variableness, neither shadow of turning. James 1:17.

Every man is brutish in his knowledge: every founder is confounded by the graven image: for his molten image is falsehood, and there is no breath in them. They are vanity, and the work of errors: in the time of their visitation they shall perish. The portion of Jacob is not like them: for he is the former of all things; and Israel is the rod of his inheritance: The LORD of hosts is his name. Jer. 10:14-16.

Professing themselves to be wise, they became fools, and changed the glory of the uncorruptible God into an image made like to corruptible man, and to birds, and four-footed beasts, and creeping things. Wherefore God also gave them up to uncleanness through the lusts of their own hearts. Rom. 1:21-30.

Avoiding profane and vain babblings, and oppositions of science falsely so called: Which some professing have erred concerning the faith 1 Tim. 6:20-21.

Neither give heed to fables and endless genealogies, which minister questions, rather than godly edifying which is in faith: so do. 1 Tim. 1:4.

The voice of thy thunder was in the heaven: the lightnings lightened the world: the earth trembled and shook. Ps. 77:18.

He watereth the hills from his chambers. Ps. 104:13.

Then the priest of Jupiter, which was before their city, brought oxen and garlands unto the gates, and would have done sacrifice with the people.
Acts 14:11-13.

Know ye not that they which run in a race run all, but one receiveth the prize? So run, that ye may obtain. And every man that striveth for the mastery is temperate in all things. Now they do it to obtain a corruptible crown; but we an incorruptible. I therefore so run, not as uncertainly; so fight I, not as one that beateth the air: But I keep under my body, and bring it into subjection: lest that by any means, when I have preached to others, I myself should be a castaway.   1 Cor. 9:24-27.

Bodily exercise profiteth little: but godliness if profitable unto all things, having promise of the life that now is, and of that which is to come.   1 Tim. 4:8.

Why do thy disciples trangress the tradition of the elders? . . . But he answered and said unto them, Why do ye also transgress the commandment of God by your tradition? . . . Thus have ye made the commandment of God of none effect by your tradition.   Matt. 15:2, 3, 6.

1 Tim. 6:20.

Beware lest any man spoil you through philosophy and vain deceit, after the tradition of men, after the rudiments of the world, and not after Christ.   Col. 2:8.

All therefore whatsoever they bid you observe, that observe and do; but do not ye after their works: for they say, and do not.   Matt. 23:3.
Of the tree of the knowledge of good and evil, thou shalt not eat of it: for in the day that thou eatest thereof thou shalt surely die.
Gen. 2:17.

Then certain of the people were so forward herein, that they went to the king, who gave them licence to do after the ordinances of the heathen: Whereupon they built a place of exercise at Jerusalem according to the customs of the heathen: And made themselves uncircumcised, and forsook the holy covenant, and joined themselves to the heathen, and were sold to do mischief.
1 Maccabees 1:13-15.

Israel's departure from the Lord during the period of the Greek influence was so great that they were not entrusted with the spirit of prophecy as aforetime.

Dan. 10:20.
Dan. 11:3.

The Greeks offered sacrifices, but of what value were they when they accepted not the sacrifice of the slain Lamb of God? The spirit of prophecy was cherished, but while God's prophets mingled with the people, the Greek prophetess, a maiden of questionable character, was secluded from the people, and received her inspiration from a vapor that poured from a rent in a rock over which the temple of Delphi was built.

There was a priesthood, the duties of whose members were to reveal the will of the gods. The sacred feasts of Jehovah's people were replaced by the national games of the Greeks. As the passover and the feast of tabernacles called the Hebrew race together, and promoted unity and a love of God, so the Greek games gathered that people together, promoting one common language, religion, and law. God's people met for spiritual worship; the Greeks for physical or intellectual enjoyment.

The history of Greece is the history of physical and intellectual culture. The people admired grace and beauty, and her literary minds [208] worshiped the intellect. Plato, the greatest of Greek philosophers, lived about four hundred years before Christ, and his teachings have led the thoughts of writers in every age since then. The Jews mingled the teachings of the Bible with the philosophy of Plato, and that formed the traditions of men, against which Christ so often warned His followers. The false philosophy, and the "science falsely so called" of Paul's time, was Greek teaching, which breathed the spirit of Plato and his students.

Plato's writings have replaced the Bible with many, and a large number of modern writers, of both prose and poetry, recognize him as their intellectual leader. The philosophy of this man was often good, and he admired truth; but the error lay in admiring or assenting to truth, and failing to live it out. His followers came under the condemnation of Christ, together with the Pharisees, of whom He said, "They *say,* but do not."

Here, in Greek religion and Greek learning, was the most subtle form of that mixture of truth and error which Satan offered at the tree of the knowledge of good and evil, which existed from the days of Eden to the time of Greece. Babylon enslaved the bodies of God's people, Medo-Persia made laws to slay them, but Greece captured their minds, and enslaved them to her ideas. She counterfeited so neatly, so adroitly, the spiritual teachings of the Old Testament; and so quietly, yet so surely, wound her tendrils about God's people, that her slavery was far worse than that of Egypt or Babylon. It is this influence which must be taken into consideration while following the history of the Greeks as given by Gabriel. [209]

The angel said, "When I am gone forth [from Persia], lo, the prince of Grecia shall come." And of Greece, he says, "A mighty king shall stand up, that shall rule with great dominion, and do according to his will." It is in this language that Alexander is introduced in the divine records. He was not a Greek, but a Macedonian, the son of Philip of Macedon. He stands in history as one of those strong characters whom God uses in spite of the fact that, they are unacquainted with Him, and know not His manner of working. Alexander, in Greek history, corresponds in some ways to Cyrus the Persian.

Alexander, as a boy; showed an indomitable will, and as he grew to manhood the trait strengthened. He was educated by Aristotle, the illustrious pupil of Plato, in the wisdom of the Greeks. When twenty years of age, Philip of Macedon died, leaving the government to Alexander. This was the year 336 B. C. Alexander united the independent states of [210] Greece, and placed himself at the head of their amphictyonic council. The Greeks were ambitious, and the new general organized an army for foreign conquest.

The third kingdom was represented by a leopard with four wings on its back. This symbol covered the time not only that Alexander was king, but during its divided state as well. The swiftness of conquest is well represented by the wings of a fowl; the cunning, insinuating nature by the lithe form of the leopard; and the mingling together of truth and error in its doctrines and practices by the spots. "Can the leopard change his spots?" No more could Greece give truth without a portion of the false; no more can truth and error be separated

Vainly puffed up by his fleshly mind
Col. 2:18.

I am the LORD, and there is none else, there is no God beside me: I girded thee, though thou hast not known me. Isa. 45:5.

The most High ruleth in the kingdom of men, and giveth it to whomsoever he will.
Dan. 4:32.

Therefore that he goat waxed very great.
Dan. 8:8.

I have even called thee by thy name: I have surnamed thee, though thou hast not known me. I am the LORD, and there is none else, there is no God beside me: I girded thee, though thou hast not known me. Isa. 45:4-5.

Jehovah God gave commandment unto the man, saying: Of every of the trees of the garden eating thou mayest eat: But of the tree of the knowledge of good and evil thou shalt not eat of it, for on the day that thou eatest thereof, dying thou shalt die.
Gen. 2:16, 17 [Spurrell's trans].

Jehovah God layeth a charge on the man, saying, Of every tree of the garden eating thou dost eat: and of the tree of knowledge of good and evil, thou dost not eat of it, for in the day of thine eating of it-dying thou dost die.
Gen. 2:16, 17 [Young's trans].

Even a child is known by his doings, whether his work be pure, and whether it be right.
Prov. 20:11.

He seeth that wise men die, like-wise the fool and the brutish person perish, and leave their wealth to others. Ps. 49:10.

After this I beheld, and lo another, like a leopard, which had upon the back of it four wings of a fowl; the beast had also four heads; and dominion was given to it. Dan. 7:6.

A leopard shall watch over their cities: every one that goeth out thence shall be torn in pieces.
Jer. 5:6.

A leopard by the way will I observe them.
Hosea 13:7.

Can the Ethiopian change his skin, or the leopard his spots? then may ye also do good, that are accustomed to do evil. Jer. 13:23.

I turned myself to behold wisdom, and madness, and folly: for what can the man do that cometh after the king? even that which hath been already done. Then I saw that wisdom excelleth folly, as far as light excelleth darkness.
Eccl. 2:12-13.

As I was considering, behold, an he goat came from the west on the face of the whole earth, and none touched him in the earth. And the goat had a notable horn between his eyes.

Dan. 8:5 [margin].

Another third kingdom of brass, which shall bear rule over all the earth.   Dan. 2:39.

Therefore the he goat waxed very great: and when he was strong, the great horn was broken; and for it came up four notable ones toward the four winds of heaven.   Dan. 8:8.

He that hath no rule over his own spirit is like a city that is broken down, and without walls.

Prov. 25:28.

Wine is a mocker, strong drink is raging: and whosoever is deceived thereby is not wise.

Prov. 20:1.

And the Gentiles shall come to thy light, and kings to the brightness of thy rising.

Isa. 60:3.

Arise, O LORD, disappoint him, cast him down: deliver my soul from the wicked, which is thy sword: From men which are thy hand, O LORD, from men of the world, which have their portion in this life, and whose belly thou fillest with thy hid treasure.   Ps. 17:13-14.

Thou shalt make holy garments for Aaron thy brother for glory and for beauty.   Ex. 28:2.

Kings shall be thy nursing fathers, and their queens thy nursing mothers: they shall bow down to thee with their face toward the earth, and lick up the dust of thy feet; and thou shalt know that I am the LORD: for they shall not be ashamed that wait for me.   Isa. 49:23.

Dan. 2:31-39.
Dan. 8:3-8.
Dan. 8:20, 21.
Dan. 11:2-4.

He shall break in pieces mighty men without number, and set others in their stead.

Job 34:24.

Dan. 4:32.

Behold, I stand at the door, and knock: if any man hear my voice, and open the door, I will come in to him, and will sup with him, and he with me.

Rev. 3:20.

in that system of education founded upon the wisdom of the Greeks—her philosophy, her myths, and her nature teaching.

Again Daniel saw the progress of this third nation, as a rough goat coming from the west without touching the earth. This marks the rapidity of the conquests carried on by Alexander. It was Granicus, Asia Minor, Issus, Tyre, Gaza, with the surrender of all Egypt; Arbela, Babylon, Susa, Bactria, and India—all in the space of eight short years. Having conquered those who opposed him, he planned to unite the extensive territory over which he bore sway. He was an organizer and diplomat as well as a general. By marrying a princess of Babylon, and giving several members of the royal family of Persia in marriage to his generals, he sought to win the favor of the conquered races. It was while in Babylon, directing affairs in that ancient Eastern capital, that Alexander died, probably [211] as a result of intemperance and excess. He was still a young man, but the nations of the world bowed at his feet.

In following the rapid conquests of Alexander,—symbolized by the goat which touched not the ground,—no mention has been made of the Jews. As God brought Nebuchadnezzar and Cyrus in direct contact, with His people, that they might know the God of heaven, so He permitted Alexander to learn of Him. While that conqueror was passing from Tyre, after its surrender, toward Gaza, which guards the entrance into Egypt, he stopped at Jerusalem. Josephus states that great consternation filled the city when it was known that the Greek warrior was coming. But the high priest, Juddas, had a dream in which he was bidden to go out to meet Alexander, arrayed in his priestly garments, and accompanied by the temple officers clad in white.

When Alexander met this company, much to the surprise of his army and generals, he bowed to the ground to worship the God whose name was on the miter worn by the high priest. He then accompanied the high priest to the temple at Jerusalem, where the sacrifices were explained; also the prophecies of Daniel concerning the rise and fall of Babylon, the conquests of Medo-Persia and its subsequent fall, and the

Alexander bowed to the ground to worship the God whose name was on the miter worn by the high priest.

rise of a third empire. Daniel, who had in person witnessed before Nebuchadnezzar and Cyrus, was then quoted to Alexander. The mighty conqueror was in the presence of the Spirit of God, and was given the message that the Most High ruleth in the kingdom of men, and giveth it to whomsoever he will. Would he [212] bow in submission, and let God conquer for him? This was the opportune moment in his life.

Alexander acknowledged God, but left Jerusalem and pushed forward in battle. Gaza fell. Egypt was entered, and there, in order to gratify a selfish pride, he had himself proclaimed son of Jupiter Ammon. He who might have become

Behold, what manner of love the Father hath bestowed upon us, that we should be called the sons of God.   1 John 3:1.

Who changed the truth of God into a lie, and worshiped and served the creature more than the Creator, who is blessed forever. Amen.
                    Rom. 1:25.

All are of the dust, and all turn to dust again.
                    Eccl. 3:18-20.

He that is of the earth is earthly.
John 3:31.

3. And a mighty king shall stand up, that shall rule with great dominion, and do according to his will.
Dan. 11:3.

Choose you this day whom ye will serve.
Joshua 24:13.

2 Cor. 4:4.
Eph. 2:2, 3.
Phil. 2:5.
Matt. 12:30.

If the son therefore shall make you free, ye shall be free indeed.
John 8:36.

I fear, lest by any means, as the serpent beguiled Eve through his subtility, so your minds should be corrupted from the simplicity that is in Christ.
2 Cor. 11:3.

Behold, the eyes of the Lord God are upon the sinful kingdom, and I will destroy it from off the face of the earth.
Amos 9:8.

4. And when he shall stand up, his kingdom shall be broken, and shall be divided toward the four winds of heaven; and not to his posterity, nor according to his dominion which he ruled: for his kingdom shall be plucked up, even for others beside those.
Dan. 11:4.

Therefore the he goat waxed very great: and when he was strong, the great horn was broken; and for it came up four notable ones toward the four winds of heaven.
Dan. 8:8.

5. And the king of the south shall be strong, and one of his princes; and he shall be strong above him, and have dominion; his dominion shall be a great dominion.
Dan. 11:5.

Hab. 2:5-7.

a son of God chose rather to be called the son of Jupiter. The result of Greek education and learning is fully exemplified in this one act. The outcome of such a choice—a fit consummation of all Greek teaching—was met at Babylon when the king, at his very prime, laid down and died with no hope of the future. It is a sad but impressive commentary for those who seek the ways of the world in preference to the truths of God.

One thing which the inspired historian notes, is, that he would do "according to his will." When man makes such a resolution, it means that he has been offered a choice between God and Satan, and has chosen the latter. There are but minds in the universe, and he who rejects God may claim that he exercises his own mind, but it means that he is swayed by the mind of the enemy of God. "Let this mind be in you which was also in Christ Jesus," for it brings liberty. The spirit which wishes to exalt self is imitating the philosophy of the Greeks, and its result is death; for Greek philosophy is but a continuation of the philosophy used to deceive Adam and Eve in Eden, at the tree of the knowledge of good and evil.

Alexander left no heirs to the throne who could hold the reins of government. His eldest son was a child of five. A number of strong men had acted as generals of the army during the march through Asia, and on the death of the emperor eight of these contended for supremacy. None, however, were strong enough to subdue all the others. Nearly twenty years were spent in war and contention. Finally it was decided that Ptolemy should hold Egypt; Seleucus Syria and the east; Lysimachus Thrace and Asia Minor, and Cassander Greece. The territory of Alexander was divided, but "not to his posterity;" neither was the strength of these four equal to that of Alexander, and the four partitions lasted but a few years. [214] Greece, which was under the rule of Cassander, was taken by Lysimachus, thus uniting the western and northern divisions.

In 281 B. C., after intrigues too numerous to mention, Seleucus met Lysimachus and slew him in battle. This reduced the four divisions to two, the rulers of which were afterward distinguished as kings of the north and the south. Seleucus, the king of the north, now held territory which had formerly belonged to three generals, while Ptolemy retained the southern division. This agrees with the words of Gabriel to Daniel. The fifth verse, according to Spurrell, reads: "Then shall the king of the south, even one of his [Alexander's] princes, be strong; yet shall another exceed him in strength and have dominion; a grand dominion shall be his dominion.'

The Ptolemy who gained Egypt was surnamed Soter, or Saviour, and on his death he was succeeded by his son, Ptolemy Philadelphus. The Seleucus who gained the three divisions was succeeded by his son Antiochus Sotor, who was killed by the Gauls in Asia Minor. The third in the line of Greco-Syriac kings was Antiochus Theos, who was reigning in Syria while Ptolemy Philadelphus reigned on the Egyptian throne.

There is, however, something aside from the mere succession of kings which is worthy of notice. Gabriel gave Daniel the framework of the history of Greece. We have in the inspired record something which corresponds to the skeleton in the human body, and the flesh and organs of life need to be put in. These nations which were then in existence were a shelter, [215] perhaps, a scaffolding, built about God's people, offering them another opportunity to work. The Spirit of God was working in the courts of monarchs as faithfully as ever. At the same time the controversy between truth and error never for a moment abated.

It might seem to the casual observer that Greece was not in reality a ruling power in the sense that Babylon and Medo-Persia were universal monarchies. Let us see. From the first it has been noted that Greece was an intellectual ruler rather than a power which held the bodies of men in slavery. If we may personify Greek *intellect* in an abstract way, we may say that Alexander was the tool in God's hand for building up a kingdom where it might hold sway. Alexander did this work well; and while he individually fell, the Greek language, learning, and customs were introduced

He leadeth counsellors away spoiled, and maketh the judges fools. He looseth the bond of kings, and girdeth their loins with a girdle. He leadeth princes away spoiled, and overthroweth the mighty. Job 12:17-19.

When they went from one nation to another, from one kingdom to another people; He suffered no man to do them wrong: yea, he reproved kings for their sakes. Ps. 105:13-14.

God is known in her palaces for a refuge. For, lo, the kings were assembled, they passed by together. They saw it, and so they marveled: they were troubled, and hasted away. Ps. 48:3-5.

Another third kingdom of brass, which shall bear rule over all the earth. Dan. 2:39.

1 Maccabees 1:28.
1 Maccabees 1:39-45.

The daughter of Egypt shall be confounded; she shall be delivered into the hand of the people of the north. The LORD of hosts, the God of Israel, saith; Behold, I will punish the multitude of No, and Pharaoh, and Egypt, with their gods, and their kings; even Pharaoh, and all them that trust in him. Jer. 46:24-25.

He went to the king, not to be an accuser of his countrymen, but seeking the good of all, both publick and private: For he saw that it was impossible that the state should continue quiet, and Simon leave his folly, unless the king did look thereunto. But after the death of Seleucus, when Antiochus, called Epiphanes, took the kingdom, Jason the brother of Onias laboured underhand to be high priest, Promising unto the king by intercession three hundred and threescore talents of silver, and of another revenue eighty talents: Beside this, he promised to assign an hundred and fifty more, if he might have licence to set him up a place for exercise, and for the training up of youth in the fashions of the heathen, and to write them of Jerusalem by the name of Antiochians. Which when the king had granted, and he had gotten into his hand the rule he forthwith brought his own nation to Greekish fashion. . . . For he built gladly a place of exercise under the tower itself, and brought the chief young men under his subjection, and made them wear a hat. Now such was the height of Greek fashions, and increase of heathenish manners, through the exceeding profaneness of Jason, that ungodly wretch, and no high priest; That the priests had no courage to serve any more at the altar, but despising the temple, and neglecting the sacrifices, hastened to be partakers of the unlawful allowance in the place of exercise, after the game of Discus called them forth; Not setting by the honours of their fathers, but liking the glory of the Grecians best of all. By reason whereof sore calamity came upon them: for they had them to be their enemies and avengers, whose custom they followed so earnestly, and unto whom they desired to be like in all things.   2 Maccabees 4:5-16.

He beholdeth all high things: He is a king over all the children of pride.   Job 41:34.

Mischief shall come upon mischief, and rumour shall be upon rumour; then shall they seek a vision of the prophet; but the law shall perish from the priest, and counsel from the ancients.
                              Eze. 7:26.

Her gates are sunk into the ground; he hath destroyed and broken her bars: her king and her princes are among the Gentiles: the law is no more; her prophets also find no vision from the LORD.   Lam. 2:9.

Where there is no vision, the people perish: but he that keepeth the law, happy is he.
                              Prov. 29:18.

Take heed to thyself that thou be not snared by following them, after that they be destroyed from before thee; and that thou enquire not after their gods, saying, How did these nations serve their gods? even so will I do likewise.   Deut. 12:30.

into all countries where his arms had opened the way. The Greek religion, with its mysteries, was accepted in Syria and Asia Minor; Greek games were celebrated in the eastern provinces. But Greek education took a position ahead even of her religion, and Greek teachers and scholars followed in the wake of the conqueror. The Greek language was almost universally used, and Greek [216] books were in demand. The city of Alexandria, in Egypt, was founded by Alexander, and it became the center of Greek learning. Egyptian idolatry and Greek philosophy sat enthroned beside each other. As the Encyclopedia Britannica states it, "In Egypt a Greek aristocracy of office, birth, and *intellect* existed side by side with a distinct native life."

Israel had once been miraculously delivered from physical bondage in Egypt. They had been warned against fleeing to Egypt for protection in the days of Nebuchadnezzar at the siege of Jerusalem. They may have escaped the bondage of those earlier times, but they were captured by the learning of the Greeks. In the days of Ptolemy Soter, hosts of Jews flocked into Egypt, and those who remained in Jerusalem and Palestine imbibed many of the ideas of the Greeks.

It has been stated that the history of Greece fills the time between the prophecy of Malachi and John the Baptist. We are now ready to appreciate the reason why Israel was so long without the sound of a prophet's voice. God gave Israel a system of education separate and distinct from the systems of all other nations; a system which, if followed, would forever make it impossible for the people to go into captivity. But Israel often gave up her God-given system for the teaching of heathen nations.

When the Jews returned from Babylon, they were strongly tinctured with Babylonian ideas of education and religion. This prepared them to accept with readiness the teachings of the Greeks. The rabbis of Jerusalem mingled the principles of Greek philosophy so thoroughly [217] with the statutes of Jehovah, which they were commanded to teach the children, that from the death of Malachi to the

Priests watching Grecian games.

Not long after this the king sent an old man of Athens to compel the Jews to depart from the laws of their fathers, and not to live after the laws of God: And to pollute also the temple in Jerusalem, and to call it the temple of Jupiter Olympius; and that in Garizim, of Jupiter the Defender of strangers, as they did desire that dwelt in the place. The coming in of this mischief was sore and grievous to the people: For the temple was filled with riot and revelling by the Gentiles, who dallied with harlots, and had to do with women within the circuit of the holy places, and besides that brought in things that were not lawful. The altar also was filled with profane things, which the law forbiddeth. Neither was it lawful for a man to keep sabbath days or ancient fasts, or to profess himself at all to be a Jew.

2 Maccabees 6:1-6.

Thous shalt call his name John.

Luke 1:13, 15, 63.

And the child grew, and waxed strong in spirit, and was in the deserts till the day of his shewing unto Israel. Luke 1:80.

In those days came John the Baptist, preaching in the wilderness of Judea. Matt. 3:1.

The Jews marveled, saying, How knoweth this man letters, having never learned? Jesus answered them, and said, My doctrine is not mine, but his that sent me. John 7:15, 16.

Then stood there up one in the council, a Pharisee, named Gamaliel, a doctor of the law, had in reputation among all the people, and commanded to put the apostles forth a little space.

Acts 5:34.

I am verily a man which am a Jew, born in Tarsus, a city in Cilicia, yet brought up in this city at the feet of Gamaliel, and taught according to the perfect manner of the law of the fathers, and was zealous toward God, as ye all are this day.

Acts 22:3.

Ex. 14:13.

Even his eternal power and Godhead; so that they are without excuse: Because that, when they knew God, they glorified him not as God, neither were thankful; but became vain in their imaginations, and their foolish heart was darkened. Professing themselves to be wise, they became fools.

Rom. 1:20-22.

But I would ye should understand, brethren, that the things which happened unto me have fallen out rather unto the furtherance of the gospel; So that my bonds in Christ are manifest in all the palace, and in all other places. Phil. 1:12-13.

birth of John the Baptist there was not a family in Judah to whom the education of a prophet could be intrusted.

The Greek games were performed in Jerusalem itself, and Jewish youth, dressed only in the scarf and broad hat, in imitation of the god Hermes, wrestled like the Athenian athletes. It is stated by Dr. Mears that the priests, when the signal was given for the sports, left their work in the temple to watch the games. Greek names replaced the Jewish in many instances, and even priests intermarried with the Greeks. It is no wonder that Gabriel gave specific instruction concerning the name to be given the babe of Zacharias and Elizabeth, for although there was once a time when every child in Israel was named under the inspiration of the Spirit, the Israelites had now chosen Greece in the place of God.

The whole Jewish teaching was Hellenized; and when John the Baptist was born, his mother and father were commanded to leave the city of Jerusalem, and educate the child in the desert, away from the influence of the schools and the society of the Jews. Christ himself never entered the schools of His day, because of the mixture of the truth of God with heathen philosophy. Greek teaching exalted nature; but the Son of God could not hear the voice of the Father in the teachings of the schools, and He wandered through the woods alone, or in company with His mother. Then it was that nature, the great object lesson of the Creator, was opened to His expanding mind. Other [218] Jewish youth sat at the feet of the rabbis, learning what the spirit of the Greeks taught, and they crucified the Lord of life.

It is a wonderful thing to man, who is so limited in means, to watch the workings of God, who is so limitless in resources. When the Jews fled to Egypt, then God took advantage of their presence there, and turned it to His glory. Ptolemy Philadelphus founded the Alexandrian Library, and it was he who encouraged the translation of the Old Testament into Greek. Thus the prophecies concerning the promised Messiah were put into the universal language nearly three hundred years before the birth of Christ. The world might become intoxicated with the Greek philosophy, but God left man without excuse by placing the word of life in the household tongue of the nations. Satan may scheme, and his agents on earth may be wise, but they can do nothing against the truth without in that very act promoting the truth. While the dark wings of paganism were drawing closer and closer about the world, to shut out if possible the light of heaven, the word of God, as a lighted candle, was shining under that darkness, and proclaiming the advent of the Desire of all ages.

The first verses in the history of Greece (Dan. 11:3-5) bring the student face to face with that country as an intellectual power, and reveal the secret of her strength to be in her language and philosophy. She conquered the world by bringing all minds under her control. It was the plan of the enemy of truth to subjugate minds to a false philosophy; and since this was the scheme upon which he worked in

Greece, it was under this same national influence that the truth which frees the mind was given to the world. How far-reaching, then, were the purposes of God.

Another great principle lies side by side with the one given in those first verses. This second, which is hidden in verses six to thirteen, has to do with the working out of those same principles through the government as a channel. The kingdom of Alexander resolved itself into two divisions, a northern and a southern. Both were Hellenized, but the northern represented more truly the Greek principles, while the southern division was strongly tinctured with the old Egyptian ideas of both government and religion. It was the northern division which carried forward the work of the prophecy as symbolized by the leopard and the rough goat, and it was from the northern division that the little horn of Daniel eight proceeded. Consequently it must be right to conclude that it is the Greco-Syriac division, rather than the Egyptian division, that will do the work of which Alexander was the forerunner. Nevertheless there will be throughout the ages until the end of time a strength rising from the south and opposing the northern power. This will again be seen in the Mohammedan work of the Middle Ages during the su-

2 Cor. 10:4, 5.

For all the Athenians and strangers which were there spent their time in nothing else, but either to tell, or to hear some new thing.

Acts 17:21.

For the Jews require a sign, and the Greeks seek after wisdom: But we preach Christ crucified, unto the Jews a stumblingblock, and unto the Greeks foolishness; But unto them which are called, both Jews and Greeks, Christ the power of God, and the wisdom of God. Because the foolishness of God is wiser than men; and the weakness of God is stronger than men.

1 Cor. 1:22-25.

The king of the south shall be strong, and one of his princes; and he shall be strong above him, and have dominion; his dominion shall be a great dominiom.

Dan. 11:5.

Out of one of them came forth a little horn, which waxed exceeding great, toward the south; and toward the east, and toward the pleasant land.

Dan. 8:9.

Thou art of purer eyes than to behold evil, and canst not look on iniquity: wherefore lookest thou upon them that deal treacherously, and holdest thy tongue when the wicked devoureth the man that is more righteous than he? And makest men as the fishes of the sea, as the creeping things, that have no ruler over them? They take up all of them with the angle, they catch them in their net, and gather them in their drag: therefore they rejoice and are glad. Therefore they sacrifice unto their net, and burn incense unto their drag; because by them their portion is fat, and their meat plenteous.

Hab. 1:13-16.

Rev. 9:1-21.

And I say unto you, That many shall come from the east and west, and shall sit down with Abraham, and Isaac, and Jacob, in the kingdom of heaven.   Matt. 8:11.

Out of the south cometh the whirlwind: and cold out of the north. . . Fair weather cometh out of the north: with God is terrible majesty.
Job 37:9, 22.

I saw the beast, and the kings of the earth, and their armies, gathered together to make war against him that sat on the horse, and against his army.   Rev. 19:19.

He gathered them together into a place called in the Hebrew tongue Armageddon.
Rev. 16:16.

6. And in the end of years they shall join themselves together; for the king's daughter of the south shall come to the king of the north to make an agreement: but she shall not retain the power of the arm; neither shall he stand, nor his arm: but she shall be given up, and they that brought her, and he that begat her, and he that strengthened her in these times.   Dan. 11:6.

They shall mingle themselves with the seed of men: but they shall not cleave one to another, even as iron is not mixed with clay.
Dan. 2:43.

And I say unto you, Whosoever shall put away his wife, except it be for fornication, and shall marry another, committeth adultery: and whoso marrieth her which is put away doth commit adultery.   Matt. 19:9.

The curse of the LORD is in the house of the wicked: but he blesseth the habitation of the just.
Prov. 3:33.

Jealousy is cruel as the grave: the coals thereof are coals of fire, which hath a most vehement flame.
Song of Sol. 8:6.

7. But out of a branch of her roots shall one stand up in his estate, which shall come with an army, and shall enter into the fortress of the king of the north, and shall deal against them, and shall prevail.

premacy of the fourth beast. But we must watch the working out of the principle during the life of the third kingdom, as that is introductory in itself to the future work.

History reveals the fact that the greatest strength in government is found in those powers whose territory extends from east to west, and [220] that nations which try to govern territory extending far to the north and the south have trouble. It is in recognition of this fact that each universal empire has progressed mainly from east to west, and each succeeding kingdom has gone farther to the west than the preceding one. This continues until the globe is encircled, and all the kings of the earth finally meet in the great battle of Armageddon.

In spite of this controlling principle among nations, and in face of the decree of the Holy Watcher, the north and the south attempted to unite. Worldly policy of intermarriage was followed, and as Spurrell renders verse 6, "After some years they [the kings of the north and the south] shall be associated; for the daughter of the king of the south [Berenice, daughter of Ptolemy Philadelphus] shall come to the king of the north [Antiochus Theos] to make agreements." Antiochus put away his lawful wife, Laodice, in order to marry Berenice, and the results of this transgression of God's law are given by the.pen of Inspiration: "The arm shall not retain its strength, neither shall their offspring be established; but she shall be given up, and her attendants, and her child, and her supporters at those times." Human pen can not make the history any plainer than did Gabriel in relating it to Daniel nearly two hundred years before it occurred. Berenice lost favor in the eyes of Antiochus Theos, who thereupon recalled Laodice. The jealous wife then caused Antiochus to be poisoned, and placed her own son on the throne. Through her influence, also, Berenice, her child by Antiochus, and her Egyptian attendants [221] and supporters, were all murdered.

This aroused the royal house of Egypt, and a brother of Berenice advanced into the territory of Antiochus with a large army. "He shall rule within the fortifications of the kings of the north, and shall war against them and shall prevail." Ptolemy Euergetes, son of Ptolemy Philadelphus, is here described. He not only invaded Syria, but went to Babylon, where he found some of the Egyptian gods and molten images which Cambyses had captured during his war in Egypt. These Ptolemy returned, and for this was named Euergetes (benefactor) by his grateful people. It is said that he carried to Egypt forty thousand talents of silver and many vessels of silver and gold. Ptolemy Euergetes then returned to his own kingdom, where he outlived Antiochus Callinicus, the son of Laodice.

8. And shall also carry captives into Egypt their gods, with their princes, and with their precious vessels of silver and of gold; and he shall continue more years than the king of the north.
Dan 11:7, 8.

Yet I am the Lord thy God from the land of Egypt, and thou shalt know no god but me: for there is no Saviour beside me.   Hosea 13:4.

So the king of the south shall come into his kingdom, and shall return into his own land.
Dan. 11:9.

But trouble did not cease then. There was a natural jealousy and antipathy between the north and the south. Ptolemy Euergetes held much of Syria. On the death of Antiochus Callinicus, two sons of Callinicus undertook to regain the lost territory, and to redeem the honor of their father. The first was weak and inefficient; the younger, Antiochus Magnus, who took the throne in the course of a few years, was stronger. He is the "one" who advanced speedily, regaining much of the lost territory.

Prov. 27:4.
Amos 3:9, 10.

About the time of the accession of Antiochus Magnus to the Syrian throne, Ptolemy Philopater took the throne in Egypt. He manifested no disposition to invade the territory of the king of the north, being indolent, and a great lover [222] of luxury and ease, but he was aroused by the prospects of an invasion of Egypt, his own throne being threatened by Antiochus Magnus. Antiochus was supported by an immense army, but it fell into the hands of Ptolemy Philopater, who, elated by his victory, returned to his capital to feast. Although he had cast down ten thousand soldiers, yet he did not profit by the victory. Nothing was gained; it was but a merciless slaughter of human beings a contest for brute supremacy, which is hateful in the sight of God and man. The difference is striking between such warfare and the progress of the mighty generals whom God used to establish kingdoms and punish kings.

10. But his sons shall be stirred up, and shall assemble a multitude of great forces: and one shall certainly come, and overflow, and pass through: then shall he return, and be stirred up, even to his fortress.
11. And the king of the south shall be moved with choler, and shall come forth and fight with him, even with the king of the north: and he shall set forth a great multitude; but the multitude shall be given into his hand.
12. And when he hath taken away the multitude, his heart shall be lifted up; and he shall cast down many ten thousands: but he shall not be strengthened by it.
Dan. 11:10-12.
Now the Egyptians are men, and not God; and their horses flesh, and not spirit. When the LORD shall stretch out his hand, both he that helpeth shall fall, and he that is holpen shall fall down, and they all shall fail together.
Isa 31:3.

Every man is brutish by his knowledge; every founder is confounded by the graven image: for his molten image is falsehood, and there is no breath in them. They are vanity, the work of errors: in the time of their visitation they shall perish.
Jer. 51:17-18.

Ptolemy Philopater did even worse things, for in self-esteem he entered Jerusalem, and attempted to profane the

2 Chron. 26:16-23.

Woe to the rebellious children, saith the LORD, that take counsel, but not of me; and that cover with a covering, but not of my spirit, that they may add sin to sin: That walk to go down into Egypt, and have not asked at my mouth; to strengthen themselves in the strength of Pharaoh, and to trust in the shadow of Egypt! Therefore shall the strength of Pharaoh be your shame, and the trust in the shadow of Egypt your confusion.

Isa. 30:1-3.

Woe to them that go down to Egypt for help; and stay on horses, and trust in chariots, because they are many; and in horsemen, because they are very strong; but they look not unto the Holy One of Israel, neither seek the LORD! Yet he also is wise, and will bring evil, and will not call back his words: but will arise against the house of the evildoers, and against the help of them that work iniquity.

Isa. 31:1-2.

Neverthless God did not choose the people for the place's sake, but the place for the people's sake.

2 Maccabees 5:19.

Deut. 28:11, 12.

And God gave Solomon wisdom and understanding exceeding much, and largeness of heart, even as the sand that is on the sea shore. And Solomon's wisdom excelled the wisdom of all the children of the east country, and all the wisdom of Egypt. For he was wiser than all men; than Ethan the Ezrahite, and Heman, and Chalcol, and Darda, the sons of Mahol: and his fame was in all nations round about. And he spake three thousand proverbs: and his songs were a thousand and five. And he spake of trees, from the cedar tree that is in Lebanon even unto the hyssop that springeth out of the wall: he spake also of beasts, and of fowl, and of creeping things, and of fishes. And there came of all people to hear the wisdom of Solomon, from all kings of the earth, which had heard of his wisdom.

1 Kings 4:29-34.

2 Tim. 4:3, 4.

13. For the king of the north shall return, and shall set forth a multitude greater than the former, and shall certainly come after certain years with a great army and with much riches.

Dan. 11:13.

And in those times there shall many stand up against the king of the south: also the robbers of thy people shall exalt themselves to establish the vision; but they shall fall.

Dan. 11:14.

temple by himself offering sacrifice. The restraint offered by the priests so incensed him that he began war against them, and history states that between forty and sixty thousand Jews, who then lived in Egypt, fell by the sword. Those Jews who had sought Egypt either for protection or for the advantages of her schools and libraries, withdrew from the sheltering hand of their God, and the time came when they felt the wrath of the enemy. Through all these struggles the nation whom God had chosen might have stood as a beacon on a hill, instead of being trampled upon by every army in its marches between Egypt and Syria. Nay, more, the location of the Jews in Palestine and her capital was by divine appointment. They were at the gateway of the nations, and might have held the balance of power. Had they held aloft [223] the word of God, all nations would have bowed before their kings and paid tribute into their treasury. It was so in the days of Solomon; it might have been repeated in the days of Greek history.

Alexander's act of reverence when he met the company of priests at Jerusalem should have been an object lesson to all Judea of what God by His Spirit would cause all nations to do. But so blinded by Greek teaching were those Jewish leaders, even at that time, that they failed to see this. Instead of flocking to Alexandria for the wisdom of Greece, nations *should* have sent their youth to schools of the prophets at Jerusalem, and scholars of the world *should* have sought wisdom from those who knew the God [224] of wisdom. But it was not so. Israel then was as the church of to-day. Instead of leading by virtue of the spiritual life, she sought the wisdom of Egypt and Greece.

Peace was finally concluded between Philo- pater and Antiochus Magnus, which lasted fourteen years, until the death of Ptolemy. Ptolemy Philopater was succeeded by his son Ptolemy Epiphanes, who was in his minority. Antiochus Magnus took advantage of this seeming weakness in Egyptian affairs, and made extensive preparations to invade Egypt with the design of conquering the entire dominion of the Ptolemies. But the Most High ruleth in the kingdoms

Ptolemy entered
Jerusalem, and attempted
to profane the temple by
himself offering sacrifice.

of men, and Antiochus was brought to realize that there was another power on earth as well as in heaven.

In the fourteenth verse the voice of the fourth beast is heard; Rome placed itself on the side of the helpless king, and Antiochus found his ambition thwarted. The life of the Greek kingdom was spent. There were still many years of struggle, but it was a struggle for existence, not for added territory. But what Greece would not gain in territory she did gain as a teacher of nations, and although she finally lost all territorial supremacy, though, like the kingdom of Nebuchadnezzar, the tree was cut down, yet the roots remain unto this day. More than once, as an intellectual power, has Greece arisen.

For the time will come when they will not endure sound doctrine; but after their own lusts shall they heap to themselves teachers, having itching ears; And they shall turn away their ears from the truth, and shall be turned unto fables.

2 Tim. 4:3, 4.

As concerning the rest of the beasts, they had their dominion taken away: yet their lives were prolonged for a season and time.　　　　Dan. 7:12.

Now go, write it before them in a table, and note it in a book, that it may be for the time to come for ever and ever: That this is a rebellious people, lying children, children that will not hear the law of the LORD: Which say to the seers, See not;

and to the prophets, Prophesy not unto us right things, speak unto us smooth things, prophesy deceits.   Isa. 30:8-10.

Casting down imaginations, and every high thing that exalteth itself against the knowledge of God, and bringing into captivity every thought to the obedience of Christ.   2 Cor. 10:5.

From a child thou hast known the holy scriptures, which are able to make thee wise unto salvation through faith which is in Christ Jesus.
2 Tim. 3:15-17.
If the trumpet give an uncertain sound, who shall prepare himself to the battle?
1 Cor. 14:8.

Let us therefore fear, lest, a promise being left us of entering into his rest, any of you should seem to come short of it.   Heb. 4:1.

She had a sister called Mary, which also sat at Jesus' feet, and heard his word.
Luke 10:39.

Through faith we understand that the worlds were framed by the word of God, so that things which are seen were not made of things which do appear.   Heb. 11:3.

Without faith it is impossible to please him: for he that cometh to God must believe that he is, and that he is a rewarder of them that diligently seek him.   Heb. 11:6.

Whatsoever is not of faith is sin.
Rom. 14:23.

It is the spirit that quickeneth; the flesh profiteth nothing: the words that I speak unto you, they are spirit, and they are life.   John 6:63.
Stand fast therefore in the liberty wherewith Christ hath made us free, and be not entangled again with the yoke of bondage.   Gal. 5:1.

Sanctify them through thy truth: thy word is truth.   John 17:17.

Throughout the intellectual world she has votaries bowing before her shrine—the mind of man. Her philosophy is to-day studied under the guise of modem writers; her ideas are instilled into the minds of children, from the kindergarten to the [225] university, and students are graduated from the schools of the land knowing much more of the mythology of Greece than they do of the religion of Jesus Christ; better acquainted with Greek heroes than with the Man of Calvary. Greek learning still rules the world, and it will until the setting up of the everlasting kingdom of God—till the stone cut out without hands shall fill the earth.

As the Jews during the days of Alexander and his successors were without excuse, so the Israel of to-day has set before it the wisdom of the Eternal in contrast with the wisdom of Greece. And the message is, "Choose ye this day" at which shrine ye will bow. Sitting at the feet of Jesus, learning of Him, taking His word as the authentic history of the world, His truth as the interpreter of nature, will insure eternal life. Accepting the writings of men, human speculations regarding the history of the world, its creation, its age, placing a human interpretation upon the works of nature, and seeking to find out by experiment and speculation what must be known by faith,—this brings death; for it leads away from Christ, the center of the universe, the source of all wisdom, the great drawing power of creation. The first is the system of God, of which faith is the motive power; the second is the Greek system, which exalts human reasoning. One may not bow down to the idols of Egypt, nor drink of the wines of Babylon, but if he is entrapped by the more pleasing sophistries of Greece, his fate is the same in the end.

For this reason Eternal Truth has shone along the pathway of men in all ages to guard [226] against the enemy. In these last days, when all the evil of the past is renewed and presented to man in all its varied forms, then it is that Greek philosophy and skepticism come forth in full force. A heart filled with truth is the only safeguard against error.

CHAPTER 15

THE FOURTH KINGDOM

DANIEL 11:14-22

THE fourteenth verse of the eleventh chapter of Daniel, as we have seen, introduces a new power. Gabriel, in narrating the events connected with the history of Greece, brought that empire down to the time when the southern division was in the hands of a child, Ptolemy Epiphanes, and when two men,, Philip of Macedon and Antiochus of Syria, although jealous of each other, were willing to unite their strength in order to subdue Egypt. From a political point of view a general weakness prevailed in the once mighty empire of Alexander. Without noticing the details, the angel of prophecy speaks of the first appearance of the fourth kingdom as it comes in contact with the divisions of the third kingdom, Greece. This fourth kingdom is thus introduced: "The violent opposers [228] of thy people shall exalt themselves that the vision may stand." (Spurrell.)

Since every word is divinely given, there is a significance in the very introduction of what is about to become the mightiest kingdom of the earth, and at the same time the greatest enemy which the people of God have ever had to meet. Daniel had seen this kingdom before. In the vision of the seventh chapter, Rome was represented as a beast too terrible to name. Its characteristics were to devour, to stamp in pieces, and to break. During a part of its history it should

14. And in those times there shall many stand up against the king of the south: also the robbers of thy people shall exalt themselves to establish the vision; but they shall fall.
Dan. 11:14.

Mal. 3:5.
Prov. 11:21.

The perverseness of transgressors shall destroy them.   Prov. 11:3.

They would none of my counsel: they despised all my reproof. Therefore shall they eat of the fruit of their own way, and be filled with their own devices.   Prov. 1:30, 31.

Dan. 11:14.

It is the spirit that quickeneth; the flesh profiteth nothing: the words that I speak unto you, they are spirit, and they are life.   John 6:63.

The words of the LORD are pure words: as silver tried in a furnace of earth, purified seven times.
Ps. 12:6.

Dan. 2:40-43.
Dan. 7:7, 19.
Dan. 7:25.

Then I would know the truth of the fourth beast, which was diverse from all the others, exceeding dreadful, whose teeth were of iron, and his nails of brass; which devoured, brake in pieces, and stamped the residue with his feet.
Dan. 7:19.

And out of one of them came forth a little horn, which waxed exceeding great, toward the south, and toward the east, and toward the pleasant land. . . And in the latter time of their kingdom, when the transgressors are come to the full, a king of fierce countenance, and understanding dark sentences, shall stand up. And his power shall be mighty, but not by his own power: and he shall destroy wonderfully, and shall prosper, and practise, and shall destroy the mighty and the holy people. And through his policy also he shall cause craft to prosper in his hand; and he shall magnify himself in his heart, and by peace shall destroy many: he shall also stand up against the Prince of princes; but he shall be broken without hand.   Dan. 8:9, 23-25.

Jer. 51:34, 35.

In those times there shall many stand up against the king of the south also the children of robbers shalt exalt themselves to establish the vision; but they shall fall.   Dan. 11:14.

For whatsoever things were written aforetime were written for our learning, that we through patience and comfort of the scriptures might have hope.   Rom. 15:4.

It is the land of graven images, and they are mad upon their idols.   Jer. 50:38.

The Babylonians came to her into the bed of love, and they defiled her with their whoredom, and she was polluted with them, and her mind was alienated from them.   Eze. 23:14-18.

And upon her forehead was a name written, MYSTERY, BABYLON THE GREAT, THE MOTHER OF HARLOTS AND ABOMINATIONS OF THE EARTH.   Rev. 17:5.
Dan. 6:12.
But the prince of the kingdom of Persia withstood me one and twenty days: but, lo, Michael, one of the chief princes, came to help me; and I remained there with the kings of Persia.   Dan. 10:13.
And hath made of one blood all nations of men to dwell on all the face of the earth, and hath determined the times before appointed, and the bounds of their habitation.   Acts 17:26.

The Greeks seek after wisdom.
                    1 Cor. 1:22.

speak great words against the Most High, it should wear out the saints of God, and think to change even His laws. So troubled was the prophet over this view in his first vision that he sought for a special explanation of this fourth kingdom.

In his next vision the fourth kingdom was again shown under the symbol of a little horn, which sprang from one of the divisions of Alexander's kingdom. In this view Rome was presented in no milder form than in the previous vision. It was as a king with a "fierce countenance," "understanding dark sentences," having mighty power—a power even more than human. It was to be a scheming, underhanded government, and its most cruel practices were seen to be against God's chosen people. Yea, against Christ, the Prince of princes, the Prince of the covenant, this power should stand up. Gabriel spoke of the robbers who should exalt themselves to establish the vision—that is, to fulfill the description just given.

Putting all these thoughts together, it will be seen that Rome, the fourth kingdom, the successor [229] of Greece, would be noted for the decisive policy which it maintained. Each nation in the prophetic chain had some strong feature, and its history is recorded as an object lesson to the world, as in the days of its life it had been an object lesson to the watching multitudes of other worlds. Babylon was an example of Satan's power to establish a *religion* which counterfeited the heavenly worship. The result was the basest form of idolatry, a fornication which makes her the personification, among Bible writers, of all vileness. Medo-Persia was a type of Oriental despotism. "The law of the Medes and Persians changeth not;" this was a proverb among the nations. But it was with the kings of this nation that Gabriel and Michael wrought; it was the heads of this despotism who were kept in check by the power of the King of kings.

Greece was altogether different from the preceding two, and instead of gaining recognition because of the form of religion or government, she gained control of the world, by the power of her intellect. With her education and philosophy she gained a foothold which no other nation ever held. When Babylon was overthrown and Medo-Persia was no more, Greece lived on in the *minds* of men.

But the fourth kingdom was "diverse from all the others." As represented to John, Rome, the beast of Rev. 13:2, combined the characteristics of the leopard, the bear, and the lion. There were united the false system of the religion of ancient Babylon, the governmental tyranny of Medo-Persia, and the mixture of good and evil in the intellectual culture of Greece. When the religion, the educational system, or [230] intellectual statutes, and the governmental history of a nation are given, there remains little else worth relating. So in the one nation, Rome, is embodied the strength of all the previous nations. What wonder that it was a terrible and dreadful nation, and that except the time of its supremacy should be shortened there should be none left to witness for the truth. It is to this power that we are introduced in the fourteenth verse of the eleventh chapter of Daniel.

(For all the Athenians and strangers which were there spent their time in nothing else, but either to tell, or to hear some new thing)
Acts 17:16-21.

And the beast which I saw was like unto a leopard, and his feet were as the feet of a bear, and his mouth as the mouth of a lion: and the dragon gave him his power, and his seat, and great authority.
Rev. 13:2.

The king that faithfully judgeth the poor, his throne shall be established for ever.
Prov 29:14.

And except those days should be shortened, there should no flesh be saved: but for the elect's sake those days shall be shortened.
Matt. 24:22.

Righteousness exalteth a nation: but sin is a reproach to any people.
Prov. 14:34.

It was in the year 201 B. C. that the child, Ptolemy Epiphanes, fell heir to the throne of Egypt, and the kings of Macedon and Syria planned his overthrow and the division of his empire. It was then that Rome arose to promi-

The way of man is froward and strange: but as for the pure, his work is right.
Prov. 21:8.

I stood upon the sand of the sea, and saw a beast rise up out of the sea, having seven heads and ten horns, and upon his horns ten crowns, and upon his heads the name of blasphemy.
Rev 13:1.

Is this your joyous city, whose antiquity is of ancient days? her own feet shall carry her afar off to sojourn.   Isa. 23:7.

Rome like other nations had a history, long before its connection with the people of God, at which time it is noticed in prophecy. Babylon dates from the tower of Babel which Ninrod and others built.

Dan. 11:14 [margin].
Rev. 13:2.

And the fourth kingdom shall be strong as iron: forasmuch as iron breaketh in pieces and subdueth all things: and as iron that breaketh all these, shall it break in pieces and bruise.   Dan. 2:40.

This matter is by the decree of the watchers, and the demand by the word of the holy ones: to the intent that the living may know that the most High ruleth in the kingdom of men, and giveth it to whomsoever he will, and setteth up over it the basest of men.   Dan. 4:17.

Ps. 22:27, 28.

Thou sealest up the sum, full of wisdom, and perfect in beauty.   Eze. 28:12.

Ps. 105:5.
We can do nothing against the truth, but for the truth.   2 Cor. 13:8.

And in the days of these kings shall the God of heaven set up a kingdom.   Dan. 2:44.

And the beast was taken, and with him the false prophet that wrought miracles before him...These both were cast alive into a lake of fire burning with brimstone.   Rev. 19:20.

Where the word of a king is, there is power: and who may say unto him, What doest thou?
                                                Eccl. 8:4.
The governor answered and said unto them, Whether of the twain will ye that I release unto you? They said, Barabbas.   Mat 27:21:.

nence before the prophet's eye. But Rome had already been in existence for years, and during [231] those years had been accumulating strength to enable her to enter the arena with a bound when the proper time should come. The traditional history of Rome dates as far back as the middle of the eighth century before Christ. That was before the days of Nebuchadnezzar and the glories of Babylon. In the days when Isaiah began to prophesy, then Rome was founded. It was said to be the home of a band of robbers and outlaws, and one of the first acts was the theft of the women of a neighboring city as wives for these early settlers. So if Romans are called the children of robbers, the character can not be denied. The Romans were a stalwart, sturdy race, and from the first began the development of a strong central government. In this undertaking men were aided by the prince of this world, the devil himself: for the dragon, that old serpent, called the devil and Satan, gave the fourth beast "his power, and his seat, and great authority."

The force of all history is lost unless the student recognizes each nation as an actor in the great plan of redemption—one of the participants in the great controversy between Christ and Satan. As the plans of the arch enemy had failed to carry in the history of Babylon, Medo-Persia and Greece, he now attempted with redoubled vigor to thwart the plans of God. He chose for this purpose the seven-hilled city. His plans were deep laid, and the structure that he reared was builded on a firm foundation. Like a lighthouse off some rocky coast, the great planner hoped it would stand the mighty dashings of the waves of truth. It was his last, his supreme effort, for it is this kingdom in one [232] of its manifestations which stands until the end of time.

In its earliest days Rome was ruled by kings, but it was impossible for a Western king to imitate the customs of the Oriental monarchies. Greek governments spanned the gulf between early despotism and the liberality of more modern Western nations. There were two classes of men in Rome, and they both demanded representation in the government. At the end of two hundred and fifty years the kings were dethroned, and consuls substituted. Two consuls from the 'wealthy class, the patricians, held the reins of government. For the next two centuries there was a struggle between patricians and plebeians for equal rights. The principles of republicanism were struggling for birth. Gradually the patricians lost power, until at last the government rested in the hands of the people—that is citizens of Rome. But there were conquered cities, especially in the peninsula of Italy. "Roman dominion in Italy was a dominion of a city over cities." Finally rights of citizenship were granted to most of these.

God's government is a representative government, and while He sits as King of kings, He bears sway by common consent, and His subjects from all the worlds have representatives in the councils of heaven. Satan, as prince of this world, was a representative in those days in that council. In Rome he attempted to counterfeit that phase of the divine government.

It was as a republic that Rome began her career as a conquering nation. Her constitution was the result of a gradual growth of two [233] centuries. Having her authority recognized throughout Italy, of which Rome was the center, she began acquiring territory by force of arms. Carthage, a rival city on the south of the Mediterranean, was the first point of attack, and for one hundred years Rome fought for supremacy. It was a bitter struggle, which could end in nothing less than the annihilation of one of the contending parties. Ridpath aptly expresses the policy of the government when he says. "They [the Romans] took what they could and then took the remainder."

During the years when Rome hovered over Carthage, like an eagle ready to descend upon its prey, she was always carrying on wars of aggression in other directions. Both the West and the East were invaded. Spain was made a subjected province; all the citizens were taxed; the silver and gold mines, the wealth of that county, were confiscated as state property, and no city was allowed to fortify itself without the consent of Rome. This was so-called republicanism—the equal rights of men—as understood and practiced by Rome.

The rich man's wealth is his strong city: the destruction of the poor is their poverty.
Prov 10:15.

But ye have despised the poor. Do not rich men oppress you, and draw you before the judgment seats?
James 2:6.

The rich ruleth over the poor, and the borrower is servant to the lender. Prov. 22:7.

Acts 21:39.

And the woman which thou sawest is that great city, which reigneth over the kings of the earth.
Rev. 17:18.

Now there was a day when the sons of God came to present themselves before the LORD, and Satan came also among them. Job 1:6.

Hereafter I will not talk much with you: for the prince of this world cometh, and hath nothing in me. John 14:30.

15. So the king of the north shall come, and cast up a mount, and take the most fenced cities: and the arms of the south shall not withstand, neither his chosen people, neither shall there be any strength to withstand.
Dan. 11:15.

Which waxed exceeding great, toward the south, and toward the east, and toward the pleasant land.
Dan. 8:9.

There is a generation, whose teeth are as swords, and their jaw teeth as knives, to devour the poor from off the earth, and the needy from among men.
Prov. 30:14.

Hab. 1:8.
Javan, Tubal, and Meshech, they were thy merchants: they traded the persons of men and vessels of brass in thy market.   Ezek. 27:13.

Through his policy also he shall cause draft to prosper in his hand.
Dan. 8:25.

All this have I seen, and applied my heart unto every work that is done under the sun: there is a time wherein one man ruleth over another to his own hurt.   Eccl. 8:9.

For man also knoweth not his time: as the fishes that are taken in an evil net, and as the birds that are caught in the snare; so are the sons of men snared in an evil time, when it falleth suddenly upon them.   Eccl. 9:12.

Render therefore to all their dues: tribute to whom tribute is due; custom to whom custom; fear to whom fear; honour to whom honour.
Rom 13:6-7.

Matt. 17:24-27.

Woe to thee, O land, when thy king is a child.
Eccl. 10:16.

Therefore also will I make thee sick in smiting thee, in making thee desolate because of thy sins.
Micah 6:13.

And out of one of them came forth a little horn, which waxed exceeding great, toward the south, and toward the east, and toward the pleasant land.
Dan. 8:9.

When the righteous are in authority, the people rejoice: but when the wicked beareth rule, the people mourn.   Prov. 29:2.

If thou seest the oppression of the poor, and violent perverting of judgment and justice in a province, marvel not at the matter: for he that is higher than the highest regardeth; and there be higher than they.   Eccl. 5:8.

If the Son therefore shall make you free, ye shall be free indeed.   John 8:36

The inhabitants of Corsica and Sardinia were sold in the slave markets of Rome, and so numerous were these slaves, says Livy, that "Sardinians for sale" became a proverbial expression for anything cheap. This also was Roman republicanism. Macedonia and Greece were in a state of turmoil, and Rome interfered. After conferences and wars, independence was proclaimed to all Greeks. This was one of the policy schemes by which the republic worked, but liberty lasted for only a brief space. A few years later all those Macedonians who were able [234] to govern themselves were carried to Rome, while those left were inexperienced men who soon played into the hands of the Roman senate. One hundred and fifty thousand Greeks were sold as slaves, and the treasures taken paid all expenses contracted during the war. So high was the tribute exacted from subjected provinces that it relieved Roman citizens of all taxes for future wars. This was independence as granted subjected provinces by the republic of Rome.

The family of Antiochus was still bearing sway in the Eastern world. It was Antiochus IV who proposed to unite with Philip V of Macedon against the young king of Egypt when Rome interfered. But mild interference was never enough for Rome, although she sometimes assumed to play that role for a time. Antiochus the Great in the single battle of Magnesia (B. C. 190) lost all his conquests in Asia Minor. He was obliged to pay three thousand talents, and an annual subsidy of one thousand talents, for twelve years.

Rome controlled Egypt because the education of the heir to the throne was in the hands of a Roman senator, and a Roman army stood ready to defend the country against all attacks from the north or east. Roman power thus encircled the Mediterranean.

The liberty granted to conquered nations was a myth. Rome was a republic only in name. It was as impossible for Rome to grant liberty to her dependencies as it would be for Satan himself to manifest the attributes of God. Any nation, that departs from the principles of liberty of conscience, it matters not what its pretensions, [235] nor the wording of its constitution, nor the will of some of its people, will find it impossible to maintain a republic other than in name. This is true also in individual experience. Liberty is known only when Christ is enthroned in the heart.

There are always certain other results which accompany wars of conquest. For instance, this policy demands a large army. In the early days of Rome the army was made up of men who left the plow and the shop for the defense of their country, and when war was over, returned to their homes and their trades; but as war became a regular business, generals found it to their advantage to keep their soldiers in readiness. The army was not so much a servant of the state as an attache to the person of some successful general, whom it regarded as its patron. The way was thus open for military despotism, and Rome experienced that form of government more than once.

The senate, supposed to represent the people, became a corporation greedy for gain and enriched by the spoils of war.. Senatorial favorites received rich provinces to govern, and bribery was almost universally practiced. "The power of the purse" was in the hands of the senate alone. To their influence may be added the constant and steady growth of the cities, and the decline of the rural population, a practice always ruinous to republicanism, and one always encouraged by a false system of education and religion.

Tradition made the Romans the descendants of the god of war, Mars, the Bruiser, and they were true to the character. [236] Said the inspired penman, "It shall break in pieces and bruise." Christ came to Rome as the Prince of peace, the binder up of wounds, the healer of the broken-hearted.

The religion of Rome was secondary to its government. That is, the state was the one allabsorbing institution. A man in Rome was great, not because of any character he bore or deed he had done, but for the simple fact that he was a Roman citizen. Name took the place of character. Here is seen the reverse of truth. With God it is character which gives the name; with Rome it was name independent of character.

Although religion was subservient to the state, yet the form of religion in Rome played an important part in its

Woe to the multitude of many people, which make a noise like the noise of the seas; and to the rushing of nations, that make a rushing like the rushing of mighty waters! The nations shall rush like the rushing of many waters: but God shall rebuke them, and they shall flee far off, and shall be chased as the chaff of the mountains before the wind, and like a rolling thing before the whirlwind. Isa. 17:12-13.

God hath spoken once; twice have I heard this; that power belongeth unto God. Ps. 62:11.

Woe unto them that draw iniquity with cords of vanity, and sin as it were with a cart rope. Isa. 5:18.

He that loveth silver shall not be satisfied with silver; nor he that loveth abundance with increase: this is also vanity. Eccl. 5:10.

His sons walked not in his ways, but turned aside after lucre, and took bribes, and perverted judgment. 1 Sam. 8:3.

They that trust in their wealth, and boast themselves in the multitude of their riches; None of them can by any means redeem his brother, nor give to God a ransom for him. Ps. 49:6-7.

Moreover the profit of the earth is for all: the king himself is served by the field. Eccl. 5:9.

It shall break in pieces and consume all these kingdoms, and it shall stand for ever. Dan. 2:44.

He hath sent me to heal the broken hearted. Luke 4:18.

Acts 22:25-29.
Acts 23:27.
Acts 16:37, 38.

And he said, Thy name shall be called no more Jacob, but Israel: for as a prince hast thou power with God and with men, and hast prevailed. Gen. 32:28.

The dragon gave him his power, and his seat, and great authority. Rev. 13:2.

Now these be the last words of David. . . The anointed of the God of Jacob, and the sweet psalmist of Israel, said.
2 Sam. 23:1.

1 Cor. 8:5.

Who changed the truth of God into a lie, and worshipped and served the creature more than the Creator, who is blessed for ever. Amen.
Rom. 1:25.

Now therefore send, and gather to me all Israel unto mount Carmel, and the prophets of Baal four hundred and fifty, and the prophets of the groves four hundred, which eat at Jezebel's table.
1 Kings 18:19.

And as Paul was to be led into the castle, he said unto the chief captain, May I speak unto thee? Who said, Canst thou speak Greek?
Acts 21:37.

A wise servant shall have rule over a son that causeth shame, and shall have part of the inheritance among the brethren.
Prov. 17:2.

Let both grow together until the harvest: and in the time of harvest I will say to the reapers, Gather ye together first the tares, and bind them in bundles to burn them: but gather the wheat into my barn.
Matt. 13:30.

Gen. 2:17.

There is a way that seemeth right unto a man, but the end thereof are the ways of death.
Prov. 16:25.

Thou shalt remember all the way which the LORD thy God led thee these forty years in the wilderness, to humble thee, and to prove thee, to know what was in thine heart, whether thou wouldest keep his commandments, or no.
Deut. 8:2.

I know that, whatsoever God doeth, it shall be for ever: nothing can be put to it, nor any thing taken from it: and God doeth it, that men should fear before him.
Eccl. 3:14.

history, especially in the second or papal phase. Since the papacy was a continuation of paganism, it is necessary to notice its leading features. There were no sweet singers, as David the Bethlehemite; the nature study of the Greeks was also lacking. There were gods many and lords many, but a sternness characterized all worship. Man was dei- - fled and canonized. The very name Augustus, which was applied to a long line of emperors, meant *divine*.

In the Roman temples a body of priests performed the sacred rites, but they were appointed by the state. The highest religious officer during the life of paganism was the Pontifex Maximus, the pope of paganism, and he was a civil officer. The religious hierarchy, consisting of priests, augurs, vestals, and the Pontifex Maximus, paved the way for the papal hierarchy of later days, just as the transition from republicanism to imperialism [237] opened the gate for papal supremacy.

In literature and education Rome borrowed largely from Greece, so that the intellectual supremacy of that nation must be traced to Greece, although the man of learning was often a slave sold in the markets of his captors.

It was, however, the education which prevailed in Greece, and which was copied by Rome, that trained a class of citizens for warfare, for tryanny, and for the papacy.

Roman law is extolled as the basis of all civil law to-day. It was developed gradually as before stated, and the wheat of truth was mingled with the tares of error. It was good and evil, like the tree of which Adam partook in the garden. This is seen in latter-day applications [238] of those laws. The Greek worship of mind or reason, applied to Roman love of law, made the lawyer of Rome the forefather of that class of reasoners who to-day sway the world by argument rather than by the rule of justice.

Satan has but one plan—that is the development of sin; God has but one—the unfolding of truth and love. All history is an object lesson, showing how God thwarts the thousand ways by which the devil tries to carry out his plans, and national history is but individual experience on a large scale.

Satan has but one plan—
that is
the development of sin.

God has but one plan—
the unfolding
of love and truth.

Students very often read the story of nations, forgetting that they have before them a picture of their own lives. National history, rather than individual experience, is given in prophecy, because it is like a magnified view thrown on the canvas, revealing details that would be overlooked in the study of one man. It should be remembered that when principles are referred to, such as republicanism, Protestantism, monarchy, papacy, liberty, or oppression, each has an application to man dealing with man, to church members dealing with one another, and to nation dealing with nation.

With these facts in mind, the prophecies of Daniel concerning Rome may be understood. It seems that Gabriel called attention to the fourth kingdom, not at the beginning of its existence, but at the time when all the principles previously set forth were well developed, and in just the stage

When he giveth quietness, who then can make trouble? and when he hideth his face, who then can behold him? whether it be done against a nation, or against a man only. Job 34:29.

Where the Spirit of the Lord is, there is liberty. 2 Cor. 3:17.

But Jesus called them unto him, and said, Ye know that the princes of the Gentiles exercise dominion over them, and they that are great exercise authority upon them. But it shall not be so among you: but whosoever will be great among you, let him be your minister; And whosoever will be chief among you, let him be your servant. Matt. 20:25-27.

I will show thee that which is noted in the Scripture of truth.

Dan. 10:21.

They eat the bread of wickedness, and drink the wine of violence. . . . The way of the wicked is a darkness: they know not at what they stumble.

Prov. 4:17-19.

We wrestle not against flesh and blood, but against principalities, against powers, against the rulers of the darkness of this world, against spiritual wickedness in high places.

Eph. 6:12.

Associate yourselves, O ye people, and ye shall be broken in pieces; and give ear, all ye of far countries: gird yourselves, and ye shall be broken in pieces; gird yourselves, and ye shall be broken in pieces.

Isa. 8:9.

16. *But he that cometh against him shall do according to his own will, and none shall stand before him: and he shall stand in the glorious land, which by his hand shall be consumed.*

Dan. 11:16.

The people of the prince that shall come shall destroy the city and the sanctuary.

Dan. 9:26.

Tell us therefore, What thinkest thou? Is it lawful to give tribute unto Caesar, or not? But Jesus perceived their wickedness, and said, Why tempt ye me, ye hypocrites Shew me the tribute money. And they brought unto him a penny. And he saith unto them, Whose is this image and superscription They say unto him, Caesar's. Then saith he unto them, Render therefore unto Caesar the things which are Caesar's; and unto God the things that are God's.

Matt. 22:17-21.

For so hath the Lord commanded us, saying, I have set thee to be a light of the Gentiles, that thou shouldest be for salvation unto the ends of the earth.

Acts 13:47.

Acts 17:24, 25.

to grow rapidly when the proper environments should be offered. The republic was in reality dead, although its corpse was yet unburied, and men were unwilling to acknowledge that life had really departed. During the [239] transition period between the republic and the full-fledged empire of the twentieth verse, a number of actors took a prominent part. It was a time of severe contest between men to see who could best serve the purpose of the controller of affairs who stood behind the throne of earthly monarchs. As the republic lost power, a corporation composed of Caesar, Pompey, and Crassus took the reins of government. Crassus controlled the money, Pompey had the army, and Caesar was the master mind.

The Roman army, with Pompey as leader, swept through Asia Minor and Syria, and the entire kingdom of the Seleucidae fell at his feet. Antioch and every fortified station of the Eastern empire crumbled as he advanced. Pompey, called upon to decide between rulers of the Jews, entered Jerusalem, and, as in times past, the knowledge of the God of Israel was made known to the nation which was leading the world. Pompey, however, acted very differently from Alexander. He entered the city by force after a siege of three months; the walls were demolished and the Jews put under tribute to the Roman government. Rome now stood "in the glorious land which by his hand shall be consumed." This was in B. C. 63.

The wisdom of God in choosing Palestine as the home of the Jews is recognized more and more as history progresses. There was no mistake in the location, and there was no lowering of the standard set for that nation. In the days of Roman supremacy, as in the days of Solomon, it was the divine will that Israel should be the light of the world. They were entrusted with the sacred oracles of truth, and each nation [240] was brought to them as to a fountain of living water. Had the Hebrew race been true to its appointed duty, the history of the whole world would read differently. Rome came to Jerusalem—came because sent of God, but the well was a cracked and leaky cistern, and the soul-thirst of the nation could not be quenched. As a result, Rome enslaved the Jews: the power of life which repels the enemy was *lacking*.

It was during the rule of the first triumvirate that Egypt, the kingdom of the south, was again entered by Rome. The Roman senate, in whose charge Cleopatra and her brother, Ptolemy Dionysius, had been placed by their father, had requested Pompey to visit Egypt to settle difficulties. Pompey, however, was slain while crossing to the land in a small boat. Caesar entered Alexandria shortly afterward, and espoused the cause of Cleopatra, who had been obliged to flee from the capital. Caesar was victorious over the ruling faction in Alexandria, and before leaving the city, enthroned Cleopatra and graced his triumph in Rome with Arsinoe, a representative of the royal family of the Ptolemies. History states that Caesar spent some nine months in Egypt, which was unusual for this general, as his rapid movements from place to place were one secret of his success.

Cesar as a general stood in a position to accomplish for the fourth kingdom what Nebuchadnezzar, Cyrus, and Alexander had done for the former three, but we have no record that he even acknowledged God as a ruler of nations. He was fascinated and corrupted by the queen of Egypt. The seventeenth verse, which describes [241] a particular event in history, also symbolizes the corrupting influence of Egypt whenever the north came in touch with the south. Egypt was a blight to men and nations alike, from the days of Abraham to Caesar and its influence still lives, a type of sin and bondage.

Leaving Egypt, Caesar passed along the coast of Palestine and Asia Minor, receiving the submission of all peoples, with such rapidity that he sent the famous despatch to Rome, "I came, I saw, I conquered" *(Veni, Vidi, Vici)*. He returned to Rome, where he altered laws, strengthened the senate, settled disturbances in the army, and later brought western Africa, which had revolted, into submission.

Caesar was an organizer as well as a warrior, and displayed greater liberality and breadth of ideas than any previous ruler. Roman franchise was granted to the citizens of many cities hitherto excluded, and all scientific men, of

For my people have committed two evils; they have forsaken me the fountain of living waters, and hewed them out cisterns, broken cisterns, that can hold no water.

Jer. 2:13.

Yea, the light of the wicked shall be put out, and the spark of his fire shall not shine.

Job 18:5.

The good man is perished out of the earth: and there is none upright among men: they all lie in wait for blood; they hunt every man his brother with a net. That they may do evil with both hands earnestly, the prince asketh, and the judge asketh for a reward; and the great man, he uttereth his mischievous desire: so they wrap it up. The best of them is as a brier: the most upright is sharper than a thorn hedge: the day of thy watchmen and thy visitation cometh; now shall be their perplexity.

Micah 7:2-4.

And he said, It is a light thing that thou shouldest be my servant to raise up the tribes of Jacob, and to restore the preserved of Israel: I will also give thee for a light to the Gentiles, that thou mayest be my salvation unto the end of the earth.

Isa. 49:6.

17. He shall also set his face to enter with the strength of his whole kingdom, and upright ones with him; thus shall he do: and he shall give him the daughter of women, corrupting her: but she shall not stand on his side, neither be for him.

Dan. 11:17.

As a jewel of gold in a swine's snout, so is a fair woman's which is without discretion.

Prov. 11:22.

Prov. 7:4, 5.
Eccl. 7:26.

Eze. 29:3, 6, 7.
2 Kings 18:21.
Matt. 2:15.

Thus I will make thy lewdness to cease from thee, and thy whoredom brought from the land of Egypt.

Eze. 23:27.

18. After this shall he turn his face unto the isles, and shall take many: but a prince for his own behalf shall cause the reproach offered by him to cease; without his own reproach he shall cause it to turn upon him.

19. Then he shall turn his face toward the fort of his own land: but he shall stumble and fall, and not be found.

Dan. 11:18, 19.

And I will punish the world for their evil, and the wicked for their iniquity; and I will cause the arrogancy of the proud to cease, and will lay low the haughtiness of the terrible.

Isa. 13:11.

Thou art weighed in the balances, and art found wanting.

Dan. 5:27.

1 Sam. 8:19, 20.

So man lieth down, and riseth not: till the heavens be no more, they shall not awake, nor be raised out of their sleep.

Job 14:12.

There is no man that hath power over the spirit to retain the spirit; neither hath he power in the day of death: and there is no discharge in that war; neither shall wickedness deliver those that are given to it.

Eccl. 8:8.

20. Then shall stand up in his estate a raiser of taxes in the glory of the kingdom: but within few days he shall be destroyed, neither in anger, nor in battle.

Dan. 11:20.

And it came to pass in those days, that there went out a decree from Caesar Augustus, that all the world should be taxed. . . And all went to be taxed, every one into his own city. And Joseph also went up from Galilee, out of the city of Nazareth, into Judaea, unto the city of David, which is called Bethlehem; (because he was of the house and lineage of David:) To be taxed with Mary his espoused wife, being great with child. And so it was, that, while they were there, the days were accomplished that she should be delivered. And she brought forth her firstborn

whatever nationality, were equally honored. Still greater plans for Roman improvement were found among his papers after his death. He was nearing the pinnacle of earthly fame when he fell, pierced by a score of daggers, in the presence of the senate which he controlled. He "stumbled and fell," leaving no heir to the throne. Another great man had passed from the scene of action. Heaven was watching, for the birth of the Son of Man was near at hand.

It was the year 44 B.C. when the plans of Julius Caesar were cut short by his untimely death. Republicanism was so far gone that the government fell into the hands of the strongest men, those who had military support.

Lepidus, one of the second triumvirates, soon [242] died; Antony, a second member, enamored by Cleopatra, and entrapped in the net of Egyptian darkness, cast himself upon his own sword and died; Octavius, an adopted son of Julius Caesar, alone remained. Says Gibbon: "A martial nobility and stubborn commons, possessed of arms, tenacious of property, and collected into constitutional assemblies, form the only balance capable of preserving a free constitution against the enterprises of an aspiring prince." Rome had none of these; every barrier of the Roman constitution had been leveled by the ambition of Octavius, called Caesar Augustus. Furthermore, the provinces had so long been oppressed by the scheming ministers of the republic that they gladly welcomed a one-man power. Augustus restored the senate to its former dignity, it is true, but "the principles of a free constitution are irrevocably lost when the legislative power is nominated by the executive." So Octavius was proclaimed emperor of Rome by the unanimous vote of that same servile senate.

Thus was Caesar Augustus, the raiser of taxes, brought to the head of the fourth kingdom.

After centuries of strife and turmoil, wars, bloodshed, and oppression, the world lay passive [243] at the feet of the Roman emperor. One government encircled the Mediterranean; from the Atlantic to the Indian Ocean one power bore sway. It would seem that earthly government had achieved its highest ambition. Satan exulted, and rested in the hope that at last victory was his. But the moment of his quiet resting was the calm preceding his greatest struggles. So quiet was the nation that the lifting of a hand in rebellion in any of its most distant parts would send a throb to the center, which would be answered by the return of the legions.

Then it was that in the little town of Bethlehem Ephratah, where Mary and Joseph, peasants of the hill town of Nazareth, had gone to be taxed in obedience to the command of this same Augustus, was born a Saviour, even Christ the Lord. The very condition which caused Satan to exult were the conditions most favorable to Christ when He came to tabernacle among men. He whom Satan had opposed since the rebellion in heaven; He, the Prince of the worlds throughout space, "was made in the likeness of man," and came into the world a helpless babe. The simple shepherds on the hillside near Bethlehem, tending their sheep where David had often tended his flocks, heard the angel choir proclaim the birth of the world's Redeemer. Wise men in the eastern limits of the vast empire of Augustus, having read the prophecies, were watching for His star, and they, too, beheld a shining company of angels, and knew that God dwelt with men. But the rest of the empire slept on unconscious of His nearness.

Bethlehem, the place of His birth, was dear to the memory of every true Jew. It was there [244] that God met their father Jacob as he left home, a fugitive and alone. It was named Bethel,—the house of God, for said Jacob, "Surely God is in this place, and I knew it not." Jacob came to the same spot and paid tithe of his gain while with Laban. Deborah, Rachel's nurse, was buried there. It was in Bethlehem that Abraham pitched his tent when he first entered the promised land. David, the chosen of God, was anointed there. The well of Bethlehem was noted, a fit symbol of Him who was born in [245] Bethlehem and offers the water of life to all.

son, and wrapped him in swaddling clothes, and laid him in a manger; because there was no room for them in the inn. And there were in the same country shepherds abiding in the field, keeping watch over their flock by night. And, lo, the angel of the Lord came upon them, and the glory of the Lord shone round about them: and they were sore afraid.
Luke 2:1-9.

Micah 5:2.

And the angel said unto them, Fear not: for, behold, I bring you good tidings of great joy, which shall be to all people. For unto you is born this day in the city of David a Saviour, which is Christ the Lord. And this shall be a sign unto you; Ye shall find the babe wrapped in swaddling clothes, lying in a manger. And suddenly there was with the angel a multitude of the heavenly host praising God, and saying, Glory to God in the highest, and on earth peace, good will toward men.
Luke 2:10-14.

Now when Jesus was born in Bethlehem of Judaea in the days of Herod the king, behold, there came wise men from the east to Jerusalem, Saying, Where is he that is born King of the Jews? for we have seen his star in the east, and are come to worship him. . . . When they saw the star, they rejoiced with exceeding great joy. And when they were come into the house, they saw the young child with Mary his mother, and fell down, and worshipped him: and when they had opened their treasures, they presented unto him gifts; gold, and frankincense, and myrrh.
Mat 2:1, 2, 10-14.

Gen. 28:12, 19.

Yea, he had power over the angel, and prevailed: he wept, and made supplication unto him: he found him in Bethel, and there he spake with us.
Hosea 12:4.

Gen. 28:22.

Gen. 35:8.

And he went on his journeys from the south even to Bethel, unto the place where his tent had been at the beginning, between Bethel and Hai.
Gen. 13:3.

1 Sam. 16:4-13.
2 Sam. 23:14-17.
If any man thirst, let him come unto me and drink.
John 7:37.

The angel choir proclaim the birth
of the world's Redeemer.

Surely the Lord is in this place; and I knew it not.
Gen. 28:16.

By me princes rule, and nobles, even all the judges of the earth.
Prov. 8:10.

The Lord is high above all nations, and his glory above the heavens.
Ps. 113:4.

Unto us a child is born, unto us a son is given: and the government shall be upon his shoulder: and his name shall be called Wonderful, Counsellor, The mighty God, The everlasting Father, The Prince of Peace.
Isa. 9:6.

"The story of Bethlehem is an exhaustless theme." In it is hidden "the depth of the riches both of the wisdom and knowledge of God." But in spite of the sacred memories which clustered about the place, when the Christ was born but few men knew it.

All that the sacred record gives concerning Augustus, the man who held universal sway, is that he was a raiser of taxes when the kingdom was at the height of its glory, and that after a reign of a few days or years, he should end his career in peace. He had unconsciously been instrumental in preparing the way for the Prince of peace, and having done that, he passed from the scene.

"As in old time Cyrus was called to the throne of the world's empire that he might set free the captives of the Lord, so Caesar Augustus is made the agent for the fulfillment of God's purpose in bringing the mother of Jesus to Bethlehem. She is of the lineage of David, and the Son of David must be born in David's city."

Most of the life of the Saviour was spent during the reign of Tiberius, the successor of Augustus, whom Gabriel described to Daniel as a "vile person." History substantiates the description. He was not a direct heir to the throne, and he was never honored by his subjects. The tyranny of absolutism began again to manifest itself, and the principles of the Oriental monarchies were repeated. Popular assemblies entirely ceased, and the emperor usurped the right to put to death without trial. The governors of Judah reflected the [246] character of the general government. The Jews were bitterly oppressed, and as they knew the time was near for the appearance of a Saviour, they placed all their hopes upon a temporal king, one who should break the yoke of Rome and establish for them a separate kingdom. A few, perhaps, but only a few, divined the spiritual nature of the promise of a Messiah, for it was Satan's studied plan to blind men's eyes to all spiritual truth.

In Babylon he had sought to make men drunk with idolatry; working through Medo-Persia he had hoped to slay those who were faithful to their God; through the teachings of Greece he had so fascinated man with the powers of his own mind that by works of righteousness which he might do, and philosophies of his own conjecturing, he was led to forget any higher power than that which he himself possessed. But through it all a few had clung to the promise delivered to Abraham, Isaac, and Jacob. The world was ignorant of the Christ, but John the Baptist called many to repentance.

Christ's ministry was during the reign of Tiberius, and while that vile person worked, planned, mistrusted, and killed, the Man of God went about all the towns of Palestine, healing the broken-hearted, and dispensing light to all who would accept. Angels watched Him, Gabriel attended Him, and in times of special danger, shielded Him from the enemy who tracked him incessantly. Finally they nailed Him to the cross; the Jews were responsible for it, but the

For Jacob my servant's sake, and Israel mine elect, I have even called thee by thy name: I have surnamed thee, though thou hast not known me.
Isa. 45:4.

21 And in his estate shall stand up a vile person, to whom they shall not give the honour of the kingdom: but he shall come in peaceably, and obtain the kingdom by flatteries. Dan. 11:21.

He was taken from prison and from judgment.
Isa. 53:8.

But we trusted that it had been he which should have redeemed Israel: and beside all this, to day is the third day since these things were done.
Luke 24:21.

When they therefore were come together, they asked of him, saying, Lord, wilt thou at this time restore again the kingdom to Israel?
Acts 1:6.

In whom the god of this world hath blinded the minds of them which believe not, lest the light of the glorious gospel of Christ, who is the image of God, should shine unto them.
2 Cor. 4:4.

Dan. 3:4-6.
Esther 3:6, 12-14.

Col. 2:8.
1 Tim. 6:20.

Let no man beguile you of your reward in a voluntary humility and worshipping of angels, intruding into those things which he hath not seen, vainly puffed up by his fleshly mind.
Col. 2:18.

Luke 2:25, 38.
Matt. 3:5, 6.

And Jesus went about all Galilee, teaching in their synagogues, and preaching the gospel of the kingdom, and healing all manner of sickness and all manner of disease among the people. And his fame went throughout all Syria: and they brought unto him all sick people that were taken with divers diseases and torments, and those which were possessed with devils, and those which were lunatick, and those that had the palsy; and he healed them.
Matt. 4:23-24.

22. And with the arms of a flood shall they be overflown from before him, and shall be broken; yea, also the prince of the covenant.   Dan. 11:22.

Gen. 9:16.
Heb. 13:20, 21.
Acts 4:26, 27.
Acts 2:24.

John 12:20-29.
Matt. 27:38.
Matt. 27:32.
Matt. 27:54.

For God, who commanded the light to shine out of darkness, hath shined in our hearts, to give the light of the knowledge of the glory of God in the face of Jesus Christ.
                    2 Cor. 4:6.

Roman law upheld them in the act; and had it not been done by His own people, the Romans would have done it; for they had [247] reached a condition when the life of man was but lightly esteemed, and the spiritual kingdom which Christ came to set up could never have been understood by the reigning monarch. The officers of Rome nailed the Son of God to the cross. The Prince of the everlasting covenant was crushed by those who sought to confederate together; they placed Him in the tomb; they joined hands with Satan, as nation had never done before; but He broke those bands, and came forth triumphant.

Representatives from the four quarters of the globe stood near Him in His last hours. The Greeks met Him at the temple on the last great day of the feast; the thief hung beside Him on Calvary; Simon of Cyrene helped bear the cross, and the centurion, a Roman soldier, convicted, said, "Truly, this was the Son of God." The darkness which shrouded the dying form of Christ typified the condition of the Roman world. The light which shone about the tomb when the angels bade the Son of Man come forth, typified the power with which the truth should penetrate the empire as His followers went forth to preach salvation. [248]

CHAPTER 16

THE MYSTERY OF INIQUITY

DANIEL 11:23-31

THE strength of paganism had been tested. Truth, eternal truth, had dwelt in the person of the Man of Nazareth. With the death of Christ, Satan lost hope. Looking forward to His crucifixion, Jesus said, "Now is the judgment of this world; now shall the prince of this world be cast out." Satan, after his fall, had met from time to time with the representatives of other worlds. Some in that assembly, not comprehending the hideous nature of sin, had felt to question God's wisdom in expelling Satan from the heavenly courts; but when Christ's life was over, and they had seen the taunting of the enemy and his final act of murder, "the accuser of the brethren" was forever cast from the council of worlds. "When the dragon saw that [249] he was cast to the earth," he knew that his time was short, and with renewed energy he sought to overthrow the truth of God, and crush those who adhered to it. The remaining portion of the eleventh chapter of Daniel clearly reveals the true character of these statements.

After the ascension of Christ, His disciples spread the gospel throughout Judea and all Palestine, and many who heard the word spoken with power on the day of pentecost went into their own countries to proclaim the truth as it was in Christ. In less than thirty years the world was warned. But the Jews were exclusive, even the disciples had not yet lost the idea that Christ was the Saviour of the Hebrew race, not the healer of all mankind. Persecutions in Jerusalem scattered the believers, and then they went everywhere preaching the salvation of God. Quietly, yet steadily, the life-giving current of the stream of Christianity pen-

I am the way, the truth, and the life: no man cometh unto the Father, but by me.   John 14:6.

That through death he might destroy him that had the power of death, that is, the devil.
                                                          Heb. 2:14.

1 John 3:5.

Now there was a day when the sons of God came to present themselves before the LORD, and Satan came also among them.   Job 1:6.

I saw the LORD sitting on his throne, and all the host of heaven standing by him on his right hand and on his left. And the LORD said, Who shall persuade Ahab, that he may go up and fall at Ramothgilead? And one said on this manner, and another said on that manner. And there came forth a spirit, and stood before the LORD, and said, I will persuade him. And the LORD said unto him, Wherewith? And he said, I will go forth, and I will be a lying spirit in the mouth of all his prophets.   1 Kings 22:19-22.

The accuser of our brethren is cast down, which accused them before our God day and night.
                                                          Rev. 12:10.

Woe to the inhabiters of the earth and of the sea! for the devil is come down unto you, having great wrath, because he knoweth that he hath but a short time.   Rev. 12:12.

How hear we every man in our own tongue, wherein we were born?   Acts 2:8-11.

The hope of the gospel, which ye have heard, and which was preached to every creature which is under heaven.   Col. 1:6, 23.

Therefore they that were scattered abroad went every where preaching the word.
                                                          Acts 8:4.

First, I thank my God through Jesus Christ for you all, that your faith is spoken of throughout the whole world.   Rom. 1:8.

First, I thank my God through Jesus Christ for you all, that your faith is spoken of throughout the whole world.   Rom. 1:8.

Where there is neither Greek nor Jew, circumcision nor uncircumcision, Barbarian, Scythian, bond nor free: but Christ is all, and in all.
Col. 3:11.

And when he was demanded of the Pharisees, when the kingdom of God should come, he answered them and said, The kingdom of God cometh not with observation: Neither shall they say, Lo here! or, lo there! for, behold, the kingdom of God is within you. Luke 17:20, 21.

To whom God would make known what is the riches of the glory of this mystery among the Gentiles; which is Christ in you, the hope of glory. Col. 1:27.
Gal. 2:20.

But I see another law in my members, warring against the law of my mind, and bringing me into captivity to the law of sin which is in my members. Rom. 7:18-25.

Because the carnal mind is enmity against God; for it is not subject to the law of God, neither indeed can be. Rom. 8:7.

Let us lay aside every weight, and the sin which doth so easily beset us, and let us run with patience the race that is set before us. Heb. 12:1.

Men that have hazarded their lives for the name of our Lord Jesus Christ. Acts 15:26.
2 Cor. 11:25-28.

I am married unto you: and I will take you one of a city, and two of a family, and I will bring you to Zion. Jer. 3:14.

Who hath delivered us from the power of darkness, and hath translated us into the kingdom of his dear Son. Col. 1:13.

It seemed good to the Holy Ghost, and to us, to lay upon you no greater burden than these necessary things; That ye abstain from meats offered to idols, and from blood, and from things strangled, and from fornication: from which if ye keep yourselves, ye shall do well. Fare ye well.
Acts 15:28-29.
Gal. 4:9, 10.

Take ye therefore good heed unto yourselves; for ye saw no manner of similitude on the day that the Lord spake unto you in Horeb out of the midst of the fire. Deut. 4:15-19.
Ex. 20:3-5.
But when ye pray, use not vain repetitions, as the heathen do. Matt. 6:7.

Now when they saw the boldness of Peter and John, and perceived that they were unlearned and ignorant men, they marvelled; and they took knowledge of them, that they had been with Jesus. Acts 4:13.

etrated to the remotest corners of the vast Roman empire. All nationalities were for the first time in all history united in Him, for with Him and His followers there was neither "Greek nor Jew, circumcision nor uncircumcision, barbarian, Scythian, bond nor free, but Christ was all and in all."

As the truth spread, it was the growth of an empire, a spiritual kingdom within the confines of earth's strongest monarchy. It was with the whole church as with each individual within the church, a spiritual life, a new man, circled about by a human form. Well would it have been for the progress of truth if all oppression of the spiritual by the temporal had been only when the state opposed the church. Instead, the [250] greatest, the only effectual, drawback to the spread of the truth has been caused in individual experience when the physical man has limited the development of the spiritual.

The early church was zealous; their first love was strong, and the greatest difficulties were met and surmounted. Sometimes it meant an entire household, but often only one or two members of the home circle, stepped out of the darkness of paganism to stand for the truth of God against all the attacks of the enemy. Mothers watched their children with the greatest care, for every custom and practice of the people from their waking moment to the time when they committed themselves to sleep, from birth to death, was associated with the worship of some god.

One peculiar thing about the new sect, as they were viewed by the pagans, was the absence of images and forms which the senses could comprehend. When Christians gath- red for worship, there was no altar, no god, no incense. When the Christians prayed, there was no priesthood, no vain repetition of words, no offerings, but a simple petition in the name of Christ. An invisible power seemed to have taken control of the new converts, a power which never quailed, and which no pagan votary could gainsay. The life which God had so long searched for among the Jews was found among the early Christians.

The enemy of truth had sought by every means to blind the eyes of the Jews to the love of God; he had worked through every government for their destruction, and when their nation was at its lowest point, when spiritual vitality [251] was almost exhausted, Christ came in person to revive their fainting hope. Then Satan used every device to deceive the Son of Man. He tempted Him in all points where human nature can be tempted; he sought to ensnare Him with petty trials; he sought to induce Him to accept high worldly honors; but he failed in all, and when he thought he had gained the victory by His crucifixion, he found it was only the physical form which could be thus bound, and that only for a time. An eternal spirit dwelt in mortal clay, and the bands of death were broken by His resurrection. Now from the midst of that down-trodden people, that despised race, from the very foot of the ignominious cross, God chose a people and sent them forth to conquer the world. "Such knowledge is too wonderful for me; it is high, I can not attain unto it." What wonder that the world awoke with a start, and that Satan sought new devices for the overthrow of truth.

Outward pressure, though tried again and again, had proved unavailing in stamping out the truth. In the fiery furnace was seen the form of a Fourth; from the lions' den came forth a prime minister; from Joseph's new sepulcher arose a conqueror. Babylon, Persia, Greece, and Rome had attempted the overthrow of truth, but there had been a constantly increasing grandeur in place of defeat. A new plan was devised by Satan. If paganism could be placed in the heart, while Christian principles were acknowledged outwardly, the overthrow would be certain; for destruction worketh from within, outward, It was a repetition of Balaam's plan. [252]

Paul, the great teacher of righteousness, as he visited from place to place among the saints, wrote thus to the Thessalonians: "The mystery of iniquity doth already work." "Let no man deceive you by any means; for that day shall not come, except there come a falling away first, and that man of sin be revealed, the son of perdition; who opposeth and exalteth himself above all that is called God, or that is worshiped; so that he as God sitteth in the temple of God, showing himself that he is God." This is Paul's description

I know you, that ye have not the love of God in you. . . . How can ye believe, which receive honor one of another, and seek not the honor that commeth from God only? John 5:42-44.

The whole world lieth in wickedness. 1 John 5:19.

For we have not an high priest which cannot be touched with the feeling of our infirmities; but was in all points tempted like as we are, yet without sin. Heb. 4:15.

Hereafter I will not talk much with you: for the prince of this world cometh, and hath nothing in me. John 14:30.

Go ye therefore, and teach all nations, baptizing them in the name of the Father, and of the Son, and of the Holy Ghost: Teaching them to observe all things whatsoever I have commanded you: and, lo, I am with you alway, even unto the end of the world. Amen. Matt. 28:19-20.

And the serpent cast out of his mouth water as a flood after the woman, that he might cause her to be carried away of the flood. Rev. 12:15.

Dan. 3:25.
Dan. 6:22.
Luke 24:5, 6.

But there were false prophets also among the people, even as there shall be false teachers among you, who privily shall bring in damnable heresies, even denying the Lord that bought them, and bring upon themselves swift destruction. 2 Peter 2:1.

As he thinketh in his heart, so is he: Eat and drink, saith he to thee; but his heart is not with thee. Prov. 23:7.

I have a few things against thee, because thou hast there them that hold the doctrine of Balaam, who taught Balac to cast a stumblingblock before the children of Israel, to eat things sacrificed unto idols, and to commit fornication. Rev. 2:14.

I wrote unto the church: but Diotrephes, who loveth to have the preeminent among them, receiveth us not. Wherefore, if I come, I will remember his deeds which he doeth, prating against us with malicious words: and not content therewith, neither doth himself receive the brethren, and fordiddeth them that would, and casteth them out of the church. 3 John 9:10.

Only he who has within his own being the mystery of godliness will stand against the mystery of iniquity.

of the mystery of iniquity, the fourth beast of the vision of the seventh chapter of Daniel.

Then it was that into that church, noted for its purity, crept the life of paganism. Sheltered in the folds of the Christian garb lay the serpent, the old dragon. As the birth of Christ, the incarnation of God, was a mystery, and is today a mystery which none can fathom, it was met by another mystery, a mystery of iniquity whose machinations are too strong for the human mind to understand. It will deceive if possible the very elect. Only he whose eye is lightened by truth, whose heart is the abiding place of the Son of God; in other words, only he who has within his own being the mystery of godliness, will stand against the mystery of iniquity.

In Paul's day, that is, in the first century after [253] Christ, that power was at work. Hitherto the history as recorded in the book of Daniel dealt with earthly kingdoms, but from this time on history handles this "mystery of iniquity" which worked through the various governments. The distinction between the various kingdoms of the north and the south remains as it was in the past, but we pass from governments as governments to a power which is swaying these governments. On one side in this controversy is the church of God; on the other side is the mystery of iniquity, which often lays hold of earthly governments for the purpose of destroying the church.

The expression "church of God" does not refer to denominational names or lines. From the days of Christ until the present, there has been a true church. Its members have often been scattered as far as human eye could discern, but on the record books of heaven they have been recognized as a single company.

The characteristic which marks the true church is adherence to the commandments of the God of heaven. Wherever a people have been true to these, God has honored them with His presence. Moreover, to each denomination which has arisen, there have been offered the same opportunities which were offered to the four succeeding nations as they arose; that is, the privilege of walking in all

---

Without controversy great is the mystery of godliness: God was manifest in the flesh, justified in the Spirit, seen of angels, preached unto the Gentiles, believed on in the world, received up into glory.   1. Tim 3:16.

That ye might be filled with all the fullness of God.   Eph. 3:19.

For there shall arise false Christs, and false prophets, and shall shew great signs and wonders; insomuch that, if it were possible, they shall deceive the very elect.   Matt. 24:24.

The woman which thou sawest is that great city, which reigneth over the kings of the earth.
                                                        Rev. 17:18.

I saw a woman sit upon a scarlet coloured beast, full of names of blasphemy, having seven heads and ten horns. . . . And I saw the woman drunken with the blood of the saints, and with the blood of the martyrs of Jesus.   Rev. 17:3, 6.

God is no respecter of persons: but in every nation he that feareth him, and worketh righteousness, is accepted with him.   Acts 10:34, 35.

In that time shall the present be brought unto the LORD of hosts of a people scattered and peeled, and from a people terrible from their beginning hitherto; a nation meted out and trodden under foot.
                                                        Isa. 18:7.

Whosoever committeth sin transgresseth also the law: for sin is the transgression of the law.
                                                        1 John 3:4.

Ps. 1:1-3.

Here is the patience of the saints, here are they that keep the commandments of God, and the faith of Jesus.   Rev. 14:12.

O that thou hadst hearkened to my commandments! then had thy peace been as a river, and thy righteousness as the waves of the sea.
                                                        Isa. 48:18.

the light, and by that very act becoming an everlasting company. As truth was rejected by the nations and they fell, so truth has been rejected by one denomination after another, and they have fallen, another people taking the vacant place. This succession will be kept up until a remnant people [254] who will keep the commandments of God and the faith of Jesus, shall be made up. They will enter the eternal city to reign with Christ. It is this struggle that was revealed to Daniel in the latter part of his last vision. The history of Rome becomes the history of religious controversy, and the struggle between truth and error is greater than ever before.

The history of the church, as given to John, contains more details than the words of Gabriel to Daniel. To His followers of the first century, God says, "Thou hast left thy first love. Remember, therefore, from whence thou art fallen, and repent, and do the first works." Of the church in the second and third centuries, He says, "I know thy works, and tribulation, and poverty (but thou art rich). . . . Fear none of those things which thou shalt suffer: behold, the devil shall cast some of you into prison, that ye may be tried; and ye shall have tribulation." Christianity and paganism were in open conflict for three centuries following the birth of Christ, and at times the serpent reared his head to smite the truth to the ground. Some of the followers of Christ were persecuted, and others grew cold and indifferent. But there was a power in the gospel which the pagans could not withstand. As its followers increased, their influence was felt even in political circles.

The close of the third century of the Christian era found the government of Rome greatly weakened. The evils of the empire, its oppression and cruelty, made it almost impossible for the emperor to control affairs. Authority was in the hands of the army, which seated and unseated [255] rulers at will. Barbarian hordes pressed the empire on all sides, and the downfall of Rome was imminent. Some radical change was necessary to prevent complete disruption, and Diocletian, the reigning emperor, conceived the idea of partitioning the territory. Consequently he associated with himself a

Therefore to him that knoweth to do good, and doeth it not, to him it is sin. James 4:17.

Jer. 17:24, 25.
Jer. 51:9.

Her priests have violated my law, and have profaned mine holy things: they have put no difference between the holy and profane, neither have they shewed difference between the unclean and the clean, and have hid their eyes from my sabbaths, and I am profaned among them. Eze. 22:26.

The dragon was wroth with the woman, and went to make war with the remnant of her seed, which keep the commandments of God, and have the testimony of Jesus Christ. Rev. 12:17.

Then shall be great tribulation, such as was not since the beginning of the world to this time, no, nor ever shall be. Matt. 24:21.

I have somewhat against thee, because thou hast left thy first love. Rev. 2:4.

O Israel, return unto the LORD thy God; for thou hast fallen by thine iniquity. Take with you words, and turn to the LORD: say unto him, Take away all iniquity, and receive us graciously: so will we render the calves of our lips. Hosea 14:1-2.

That the trial of your faith, being much more precious than of gold that perisheth, though it be tried with fire, might be found unto praise and honour and glory at the appearing of Jesus Christ. 1 Peter 1:7.

I will put enmity between thee and the woman, and between thy seed and her seed; it shall bruise thy head, and thou shalt bruise his heel. Gen. 3:15.

Because iniquity shall abound, the love of many shall wax cold. Matt. 14:12.

Rev. 6:2.
So that my bonds in Christ are manifest in all Caesar's court, and in all other places. Phil. 1:13 [margin].
Phil. 4:22.

For the wickedness of their doings I will drive them out of mine house, I will love them no more: all their princes are revolters. . . My God will cast them away, because they did not hearken unto him. Hosea 9:15.

Even as I have seen, they that plow iniquity, and sow wickedness, reap the same. By the blast of God they perish, and by the breath of his nostrils are they consumed. Job 4:8, 9.

Where no counsel is, the people fall: but in the multitude of counselors there is safety. Prov. 11:14.

They have deeply corrupted themselber, as in the days of Gibeah: therefore he will remember their iniquity, he will visit their sins. Hosea 9:9.

For they know not to do right, saith the Lord, who store up violence and robbery in their palaces. Amos 3:10.

They have set up kings, but not by me: they have made princes, and I knew it not: of their silver and their gold have they made them idols, that they may be cut off. Hosea 8:4.

23. And after the league made with him he shall work deceitfully: for he shall come up, and shall become strong with a small people.
24. He shall enter peaceably even upon the fattest places of the province; and he shall do that which his fathers have not done, nor his fathers' fathers; he shall scatter among them the prey, and spoil, and riches: yea, and he shall forecast his devices against the strong holds, even for a time.
Dan. 11:23, 24.

Her princes in the midst thereof are like wolves ravening the prey, to shed blood, and to destroy souls, to get dishonest gain. Eze. 22:27.

And saying, Alas, alas, that great city, that was clothed in fine linen, and purple, and scarlet, and decked with gold, and precious stones, and pearls! Rev. 18:16.

Take the helmet of salvation, and the sword of the Spirit, which is the word of God. Eph. 6:17

Not every one that saith unto me, Lord, Lord, shall enter into the kingdom of heaven; but he that doeth the will of my Father which is in heaven. Matt. 7:21.

When Ephraim spake trembling, he exalted himself in Israel; but when he offended in Baal, he died. Hosea 13:1.

I am the LORD: that is my name: and my glory will I not give to another, neither my praise to graven images. Isa. 42:8.

Beware of false prophets, which come to you in sheep's clothing, but inwardly they are ravening wolves. Matt. 7:15.

They consider not in their hearts that I remember all their wickedness: now their own doings have beset them about. Hosea 7:2.

man by the name of Maximian, giving him the title of Augustus. Each of the two emperors chose an assistant, called a Caesar, whose duty it was to guard the frontiers. According to the plan of Diocletian, the Caesars should become emperors on the death of the Augusti, and then other Caesars would be appointed. For a while the four who stood at the head of the Roman empire worked together in harmony, but through a variety of complications war broke out.

Constantine was a Caesar in the western division of the empire, and marching toward the East, he subdued, one by one, all rivals in the government. It was about the year 312 A. D. when, confronted by bitter foes, whose strength he recognized, this rising light assumed a policy never before followed.

There were many Christians scattered throughout the empire who refused to fight under the banner of paganism. With these Constantine made a league. The story of his conversion is variously told, and perhaps the details are unimportant. The fact remains that he acknowledged the God of the Christians, proclaimed himself a follower of Christ, and immediately Christians from all over the empire flocked into his army, devout followers of the general who now fought in the name of Christianity.

Speaking of the use of the cross, Gibbon [256] says: "This same symbol sanctified the arms of the soldiers of Constantine; the cross glittered in their helmets, was engraved on their shields, was interwoven into their banners; and the consecrated emblems which adorned the person of the emperor himself were distinguished only by the richer materials and more exquisite workmanship." The standard which was borne before this (Christian) army "supported a crown of gold, which inclosed the mysterious monogram, at once expressive of the figure of the cross, and the initial letter of the name of Christ."

The humble followers of Christ, who immediately after His ascension had gone forth "conquering and to conquer," carrying with them His words, the sword of the Spirit, had been replaced by an army with helmet and sword, led by a commander who bound together the emblems of the cross and his own name.

The clothing of paganism in Christian 'garments was never more complete than in the days of Constantine. The mystery of iniquity was [257] hard at work. Constantine conquered the Roman world; he sat as sole monarch of the empire which had been tottering in the hands of his predecessors. The Praetorian guard, which had been the terror as well as the protection of other emperors, was forever suppressed by Constantine. The dignity of the senate and people of Rome received a fatal blow, and they were thereafter subject alike to the insults or neglect of their master, who resided in the new capital, Constantinople.

The cross glittered in their helmets, was engraved on their shields, was interwoven into their banners.

The character of Constantine, that first Christian emperor, is aptly described by Gibbon. In discussing the reason why he delayed baptism until he was on his death-bed, he says: "The sublime theory of the gospel had made a much fainter impression on the *heart* than on the understanding of Constantine himself. He pursued the great object of his ambition through the dark and bloody paths of war and policy; and after the victory, he abandoned himself without moderation to the abuse of his fortune. Instead of asserting his just superiority above the imperfect heroism and profane philosophy of Trajan and the Antonines, the mature age of Constantine forfeited the reputation which he had acquired in his youth. As he gradually advanced in the knowledge of truth, he proportionately declined in the practice of virtue; and the same year of his reign in which he convened the Council of Nice, was polluted by the execution, or rather murder, of his eldest son. . . . The gratitude of the church has exalted the virtues and excused the failings of a

Ye who turn judgment to wormwood, and leave off righteousness in the earth, . . . For I know your manifold transgressions and your mighty sins: they afflict the just, they take a bribe, and they turn aside the poor in the gate from their right. Therefore the prudent shall keep silence in that time; for it is an evil time.
Amos 5:12-13.

How long halt ye between two opinions? if the LORD be God, follow him: but if Baal, then follow him. 1 Kings 18:21.

I have written to him the great things of my law, but they were counted as a strange thing.
Hosea 8:12.

I found Israel like grapes in the wilderness; I saw your fathers as the firstripe in the fig tree at her first time: but they went to Baalpeor, and separated themselves unto that shame; and their abominations were according as they loved.
Hosea 9:10.

Their heart is divided; now shall they be found faulty: he shall break down their altars, he shall spoil their images. Hosea 10:2.

No man can serve two masters: for either he will hate the one, and love the other; or else he will hold to the one, and despise the other. Ye cannot serve God and mammon.   Matt. 6:24.

Woe unto you, scribes and Pharisees, hypocrites! for ye are like unto whited sepulchres, which indeed appear beautiful outward, but are within full of dead men's bones, and of all uncleanness. Even so ye also outwardly appear righteous unto men, but within ye are full of hypocrisy and iniquity.   Matt. 23:27-28.

Full well ye reject the commandment of God, that ye may keep your own tradition.   Mark 7:9.

In vain they do worship me, teaching for doctrines the commandments of men.   Matt. 15:9.

Think not that I am come to destroy the law, or the prophets: I am not come to destroy, but to fulfil. For verily I say unto you, Till heaven and earth pass, one jot or one tittle shall in no wise pass from the law, till all be fulfilled.   Matt. 5:17-18.

Israel hath cast off the thing that is good: the enemy shall pursue him.   Hosea 8:3.

I saw a woman sit upon a scarlet coloured beast, full of names of blasphemy, having seven heads and ten horns. . . . And the woman which thou sawest is that great city, which reigneth over the kings of the earth.   Rev. 17:3, 18.

The way of the wicked is as darkness: they know not at what they stumble.   Prov. 4:19.

O thou that art situate at the entry of the sea, which art a merchant of the people for many isles. . . . Thy borders are in the midst of the seas.   Eze. 27:3.

Though he be fruitful among his brethren, an east wind shall come, the wind of the LORD shall come up from the wilderness, and his spring shall become dry, and his fountain shall be dried up: he shall spoil the treasure of all pleasant vessels.   Hosea 13:15.

Yea, and he shall forecast his devices against the strong holds, even for a time.   Dan. 11:24:

generous patron, who seated Christianity on the throne of the Roman world; and the Greeks, who celebrate [258] the festival of the imperial saint, seldom mention the name of Constantine without adding the title of *Equal to the Apostles.*" These words alone offer a sad commentary on the decline of Christian virtue since the days of Christ. He who claimed the power of Christianity was less virtuous than the heroic pagan Trajan, and such pagan philosophers as the Antonines.

The first religious laws ever passed by Christians were edicts of Constantine. In 312 the edict of Milan granted universal toleration; in 321 the first law for the worship of Sunday was published; in 325 was convened at Nice the first ecumenical council, which formulated a creed for the world. Then began the conflict which tore the church asunder and exposed it to open shame. About the reign of Constantine cluster events of the greatest interest, not to Rome only, but to the church of God and to the world. It was the first and perhaps the greatest object lesson illustrating the effects of the elevation of Christianity in name to the throne of the world.

In the wake of this reign followed the years of darkness for all Europe, when antichrist reigned supreme. Constantine indeed performed that which neither his father nor his father's fathers had performed. He left to his heirs "a new capital, a new policy, and a new religion." No one had before dared to think that the capital could be removed from Rome. Constantine selected the site of Constantinople with more than human wisdom. It is formed by nature to be the center and capital of a great monarchy. It has been the contested point among the nations of Europe since the [259] continent has had nations to contend, and according to the prophecy of Daniel, it will be the bone of contention to the end of time. It is a fact worth noting that the city was founded in the year 330 B. C., exactly three hundred and sixty years, "a time," after the victory of Octavius over Antony at Actium, which placed him as sole ruler on the Roman throne.

The new policy was the outworking of a union of church and state. The kingdoms of the past had followed a policy somewhat similar to one another. Government was with them the central object. This was seen in its strongest light in pagan Rome, but with Constantine the policy changed. Paganism as paganism was laid low, and the "mystery of iniquity" was enthroned. The world was given Christianity, not as it came from the life of Him whose name it bore, but as it was corrupted and polluted by human and satanic minds. Gibbon says that hereafter the historian will describe "political institutions" before relating wars, and that "he will adopt the division unknown to the ancients of *civil* and *ecclesiastical affairs*." That is, future history must deal with church and state, and not with kingdoms such as Babylon, Medo-Persia, and Greece. [260]

History has changed. The devil is going about seeking whom he may devour, and the calm, determined plans for conquering the world which marked the nations before the days of Christ, have been replaced by a desperation that

Because, even because they have seduced my people, saying, Peace; and there was no peace; and one built up a wall, and, lo, others daubed it with untempered morter: Say unto them which daub it with untempered morter, that it shall fall: there shall be an overflowing shower; and ye, O great hailstones, shall fall; and a stormy wind shall rend it. Eze. 13:10-12.

Ye adulterers and adulteresses, know ye not that the friendship of the world is enmity with God? whosoever therefore will be a friend of the world is the enemy of God. James 4:4.

My people ask counsel at their stocks, and their staff declareth unto them: for the spirit of whoredoms hath caused them to err, and they have gone a whoring from under their God. Hosea 4:12.

"Let all the judges and town people, and the occupation of all trades rest on the venerable day of the sun: but let those who situated in the country freely and at full liberty attend to the business of agriculture: because it often happens that no other day is so fit for sowing corn and planting vines: lest the critical moment being let slip, men should lose the commodities granted by heaven."

The First Sunday Law.

Be sober, be vigilant; because your adversary the devil, as a roaring lion, walketh about, seeking whom he may devour. 1 Peter 5:8.

Therefore rejoice, ye heavens, and ye that dwell in them. Woe to the inhabiters of the earth and of the sea! for the devil is come down unto you, having great wrath, because he knoweth that he hath but a short time. Rev. 12:12.

The dragon was wroth with the woman, and went to make war with the remnant of her seed, which keep the commandments of God, and have the testimony of Jesus Christ. Rev. 12:17.

Be not deceived; God is not mocked: for whatsoever a man soweth, that shall he also reap. Gal. 6:7.

Can two walk together, except they be agreed? Amos 3:3.

Her priests have polluted the sanctuary, they have done violence to the law. Zeph. 3:4.

The priest's lips should keep knowledge, and they should seek the law at his mouth: for he is the messenger of the LORD of hosts. But ye are departed out of the way; ye have caused many to stumble at the law; ye have corrupted the covenant of Levi, saith the LORD of hosts. Mal. 2:7-8.

Because my people hath forgotten me, they have burned incense to vanity, and they have caused them to stumble in their ways from the ancient paths, to walk in paths, in a way not cast up. Jer. 18:15.

The shepherds fed themselves, and fed not my flock. Eze. 34:8.

In their setting of their threshold by my thresholds, and their post by my posts, and the wall between me and them, they have even defiled my holy name by their abominations that they have committed. Eze. 43:8.

Jer. 23:28-32.
Rom. 11:33-36.

Seemeth it a small thing unto you to have eaten up the good pasture, but ye must tread down with your feet the residue of your pastures? and to have drunk of the deep waters, but ye must foul the residue with your feet? And as for my flock, they eat that which ye have trodden with your feet; and they drink that which ye have fouled with your feet. Therefore thus saith the Lord GOD unto them; Behold, I, even I, will judge between the fat cattle and between the lean cattle. Because ye have thrust with side and with shoulder, and pushed all the diseased with your horns, till ye have scattered them abroad; ... And ye my flock,

means the utter destruction, if possible, of all who serve the God of heaven. Any means is lawful in the hands of the prince of this world, and the greater the number who fall, the lighter the burden which he, the arch enemy, must bear in the days of the final reckoning. The acts of Constantine started a series of movements which developed rapidly into the antichrist of the Dark Ages.

The council held at Nice was an important gathering alike to the church and the nation, for since the two have joined hands, whatever affects one affects the other.

The Christian world was torn asunder by theological factions. Alexandria, the center of all philosophical study, was also the center of theological activity. Here is where the Greek influence was most forcibly felt. Athanasius, the leader of one faction, was archdeacon, and [261] afterward bishop of Alexandria, and his opponent, Arius, was presbyter in the same city.

Paganism and Christianity met on the battlefield when Constantine contended for the throne of Rome; paganism and Christianity met in more deadly conflict in Alexandria, where Christian and pagan schools stood side by side. Here it was that such men as Origen and Clement, recognized Fathers of the church, adopted the philosophy of the Greeks, and applied to the study of the Bible the same methods which were common in the study of Homer and other Greek writers. Higher criticism had its birth in Alexandria. It was the result of a mingling of the truths taught by Christ and the false philosophy of the Greeks. It was an attempt to interpret divine writings by the human intellect, a revival of the philosophy of Plato. These teachers, by introducing Greek philosophy into the schools which were nominally Christian, opened the avenue for the theological controversies which shook the Roman world, and finally established the mystery of iniquity.

So from this false teaching of the Word in Alexandria came two leaders—Athanasius and Arius. Each had his following, and yet no man could clearly define the disputed point over which they wrangled. So great was the controversy that the Council of Nice was called to settle the dispute, and deliver to the church an orthodox creed. The emperor Constantine called the council, and was present in person. At this council the creed of Athanasius was recognized as orthodox, and Arius and his followers were pronounced heretics.

But announcing a creed is one thing, and having [262] it adopted is another. The orthodox creed was published to the world, and then began the fight. In this strife armies fought and much blood was shed. But in spite of the fact that Arianism was heresy, the doctrine spread. It was popular among the barbarian tribes who invaded the western division of the Roman empire. The Vandals, who settled in Africa, were among the followers of Arius, and so also were the Heruli and Ostrogoths who settled in Italy. But while Arianism spread through Africa, Sardinia, and Spain, and was present at times in Italy, the recognized religion of the Roman emperor and the empire itself, the northern kingdom, which now had its seat at Constantinople, was the Catholic faith, as proclaimed at Nice. As Constantine was the representative of this northern division in his day, so later, between 527 and 565, Justinian became champion of the Catholic cause.

According to the vision of the seventh chapter of Daniel, the Roman kingdom would be divided into ten parts, represented by the ten horns of the fourth beast, and three of these kingdoms should be plucked up by another power. It is this part of the history, of the fourth kingdom which is related in the eleventh chapter of Daniel, beginning with the twentyfifth verse.

Justinian's reign was the most brilliant period of Byzantine history after the death of Constantine, and historians agree that among his greatest military achievements must be classed his exploits against the south. The success of Justinian was due to the services throughout the greater part of his reign, of the celebrated [263] general Belisarius. He was the tool in the hands of the emperor for crushing out heresy.

The Vandals were Arians, but Hilderis, the grandson of their chief warrior, the noted Genseric, favored the Catholic faith. The disaffection of his subjects made it possible for Hilderis to be dethroned by Gelimer, who had some title to the Vandal throne. Under pretense of protecting the

the flock of my pasture, are men, and I am your God, saith the Lord GOD.

Eze. 34:18-21,31.

There is a conspiracy of her prophets in the midst thereof, like a roaring lion ravening the prey; they have devoured souls.   Eze. 22:25.

Her princes in the midst thereof are like wolves ravening the prey, to shed blood, and to destroy souls, to get dishonest gain.   Eze. 22:27.

They build up Zion with blood, and Jerusalem with iniquity. The heads thereof judge for reward, and the priests thereof teach for hire, and the prophets thereof divine for money: yet will they lean upon the LORD, and say, Is not the LORD among us? none evil can come upon us.

Micah 3:10-11.

Thus saith the LORD; For three transgressions of Judah, and for four, I will not turn away the punishment thereof; because they have despised the law of the LORD, and have not kept his commandments, and their lies caused them to err, after the which their fathers have walked.

Amos 2:4.

Judah hath dealt treacherously, and an abomination is committed in Israel and in Jerusalem; for Judah hath profaned the holiness of the LORD which he loved, and hath married the daughter of a strange god.   Mal. 2:11.

25. And he shall stir up his power and his courage against the king of the south with a great army; and the king of the south shall be stirred up to battle with a very great and mighty army; but he shall not stand: for they shall forecast devices against him.
26. Yea, they that feed of the portion of his meat shall destroy him, and his army shall overflow: and many shall fall down slain.
27. And both these kings' hearts shall be to do mischief, and they shall speak lies at one table; but it shall not prosper: for yet the end shall be at the time appointed.

Dan 11:25-27.

For thy violence against thy brother Jacob shame shall cover thee, and thou shalt be cut off for ever.

Obadiah 10.

But this I confess unto thee, that after the way which they call heresy, so worship I the God of my fathers, believing all things which are written in the law and in the prophets.

Acts 24:14.

An hypocrite with his mouth destroyeth his neighbor. Prov. 11:9.

O thou that art named the house of Jacob, is the spirit of the LORD straitened? are these his doings? do not my words do good to him that walketh uprightly? Even of late my people is risen up as an enemy: ye pull off the robe with the garment from them that pass by securely as men averse from war. The women of my people have ye cast out from their pleasant houses; from their children have ye taken away my glory for ever. Arise ye, and depart; for this is not your rest: because it is polluted, it shall destroy you, even with a sore destruction. If a man walking in the spirit and falsehood do lie, saying, I will prophesy unto thee of wine and of strong drink; he shall even be the prophet of this people.

Micah 2:7-11.

How canst thou say, I am not polluted, I have not gone after Baalim? see thy way in the valley, know what thou hast done: thou art a swift dromedary traversing her ways; A wild ass used to the wilderness, that snuffeth up the wind at her pleasure; in her occasion who can turn her away? all they that seek her will not weary themselves; in her month they shall find her. Withhold thy foot from being unshod, and thy throat from thirst: but thou saidst, There is no hope: no; for I have loved strangers, and after them will I go.

Jer. 2:23-25.

Behold, the eyes of the Lord God are upon the sinful kingdom. Amos 9:8.

Rejoice not, O Israel, for joy, as other people: for thou hast gone a whoring from thy God, thou hast loved a reward upon every cornfloor.

Hosea 9:1.

Ephraim is joined to idols: let him alone.

Hosea 4:17.

28. Then shall he return into his land with great riches; and his heart shall be against the holy covenant; and he shall do exploits, and return to his own land.
29. At the time appointed he shall return, and come toward the south; but it shall not be as the former, or as the latter.

Dan. 11:28, 29.

The ark was not among these holy vessels, for at the time of the Babylonian captivity, "the prophet, being warned of God, commanded the tabernacle and the ark to go with him, as he went forth into the mountain, where Moses climbed up, and saw

dethroned Hilderis, the emperor Justinian prepared for a war in Africa. While still undecided as to the advisability of making the attack because of the weakness of the Roman army and the cost of the undertaking, his purpose was confirmed by the words of a Catholic bishop. Said he in prophetic tones, "It is the will of Heaven, O emperor, that you should not abandon your holy enterprise for the deliverance of the African church. The God of battles will march before your standard, and disperse your enemies, who are the enemies of His Son." This was sufficient, and the "*holy*" war for the extermination of Arianism was undertaken.

A force of Romans, the largest Belisarius could command from the weakened empire, aided by recruits from the east, landed in Africa. The Vandal army numbered 160,000 fighting men. Belisarius was hastened in his march toward Carthage by enemies of Gelimer and friends of the Catholic creed. The armies met near the city, and victory came to the Romans through the folly and rashness of the brother of the Vandal king. Gelimer fled, and Carthage opened her gates and admitted Belisarius and his army. "The Arians, conscious that their reign had expired, resigned the [264] temple to the Catholics, who rescued their saint from profane hands, performed the holy rites, and loudly proclaimed the creed of Athanasius and Justinian." The Catholic faith triumphed. Arianism fell, and Sardinia and Corsica surrendered, and the other islands of the Mediterranean yielded to the arms and creed of Justinian.

In the autumn of 534 Justinian granted a triumph to Belisarius. Gibbon thus describes the scene: "From the palace of Belisarius the procession was conducted through the streets to the hippodrome. . . . The wealth of nations was displayed, the trophies of martial or effeminate luxury; rich armor: golden thrones, and the chariots of state which had been used by the Vandal queen; the massive furniture of the [265] royal banquet, the splendor of precious stones, the elegant forms of statues and vases, the more substantial treasures of gold, and the holy vessels of the Jewish temple, which, after their long peregrination, were respectfully deposited in the Christian church of Jerusalem. A long train

From the palace of Belisarius
the procession was conducted
through the streets.

of the noblest Vandals reluctantly exposed their lofty stature and manly countenance."

"The Arians deplored the ruin of their church which had been triumphant above a century in Africa; and they were justly provoked by the laws of the conqueror, which interdicted the baptism of their children; and the exercise of all religious worship." It is not much to be wondered at that those who remained plotted against the government and the general who represented Justinian. The loss of life was terrible in those wars for the supremacy of one creed above another, and the path to the papal crown was bloodstained. It is stated that five million Africans were consumed by the wars and government of the emperor Justinian.

For the sake of brevity, the wars between the Catholic empire and the Vandals may be taken as an illustration of the

the heritage of God. And when Jeremy came thither, he found an hollow cave, wherein he laid the tabernacle, and the ark, and the altar of incense, and so stopped the door. And some of those that followed him came to mark the way, but they could not find it. Which when Jeremy perceived, he blamed them, saying, As for that place, it shall be unknown until the time that God gather his people again together, and receive them unto mercy. Then shall the Lord shew them these things, and the glory of the Lord shall appear, and the cloud also, as it was shewed under Moses, and as when Solomon desired that the place might be honourably sanctified."

2 Maccabes 2:4-8.

30. For the ships of Chittim shall come against him: therefore he shall be grieved, and return, and have indignation against the holy covenant: so shall he do; he shall even return, and have intelligence with them that forsake the holy covenant.

Dan 11:30.

The pride of thine heart hath deceived thee, thou that dwellest in the clefts of the rock, whose habitation is high; that saith in his heart, Who shall bring me down to the ground? Though thou exalt thyself as the eagle, and though thou set thy nest among the stars, thence will I bring thee down, saith the LORD.

Obadiah 3-4.

31. And arms shall stand on his part, and they shall pollute the sanctuary of strength, and shall take away the daily sacrifice, and they shall place the abomination that maketh desolate.

Dan 11:31.

Hath a nation changed their gods, which are yet no gods? but my people have changed their glory for that which doth not profit. Be astonished, O ye heavens, at this, and be horribly afraid, be ye very desolate, saith the LORD. For my people have committed two evils; they have forsaken me the fountain of living waters, and hewed them out cisterns, broken cisterns, that can hold no water.

Jer. 2:11-13.

Thus saith the LORD concerning the prophets that make my people err, that bite with their teeth, and cry, Peace; and he that putteth not into their mouths, they even prepare war against him. Therefore night shall be unto you, that ye shall not have a vision; and it shall be dark unto you, that ye shall not divine; and the sun shall go down over the prophets, and the day shall be dark over them. Then shall the seers be ashamed, and the diviners confounded: yea, they shall all cover their lips; for there is no answer of God.

Micah 3:5-7.

extermination of the other two kingdoms—the Heruli and the Ostrogoths. Justinian was reigning emperor, and most of the work was done by Belisarius, between the years 533 and 538.

The last contest with paganism was in 508 when the French and Britons accepted Christianity; the "daily" spoken of in Daniel had been taken away. By 538 the way was clear for the papacy to sit enthroned in Rome. The new capital established by Constantine left Rome free to be occupied by the head of the church. [266]

The new religion—Christianity—we have seen mingled with paganism, which it crushed, and gave birth to the papacy. The new policy, a union of church and state, gave civil aid to that paganized Christianity called the papacy. The harvest of the seed sown in the days of Constantine was reaped in the reign of Justinian, whose military and civil power supported "the abomination that maketh desolate."

A striking feature of this history is the fact that the very code of law which Rome has bequeathed as a legacy to later times, is the work of this same Justinian. Is it to be wondered at that the laws of this emperor, who reigned at the time when the papacy was formed, and who was the one that supported it by arms, should contain some principles of the papacy? Fisher says, "Humane principles are incorporated into the civil law, but likewise *the despotic system of imperialism.*" The laws of Justinian form the basis of national laws to-day; likewise the religion of Justinian is the recognized religion of most countries to-day.

Constantine and Justinian were the two men instrumental above all others in forming the papacy, and giving it civil power. The contest between Arianism and the orthodox Catholicism was the means of enthroning the papacy. A power soon to be recognized as the personification of all tyranny swayed the scepter of Rome, and the followers of the One who proclaimed a covenant of peace to Israel, would for the period of 1200 years struggle for existence.

Every principle of truth was crushed, and with 538 was ushered in the Dark Ages. [267]

THE WORK OF THE MYSTERY OF INIQUITY

DANIEL 11:32-45

As the year 457 B. C. was an important date in Jewish history, so 538 A. D. is a mile-post in the history of the Christian church. The former, dating from the decree to restore and build Jerusalem, marks the beginning of one great prophetic period, the 2300 days of Dan. 8:14. The latter, which witnessed the setting up of the papacy, is the date from which to reckon that other prophetic period, "a time and times and the dividing of time," or the twelve hundred and sixty days of Dan. 7:25. It is the period during which the little horn, that plucked up three of the ten divisions of the Roman empire, should bear sway. It is to the beginning of this period, the year 538, that the thirty-first verse of the eleventh chapter of Daniel brings the history. [268]

The fully developed papacy was not the work of one nor of two years any more than the universal power of Babylon, Medo-Persia, or Greece was an immediate acquisition As those kingdoms grew in power, so papal Rome grew in power. According to Rev. 13:2, the dragon gave the beast his power and his seat and great authority. The work of Constantine and Justinian in gaining power for this new organization was parallel to the conquests of Cyrus, Alexander, and Caesar in their conquests for their respective nations. The seat of the pagan Roman government was removed to Constantinople, thereby giving room for the papacy to

Ezra 7:11-26.

And arms shall stand on his part, and they shall pollute the sanctuary of strength, and shall take away the daily sacrifice, and they shall place the abomination that maketh desolate.

Dan 11:31.

From the time that the daily sacrifice shall be taken away, to set up the abomination, etc., that astonisheth, there shall be a thousand two hundred and ninety days.

Dan. 12:11 [margin].

Let no man deceive you by any means: for that day shall not come, except there come a falling away first, and that man of sin be revealed, the son of perdition; Who opposeth and exalteth himself above all that is called God, or that is worshipped; so that he as God sitteth in the temple of God, shewing himself that he is God. Remember ye not, that, when I was yet with you, I told you these things? And now ye know what withholdeth that he might be revealed in his time. For the mystery of iniquity doth already work: only he who now letteth will let, until he be taken out of the way.

2 Thess. 2:3-7.

Rev.13:2.
Isa. 44:27, 28.
Isa. 45:1-5.

Violence is risen up into a rod of wickedness: none of them shall remain, nor of their multitude, nor of any of theirs: neither shall there be wailing for them.
Eze. 7:11.

There is that scattereth, and yet increaseth; and there is that withholdeth more than is meet, but it tendeth to poverty.
Prov. 11:24.

The Ten Commandments shown on a tablet:

Thou shalt have no other gods before me

Thou shalt not make unto thee any graven image or any likeness of any thing that is in heaven above, or that is in the earth beneath, or that is in the water under the earth: thou shalt not bow down thyself to them, nor serve them: for I the Lord thy God am a jealous God, visiting the iniquity of the fathers upon the children, unto the third and fourth generation of them that hate me; and showing mercy unto thousands of them that love me and keep my commandments.

Thou shalt not take the name of the Lord thy God in vain. for the Lord will not hold him guiltless that taketh his name in vain

Remember the Sabbath day to keep it holy. six days shalt thou labor, and do all thy work, but the seventh day is the Sabbath of the Lord, thy God: in it thou shalt not do any work, thou, nor thy son, nor thy daughter, thy man-servant, nor thy maid-servant, nor thy cattle, nor thy stranger that is within thy gates: for in six days the Lord made heaven and earth, the sea, and all that in them is, and rested the seventh day: wherefore the Lord blessed the Sabbath day, and hallowed it.

Honor thy father and thy mother, that thy days may be long upon the land which the Lord, thy God giveth thee.

Thou shalt not kill

Thou shalt not commit adultery

Thou shalt not steal

Thou shalt not bear false witness against thy neighbor

Thou shalt not covet thy neighbor's house: thou shalt not covet thy neighbor's wife, nor his man servant, nor his maid-servant, nor his ox, nor his ass, nor anything that is thy neighbor's.

2 Thess. 2:4.
Dan. 8:25.

Will a man leave the snow of Lebanon which cometh from the rock of the field? or shall the cold flowing waters that come from another place be forsaken? Jer. 18:14.

Seemeth it a small thing unto you to have eaten up the good pasture, but ye must tread down with your feet the residue of your pastures? and to have drunk of the deep waters, but ye must foul the residue with your feet? And as for my flock, they eat that which ye have trodden with your feet; and they drink that which ye have fouled with your feet. Eze. 34:18-19.

Ex. 20:8-11.

Speak thou also unto the children of Israel, saying, Verily my sabbaths ye shall keep: for it is a sign between me and you throughout your generations; that ye may know that I am the LORD that doth sanctify you. Ex. 31:13.

be seated on the throne in the city on the Tiber. As territory and a capital were gained gradually, so the *authority* of the papacy was a gradual acquisition. Each of the four universal kingdoms had a distinct policy, which was followed throughout its existence. Likewise the papacy had its policy just as clearly defined. The working of this policy in its inception is best seen in Alexandria. It was there that the two streams, paganism and Christianity, mingled their waters. The papacy had birth on the banks of the Nile: Egypt was the mother who nursed it, and as it grew, it breathed in the miasma of its surroundings. First, Christians *interpreted* the Bible according to pagan thought, and paganism, appearing to be vanquished, in reality became the conqueror.

Then the *teachings* of the Word were changed. In order to compromise with pagans, idol worship was introduced into the Christian church; the second commandment was dropped from the decalogue, and the tenth was divided to preserve [269] the number. The fourth, the keystone to the law of God, a memorial of creation and redemption, was so altered as to exalt the enemy of God above God himself. Later, the whole Bible was discarded, and as that detector of sin was suppressed, vileness and iniquity became uncontrollable. This, however, was not the whole policy of the papacy, but only one of the stones in the foundation of the structure that was being reared.

The head of the church, who was likewise a civil ruler, was exalted more and more above his fellows, until a complete ecclesiastical hierarchy was formed. By decree of a general council the head of the church was declared infallible. But even before, this faith in the new church, and especially in the *head* of the church, took the place of faith in Christ. The Virgin Mary and saints became mediators for sinful man, and forgiveness was granted by the head of the [270] church. Righteousness by works led to long pilgrimages, penance, and relic worship. Everlasting punishment was held as a threat above the heads of the common people. The darkness deepened. The inquisition was instituted to force men's consciences. Kings upon their thrones were compelled to recognize the superior authority of the power of Rome, and failure to do so meant the removal of their crowns. Subjects were absolved from allegiance to their sovereigns, and so complete was the obedience of nations to Rome, that no man dared lift his hand in opposition.

A darkness beyond comprehension settled over all the world. The light had been extinguished when God's word was banished "The noontide of the papacy was the world's moral midnight."

The power which should speak great words against the Most High, and wear out the saints of the Most High, was allotted 1260 years in which to work; but so cruel was that power that the time was shortened, lest none should survive the persecution. It was Egyptian or Babylonian bondage for the Christian church. But even as God had some in Egypt and Babylon who were followers of the light throughout the period of darkness, there was ever a little company of believers who held the Scriptures dear to their hearts, and who obeyed the commandments.

Rom. 7:7.

Who changed the truth of God into a lie, and worshipped and served the creature more than the Creator, who is blessed for ever. Amen.
Rom. 1:25.

For thou hast said in thine heart, I will ascend into heaven, I will exalt my throne above the stars of God. Isa. 14:13.

2 Thess. 2:8.

There is one God and one mediator between God and men, the man Christ Jesus.
1 Tim. 2:5.

Isa. 29:13-25.

Not of works, lest any man should boast.
Eph. 2:9.

Behold, the darkness shall cover the earth, and gross darkness the people.
Isa. 60:2.

Hosea 6:9.

In thee are men that carry tales to shed blood.
Eze. 22:9.

Rev. 13:7, 8.

Who hate the good, and love the evil; who pluck off their skin from off them, and their flesh from off their bones; Who also eat the flesh of my people, and flay their skin from off them; and they break their bones, and chop them in pieces, as for the pot, and as flesh within the caldron.
Micah 3:2-3.

But if thine eye be evil, thy whole body shall be full of darkness. If therefore the light that is in thee be darkness, how great is that darkness!
Matt. 6:23.

Dan. 7:25.

Then shall be great tribulation, such as was not since the beginning of the world to this time, no, nor ever shall be. And except those days should be shortened, there should no flesh be saved: but for the elect's sake those days shall be shortened.
Matt. 24:21-22.

32. And such as do wickedly against the covenant shall he corrupt by flatteries: but the people that do know their God shall be strong, and do exploits.
Dan. 11:32.

Yet I have left me seven thousand in Israel, all the knees which have not bowed unto Baal, and every mouth which hath not kissed him.

1 Kings 19:9, 10, 18.

The ear that heareth the reproof of life abideth among the wise. Prov. 15:31.

33. And they that understand among the people shall instruct many: yet they shall fall by the sword, and by flame, by captivity, and by spoil, many days.

Dan 11:33.

Precious in the sight of the Lord is the death of his saints. Ps. 116:15.

The earth helped the woman, and the earth opened her mouth, and swallowed up the flood which the dragon cast out of his mouth.

Rev. 12:16.

And it shall come to pass, that as ye were a curse among the heathen, O house of Judah, and house of Israel; so will I save you, and ye shall be a blessing: fear not, but let your hands be strong.

Zech. 8:13.

34. Now when they shall fall, they shall be holpen with a little help: but many shall cleave to them with flatteries.
35. And some of them of understanding shall fall, to try them, and to purge, and to make them white, even to the time of the end: because it is yet for a time appointed. Dan 11:34, 35.

And in very deed for this cause have I raised thee up, for to shew in thee my power; and that my name may be declared throughout all the earth.

Ex. 9:16.

Surely the wrath of man shall praise thee: the remainder of wrath shalt thou restrain.

Ps. 76:10.

In that day shall ye say, Praise the LORD, call upon his name, declare his doings among the people, make mention that his name is exalted.

Isa. 12:4.

Sing praises to the LORD, which dwelleth in Zion: declare among the people his doings. When he maketh inquisition for blood, he remembereth them: he forgetteth not the cry of the humble. Ps. 9:11-12:.

We ought to obey God rather than men.

Acts 5:29.

The Waldenses could trace their ancestry back to the days of Paul, and from Asia Minor, where that apostle first preached, to the wild retreat in the mountains of Italy, there were faithful Sabbath-keepers. The power on the [271] throne might change the day of worship, but there were always some who obeyed God rather than man. As Gabriel told Daniel, "They that understand among the people shall instruct many; yet they shall fall by the sword, and by flame, by captivity, and by spoil." Though thousands fell because they dared lift the voice against the powers that be, yet God watched their numbers and counted each one who gave his life.

There is no more wonderful record of deliverance from bondage than that which God wrought for His church at the close of the period of persecution. Israel's deliverance from Egypt, when a multitude marched, through the Red Sea on dry land, was marvelous; the deliverance from Babylon was a wonder in the eyes of the world; but the birth of Protestantism—the deliverance from the darkness of the Middle Ages—surpassed all others.

In the twelfth chapter of Revelation, where the same deliverance is mentioned, it is stated that the earth helped the woman—-the church. And it did indeed. Powers that were wholly unaccountable for the good they were doing, were used by the Father to break those bands that Satan had placed around the truth. The suppression of the Bible had led to the suppression of all learning. There were no schools for the masses; there were no books, no papers; physicians were forbidden to practice medicine, lest they should take money which would otherwise go into the coffers of the church. Should any man dare to advance learning, or cross the beaten paths made by the church, he was led to the stake. But it could not always be so. God [272] made use of the Moors, who had accepted Mohammedanism, to help deliver His people. Schools were established by them in Spain and western Asia. The sciences were taught, and from these schools the light of learning broke into Europe.

Wycliffe, called "the Morning Star of the Reformation," in the fourteenth century translated the Bible into

English. He wrote tracts showing the fallacy of the papal system. In England, he like Daniel of old, was in close touch with the king, and the light of the gospel was having its effect. To the ruler on the throne and the students in the universities, Wycliffe gave the gospel. His followers, known as Lollards, were bitterly persecuted, but never wholly exterminated; and it was their descendants who, as Puritans, brought Protestantism to America,

Huss and Jerome in Bohemia lifted their voices against papal dogmas, and later Luther, the German monk, proclaimed liberty of conscience and salvation alone by faith in Jesus Christ. He had found a copy of the Bible chained in a cell of one of the German monasteries, and the spark there kindled, lighted a fire which Rome was unable to extinguish.

The Word of God became the lesson book for the German nation. Luther was assisted in his work of reform by Melanchthon, the noted teacher in Wittenberg. Other schools were established throughout Germany; teachers were educated, and before the death of Luther the German nation sat at the feet of Protestant teachers; so rapid was the work when the Word of God was opened to mankind. The Reformation [273] marched on to victory. Rome retreated into narrower and still narrower bounds, not before the sword, but before the onward march of truth. Into every nation of Europe the light shone, and America was founded upon the principles which had their birth in Germany.

The papacy quivered before the blow; and had each nation accepted the Reformation as it came to it, it would have been but a short time until history would have been at an end. God was in the Reformation, offering to modern nations the same deliverance which was held out to the Jews when they were granted an opportunity to return from Babylon to Jerusalem. The everlasting covenant was repeated, but men in the sixteenth and seventeenth centuries treated it as the Jews did the decree to leave Babylon. When once the principles of the Reformation—liberty of conscience and the equal rights of all men—were presented to a nation, and were refused, that nation sank back into

Cry aloud, spare not, lift up thy voice like a trumpet, and shew my people their transgression, and the house of Jacob their sins. Isa 58:1.

Is not my word like as a fire? saith the LORD; and like a hammer that breaketh the rock in pieces? Jer. 23:29.

And that from a child thou hast known the holy scriptures, which are able to make thee wise unto salvation through faith which is in Christ Jesus. All scripture is given by inspiration of God, and is profitable for doctrine, for reproof, for correction, for instruction in righteousness. 2 Tim. 3:15-16.

Thou through thy commandments hast made me wiser than mine enemies: for they are ever with me. I have more understanding than all my teachers: for thy testimonies are my meditation. I understand more than the ancients, because I keep thy precepts. Ps 119:98-100.

Keep thereforw and do them: for this is your wisdom and your understanding in the sight of the nations, which shall hear all these statutes. Deut. 4:5-7.

But the path of the just is as the shining light, that shineth more and more unto the perfect day. Prov. 4:18.

I have showed thee new things from this time, even hidden things, and thou didst not know them. Isa 48:6.

Thus saith the LORD, the Redeemer of Israel, and his Holy One, to him whom man despiseth, to him whom the nation abhorreth, to a servant of rulers, Kings shall see and arise, princes also shall worship, because of the LORD that is faithful, and the Holy One of Israel, and he shall choose thee. Isa 49:7.

The ox knoweth his owner, and the ass his master's crib: but Israel doth not know, my people doth not consider. Isa. 1:3.

36. And the king shall do according to his will; and he shall exalt himself, and magnify himself above every god, and shall speak marvellous things against the God of gods, and shall prosper till the indignation be accomplished: for that that is determined shall be done.

Dan 11:36.

How is the faithful city become an harlot! it was full of judgment; righteousness lodged in it; but now murderers. Thy silver is become dross, thy wine mixed with water: Thy princes are rebellious, and companions of thieves: every one loveth gifts, and followeth after rewards: they judge not the fatherless, neither doth the cause of the widow come unto them.

Isa. 1:21-23.

37. Neither shall he regard the God of his fathers, nor the desire of women, nor regard any god: for he shall magnify himself above all.
38. But in his estate shall he honour the God of forces: and a god whom his fathers knew not shall he honour with gold, and silver, and with precious stones, and pleasant things.
39. Thus shall he do in the most strong holds with a strange god, whom he shall acknowledge and increase with glory: and he shall cause them to rule over many, and shall divide the land for gain.

Dan 11:37-39.

The fool hath said in his heart, There is no God. Corrupt are they, and have done abominable iniquity: there is none that doeth good.   Ps. 53:1.

Pharaoh said, Who is the LORD, that I should obey his voice to let Israel go? I know not the LORD, neither will I let Israel go.   Ex. 5:2.

Woe to her that is filthy and polluted, to the oppressing city! She obeyed not the voice; she received not correction; she trusted not in the LORD; she drew not near to her God. Her princes within her are roaring lions; her judges are evening wolves; they gnaw not the bones till the morrow. Her prophets are light and treacherous persons: her priests have polluted the sanctuary, they have done violence to the law.

Zeph. 3:1-4.

the arms of the papacy, and carried to their completion the principles of that government.

Such was the history of France. The experience of that nation stands as an object lesson to the world. Truth had been proclaimed within her borders, but again the papacy rose up to do according to his will. It is in that country that verses 36-39 of the eleventh chapter of Daniel were fulfilled. Having rejected light, the intensity of the darkness into which men fell was beyond description.

Scott, in the life of Napoleon, speaking of France in the year 1793, just a few years before the expiration of the allotted time (verse 36), says: "The world for the first time heard an [274] assembly of men, born and educated in civilization, and assuming to govern one of the finest European nations, uplift their united voices to deny the most solemn truth which man's soul receives, and renounce unanimously the belief and worship of the Deity." "France stands apart in the world's history as the single state which, by the decree of her legislative assembly, pronounced that there was no God, and of which the entire population of the capital, and a vast majority elsewhere, women as well as men, danced and sang with joy in accepting the announcement. This was atheism—the logical result of the position taken in Alexandria when Christians assumed the garb of pagan philosophers. God's Word was treated as a product of the human mind. Atheism in the individual is likewise the result of treating the Scriptures in the same manner."

Still further quotations from the history of those times will show how completely God was rejected, and the worship of the human intellect was substituted.

One day "the doors of the Convention were thrown open to a band of musicians, preceded by whom the members of the municipal body entered in solemn procession, singing a hymn in praise of *Liberty,* and escorting a veiled female, whom they termed the 'Goddess of Reason.'" On unveiling the creature, she was found to be a prostitute opera singer. This was the fittest representation France could find of the reason which she exalted. Perhaps it was hard to understand, when noting the policy of Greece in elevating human reason, what the result of such a course would be. The history of [275] France in the days of the Revolution is a thorough exemplification of that result.

Men to-day exalt reason above God; they deign to give private interpretation to the divine Word: they offer all sorts of theories contradictory to a "thus saith the Lord," and even professed Christians follow the Greek intellect, studying the philosophy themselves, and teaching it to their children, apparently unconscious of the fact that this is papal and only papal, and that its ultimate result may be read in the awful annals of France.

Having enthroned the "Goddess of Reason," France passed laws which clearly reveal the result of such worship. The two institutions which date back to Eden, and which are inseparably connected with the worship of Jehovah, were defamed. The week was changed by a decree so as to completely abolish all resemblance to former times, and for a brief space France rested one day in ten instead of observing the weekly Sabbath. The law of marriage was repealed, and that safeguard to society completely disregarded.

The papacy in France was fast paving the road to self-annihilation. Human intellect worshiped brings death. The French Revolution of 1798, the Massacre of St. Bartholomew, and the Reign of Terror tell the dreadful story of destruction. The entire history of this period is an object lesson to the world of the final destruction of nations when the Spirit of God is withdrawn, because those in authority refuse to worship Jehovah, choosing rather to exalt the "Goddess of Reason."

Complete overthrow stared France in the face [276] until the control of affairs was assumed by the young military officer, Napoleon Bonaparte. Out of chaos he led the nation through bloodshed to a place of honor among the nations of Europe.

The cause of the struggle, which cost thousands of lives, was the *attempt* to suppress both civil and religious rights. The Reformation in Germany in the sixteenth cen-

Casting down reasonings and every thing that exalteth itself against the knowledge of God, and bringing into captivity every thought to the obedience of Christ. 2 Cor. 10:5.

His mischief shall return upon his own head, and his violent dealing shall come down upon his own pate. I will praise the LORD according to his righteousness: and will sing praise to the name of the LORD most high. Ps. 7:16-17.

Your words have been stout against me, saith the LORD. Yet ye say, What have we spoken so much against thee? Ye have said, It is vain to serve God: and what profit is it that we have kept his ordinance, and that we have walked mournfully before the LORD of hosts? Mal. 3:13-15.

Because they had not executed my judgments, but had despised my statutes, and had polluted my sabbaths, and their eyes were after their fathers' idols. Eze. 20:24.

What evil thing is this that ye do, and profane the sabbath day? Did not your fathers thus, and did not our God bring all this evil upon us, and upon this city? yet ye bring more wrath upon Israel by profaning the sabbath. Neh. 13:17-18.

Thou hast despised mine holy things, and hast profaned my sabbaths. Eze. 22:8.

1 Tim. 4:1-3.
In thee have they taken gifts to shed blood; thou hast taken usury and increase, and thou hast greedily gained of thy neighbours by extortion, and hast forgotten me, saith the Lord GOD. Behold, therefore I have smitten mine hand at thy dishonest gain which thou hast made, and at thy blood which hath been in the midst of thee. Can thine heart endure, or can thine hands be strong, in the days that I shall deal with thee? I the LORD have spoken it, and will do it. Eze. 22:12-14.

Jer. 25:29-33.

Behold these are the ungodly, who prosper in the world; they increase in riches. . . When I thought to know this, it was too painful for me; until I went into the sanctuary of God; then understood I their end. Ps. 73:9-17.

God reigneth over the heathen: God sitteth upon the throne of his holiness. The princes of the people are gathered together, even the people of the God of Abraham: for the shields of the earth belong unto God: he is greatly exalted.

Ps. 47:8-9.

Deut. 28:53-57.
Job 30:3-8.

Even all nations shall say, Wherefore hath the LORD done thus unto this land? what meaneth the heat of this great anger? Then men shall say, Because they have forsaken the covenant of the LORD. Deut. 29:24-25.

He ruleth by his power for ever; his eyes behold the nations: let not the rebellious exalt themselves. Ps. 66:7.

The noise of a multitude in the mountains, like as of a great people; a tumultuous noise of the kingdoms of nations gathered together: the Lord of hosts mustereth the host of the battle.

Isa. 13:4,5.

Isa. 8:7.

I will send him against an hypocritical nation, and against the people of my wrath will I give him a charge, to take the spoil, and to take the prey, and to tread them down like the mire of the streets. Howbeit he meaneth not so, neither doth his heart think so; but it is in his heart to destroy and cut off nations not a few. For he saith, Are not my princes altogether kings? Is not Calno as Carchemish? is not Hamath as Arpad? is not Samaria as Damascus? As my hand hath found the kingdoms of the idols, and whose graven images did excel them of Jerusalem and of Samaria.

Isa. 10:6-10.

Behold, the Lord, the LORD of hosts, shall lop the bough with terror: and the high ones of stature shall be hewn down, and the haughty shall be humbled. And he shall cut down the thickets of the forest with iron, and Lebanon shall fall by a mighty one.

Isa. 10:33-34.

tury struck a death-blow to feudalism and the monarchy. France was the battle-ground where papal tyranny wrestled with Protestantism and republicanism. Absolute monarchy always accompanies and supports the policy of the papacy, whether in a pagan or a nominally Christian nation. Democracy in principle is the form of government assumed by any nation when the light of truth is accepted.

When the Reformation was rejected by France, the tyranny of the monarchy knew no bounds. Two thirds of the land of the state was in the hands of the clergy and nobles; the king passed laws taxing his subjects against all protests from Parliament; warrants for arrest and imprisonment were issued by his authority alone; "famine prevailed in every province, and the bark of the trees was the daily food for hundreds of thousands." The oppression was unendurable, and men, frenzied until they were more demon than human, rose in revolt.

In America the principles of the Reformation had been put into practice with comparative ease. But France, having once rejected light, waded through blood in her demand for freedom.

Then appeared Napoleon. With the rapid movements of a master mind he carried victory [277] for the French arms throughout Europe. The army was the controlling element; nobles and clergy were alike powerless, and the common people had exhausted themselves without avail during the terrors of the past few years. He defeated the Austrians and captured Milan; he forced the pope, and various cities of Italy, to purchase peace by giving up their art collections. He organized a republic in Northern Italy, and compelled Austria to cede its Belgian provinces to France. He conducted an expedition to Egypt, hoping to gain control of the eastern Mediterranean. On the way he captured Malta, and then gained a victory over the Mohammedans of Egypt near the pyramids. Near the Nile, however, Bonaparte was met and defeated by Lord Nelson, the greatest of English naval officers. England, jealous of the rapid progress now being made by Napoleon, had opposed his progress in

Egypt. Later he defeated the Turks of Egypt at Aboukir. In 1799 a constitution was adopted in France, and Napoleon was chosen First Consul, with two assistants. France had attempted to copy the Constitution of the United States, but the effort failed. The constitution of 1799 established a centralized government, and deprived the people of liberty and self-government. *"Equality, not liberty,* was all that the cause of France now represented."

The reforms of Napoleon are worthy of tice. Says the historian, "He personally participated in the religious ceremonies which attended the formal restoration of the old system of worship where the Goddess of Reason had been enthroned with atheistic orgies." [278]

"Full toleration was secured for non-Catholics." It was Berthier, who in 1798 made the pope a prisoner, thus fulfilling the prophecy concerning the 1260 years of papal supremacy.

The reforms of Napoleon, however, tended only toward monarchy, and while the people pleaded for republicanism, the pride of the man overruled, and he bent his energies toward his own exaltation. He was proclaimed emperor in 1804, and, in imitation of Charlemagne, he received a crown from Pope Pius VII in Notre Dame. Freedom seemed again to be defeated. Partial acceptance of truth brings only tyranny. This is individual as well as national experience.

The establishment of the principles of the Reformation, as seen in the adoption of the Constitution of the United States, was the result of Puritan faith and courage to follow in that light which led away from the papacy. The struggle of France is a warning to those who see no harm in harboring the principles of antichrist, or those who, having known the truth of civil and religious liberty, turn again to the bondage of error.

At the time of the end (1798), the kings of the north and the south again contended. From the founding of Constantinople by Constantine in 330, the power which held that city had maintained control of the Mediterranean, for Constantinople is recognized by all nations as the key to both Asia and Europe. In the time of the end, history will again center about this city.

When the LORD shall stretch out his hand, both he that helpeth shall fall, and he that is holpen shall fall down, and they all shall fail together. Isa. 31:3.

For it is a day of trouble, and of treading down, and of perplexity by the Lord GOD of hosts in the valley of vision, breaking down the walls, and of crying to the mountains. Isa. 22:5.

So are the paths of all that forget God: and the hypocrite's hope shall perish. Job 8:13.

He did that which was right in the sight of the Lord, but not with a perfect heart. 2 Chron. 25:2.

And I saw one of his heads as it were wounded to death; and his deadly wound was healed: and all the world wondered after the beast. ... He that leadeth into captivity shall go into captivity: he that killeth with the sword must be killed with the sword. Here is the patience and the faith of the saints. Rev. 13:3,10.

Their webs shall not become garments, neither shall they cover themselves with their works: their works are works of iniquity, and the act of violence is in their hands. Their feet run to evil, and they make haste to shed innocent blood: their thoughts are thoughts of iniquity; wasting and destruction are in their paths. The way of peace they know not; and there is no judgment in their goings: they have made them crooked paths: whosoever goeth therein shall not know peace. Isa. 59:6-8.

Rejoice not thou, whole Palestina, because the rod of him that smote thee is broken: for out of the serpent's root shall come forth a cockatrice, and his fruit shall be a fiery flying serpent. Isa. 14:29.

40. And at the time of the end shall the king of the south push at him: and the king of the north shall come against him like a whirlwind, with chariots, and with horsemen, and with many ships; and he shall enter into the countries, and shall overflow and pass over. Dan. 11:40.

Hast thou not heard long ago, how I have done it; and of ancient times, that I have formed it? now have I brought it to pass, that thou shouldest be to lay waste defenced cities into ruinous heaps. Isa. 37:26.

"God is most great;
Mohammed is God's apostle.
Come to prayer;
Come to security."

The Mohammedan
day-call to prayer.

As in times past, so again we are obliged to trace far back to find the source of events which now appear in full view. About the time [279-280] that the papacy was growing into a full-fledged monarchy, recognized among nations of the earth, another power had birth. This new work of Satan came in the form of Mohammedanism, which to-day holds about one-sixth of the world's population in its grasp. The new doctrine originated in Arabia, from whence it spread as a smoke from the bottomless pit. Syria fell under its power, but Egypt became the center of its influence. The banks of the Nile have fed every form of idolatry.

Mohammedanism is but another form of Egyptian darkness. By the power of the sword the followers of Mohammed strove to enter Europe. The western horn of the Crescent, the Moslem symbol, was extended into Spain in the early part of the eighth century, and for a time all Europe was threatened, but the battle of Tours (732) stopped the progress of the conquerors. In 1453, however, Constantinople was captured, and has since remained in the hands of the Turks, the boldest advocates of the doctrine of Mohammed. As the *founding* of Constantinople is a guidepost in history, so the capture of that city in 1453 is another landmark. One of the greatest checks received by the papacy was due to the influx into Italy of Greek scholars, driven from Constantinople by the incoming Mohammedans. The discovery of America was due to the closing of the eastern passage to the rich islands of the Indian Ocean by the Mohammedans in Constantinople and Asia Minor, and so in more ways than is usually thought, [281] God worked to advance truth through those who were ignorant of His truth.

God's plans are never defeated. While Satan closed the passage to the eastern world, God used that act as a key to open the door to the great western world. Thus it is in the Lord's work, from seeming defeat often comes the greatest victory. When the Saviour hung upon the cross, Satan exulted; but what he thought to be the hour of his greatest triumph proved to be but the death knell of his eternal ruin. The cross was the Saviour's greatest victory,

And he opened the bottomless pit; and there arose a smoke out of the pit, as the smoke of a great furnace; and the sun and the air were darkened by reason of the smoke of the pit. And there came out of the smoke locusts upon the earth: and unto them was given power, as the scorpions of the earth have power. Rev. 9:2-3.

And the spirit of Egypt shall fail in the midst thereof; and I will destroy the counsel thereof: and they shall seek to the idols, and to the charmers, and to them that have familiar spirits, and to the wizards. And the Egyptians will I give over into the hand of a cruel lord; and a fierce king shall rule over them, saith the Lord, the LORD of hosts. Isa. 19:3-4.

Looking unto Jesus, the author and finisher of our faith.

The fortress also shall cease from Ephraim, and the kingdom from Damascus, and the remnant of Syria: they shall be as the glory of the children of Israel, saith the LORD of hosts. Isa. 17:3.

Therefore thus saith the Lord GOD; Behold, I am against thee, O Tyrus, and will cause many nations to come up against thee, as the sea causeth his waves to come up. Eze. 26:3.

She is broken that was the gates of the people. Eze. 26:2.

Set thee up waymarks, make thee high heaps: set thine heart toward the highway, even the way which thou wentest. Jer. 31:21.

The LORD shall go forth as a mighty man, he shall stir up jealousy like a man of war: he shall cry, yea, roar; he shall prevail against his enemies. Isa. 42:13.

The one preach Christ of contention, not sincerely, supposing to add affliction to my bonds: what then? notwithstanding, every way, whether in pretence, or in truth, Christ is preached; and I therein do rejoice, yea, and will rejoice. Phil.1:16-19.

and will be the science and song of the redeemed throughout the ceaseless ages of eternity.

Not only Egypt, but Syria and Turkey in Europe, belong to the Mohammedans, and he has entered the "glorious land," and a Moslem mosque occupies the site where once stood the temple of Solomon. This spot where Abraham offered Isaac, and David met the Lord, is sacred to every child of God; but it will be held by unholy hands until "He comes whose right it is to rule." Edom, Moab, and Ammon, however, escaped the hand of this conquering power, and these countries receive an annual tribute from the Turks who pass in caravans on their way to Mecca.

The ambition of Napoleon to establish the authority of Europe in Egypt might have been the beginning of the last struggle between the north and the south. Even in his day Russia and France made friends, but the time had not yet come for the Turk to take his departure from Europe, and England took the part of Egypt against the arms of Napoleon. Napoleon recognized the strength of Constantinople, so [282] also did Russia, and there has been constant jealousy among the nations of Europe lest one should outwit the others, and become the possessor of that stronghold.

Every eye is centered on that spot, and has been for years. Turkey is known universally as the "Sick Man of the East," and the only reason he does not die is because intoxicants are administered, figuratively speaking, first by one nation then by another. The time will come when he will remove from Constantinople, and take up his abode in Palestine; that is, plant his tabernacles between the Mediterranean and Red Seas. Even the Turks themselves are looking forward to the time when they will have to remove their capital from Constantinople to Jerusalem. Time and again the world has been brought to realize that the end of all things is near at hand, for all know that when the Turk steps out of Constantinople, there will be a general breaking up of Europe. They may not name this impending conflict the battle of Armageddon, but God has so named it. In the Crimean war of 1853—1856, the world trembled for Turkey, and, lest the crisis should be precipitated, England and France came to the rescue, and Russia was bidden to stand back. In the Russo-Turkish war of 1877, the powers of Europe united to sustain the life of the *sick man.*

"I saw four angels standing on the four corners of the earth, holding the four winds of the earth, that the winds should not blow on the earth, nor on the sea, nor on any tree, and I saw another angel ascending from the east, having the seal of the living God; and he cried with a loud voice to the four angels, to whom it was [283] given to hurt the earth and the sea saying, 'Hurt not the earth, neither the sea, nor the trees, till we have sealed the servants of our God in their foreheads." These angels now hold the winds of strife, waiting for the church of God to prepare for His coming. The sealing angel goes through Jerusalem (the church) to place the seal of the living God on the foreheads of the faithful, and while this work goes forward, Turkey stands as a national guide-post to the world, that men may know what is going on in the sanctuary above.

God's eye is upon His people, and He never leaves Himself without a witness in the world. No man knows when Turkey will take its departure from Europe, but when that move is made, earth's history will be short. Then the sealing angel that was commissioned to seal the servants of God will return" to heaven with the message, "I have done as Thou hast commanded me." Our great High Priest will then cast His censer into the earth, and pronounce the irrevocable sentence, "He that is unjust, let him be unjust still: and he which is filthy, let him be filthy still: and he that is righteous, let him be righteous still: and he that is holy, let him be holy still." To-day is "the day of preparation." The fate of Babylon, Medo-Persia, Greece, and Rome is recorded for the edification of the nations of to-day, and the lessons taught by all center in the events just before us. While the world watches Turkey, let the servant of God watch the movements of His great High Priest whose ministry for sin is almost over. [284]

And after these things I saw four angels standing on the four corners of the earth, holding the four winds of the earth, that the wind should not blow on the earth, nor on the sea, nor on any tree. And I saw another angel ascending from the east, having the seal of the living God: and he cried with a loud voice to the four angels, to whom it was given to hurt the earth and the sea.

Rev. 7:1-2.

CHAPTER 18

THE CLOSING SCENE

DANIEL 12

DANIEL, the man greatly beloved of God, was several times given a view of the history of the world; but the last vision covered the whole period in detail, and Gabriel did not leave the prophet until he had revealed to him the consummation of all things. Daniel is a latter-day prophet, and gave a history of the period intervening between his own day and the present time, but it was upon the closing events that special emphasis was laid. Four times in his prophecies the expression, "time of the end," is repeated; "the latter days" is used twice, [285] and the expressions "the end of the indignation" and "for many days" each appear once, the closing words of Gabriel were, "Thou shalt rest and stand in thy lot at the end of the days." Thus nine times in the course of the book, attention is called to the fact that the prophecy pointed directly to the closing history of this world.

When the last vision began, the prophet was beside the River Tigris. It was the third year of the sole reign of Cyrus, the Persian. Beginning with the times in which he lived, Gabriel carried the prophet through the history of Persia; he spread out before his vision the conquests of Alexander and the division of his empire; he saw the workings of Greek literature and art, and watched this influence spread into Italy, there moulding the fourth kingdom, and finally blending with the truth in such a manner as to form the papacy. Daniel saw antichrist upheld by arms on the throne of Rome; he was carried through the Dark Ages; he watched, and lo, the darkness scattered before the truth as proclaimed by the Reformers. Like a sudden clearing after a storm, the clouds rolled

Dan. 10:11-19.
Dan. 2:31-45.
Dan. 7:1-27.
Dan. 8:1-27.
Dan. 9:24-27.
Dan. 11:1-45.

But there is a God in heaven that revealeth secrets, and maketh known to the king Nebuchadnezzar what shall be in the latter days. Thy dream, and the visions of thy head upon thy bed, are these. Dan. 2:28.

Dan. 10:14.
Dan. 12:13.
Dan. 8:17.
Dan. 11:35.
Dan. 12:4, 9.
Dan. 8:19.

Yea, saith the Spirit, that they may rest from their labours; and their works do follow them. Rev. 14:13.

In the third year of Cyrus king of Persia a thing was revealed unto Daniel, whose name was called Belteshazzar; and the thing was true, but the time appointed was long: and he understood the thing and had understanding of the vision. . . . And in the four and twentieth day of the first month, as I was by the side of the great river, which is Hiddekel. Dan. 10:1, 4.

Surely the Lord God will do nothing, but he revealeth his secret unto his servants the prophets. Amos 3:7.

The secret things belong unto the LORD our God: but those things which are revealed belong unto us and to our children for ever, that we may do all the words of this law. Deut. 29:29.

Ye were sometimes darkness, but now are ye light in the Lord: walk as children of light. . . . And have no fellowship with the unfruitfull works of darkness, but rather reprove them.
Eph. 5:8, 11.

Unto you that fear my name shall the Sun of righteousness arise with healing in his wings.
Mal. 4:2.

And their dead bodies shall lie in the street of the great city, which spiritually is called Sodom and Egypt, where also our Lord was crucified.
Rev. 11:8.

This I say therefore, and testify in the Lord, that ye henceforth walk not as other Gentiles walk, in the vanity of their mind, Having the understanding darkened, being alienated from the life of God through the ignorance that is in them, because of the blindness of their heart: Who being past feeling have given themselves over unto lasciviousness, to work all uncleanness with greediness.
Eph. 4:17-19.

And the sixth angel poured out his vial upon the great river Euphrates; and the water thereof was dried up, that the way of the kings of the east might be prepared.
Rev. 16:12.

And he shall plant the tabernacles of his palace between the seas in the glorious holy mountain; yet he shall come to his end, and none shall help him.
Dan. 11:45.

And I answered again, and said unto him, What be these two olive branches which through the two golden pipes empty the golden oil out of themselves?
Zech. 4:12.

I, even I only, am left: and they seek my life, to take it away. . . . Yet I have left me seven thousand in Israel, all the knees which have not bowed unto Baal and every mouth which hath not kissed him.
1 Kings 19:14, 18.

Then shall we know, if we follow on to know the Lord: his going forth is prepared as the morning.
Hosea 6:3.

Your iniquities have separated between you and your God, and your sins have hid his face from you.
Isa. 59:2.

The path of the just is as the shining light, that shineth more and more unto the perfect day.
Prov. 4:18.

Dan. 8:14.

back, and the Sun of Righteousness shone forth; but again the darkness gathered, and France, that nation of Europe which was a battle-field where Protestantism contended with the papacy, almost ceased to exist, so bitter was the struggle between the principles of -truth and of error.

The very existence of God was denied, and for a time eternal ruin hung like a pall over that country. God's wrath was stayed, but as a person stricken by some loathsome disease may [286] live, yet ever bear in his body the effects of the illness, so France coming out of the struggle is still scarred with the awfulness of her sin. The prophetic guide carried the prophet still farther, and revealed the contest between modem nations; he saw the final struggle between the north and the south, and pointed to Constantinople as the seat of contention in the last days. Nations should turn their gaze toward the present occupants of that city and patiently await the removal of the Turk into the "glorious land." For "he shall come to his end and none shall help him."

The prophet had watched with intense interest the people upon whom had shone the light of heaven. From Babylon to the end of time a golden stream connected heaven and earth, as if the heavens were open and the dove of peace was descending. At times the stream narrowed to a mere hair-line of light, but it was never wholly extinguished; then the prophet saw it broaden until it lightened the whole world.

That light followed the Jews for hundreds of years, but in the days preceding the Saviour's birth there were but a few souls that bound earth and heaven together. With the advent of Christ a flood of light filled the earth, but again the darkness almost covered the face of the sun. The streams of light were numerous as the Christians scattered throughout the earth, but gradually as the prophet followed these in vision, they grew dim and dimmer. In the days of Luther and the Reformers the stream widened, and again the light flashed like streaks of lightning, piercing the darkness. But days of clear shining were comparatively few. [287]

The close of the prophetic period of 2300 days brought men to important changes in the heavenly sanctuary. Through all time Christ had pleaded for His people, and whether they were many or few, His love was always the same. Finally the great High Priest entered within the holy of holies. To Daniel the scene of the investigative judgment had been revealed. He had seen the Son approach the An-

With the advent of Christ a flood of light filled the earth.

cient of Days; the books of heaven were opened and the records examined. Over and over again the nail-pierced hands had been raised before the great Judge, as the name of some repentant soul was read, and the Intercessor had cried, "Pardon, Father! My blood! My blood," and the scarred character, the marred record, was covered by the life of the Son of Man. Daniel had seen this. He knew that God's people [288] must pass in review before the Judge of worlds, but at the end of the last vision there is another scene presented.

While men are watching the movements of nations; while they cry, "Peace and safety," and yet prepare for war, the angel of God is seen by Daniel to pass through the earth, and place a seal upon the foreheads of those to whom

The temple of God was opened in heaven, and there was seen in his temple the ark of his testament. Rev. 11:19.

The LORD hath appeared of old unto me, saying, Yea, I have loved thee with an everlasting love: therefore with lovingkindness have I drawn thee. Jer. 31:3.

The Ancient pf Days did sit. . . . The judgment was set, and the books were opened. Dan. 7:9, 10.

And she brought forth her firstborn son, and wrapped him in swaddling clothes, and laid him in a manger; because there was no room for them in the inn. And there were in the same country shepherds abiding in the field, keeping watch over their flock by night. And, lo, the angel of the Lord came upon them, and the glory of the Lord shone round about them: and they were sore afraid. And the angel said unto them, Fear not: for, behold, I bring you good tidings of great joy, which shall be to all people. For unto you is born this day in the city of David a Saviour, which is Christ the Lord. And this shall be a sign unto you; Ye shall find the babe wrapped in swaddling clothes, lying in a manger. Luke 2:7-12.

He that overcometh, the same shall be clothed in white raiment; and I will not blot out his name out of the book of life, but I will confess his name before my Father, and before his angels. Rev. 3:5.

Behold, I have graven thee upon the palms of my hands; thy walls are continually before me. Isa. 49:16.

He hath clothed me with the garments of salvation, he hath covered me with the robe of righteousness. Isa. 61:10.

When they shall say, Peace and safety; then sudden destruction cometh upon them. 1 Thess. 5:3.

The Son of man shall send forth his angels, and they shall gather out of his kingdom all things that offend, and them which do iniquity. Matt. 13:41.

2. And many of them that sleep in the dust of the earth shall awake, some to everlasting life, and some to shame and everlasting contempt.
Dan. 12:2.

1. And at that time shall Michael stand up, the great prince which standeth for the children of thy people: and there shall be a time of trouble, such as never was since there was a nation even to that same time: and at that time thy people shall be delivered, every one that shall be found written in the book.
Dan 12:1.

Rev. 22:11.
Prov. 1:24-28.
Gen. 22:1, 2.
Gen. 32:24-30.

For thus saith the LORD; We have heard a voice of trembling, of fear, and not of peace. Ask ye now, and see whether a man doth travail with child? wherefore do I see every man with his hands on his loins, as a woman in travail, and all faces are turned into paleness? Alas! for that day is great, so that none is like it: it is even the time of Jacob's trouble; but he shall be saved out of it.
Jer 30:5-7.

In that day shall there be a great mourning in Jerusalem, as the mourning of Hadadrimmon in the valley of Megiddon. And the land shall mourn, every family apart; the family of the house of David apart, and their wives apart; the family of the house of Nathan apart, and their wives apart.... All the families that remain, every family apart, and their wives apart.
Zech. 12:11-14.

Are ye able to drink of the cup that I shall drink of, and to be baptized with the baptism that I am baptized with They say unto him, We are able. And he saith unto them, Ye shall drink indeed of my cup, and be baptized with the baptism that I am baptized with: but to sit on my right hand, and on my left, is not mine to give, but it shall be given to them for whom it is prepared of my Father.
Matt 20:22-23.

But they that escape of them shall escape, and shall be on the mountains like doves of the valleys, all of them mourning, every one for his iniquity.
Eze. 7:16.

Because thou hast made the LORD, which is my refuge, even the most High, thy habitation; There shall no evil befall thee, neither shall any plague come nigh thy dwelling. For he shall give his angels charge over thee, to keep thee in all thy ways.
Ps. 91:9-11.

these heavenly rays extend. So long as the angel finds any of these faithful ones, Christ still intercedes, but at last the messenger wings his way toward heaven. Throughout the vast kingdom of Jehovah echoes the sound, "It is done," and Christ from the inner sanctuary rises and proclaims, "*It is done.*" He lays aside His priestly garments, and prepares to set in order His kingdom.

His mediatorial work is over; the door from whence has streamed those rays of light and mercy is closed forever. Those who have been sealed must now stand wholly by faith, clinging to God alone during a "time of trouble such as never was since there was a nation."

Daniel had watched men pass through trials. He had seen Israel tried, and men in all ages who were true to God tested on the point of faith, but in all previous instances the test had been lightened by a mediator. Now there is no intercessor, and man stands alone. Mercy is no longer sheltering him. It is another night in Gethsemane, another day of Calvary.

Again the words are uttered, not by one lone man, but by multitudes, "My God, my God, why hast thou forsaken me?" The sweat drops of blood roll from other foreheads; the crown of thorns can be pressed unheeded into many a [289] brow; Calvary's nails can be driven without added pain. The burden of heart-searching is great among the faithful few, as they remember that one unconfessed sin means death. The mother of Zebedee's children asked for her sons a place on the right and on the left of the King on His throne. The Saviour said that place belonged to him who should drink of the cup of which He Himself must drink. That is the cup which is drained to the bitter dregs by the remnant people in the time of trouble, for they are the ones who shall occupy the position mentioned by the mother of James and John.

The faithful sealed followers are not the only ones who know that probation has ended, for upon the wicked the seventh plague is falling, and from it none escape. The time of trouble to the wicked will be terrible, for they drink to the dregs the cup of God's wrath. "A thousand shall fall at thy side and ten thousand at thy right hand," but the righteous do not feel the effects of the plague. The mountains shall shake and the islands flee away. Then it is that the grave yields up part of its dead. At the resurrection of Christ a multitude from all ages came from their graves; they were seen in Jerusalem, and presented by Jesus as a waveoffering on His return to heaven.

So just before His second coming the earth gives up some of those who have slumbered in its bosom. Those who pierced Christ when He hung on the cross, those who mocked and derided Him during His trial, will arise to see Him as He comes triumphant with the host of heaven. Likewise those who under the last message have fallen asleep in Jesus, will come [290] forth to welcome Him for whom they looked and lived. These come forth to everlasting life, but the first class will be slain by the brightness of His coming.

The kingly garments are put on, and the Saviour prepares to gather His people. Throughout heaven the preparation goes on. Angels hurry to and fro, and the inhabitants of the unfallen worlds watch with eagerness. As the company forms to accompany the King, the law of God, the ten commandments, the foundation of His throne, is hung upon the sky in view of the startled multitudes of earth. "His righteousness hath He openly showed in the sight of the heathen." Men who have scoffed and derided those who obeyed this law, now see it written in the heavens.

Again the most brilliant rainbow is painted on the threatening clouds which overhang the earth. Mercy and justice mingled in all God's dealings with men until they utterly turned from Him. To the waiting company this is a renewal of the everlasting covenant made to the fathers that the inheritance should belong to the faithful. Over and over again that same symbol of the everlasting covenant has been hung in the sky, but men have not heard the voice of Jehovah as He spoke in the bow. "The heavens declare the glory of God," but while suns, planets, and systems have been studied by scientists, they have failed to see that in them all God has pictured the organization of His church, and the story of His love to man.

And the graves were opened; and many bodies of the saints which slept arose, And came out of the graves after his resurrection, and went into the holy city, and appeared unto many.
Matt. 27:52-53.
Eph. 4:8 [margin].

2. *And many of them that sleep in the dust of the earth shall awake, some to everlasting life, and some to shame and everlasting contempt.*
Dan 12:2.

Write, Blessed are the dead which die in the Lord from henceforth.
Rev. 14:13.

And then shall that Wicked be revealed, whom the Lord shall consume with the spirit of his mouth, and shall destroy with the brightness of his coming:
2 Thess. 2:8.

And he was clothed with a vesture dipped in blood: and his name is called The Word of God. . . . And he hath on his vesture and on his thigh a name written, KING OF KINGS, AND LORD OF LORDS.
Rev 19:13, 16.
Isa. 63:1-6.

And the armies which were in heaven followed him upon white horses, clothed in fine linen, white and clean.
Rev. 19:14.

The LORD hath made known his salvation: his righteousness hath he openly shewed in the sight of the heathen.
Ps. 98:2.

All thy commandments are righteousness.
Ps. 119:172.

The bow shall be in the cloud; and I will look upon it, that I may remember the everlasting covenant between God and every living creature of all flesh that is upon the earth.
Gen 9:16.

Through the blood of the everlasting covenant, Make you perfect in every good work to do his will, working in you that which is wellpleasing in his sight, through Jesus Christ.
Heb 13:20-21.

And above the firmament that was over their heads was the likeness of a throne, as the appearance of the bow that is in the cloud in the day of rain, so was the appearance of the brightness round about. This was the appearance of the likeness of the glory of the LORD.
Eze. 1:26, 28.

Ps. 19:1-7.

Over and over again
that same symbol of
the everlasting covenant
has been hung in the sky.

And he brought him forth abroad, and said, Look now toward heaven, and tell the stars, if thou be able to number them: and he said unto him, So shall thy seed be. Gen 15:5.

The heavens declare the glory of God; and the firmament sheweth his handywork. Ps. 19:1.

Saying, Where is he that is born King of the Jews? for we have seen his star in the east, and are come to worship him. Matt. 2:2.

Gen.22:17.

From the creation of the world, the very order and arrangement of the stars have told the plan of redemption, but man, devoid of the spirit of [291] truth, can not understand the alphabet of the celestial dome; and while the story has been repeated night after night, he has failed to see the law of God in the firmament.

Jehovah to-day points us to the stars that we may learn the lesson given to Abraham as he called him to his tent door, and traced the promise of the Saviour in the sky. The Star rose upon Israel, and *wise men* of the East, inspired by God, knew that it was the Christ star. Men, using God-given ability, have invented wonderful instruments for searching the heavens, and God has encouraged the effort in hopes that it would lead to an understanding of the divine story written there; but only the very [292] few have seen or heard the spiritual lesson which was taught.

As each sun is encircled by the worlds of its system, so each teacher of righteousness saved in the kingdom of God will be encircled by those saved by his efforts, and as every group of heavenly bodies with its suns revolves around one spot in the heavens, so all the redeemed will be gathered around Christ, the Saviour of mankind.

Daniel watched as Gabriel proceeded, and he saw the heavens depart as a scroll; he saw the sun burst forth in all its glory at midnight, a herald of the Sun of Righteousness. He heard the voice of the trumpeter as the sound rolled through the earth; he saw the righteous dead come forth in answer to the call of the God of heaven. They come forth glorified; the power of the grave is broken; the grave can not hold them. The whole earth resounds with a mighty shout of triumph as they rise to meet the Lord in the air. Multitudes from the days of Adam down to the end of time mingle with that little company who on earth were waiting and watching for His appearing. Together they pass toward the gates of heaven. The advance guard throw open the pearly gates, and again the angel choir chant the wonderful hallelujah which was sung when Christ returned with the little company on the day of His ascension.

From without come the words, "Lift up your heads, O ye gates; and be ye uplifted, ye everlasting doors; that the King of glory may enter through." From within rings forth the challenge: "Who is this king of glory?"

The accompanying host reply:— [292]

"Jehovah, mighty and victorious;

Jehovah, victorious in battle, Lift up your heads, O ye gates; And be ye uplifted, O everlasting doors; That the King of glory may enter through."

"And I looked, and lo, a Lamb stood on the mount Sion, and with Him an hundred forty and four thousand." In a hollow square before the throne are clustered those who were living when the Son of Man came in power. As they

As the host of heaven cannot be numbered, neither the sand of the sea measured: so will I multiply the seed of David my servant, and the Levites that minister unto me. Jer. 33:22.

The heaven departed as a scroll when it is rolled together. Rev. 6:14.

All the foundations of the earth are out of course. Ps. 82:5.

The Lord himself shall descend from heaven with a shout, with the voice of the archangel, and with the trump of God: and the dead in Christ shall rise first: 1 Thess. 4:16.

John 5:28, 29.
Hosea 13:14.

Who shall change our vile body, that it may be fashioned like unto his glorious body, according to the working whereby he is able even to subdue all things unto himself. Phil. 3:21.

Then we which are alive and remain shall be caught up together with them in the clouds, to meet the Lord in the air: and so shall we ever be with the Lord. 1 Thess. 4:17.

And he shall send his angels with a great sound of a trumpet, and they shall gather together his elect from the four winds, from one end of heaven to the other. Matt. 24:31.

I go to prepare a place for you. And if I go and prepare a place for you, I will come again, and receive you unto myself; that where I am, there ye may be also. John 14:2-3.

Lift up your heads, O ye gates; and be ye lift up, ye everlasting doors; and the King of glory shall come in. Who is this King of glory? The LORD strong and mighty, the LORD mighty in battle. Lift up your heads, O ye gates; even lift them up, ye everlasting doors; and the King of glory shall come in. Who is this King of glory? The LORD of hosts, he is the King of glory. Selah. Ps. 24:7-10.

Rev. 14:1.

And I saw as it were a sea of glass mingled with fire: and them that had gotten the victory over the beast, and over his image, and over his mark, and over the number of his name, stand on the sea of glass, having the harps of God. Rev. 15:2.

Rev. 13:8.

They sing the song of Moses the servant of God, and the song of the Lamb.
Rev. 15:3.

That they all may be one; as thou, Father, art in me, and I in thee, that they also may be one in us: that the world may believe that thou hast sent me.
John 17:21.

They sung as it were a new song before the throne, and before the four beasts, and the elders: and no man could learn that song but the hundred and forty and four thousand, which were redeemed from the earth.
Rev. 14:3.

They shall be as the stones of a crown, lifted up as an ensign upon his land.
Zech. 9:16.

Thou shalt also be a crown of glory in the hand of the LORD, and a royal diadem in the hand of thy God.
Isa 62:3.

They shall be mine, saith the LORD of hosts, in that day when I make up my jewels.
Mal. 3:17.

These are they which were not defiled with women; for they are virgins. These are they which follow the Lamb whithersoever he goeth.
Rev 14:4:

Zech. 3:7.
Eze. 28:16.

After this I beheld, and, lo, a great multitude, which no man could number, of all nations, and kindreds, and people, and tongues, stood before the throne, and before the Lamb, clothed with white robes, and palms in their hands.
Rev. 7:9, 10.

He shall see of the travail of his soul, and shall be satisfied.
Isa. 53:11.

Saying, I will declare thy name unto my brethren, in the midst of the church will I sing praise unto thee. And again, I will put my trust in him. And again, Behold I and the children which God hath given me.
Heb. 2:12-13.

And his brightness was as the light; he had horns coming out of his hand: and there was the hiding of his power.
Hab. 3:4.

3. And they that be wise shall shine as the brightness of the firmament; and they that turn many to righteousness as the stars for ever and ever.
Dan. 12:3.

The fruit of the righteous is a tree of life: and he that winneth souls is wise.
Prov. 11:30.

Through faith we understand that the worlds were framed by the word of God, so that things which are seen were not made of things which do appear.
Heb. 11:3.

see the Lamb slain from the foundation of the world, a song of triumph bursts from their lips. Heaven's arches ring, and, wonder of wonders, they whose experiences have seemed so varied, they who have been separated, crushed, degraded, upon whom sin had once placed its terrible hand, find that their voices blend in perfect harmony, and the song they sing is one of such pathos, such depths of joy and gratitude, that none others can join with them. Praise rings throughout heaven. Christ's image and character are perfectly reflected by this company. From the deepest depths of sin they have been raised to the pinnacle of heaven, each, like a stone in the Master's crown, reflecting His character at some certain angle. The one hundred and forty-four thousand together complete the circle of perfection.

In addition to this company, who act henceforth as the bodyguard of the King, taking the place which had been vacant since the fall of Satan and his angels, was seen another company composed of those who were martyrs, and those who had been snatched from the pit of ruin. And again there is seen an innumerable company [294] which no man can number, representing every nation, tribe, and tongue.

The number which would have peopled the earth had no sin ever entered, is gathered about the Father and the Son. Christ looks upon them, and in spite of the remembrance of the fall, and the pain and sorrow which the plan of salvation cost, when He sees the travail of His soul, He is satisfied. In the midst of His redeemed church the Saviour breaks forth into singing. The thought of sin and sorrow is blotted out. From the nail-prints in His hands stream beams of light which are "the hiding of His power." Heaven bows in adoration, for the victory is gained.

Then it is that Daniel sees the language of the heavens interpreted. The universe is composed of suns, many of them mightier than our own, and each sun is the center of a planetary system. Each planet is accompanied by its satellites, a vast circle within a circle, moving in perfect order, performing its revolution in its allotted time, making, to the ear of Jehovah, the music of the spheres. The immensity of space is filled with universes, and all revolve about the throne of God; all are held in their orbits by rays of power from His throne of life; each shines with a light reflected from Him who is the fountain of life; each is guided in its path by the eye of Him who sits on the throne.

This is the type of God's order for His church upon earth. The perfect order of the heavenly bodies is a pattern for family and church organization. Each little company should shine as a star. God looks with pleasure upon the clusters of worshipers as they [295] move in perfect order, each bending to the influence of the higher powers. As it is the power of God in the sun which holds the earth in its course, so His power, working through the highest organization on earth, controls those of smaller power. In the family, children should obey parents, and parents should obey God, even as the earth follows the sun, and the sun circles about its center—God's throne.

The perfection of this system will characterize the last church, which will have developed the character that was looked for in ancient Israel. God's people are a peculiar people, and their peculiarities are derived from the virtues of Christ, which they reflect; this fits them to become a royal priesthood. To Daniel the angel said, "They that be teachers [margin] shall shine as the brightness of the firmament." And so the prophet had the privilege of seeing a nation or company of teachers among the saved, who carried forward the work which his own race might have done. As Christ was a *teacher* who spoke with authority which none could resist, so the remnant church will be teachers by virtue of the Christ-life within them.

It was a beautiful picture, that last scene which fell upon the eyes of Daniel. So many time disappointment had been the outcome when the beginning looked so promising, but in the end it is a glorious triumph. Those who are [296] taken from the depths of sin will shine as the stars in the firmament.

"But thou, Daniel, shut up the words, and seal the book, even to the time of the end." At that time "many shall run to and fro, and knowledge shall be increased."

He is before all things, and by him all things hold together.　　　Col. 1:17, R. V. [margin].

I will instruct thee and teach thee in the way which thou shalt go: I will guide thee with mine eye.
　　　Ps. 32:8.

The husband is the head of the wife, even as Christ is the head of the church: and he is the saviour of the body.　　　Eph. 5:23.

And for the precious fruits brought forth by the sun, and for the precious things put forth by the moon.
　　　Deut. 33:14.

He cutteth out rivers among the rocks; and his eye seeth every precious thing.
　　　Job 28:10.

As also ye have acknowledged us in part, that we are your rejoicing, even as ye also are ours in the day of the Lord Jesus.　　　2 Cor. 1:14.

Children obey your parents in the Lord: for this is right.　　　Eph. 6:1.

But ye are a chosen generation, a royal priesthood, an holy nation, a peculiar people; that ye should shew forth the praises of him who hath called you out of darkness into his marvellous light.
　　　1 Peter 2:9.

The wise shall understand

What is our hope, or joy, or crown of rejoicing? Are not even ye in the presence of our Lord Jesus Christ at his coming? For ye are our glory and joy.
　　　1 Thess. 2:19-20.

Never man spake like this man.
　　　John 7:46.

And I saw as it were a sea of glass mingled with fire: and them that had gotten the victory over the beast, and over his image, and over his mark, and over the number of his name, stand on the sea of glass, having the harps of God.
　　　Rev. 15:2.

Even to the time of the end: because it is yet for a time appointed.　　　Dan. 11:35.

He shall . . . wear out the saints of the Most High, and think to change times and laws: and they shall be given into his hand until a time and times and the dividing of time.
　　　Dan. 7:25.

Rev. 11:3.
And the earth helped the woman, and the earth opened her mouth, and swallowed up the flood which the dragon cast out of his mouth.
Rev. 12:16.

The portion of time known as "the time of the end" is as distinctly marked as any other prophetic period. At its beginning the hand of oppression was removed from the

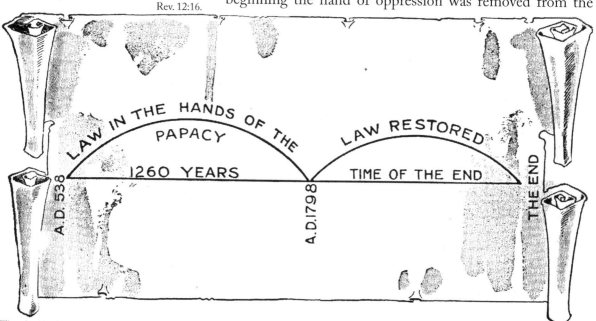

The shield of his mighty men is made red, the valiant men are in scarlet: the chariots shall be with flaming torches in the day of his preparation, and the fir trees shall be terribly shaken. The chariots shall rage in the streets, they shall justle one against another in the broad ways: they shall seem like torches, they shall run like the lightnings. He shall recount his worthies: they shall stumble in their walk; they shall make haste to the wall thereof, and the defence shall be prepared. The gates of the rivers shall be opened, and the palace shall be dissolved.
Nahum 2:3-6.

How beautiful upon the mountains are the feet of him that bringeth good tidings, that publisheth peace; that bringeth good tidings of good, that publisheth salvation; that saith unto Zion, Thy God reigneth!
Isa. 52:7.
This gospel of the kingdom shall be preached in all the world for a witness unto all nations; and then shall the end come.
Matt. 24:14.
Blessed are ye that sow beside all waters, that send forth thither the feet of the ox and the ass.
Isa. 32:20.

law of God, which had been changed, and which, in the language of Revelation, had prophesied clothed in sackcloth. At the same time the persecution of the saints had ended. Civil and religious liberty were standing full-fledged before the world, and Gabriel, seeing the freedom granted to man, explained the effects by saying, "Many shall run to and fro, and knowledge shall be increased."

Men living to-day see the fulfillment of the angel's words. Thousands of miles of railroad thread the globe, making it possible for messengers [297] of truth to pass speedily from place to place. The ocean, once an almost impassable barrier between continents, is now crossed in a few days. The printing press daily sends forth thousands of tons of matter, so that the everlasting gospel can be scattered like autumn leaves to every nation on the face of the earth. The multitude of inventions also astonishes the world. Every day witnesses the birth of some new convenience. "Men have sought out many inventions," and still the work goes on. God allows it, that His truth may be spread with rapidity, for before His coming every nation, kindred, tongue, and people must hear the warning message.

The increased knowledge of the present generation is marvelous beyond description. There is no realm of science left unexplored. This is, that man may be led to see the wonders of creation, and so desire to know more of the Creator. As the closing of the Bible in the beginning of the twelve hundred and sixty years brought darkness, intellectual and moral, so the opening of God's Word has led to intellectual as well as moral advancement. From city to city messages fly on swifter wings than carrier pigeons, while through the mysterious depths of old ocean the words of man pass, unheeded by the myriads that people the ocean caverns.

While man looks on in amazement, angels watch with intense interest to see if man will co-operate with them in using these vast facilities to forward the gospel in the earth.

God from the beginning of earth's history, has offered life to that nation which would make His Word the basis of its education. The Jews were [298] lost as a nation because of the failure to train their children according to its sacred truths; and when the Christian church inherited the promises made to the Israelites, it was upon the same condition that they should teach their children all the statutes of Jehovah.

The time of the end is the period during which the remnant people will be developed. One great means for their education will be a return to true principles of education.

As Christian education and healthful living are revealed in the first glimpse given of the prophet Daniel and his work, so, as he is about to close his earthly career, as he views the last days of earth's history, he is pointed by Christ's special messenger to a people who are true to those same foundation principles. The people who pass safely through the time of trouble, which closes this last prophetic period, will be fortified physically by strict obedience through faith to all the laws of the physical man. And mentally they will be made strong by an education of faith which separates every family from the culture of Egypt, Babylon, and Greece, and instead turns the hearts

Lo, this only have I found, that God hath made man upright; but they have sought out many inventions. Eccl. 7:29.

Jehovah's voice causeth the oaks to wither, and denudeth the trees of the woods. Surely through this his universal temple everything speaks of his glory. Ps. 29:9 [Spurrell's trans].

The entrance of thy words giveth light; it giveth understanding unto the simple. Ps. 119:130.

Curse not the king, no not in thy thought; and curse not the rich in thy bedchamber: for a bird of the air shall carry the voice, and that which hath wings shall tell the matter. Eccl. 10:20.

How then shall they call on him in whom they have not believed? and how shall they believe in him of whom they have not heard? and how shall they hear without a preacher? And how shall they preach, except they be sent? Rom. 10:14-15.

Only take heed to thyself, and keep thy soul diligently, lest thou forget the things which thine eyes have seen, and lest they depart from thy heart all the days of thy life: but teach them thy sons, and thy sons' sons. Deut. 4:9.

Therefore my people are gone into captivity, because they have no knowledge: and their honourable men are famished, and their multitude dried up with thirst. Isa. 5:13.

Ye fathers, provoke not your children to wrath: but bring them up in the nurture and admonition of the Lord. Eph. 6:4.

4. But thou, O Daniel, shut up the words, and seal the book, even to the time of the end: many shall run to and fro, and knowledge shall be increased. Dan. 12:4.

But Daniel purposed in his heart that he would not defile himself with the portion of the king's meat, nor with the wine which he drank: therefore he requested of the prince of the eunuchs that he might not defile himself. Dan. 1:8.

And take heed to yourselves, lest at any time your hearts be overcharged with surfeiting, and drunkenness, and cares of this life, and so that day come upon you unawares. . . . Watch ye therefore, and pray always, that ye may be accounted worthy to escape all these things that shall come to pass, and to stand before the Son of man. Luke 21:34, 36.

MODERN LOCOMOTIVE

MODERN AUTOMOBILE

THE FIRST LOCOMOTIVE

EARLY ENGLISH STEAM MOTOR COACH

But thou, O Daniel, shut up the words and seal the book, even to the time of the end, many shall run to and fro, and knowledge shall be in-creased.

Dan. 12:4

WIRELESS TELEGRAPH STATION

THE OLD METHOD OF TYPE-SETTING

WIRELESS TELEGRAPHY AT SEA

LINOTYPE MACHINE

THE NEW METHOD OF TYPE-SETTING

BENJ. FRANKLINS PRESS

"CLERMONT" THE FIRST STEAMBOAT

A MODERN STEAMER

MODERN PRINTING PRESS

of parents to their children, binding them all together in the love of Christ.

The time of the end, the period in which we now live, is a time when knowledge shall increase; and as the worldly wise trust more and more to their own wisdom, the faithful followers of God will separate entirely from worldly education. Now is the time for the truly wise to shine as the stars whose light is made more apparent as the darkness of iniquity deepens. It is evident that Daniel's whole attention had [299] been centered on the events which Gabriel, God's historian, had related; and when the final triumph of truth was given, it was shown that Christ Himself was near the prophet, and that angels of heaven were also listening to the record of events.

So closely bound to earth are these heavenly beings, and so strong are the ties that unite their hearts and interests to man, that when Gabriel ceased speaking, one angel called to Christ, who was again seen on the waters of the stream of time: "How long shall it be to the end of these wonders?" That was the angel's question, and Christ Himself made answer. Holding up His right hand and His left unto heaven, He "sware by Him that liveth forever that it shall be for a time, times, and a half."

Angels have waited six thousand years for the completion of the plan; they have watched generation after generation for the final number to be made up, and have seen one century after another roll round, and still the inhabitants of earth loiter. What wonder is it that when the end is made known, they call out, "How long shall it be to the end?"

Daniel had heard this same period mentioned by Gabriel, and now it was repeated by Christ, but He says, "I heard, but I understood not." The prophet's heart was heavy as he followed the history of nations to the end of time; and fearing he should still be left in doubt as to the time for the fulfillment of all he had seen, like Jacob who, in his night of wrestling, clung to the angel, he pleaded, "O my Lord, what *shall* be the end of these things?" No request yet made by this man of God had been passed by without [300] an answer. Neither was he now left in ignorance of the time. Gabriel

Here is the patience of the saints: here are they that keep the commandments of God, and the faith of Jesus. Rev. 14:12.

And he shall turn the heart of the fathers to the children, and the heart of the children to their fathers, lest I come and smite the earth with a curse. Mal. 4:6.

And ye shall not walk in the manners of the nation, which I cast out before you: for they committed all these things, and therefore I abhorred them. Lev. 20:23.

Let your light so shine before men, that they may see your good works, and glorify your Father which is in heaven. Matt. 5:16.

I am with you alway, even unto the end of the world. Matt. 28:20.
5. Then I Daniel looked, and, behold, there stood other two, the one on this side of the bank of the river, and the other on that side of the bank of the river.
6. And one said to the man clothed in linen, which was upon the waters of the river, How long shall it be to the end of these wonders? Dan 12:5, 6.

Which things the angels desire to look into. 1 Peter 1:12.

7. And I heard the man clothed in linen, which was upon the waters of the river, when he held up his right hand and his left hand unto heaven, and sware by him that liveth for ever that it shall be for a time, times, and an half; and when he shall have accomplished to scatter the power of the holy people, all these things shall be finished. Dan 12:7.

There came two angels to Sodom at even. . . . And while he lingered, the men laid hold upon his hand, and upon the hand of his wife, and upon the hand of his two daughters; the LORD being merciful unto him: and they brought him forth, and set him without the city. Gen 19:1, 16.

1 Thess. 5:4, 5.
Gen. 32:24-31.

9. And he said, Go thy way, Daniel: for the words are closed up and sealed till the time of the end. Dan. 12:9.

The eyes of the LORD are upon the righteous, and his ears are open unto their cry. Ps. 34:15.

The effectual fervent prayer of a righteous man availeth much. James 5:16.

Let thy work appear unto thy servants, and thy glory unto their children. Ps. 90:16.

O LORD, I have heard thy speech, and was afraid: O LORD, revive thy work in the midst of the years, in the midst of the years make known; in wrath remember mercy.   Hab. 3:2.

Seemeth it a small thing unto you to have eaten up the good pasture, but ye must tread down with your feet the residue of your pastures? and to have drunk of the deep waters, but ye must foul the residue with your feet?   Eze. 34:18.

If thou turn away thy foot from the sabbath, from doing thy pleasure on my holy day; and call the sabbath a delight, the holy of the LORD, honourable; and shalt honour him, not doing thine own ways, nor finding thine own pleasure, nor speaking thine own words: Then shalt thou delight thyself in the LORD.   Isa. 58:13-14.

He shall speak words against the Mosth High, and wear out the saints of the Most High, and think to change the times and the law; and they shall be given into his hand, until a time and times and half a time.   Dan. 7:25. R. V.

The temple of God was opened in heaven, and there was seen in his temple the ark of his testament.   Rev. 11:19.

I saw another angel fly in the midst of heaven, having the everlasting gospel to preach unto them that dwell on the earth, and to every nation, and kindred, and tongue, and people,   Rev. 14:6.

10. Many shall be purified, and made white, and tried; but the wicked shall do wickedly: and none of the wicked shall understand; but the wise shall understand.

11. And from the time that the daily sacrifice shall be taken away, and the abomination that maketh desolate set up, there shall be a thousand two hundred and ninety days.

12. Blessed is he that waiteth, and cometh to the thousand three hundred and five and thirty days.   *Dan. 12:10-13.*

He hath blessed; and I can not reverse it.   Num. 23:30.

Many shall be purified, and made white, and tried; but the wicked shall do wickedly: and none of the wicked shall understand; but the wise shall understand.   Dan. 12:10.

And the vision of all is become unto you as the words of a book that is sealed, which men deliver to one that is learned, saying, Read this, I pray thee: and he saith, I cannot; for it is sealed: And the book is delivered to him that is not learned, saying, Read this, I pray thee: and he saith, I am not learned.   Isa. 29:11-12.

answered the earnest inquiry in tender tones. Said he: "Go thy way, Daniel: for the words are closed up and sealed *till the time of the end;*" and then it was seen that "till the time of the end" meant the same as "a time, times, and a half," at the end of which period the great persecution should cease.

This prophetic period of twelve hundred and sixty years began in 538; the law of God was changed, and the Sabbath of the decalogue was trampled under foot of men. Both the law of God and the saints of God were bound for "a time, times, and a half" by the power which exalteth itself above Jehovah, as described in Dan. 7:25. The persecution tended only to scatter the power of the holy people; and at the time of the end both the law of God and the people were restored. The "time, times, and a half" ended in 1798. Since that time the Word of God has been freely circulated among the people. The prophecies have been studied, the judgment message of the fourteenth chapter of Revelation has been proclaimed, and in 1844, at the close of the twenty-three hundred days, light shone from the sanctuary above, revealing the true Sabbath of the Lord.

As knowledge has increased, the wonderful truths for the time of the end have spread from country to country, preparing the way for the coming of the Son of Man.

That the two prophetic periods which had so puzzled the mind of the prophet might be more perfectly understood, Gabriel said, "From the time that the daily is taken away," that is from [301] 508 A. D., "there shall be a thousand two hundred and ninety days" until the time of the end, 1798. And again, "Blessed is he that waiteth, and cometh to the thousand three hundred and five and thirty days." There is then a blessing pronounced upon those who are living in 1843 (508 + 1335 = 1843), for the seal has been removed from the prophecies, and they are understood. True it is that "many shall be purified and made white and tried," and that some will not understand, but that does not disprove the prophecies, for "the wise shall understand." In the time when all may understand some will insist that the book of Daniel is still a sealed book. The words of Christ and Gabriel witness against all such. "Whoso readeth, *let*

The appearing of Christ in the clouds of heaven.

him understand." [302] "He that hath an ear, *let him hear* what the Spirit saith unto the churches."

DANIEL'S WORK WAS OVER. The story of the world was written. His prophecy would stand until the end. He slept with his fathers, after more than seventy years of faithful service in the courts of Babylon and Shushan. Men could find no fault with him except concerning the law of his God, and Jehovah called him a "man greatly beloved."

In the last days he stands in his lot as a prophet, and the things revealed to him, together with the Revelation given to John on Patmos, and the warnings sent of God through the spirit of prophecy in the remnant church, will guide the faithful company of believers through the time of trouble, and prepare them for the appearing of Christ in the clouds of heaven. [303]

I have fought a good fight, I have finished my course, I have kept the faith.   2 Tim. 4:7, 8.

Thou shalt come to thy grave in a full age, like as a shock of corn cometh in in his season.
      Job 5:26.

13. But go thou thy way till the end be: for thou shalt rest, and stand in thy lot at the end of the days.
      Dan. 12:13.

That he might present it to himself a glorious church, not having spot, or wrinkle, or any such thing; but that it should be holy and without blemish.   Eph. 5:27.

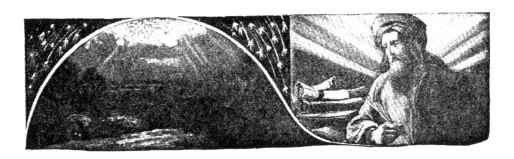

OUTLINE STUDY

THE SANCTUARY

THE heavenly sanctuary is the center of Christ's work for man. The destiny of every soul hangs upon the decisions rendered in that great tribunal. Whether he is conscious of it or not, that work concerns every soul upon the earth.

The ancient sanctuary service was given as a shadow of the work done by Christ for the fallen race, in the heavenly sanctuary. "The whole Jewish economy is a compacted prophecy of the gospel. It is the gospel in figures." The diagram given on page 262, illustrates this truth. *The subjects are not exhausted by any means;* but a few texts are given on each subject, that will serve as a guide to deeper research for those who wish to see the light that flashed from the Levitical laws and sacrificial offerings.

All the texts in the diagram are reprinted on the following pages, together with the leading thought in the texts. Let the reader ever remember that, "The entire system of Judaism was the gospel veiled."

There are precious views of the work of Christ revealed in the rays of light flashing from the Levitical laws and sacrificial offerings, that will well repay the student who will search for them.

Many to-day discard the study of the Levitical laws, because they think the gospel has no connection with the Jewish economy. All such would do well to ponder prayerfully the last two verses of the fourth chapter of John's Gospel. Moses wrote of Christ. Every statement made, every symbol given was for the one object; viz., To reveal a sin-pardoning Redeemer to fallen man. Christ said: "If ye believe not his [Moses'] writings how shall ye believe My words," . . . "for he wrote of Me;" also, "If they hear not [304] Moses and the prophets, neither will they be persuaded, though one rose from the dead." Luke 16:31. The words are true to-day, and all who will study the Levitical laws, believing that the entire system of Judaism reveals the gospel of Christ, will find their faith in the Saviour greatly strengthened by the study. As they learn to behold

Christ revealed in types, shadowed in symbols, and manifested in the revelations of the prophets, as fully as in the lessons given to the disciples, and in the wonderful miracles wrought for the children of men, their hearts will burn within them as He talks with them by the way. They will be dwelling upon the same precious truths the Saviour dwelt upon as he walked with the disciples on the way to Emmaus; when, "Beginning at Moses and all the prophets He expounded unto them in all the Scriptures the things concerning Himself." Luke 24 :13-31.

THE SECOND COMING OF CHRIST

Lev. 16:20-25. When the high priest on the day of atonement had made an end of reconciling, and had placed the sins upon the scapegoat, he laid aside his high priest's robe, and went into the court and cleansed it. So Christ, when probation closes, lays aside His priestly garments and comes into the antitypical court, the earth, to gather out of it all things that offend and do iniquity. Matt. 18:41.

Isa. 63 :1-6. Christ comes clad in garments of vengeance.

Rev. 19:16; Zeph. 2:1-3. Christ does not come to the earth in priestly robes; but in kingly garments.

THE MILLENNIUM

Lev. 16:20-22. The scapegoat was led into a desolate land, a land not inhabited. "Scapegoat" is a synonym for evil.

Job 1:7. The earth is the devil's home.

Jer. 4:23-27. The earth will be desolate. When there is "no man," animals, or birds, the devil and his angels will be the only life left upon the earth.

Isa. 24:21, 23; Jer. 4:27. This desolate condition will only be for a limited period of time.

Eze. 28 :18, 19. The devil will finally be brought to ashes on the earth.

Lev. 6:9-11. The ashes of the burnt offering left in a clean place, taught the final destruction of sin and the devil.

THE NEW EARTH

Gen. 3 :17. Earth cursed by sin.

Num. 35:33. Curse only removed by the blood of the offending party.

Lev. 17:11-13. The blood made atonement for sin.

Lev. 4:7, 18, 25, 30. The blood of every sin offering poured upon the sin-cursed earth, taught the cleansing of the earth by the blood of Christ. [305]

Jer. 9:21. The air is laden with disease germs as the result of sin.

Ex. 15:23. The water is affected by the curse. Land, air, and water are all cursed by sin.

Lev. 14:4-7. This offering made provision for the cleansing of the water, air, and ground. The blood came in contact with each. It was caught in an *earthen* vessel held over running *water;* and the bird flew through the *air* with blood upon its feathers. Hyssop, cedar wood, and wool were dipped in the blood.

Kings 4:33. The hyssop and cedar represented the two extremes of vegetation. Dipping them in the blood was but a type of the vegetation of the whole earth being cleansed by the blood of Christ.

Num. 19:6. In this offering the cleansing of the vegetation by fire was also taught. The hyssop and cedar wood were burned.

John 19:29. The cross was made of the trees of the forest. Thus the two extremes of vegetation, the hyssop and the forest trees, came in contact with the blood of Christ.

Lev. 25:23, 24. The land was never sold, but if lost in any way could be redeemed by the one nearest of kin that had power to redeem.

Ruth 2: 20. Christ is the only one near of kin to humanity that has power to redeem. Satan does not own the land; he simply has present possession. Christ alone has the right to redeem Adam's lost dominion.

THE LAW OF GOD

Ex. 25:21. The ark, the central article of furniture in the sanctuary, was made to contain the law of God.

Ex. 31:18. The tables were called tables of testimony.

Rev. 11:19. The ark containing the testimony is in the heavenly sanctuary.

SABBATH

Ex. 25 :30. Shewbread was to be continually kept upon the table in the holy place.

Chron. 9:32. Every Sabbath the priests were to prepare fresh bread.

Lev. 24 :5-9. The bread was made in twelve loaves, placed in two rows upon the table. It remained on the table a week, and was then taken off the table and eaten by the priests.

Sam. 21:6. The fresh bread was taken hot from the oven each Sabbath morning and placed upon the table.

All the work connected with the shewbread was Sabbath work; therefore all the antitypical lessons connected with it are Sabbath lessons. The bread was a type of Christ, the "living bread" John 6:51. We as members of the royal priesthood (1 Pet. 2:9) should have fresh truth from the Word of God each Sabbath day, and feed upon the truth ourselves.

Rev. 11:19. The ark in the most holy place was made to contain the law of God. John saw the ark in heaven. The Sabbath commandment, which is the basis of all Sabbath keeping, is the fourth one in the decalogue, and is found in the heavenly ark. [306]

REPENTANCE

Every sin offering taught this truth; for the sinner confessed his sins over the head of the sacrifice before its life was taken.

Lev. 4:27-31. Freedom from sin was clearly taught; the sinner's sins were "forgiven him."

FATE OF THE WICKED

Psa. 73 :12-18. When David entered the sanctuary he clearly understood the fate of the wicked. The sanctuary service taught it plainly.

Lev. 3 :14-17; Lev. 16:25. All the fat was separated from the sacrifice and burned.

Psa. 37:20. The burning of the fat symbolized the burning of sin and sinners in the fires of the last days.

Lev. 4:8-12; Lev. 6 :10, 11. Even the care of the ashes taken from the altar taught that important lesson. They were not thrown carelessly aside, but were emptied out on a "clean place" prepared for the purpose.

Mal. 4:3. The antitype will be fully met when the fires of the last day have fully consumed Satan and the wicked, and all that remains of them will be ashes upon the "clean" earth. Eze. 28:18.

CHRISTIAN HELP WORK

Ex. 22:22-24. God has a special care for the widow and orphans.

Deut. 14:29. One who cares for the stranger, the widow, and orphan will be blessed in his work.

Deut. 24 :19-22. When the grain was harvested provision was made for the poor.

Isa. 58:7-12. Spiritual and physical health come as the reward of supplying the needs of the poor and helpless.

SPIRITUAL GIFTS

Ex. 28:30. The Urim and Thummin were to be placed in the breastplate and worn by the high priest.

Num. 27:21; 1 Sam. 28:6. The high priest learned the mind of the Lord through these stones in the breastplate.

1 Sam. 23:9-12. Direct answers were given from God by means of the breastplate, representing the direct communication between God and His people, through the prophets.

"At the right and left of the breastplate were two large stones of great brilliancy. These were known as Urim and Thummin. By them the will of God was made known through the high priest. When questions were brought for decision before the Lord, a halo of light encircling the precious stone at the right was a token of the divine consent or approval, while a cloud shadowing the stone at the left was an evidence of denial or disapprobation." [307-308]

CHRISTIAN EDUCATION

Ex. 12:26, 27. One object of the types and symbols was to arouse an inquiry in the minds of the young, and these questions were to be faithfully answered by the parents.

Ex. 13:7, 8, 14. The eating of unleavened bread and the redeeming of the first-born would cause the children to inquire why it was done. The instruction given was to be in answer to the child's own inquiry.

Deut. 32:7. Instruction was to be received by questions asked parents and elders. It was the duty of the parents and elders to faithfully answer these questions.

Josh. 4:6-7. Objects were placed in conspicuous places to arouse the curiosity of the children, and the questions were to be faithfully answered.

Psa. 78: 6, 7. Faithfulness to God was to be implanted in the child by the instruction given by the parents.

Deut. 4:9-13. The knowledge of the events connected with the giving of the law of God, was especially mentioned as important in the education of the children.

Deut. 6:7-9. The conversation in the home and while engaged in the daily tasks should always be such as will educate the children in the things of God.

MINISTRATION OF ANGELS

Ex. 25:20. The golden cherubim were but a shadow or type of the cherubim "that covereth" in the sanctuary in heaven. Luke 1:19.

Ex. 36:8, 35. Cherubim were wrought in the curtains that served as "veils" and ceiling for the earthly sanctuary, and were but a type of the "thousand thousands" and "ten thousand times ten thousand" of angels that Daniel beheld in the heavenly sanctuary.

Dan. 7:9, 10. To Daniel this vast multitude of angels ministering in the heavenly sanctuary appeared as a "fiery flame." Heb. 1:7; Eze. 1:14.

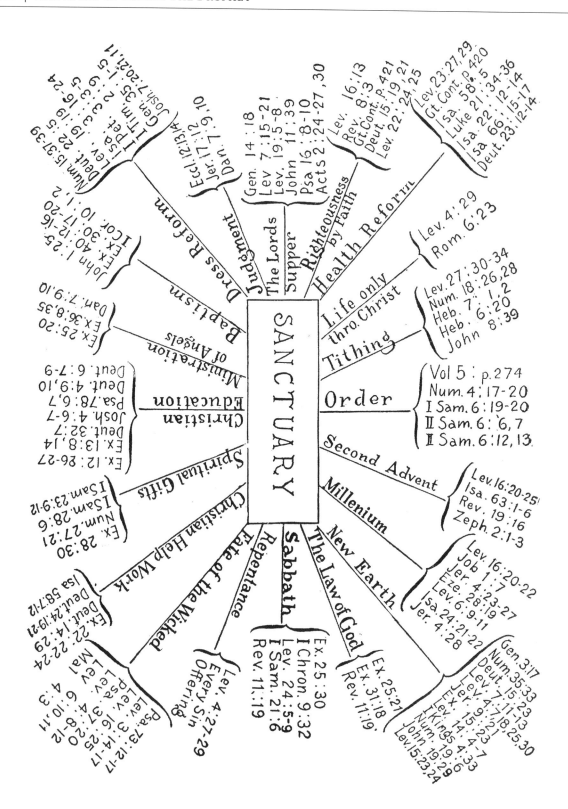

BAPTISM

John. 1: 25. There was something in the scriptures that taught the people that when the forerunner of Christ came he would baptize; for the people were expecting it.

Ex. 40 :12 16. Washing with water was a part of the ceremony in consecrating the priests.

Ex. 30:17-21. Washing with water when they served in the priests' work was so important that "death" was the penalty for neglect.

Cor. 10:1, 2. The Lord called the passage through the Red Sea baptism.

DRESS REFORM

Num. 15:37-39. Dresses were made in such a manner that as they looked at them they were reminded of the commandments of God, and encouraged to obey them. In their dress they were not to seek after their own hearts, nor their own eyes. If they did, they would copy the fashions of Babylon. [309]

Deut. 22:5. Women were forbidden to wear masculine attire.

Lev. 19:19. Garments were ever taken as an emblem of the righteousness of Christ, and when different substances as linen and wool were mingled it spoiled the figure.

Isa. 3:16-24. Foolish fashions are not confined to modern days, but have been in existence from early times. All of the fashions named here, are used in some part of the world to-day. When the "daughters of Zion" followed the fashions of the world, it caused Zion to sit upon the ground desolate. Isa. 3:26.

1 Pet.3:5. It was only a firm trust -in God that enabled the women to dress plainly and ignore the fashions of the world.

Tim. 2:9. Women should dress in modest apparel.

Gen. 35:1-5. After Jacob's daughter had been disgraced (Gen 34 :1-5), Jacob drew near to God. He then saw that their manner of dressing was like the world, and he called upon his family to change their garments and hide their ornaments.

Josh. 7:20, 21, 11. Achan coveted the Babylonish garment and lost his place in Israel.

JUDGMENT

Eccl. 12:13, 14. The law contained in the ark in the most holy place, is the standard in the Judgment. Rom. 2 :11-13.

Jer. 17 :12. The throne of God has ever been connected with the sanctuary in heaven.

Dan. 7:9, 10. Daniel was given a view of the throne of God in the heavenly sanctuary. He saw the Great Judge of the universe seated upon that throne. In His presence the books were opened and every case decided. The sanctuary is the great Judgment Hall of the universe of God.

The Lord's Supper

Gen. 14:18. Melchisedec, the great priest king of Salem, gave "bread and wine" to Abraham.

Lev. 7:15-21. The "peace offering" shadowed forth the death and resurrection of Christ. It was to be eaten on the first and second days; any one who ate the flesh the third day, by that act, virtually said he did not believe that Christ would be alive upon the third day.

Lev. 19:5-8. Any one who disregarded this injunction failed to see the object of the service, and thus "profaned the hallowed things of the Lord," and was cut off from among the people of God. The peace offering was eaten by all the people. It shadowed forth the death of Christ, while the Lord's Supper commemorates it.

John 11:39. Upon the fourth day after death the body had begun to decay.

Psa. 16:9-10. The prophets clearly revealed that Christ's body would not see corruption. It would not be in the grave the third day.

Acts 2:24-27, 30, 31. Peter quoted from the sixteenth Psalm to prove the resurrection of Christ. The people were familiar with the peace offering, which clearly taught the death and resurrection of Christ, and the converting power of God attended his words. [310]

Righteousness by Faith

Lev. 16:13. The incense shielded the priest from death when he went in before the Lord. Rev. 8:3 [margin]. Incense added to the prayers of the saints makes them acceptable to God.

Note. It was the work of the priest in the daily ministration to present before God the blood of the sin offering, also the incense which ascended with the prayers of Israel. So did Christ plead His blood before the Father in behalf of sinners, and present before Him also, with the precious fragrance of His own righteousness, the prayers of penitent believers.—"Great Controversy," p. 421.

Deut. 15:19, 21. The offerings were to be without blemish, thus representing the perfect life of Christ imputed to us.

Lev. 22: 24, 25. If any one offered an imperfect offering it was not accepted. By faith they were to see Christ's righteous character in every offering.

Health Reform

Lev. 23:27, 29. Every man was required to afflict his soul while the work was going forward. All busiess was to be laid aside, and the whole congregation of Israel were to spend the day in solemn humiliation before God, *with prayer, fasting,* and *deep searching of heart.* *"Great Controversy," p. 420.*

Isa. 58:5. To fast is to afflict the soul. The day of atonement in the type was a fast day. The appetite was held in perfect control, a type of the control of appetite God requires during the antitypical day of atonement.

Luke 21:34-36. The Saviour says that during the time of the judgment, while individuals are being "accounted" worthy or unworthy, we are to take heed least we become overchanged with surfeiting and drunkenness. Surfeiting is taking too freely of food, whether it be good or bad. Drunkenness is partaking of improper food. We are to be master, and not the slave of our appetite.

Isa. 22:12-14. In tis period when God calls to self-control, many will give loose reins to their appetite.

Isa. 66:15-17. All such will be destroyed, "consumed together saith the Lord."

Deut. 23:12-14. The Lord required strict sanitary arrangements throughout the camp, for He walked in the midst of His people.

LIFE ONLY THROUGH CHRIST

Lev. 4:29. Every sin offering slain, taught that the sinner gained life through the death of the offering. A substitute was slain and the sinner lived.

Rom. 6:23. Sin brings death; freedom from sin, life through the Saviour.

TITHING

Lev. 27:30-34. The Lord reserved as His own one-tenth of man's income. "The earth [311] is the Lord's and the fulness thereof." He has a right to claim a portion of the wealth.

Num. 18:20-28. The Lord used the tithe to support His work in the earth. It was given to the priests, and they in turn paid a tithe into the treasury.

Heb. 7 :1, 2. Abraham paid tithe to Melchisedec.

Heb. 6:20. Jesus is a priest after the order of Melchisedec.

John 8:39. If we are Abraham's seed we will do the works of Abraham—pay our tithe to support the work of Christ upon the earth. "Even so hath the Lord ordained that they that preach the gospel should live of the gospel." 1 Cor. 9:9-14.

ORDER

Num. 4: 17-20. If those appointed to carry the articles of furniture, went in to look at the furniture before it was covered, they were slain. Each was to come in their order. The priests were to cover the furniture, then the Kohathites were to bear it.

Sam. 6:19-20. The people were punished with death for disobeying and looking into the ark.

Sam. 6:6, 7. God commanded that the priests alone should touch the ark.

Sam. 6 :12, 13. When the ark was carried by the priests according to God's direction the Lord blessed them.

NOTE. The directions in regard to order in the tabernacle service were recorded that lessons might be drawn from it by all who should live upon the earth. Men were selected to do various parts of the work of setting up and taking down the tabernacle; and if one strayed in carelessly and put his hands to the work assigned to another, he was to be put to death.

We serve the same God to-day. But the death penalty has been abolished; had it not been, there would not be so much careless, disorderly work in His cause. The God of heaven is a God of order, and He requires all His followers to have rules and regulations, and to preserve order.— *"Testimonies for the Church," Vol. V, p. 274.* [312]

Questions for Study

Note.—For the benefit of those who may wish to use "The Story of Daniel the Prophet" as a text-book in either the family or the school, the following questions have been prepared. The questions are arranged in paragraphs corresponding with the paragraphs in the book.

CHAPTER 1
DANIEL AND HIS FELLOWS TESTED

1. How long ago did Daniel live? What is he called? What should be studied? Why? What is contained in Daniel's prophecies? Who bare witness to this? Quote the Saviour's words in regard to Daniel. What do these words contain? Give the object of the prophecies of Daniel.

2. What is said of the book of Daniel? How long was it sealed? When did the time of the end begin? Who will understand? What is needed with the book of Daniel to bring one in touch with God?

3. With what statement does the book of Daniel open? When? What was the result of the siege? What was carried to Babylon?

4. Of what was all this the culmination? What is essential? Of what is this captivity an object lesson? What is necessary?

5. What was God's design in separating the Jewish nation from the rest of the world? To what was Israel compared? How was the light kept burning? When the prophets were neglected what was the result? Why was Jerusalem destroyed? What proves the truth of the maxim? Why were the Jews restored?

6. How long before the days of Daniel did Hezekiah reign? What took place when he had reigned thirteen years? How much time was given him? Who visited the king? What did they see? Why did they come? What did the king lose? What message came to the king from the Lord? What would befall his descendants?

7. What was portrayed? What was done with this prophecy? What question was asked? What conclusion is drawn? How did some mothers receive the thought?

8. When was a son bom to Hezekiah and his wife? Did they regard the recent prophecy while training their son? How old was Manasseh when he began to reign? Why did he choose heathen worship?

9. What is said of Christ? When did He accept His appointed mission? Why? What course did Manasseh pursue? What came as the result?

10. What contrast is drawn? Give the names of the mothers.

11. Was the prophecy sent Hezekiah fulfilled in Manasseh's reign? What did the people say?

12. When did Jeremiah prophesy? What did God do through Jeremiah? Quote the words of the prophecy. What was given in these words?

13. What was Josiah spared from? Why? What was kept in his day? What promise was given him? What opportunity was given Josiah? How was it given? How many of Josiah's descendants reigned? What course did they all pursue?

14. Name the sons. Who reigned before Zedekiah? What is the fate of these kings? What might they have been? What became of the first one? Give the course and fate of Jehoiakim. What became of the treasures in the temple? Of the youth? Why was Jehoiakim powerless? What mistake did his parents make? How did he train his son? With what result? To what is this compared?

15. What opportunity did Zedekiah have? What was in Babylon? How long had Daniel been in Babylon when a special testimony came to Zedekiah? Repeat the message sent to Zedekiah. Did he obey? What would have been the result of his obeying the Lord? What excuse did he make?

16. What is revealed in these three sons?

17. Who was living in the same city with these kings? To whom were they related?

18. Give date of first siege of Jerusalem? How old was Daniel at this time? Who was about the same age? What is said of Daniel's mother? What did she repeat over to her son? What was Daniel taught to read? Upon what three subjects did he receive special instruction? What story was told and retold? What will dull the mind to spiritual things?

19. What is said of the Hebrew songs? What effect do such songs have upon an individual? What is said of the schools of that time? How did the holy mothers live? In what four ways did they teach their children?

20. What is said of most of the young men in the capital? Why did they excuse themselves? Who did God choose? What happened to Daniel and his companions?

21. When was the effect of home training seen? What three things placed them on the list of well-favored children? What is said of their intellectual ability? Did they lack in the sciences or essential branches?

22. What provision was made for them? In what did Daniel have unbounded confidence? Why? What is said of Daniel's education? With what was it in harmony? How much did this question mean to Daniel? What decision did he make? What purpose did he make in his heart? What expression shows there were Hebrew children 'that were not true to principle?

23. Whose council did Daniel and his companions seek? With what result? What was involved in sitting at the king's table?. What would be the result of removing the safeguard of temperance? How might they have reasoned? With whom did they leave the results?

24. What two traits of character were shown in Daniel? What request did he make? Was it an experiment with them?

25. Why did the officer hesitate? What explanation did they give to the officer? What did they urge? Was the request granted? Why? Describe their state of mind.

26. Who approved of their course? How did they appear at the end of ten days? What

bespoke physical soundness and moral purity? What were they allowed after this?

27. Was pulse and water *always* the exclusive diet of Daniel? When and why did he choose it? At what other times did he abstain from flesh, wine, etc.?

28. How does Ezekiel refer to the character of Daniel? Through what will people have to pass in these days? What does God ask them to give up? For what is this a reason? Upon [314] what did Daniel and his companions get the victory? In how many ways could Satan tempt Adam? What would have been the result of obedience? What came through the open door of appetite?

29. Where did Christ begin his work? Upon what was His first temptation in the wilderness? In withstanding this temptation what victory was gained? When will God's people be tempted as Daniel was tempted? What lies at the foundation of every reform?

30. What is embraced in being true to God? What is meant by health reform? What does it call for? What is said of too great a variety of food at the same meal? Who only are fitted to bear responsibilities in the closing work?

31. What is said of the experience of Daniel and his companions? In the midst of the evils of the court what did they exercise? What object did they have in view?

32. Who taught these Hebrew children? With whom were they connected? Who did they imitate? How did they become educated? While gaining their education what did they also receive?

33. What was the result of the examination at the end of three years? In what things did they excel the others? In what degree did they excel?

34. What is said of these youth? Why did God honor them? How did they compare with the other captives? In what five ways was their regard for God and nature's laws revealed? What is the foundation of the highest education? What is the result of faith developed in childhood?

35. What do our youth meet daily? Who will be rewarded like Daniel? What may every youth bear today?

36. For what will young men be fitted who cherish these principles? What is said of the Waldenses? Give the result of this work?

37. Give the last words of the first chapter of Daniel. How long did Daniel live in Babylon? With whom was he acquainted? How long before had Isaiah mentioned this man?

CHAPTER 2
A CONTROVERSY BETWEEN TRUTH AND ERROR

1. How are we introduced to Nebuchadnezzar in his own home? How is he spoken of in the first chapter? How in the second? Where can we trace the history of Babylon? What is embraced in this history? When will it end?

2. What is Satan's accusation? What request was made and granted? Where did he set up his rival kingdom? What had God told the people to do? What did they do? Describe the city. In what council was Satan then a representative? What was his design? After what pattern was the city modeled? Describe the government. What is the result of man being

exalted above God? What did Nebuchadnez-zar do for Babylon?

3. What is said of Nebuchadnezzar? Of Babylon? In what were the Babylonians especially proficient?

4. Of what was Babylon proud? What caused her to turn away? What was excmplified in Babylon? For what was Daniel chosen?

5. What is said of the language of the Scriptures? Of what was Nebuchadnezzar thinking when he fell asleep? With what fact was he well acquainted? When was God's opportunity to speak to him? What was spread out before the king? What [315] prevented the king from relating the dream?

6. Of whom did the king demand an interpretation? What was their answer? Why did the Lord permit this? How did the request of the wise men affect the king? What was given?

7. How long had Nebuchadnezzar been ruling? With whom had he reigned the previous two years? What position did Daniel and his fellows hold? Why did Arioch seek them? What question was asked? What reply was given? What did Daniel do? What was the result?

8. What supreme moment comes in every life? How had Daniel been prepared for this test? What probable reason is given for Daniel's not being classed with the wise men of Chaldea? How does God confound the mighty?

9. How did Daniel and his fellows spend the night? What was shown Daniel? Why did not Nebuchadnezzar see these things?

10. What was revealed in Daniel's song of praise?

11. What was developed in the schools of Babylon? With what was this contrasted? .

12. How had God taught Egyptian senators? With what words did Daniel meet the wise men of the schools of Babylon?

13. How did the king appear? Who surrounded Daniel? What words of the psalmist were exemplified?

14. Describe the condition of the king? What is said of Daniel? What opportunity did he have? What did he tell the king? To whom was the king's mind directed?

15. What was revealed in one night? Give the contrast between prof? ne and sacred history. What is said of the Scriptures?

16. How did the Lord represent Babylon? What did the Spirit of prophecy point out to the king?

17. What Scripture illustrates the weakness of Babylon? Why was that nation to be humbled? How would she seek to save herself? With what result?

18. Where is the strength of nations not found? What alone can make them strong? How do they decide their own destiny?

19. How long did Nebuchadnezzar's kingdom last? What followed?

20. Name in their order the three kingdoms that followed Babylon. How was Rome divided? What kingdom will be set up while the divisions of Rome are still in existence? How long will it continue?

21. What did the image represent? What was represented by the different grades of metals in the image? How was the division of Rome indicated in the image? How long will the division continue?

22. What beside the division was represented by the iron and clay? Where in the world's history does this begin?

23. Give the basis of government in heathen nations. What could not be separated? How is it with apostate Christianity and the State? How long will it continue? What was indicated by the stone cut out of the mountain without hands?

24. Did the king recognize the dream? Did he accept the interpretation? How did the king express his feelings? What did he say?

25. What position was given Daniel? How were his friends honored? When was the dream given? What king reigned in Judah?

26. What did God design? What were God's people compelled to do? Why? State two things said of [316] Babylon. How did the Jews lose the power of God? How did God make Himself known to the heathen king? What additional facts are stated? Why was Daniel and his companions put at the head of the empire?

27. In what position was Nebuchadnezzar? In view of this what message was sent to Zedekiah? By whom?

28. Why is the history of Babylon recorded? What is the book of Revelation? To what is the term Babylon applied? What at the present day corresponds to the relation of the Jews to the Babylon of Nebuchadnezzar's day?

29. What will be repeated to-day? What is generally accepted? State seven things toward which the world to-day is hastening.

30. What four things did God do that the Jewish nation might become a teacher of nations? From what place is He calling a people to-day? What will the principles of healthful living God Has given His people do for them? What will be the result of following God's educational principles? What is said of the principles of true government?

31. How many were true to these principles in Daniel's day? How will it be today?

CHAPTER 3
TRUE FREEDOM IN WORSHIP

1. Give the first sentence in the chapter. How long since the events recorded in the second chapter had taken place? What position did Daniel and his three friends now hold? What had these men been doing in these twenty-three years? What had happened to Jerusalem and the Jews? Where was their king? What did appearances seem to indicate?

2. What is said of Nebuchadnezzar at the time his dream was interpreted? What is said of his condition at the time he made the image? After what model was the image made? In what respect did the image differ from the one seen in the dream? What was left out? Describe the image?

3. What decree was issued by Nebuchadnezzar? Was it obeyed?

4. Who was watching with interest? Why?

5. What two facts are given in regard to Babylon? Why is the history given?

6. State one privilege of a king. One duty of subjects.

7. What was heard when the company were gathered together? Give the words of the herald. How only can we worship God? Of what are pagans ignorant? What is necessary for pagan worship? With what three things was the erection of the image in accordance?

With what three customs was the commandment to worship in harmony?

8. With what was this command to worship not in harmony? What was being done in the person of the king? How did God treat Lucifer and the angels when they refused to bow before the throne of God? How did the king of Babylon treat those who refused to bow to the image? Give the motive power in heavenly government. In human government. What is all tyranny? What is it sometimes called? What is enforced civil worship, be it true or false? With what is it always accompanied? What is it called from a civil stand point? From a religious point of view?

9. Name those who refused to worship the image? Who reported them to the king? With what words?

10. What did the king think in regard to [317] the matter? What brooks no opposition?

11. What question is given? What was offered them? What awaited traitors and rebels?

12. What five classes of individuals were spectators of the scene? Between whom was the controversy? What was at stake? For what two parties could they witness? State four important questions asked in this paragraph? How would you answer them?

13. What two important facts had these Hebrew youth learned? What answer did they give the king?

14. How did this affect the king? What command did he give? How did God begin to vindicate His faithful children?

15. Did God allow envy and hate to prevail against His people? What promise is given?

16. What was the result of casting the Hebrew youth into the fire? Quote some texts of Scripture that were fulfilled in this incident.

17. How was the king affected? What question did he ask? Give the answer. What reply did the king make?

18. How did the king recognize the form of the Son of God? What other truth did the king understand? What did he believe? What is said of these Hebrews? Of what was this miracle the result?

19. How did the king feel? What command did he give? Who were witnesses? How closely were the Hebrews examined? How had God triumphed? What was forgotten?

20. What had the Jews failed to do? How did God accomplish the work? How widely was the story told? State five important truths that were widely circulated. What became the absorbing theme? What was the result of that day's experience?

21. What does the king again acknowledge? What was the result of Daniel's interpreting the dream? What was the result of the three Hebrews being saved from the furnace?

22. What did the king at first gain? To what did it lead? What was the result? Instead of the death of three what was gained?

23. What probably was taking place in Jerusalem, at this time? What message had the prophet given Zedekiah a short time before this?

24. What seemingly strange message did the prophet give Zedekiah a little later?

25. How did Zedekiah walk? What did he lose? What only could he see? What would faith have led him to do?

26. What is said of God's commands? What always accompanies the command? If

Zedekiah had known of the decree what would he have done?

27. For what had God make provision? How were the plans frustrated? Give the pleading words of the prophet. What is said of Zedekiah? If Zedekiah had gone forth to the Chaldeans what would have been the result? What fact was made plain to him?

28. To what was Zedekiah a stranger?

29. What is said of the three Hebrews? Did they know they would be delivered from the fire? What does the lack of simple faith bring? What is God ever ready to do?

30. What is said in regard to the tests of our faith? What is said of every act? What is never closed to God's people? Who watches every movement of Satan? Why?

31. Why is the history of the three Hebrews given? Who among the captives obeyed God? What facts are stated in regard to these men?

32. What will bring strength to the will and body? What would have been the result if these youth had compromised the principles of temperance at the first? For what did faithfulness to health principles prepare them?

33. What should be studied with the third chapter of Daniel? Give parallel facts in the two Scriptures. What will be given the image? State what will take place.

34. Answer the four questions in the last paragraph of the chapter. Of what are the scenes in this chapter a miniature?

CHAPTER 4
THE MOST HIGH RULETH

1. What is the fourth chapter of Daniel? By whom written? When? To whom was it sent? How does it come to us? What was the object in writing it?

2. What is said of Nebuchadnezzar's reign? Of Nebuchadnezzar? What is he called in prophecy? Why was he successful? Relate what is said of the wars against Tyre and Egypt.

3. What was shown Ezekiel? To whom was the testimony sent? Relate the testimony.

4. Who must have been familiar with this testimony? Why? Upon what does this throw light?

5. Mention the facts stated in regard to Nebuchadnezzar. To whom did he relate the dream? Could they give the interpretation? Who was called?

6. What name had been given Daniel? What did he always retain? What opportunity was given Daniel?

7. What is said of the dream? What story had been handed down by tradition? Describe the tree seen in the dream. What strange fact is given in regard to the tree?

8. What was sheltered by the tree? What part of the tree did the king see? What is said of the roots of any tree? Upon what do the leaves and fruit depend?

9. What did Nebuchadnezzar see? What command was given? What is said of the stump of the tree?

10. What is said of this message? What had been shown the king in his former dream? Give the parting words of the angel.

11. Why did Daniel's thoughts trouble him? What did the king do? Give Daniel's words. Where did the principles of the Babylonian kingdom originate? What were they? State what is said of Babylon. What is said of tyranny in governments at the present day?

12. What did Babylon implant in all conquered territory? What was practiced? Who held full sway? What are the mysteries of Greece? What is said of the golden cup?

13. What are the nations and people of the present day doing? Where did the festivals of Christmas, Easter, and Hallowe'en originate? What is said of the root of the Babylonian tree?

14. What is said of the influence of Babylon in educational lines? Where did the principles of education in the world originate? What is prominent in the book of Daniel? What came in direct contact, every time the Hebrews met the Chaldean wise men? What two facts were shown by this? Give some of the facts stated in regard to the so-called "higher education," of to-day. What is this education?

15. What were planted in Babylon? For what was the Holy Watcher seeking? What were all nations seeking? What did they receive?

16. What was said of the leaves of the tree? [319] Of the odor? Of the plant? Against what should we guard?

17. To whom does a part of the dream apply? What would come upon Nebuchadnezzar on account of his pride? How long would this condition continue? How did Daniel exhort the king? Could the king avert this sentence? Why did it come upon the king?

18. How much probationary time was given? Give the words of Nebuchadnezzar at the end of the year. Whose words was he repeating?

While thinking these thoughts what happened to the king? What had God given the king? What could He take away? What is said of the mind? Give the words of David quoted in this paragraph.

19. If God can not save one in prosperity what does He bring? Who is clear from censure? Show how this was illustrated in the case of Nebuchadnezzar.

20. What is necessary? What experience comes alike to nations and individuals? How is this illustrated in the church? Who will be brought to confusion? What is hid in Christ? What originates with God? Who **rules?**

21. For what was God working? What did Nebuchadnezzar gain from the seven years' experience? With what Scripture quotation does the chapter close?

Chapter 5
The Last Years of the Babilonian Kingdom

1. Give the four principles that can be learned from a study of the history of Babylon as recorded in the book of Daniel? What is seen in Babylon? What were counterfeited? According to what laws was Babylon built? What was the result of the mingling of good and evil? Why was Babylon allowed to run its natural course?

2. What did God do to vindicate Himself? What three statements are made showing God's favor? Why did God send them warnings and entreaties? Of what is it a forcible commentary?

3. What would have been the result if Babylon had accepted the proffered help?

4. Of what need none be ignorant? What will give them information? What is an object-

lesson to the nations of to-day? What is said of Babylon's growth, failures and destruction?

5. What do all nations have? What record is kept? When are nations destroyed? What is said of what appears to happen by chance?

6. What does the study of the book of Daniel demand?

7. How much time between the fourth and fifth chapters of Daniel? When did Nebuchadnezzar's reign end? What is said of his reign? Who succeeded Nebuchadnezzar? What is said of the history of this period? What was the one object of all the experiences? What course did Babylon pursue?

8. How many times is Evil-merodach mentioned in the Bible? What is mentioned? Relate what was done for Jehoiachin.

9. With what was Evil-merodach familiar? Who may have been his instructor? What was delayed beyond Evil-merodach's reign? What followed his reign?

10. Who finally came to the throne? When was Belshazzar associated with him? When was the kingdom overthrown? What relation was Belshazzar to Nebuchadnezzar?

11. Where do we find Daniel? What did he see? [320]

12. What is said of the reign of Nabonadius and Belshazzar? What was well known? Who will be among the redeemed at last?

13. When did the oppression of the Jews become unbearable?

14. What instruction was given the Jews when they went into captivity? How long did the captivity last? What did God's people have to keep them from mingling with the heathen? What did the Babylonians mock? What was forbidden? What was de-

manded? What did Jeremiah say? Of what did the Babylonians boast?

15. Of what was this oppression a foretaste'? By what name are both periods called? What were the Jews obliged to do?

16. Give six important truths taught by the Tews. What was well known to the Babylonians? With what three prophets were they acquainted? What is said of Daniel? Of Ezekiel? Of Jeremiah? What nations through the spirit of prophecy knew of the fall of Babylon? What fact was known by many of these nations?

17. How did God use His people? To what is Babylon compared? What took place in 539 B. c.? Who heard the news? What message was then given? Who withdrew from Babylon? Did the Persians come? What was Cyrus doing? What prophecy was thus fulfilled?

18. What came to Babylon one spring? How was it received by the two classes? What came the next spring? What was the result?

19. What began? What fate awaited the Babylonians?

20. What had come? Who was interested? Who was asleep?

CHAPTER 6
THE HANDWRITING ON THE WALL

1. What time had arrived? Did the people know of it? How were the people spending that night? How was it in the dens of Babylon? How in the palace halls? Where were the nobles? Who else were present? What was this feast, and to whom did they drink? What did the king order? As they drank, whose blessing was invoked? Did the cup reach the king's

lips? By whose hands, and after what models, had those vessels been made? Who had watched them when taken to Babylon? Who had guarded them while there? Of what was their presence a witness? Does God let such desecrations go unnoticed?

2. What did the king see on the opposite wall? How did it affect the king? What ceased? Upon what did the one thousand guests look?

3. Who were called to read the writing? Could they read the language of Heaven? How did the four characters appear upon the wall?

4. What had been the condition of the city for several days? What had the Lord said about their earthly protection?

5. What becomes of the strongest strongholds when God's hand is laid upon them? Had the rulers of Babylon learned this lesson? Who had never owned his weakness? Who had watched the progress of affairs in this great city? Of what was it the battle-ground? Between whom was the controversy?

6. Who had mustered these forces against Babylon? Who was God using? What had God 'said about Cyrus entering the city? [321]

7. While the king and his lords were drinking, what was Cyrus doing?

8. When the Chaldeans could not read the writing on the wall, how did it affect the king? What did he know? What did the queen mother remember about Daniel?

9. Who was called into the banquet hall? What did the earthly monarch promise him? How did the prophet of God appear before the terror-stricken throng?

10. How were children named by Israel in early times? Whose names were changed by God? What is the meaning of the name, *Dan-*

iel? What had Nebuchadnezzar called him? In whose honor was this name? Did this affect the prophet? How did he speak before the king? What was this moment to them? What is said of Daniel's age? How did these rewards affect him? What did he proceed to do? How did he speak to Belshazzar?

11. What did he say? How were these words spoken? What had Belshazzar done? What had he severed? Of what is the natural breath a symbol? How had the king used his breath and powers? Where and how were these characters written?

12. How were the people affected? Give the four terrible words. What was their meaning?

13. In what way does God deal with men? What is a common belief among idolators? To whom was it familiar? How did the explanation of the writing affect the magicians?

14. Is this symbol still applicable? By whom had God sent an explanation? Give Ezekiel's explanation. When a man accepts Christ, what is written opposite his name in the books of Heaven? As long as he hides in Christ, how is he known? How does God deal with men? If the worst of sinners repent, what does God take into account?

15. How does God deal with nations? What does this explain?

16. What had God given the Babylonian monarchs? Who had long hovered over this earthly government? What had been bestowed upon them. For what purpose? What happened at last? What only could be the result? What was the last word that Daniel read?

17. How was Daniel attired? By the time this was done, what was heard?

18. What were their enemies doing while they were feasting? What had prevented Cyrus from entering the city? How did the men enter the river? When the Babylonians were feeling secure, what had they neglected to do?

19. As soon as the enemy entered the city, what happened? Did the Babylonians receive the news in time to save themselves? Toward what place did the enemy rush? What words had the prophet uttered describing the scene? Who had controled the kingdom? What did the prophet exclaim? What raged through the street? With what did they fight hand to hand?

20. What became of the king? Who took the kingdom? What had come to an end? When an individual or nation becomes lifted up in iniquity, what comes to pass?

21. What question naturally arises? What is a simple and natural answer? What had Daniel found out by the study of prophecy? Knowing this, what was his attitude towards Cyrus?

22. What was there a good reason to believe? When he was excluded from Belshazzar's council, where did he spend a portion of his time? What [322] is said of the province of Elam at this time?

23. With whom was it probable that Daniel had formed an acquaintance? On what other occasion did the priests reveal to a leading general the prophecy concerning him? What is evident from the first chapter of Ezra?

24. What does God always give those who are walking in the light? What great truth does this illustrate? Where is there always a Witness? What does the recording angel write against the unfaithful? Where is this Witness?

How may we feel? What must be rendered? What will every man reap?

25. What are nations repeating to-day? Who was an instrument in God's hands to punish Babylon? What will the next overthrow of governments usher in? For what are the nations now mustering their forces? What cry has gone forth?

CHAPTER 7
DANIEL IN THE LION'S DEN

1. What is contained in the first five chapters of Daniel? With the close of the fifth chapter, what nation is introduced? Give name and age of the ruling king. Who is associated with him? What is his position in the nation? How was this change in kingdoms represented in the image of the second chapter? Were the Medes an unknown power? Give the earliest Bible record of this nation. How were the Medes first brought in contact with the Jews? How long was this before the fall of Babylon? What can be said of their worship? What reason is given for this?

2. With what were the Medes and Persians brought in close touch? Name the elements they worshiped. Where did they establish their worship, and what was kept continually burning? In what did they believe? Quote the words of Isaiah to Cyrus. How is God's position shown in these words?

3. What was the physical condition of the Persians? Give the reason for this. What were the Medes and Persians? Where do we learn of the organization of the kingdom? Into how many provinces was the kingdom divided?

Why was this change important? Upon what did peace depend? Who were placed over the one hundred and twenty princes?

4. What appointment was made out of the usual order? What made it still more unusual? What is revealed in Daniel 8:1, 2? What probably gave him this position?

5. What is said of Daniel's character? Of what is it a witness? In what way was Daniel an example to all officeholders? What fact shows that he served God and not a man-made party? In order to be a good business man is it necessary to be a "policy man"? While prime minister, what was Daniel receiving? To what is the usual type of a statesman compared? What pleases the Lord? How may a man preserve his integrity?

6. What was Daniel's duty as chief of the presidents? Why were they to report to Daniel? What was the character of the presidents? In what respect did the Babylonian government resemble those of the present day?

7. Quote the divine description of the condition of the nation. Where will we find the details given? What are the nations of to-day? Even in the best governments, what is seen?

8. Give points of similarity between Rome [323] and Babylon. Upon what was Rome built? What other nations repeat the same story? Where may we read the details Daniel had to meet? What three things are shown in the sixth chapter of Daniel?

9. Why did the king plan to promote Daniel? What did the presidents plan to do? Give the principles of divine government from which Daniel would not swerve.

10. Was it easy to condemn Daniel? In what way could they condemn him? With whom did their underhanded ways bring them in conflict?

11. Who waited upon Darius? What did their words reveal? With what falsehood did they address the king? •

12. In whom did the king have confidence? Give the import of the decree. What made the document a law?

13. Why was God especially interested in Babylon? What is the difference between knowing God and knowing about Him? Through whom did God manifest his power? How long had Daniel witnessed for Him?

14. Describe Daniel's character. What did he realize?

15. Did he know of the decree? What course did he pursue?

16. What appointments did he keep? Tell of his spiritual life. Which life could his enemies comprehend? What parallel is drawn between Christ and Daniel? In what way was Daniel prepared to meet the nervous strain of business? What is the weight of the atmosphere? Why does it not crush us? Of what is it a type? How can we equalize the pressure of trials?

17. What course did Daniel pursue? Who were in the councils when they plotted against Daniel? What did the spies discover? What accusation was made?

18. What did the king discover? How did the king spend the day? How did they meet every argument of the king?

19. When is God's opportunity? Give Daniel's prayer. What was impossible?

20. Where did Darius and Daniel meet? Who was best fitted to enter the den? Give Darius' words to Daniel. How was the mouth of the den secured?

21. When again did Satan exult as he saw a stone laid over an entrance? Could either Christ or Daniel be held? Where was the angel? Describe Daniel's experience in the den.

22. Was there ever a time when all beasts were gentle? What made them ferocious? What will harmony with God again restore? Who was with Daniel?

23. How did the king spend the night? Give the words of the king to Daniel, and his reply.

24. What reply was given the woman at Christ's tomb? Why was Daniel protected?

25. Give the fate of Daniel's accusers. What did the nations of the world see? What effect did it have upon Darius and Cyrus? What special light was given Daniel after this experience?

26. Give Darius' decree. What decree was given by Cyrus?

27. Where can we learn the fate of evil men?

28. Give the substance of the last paragraph of the chapter.

CHAPTER 8
THE PROPHECY OF DANIEL –
THE JUDGMENT SCENE

1. What is dealt with in the first half of the book of Daniel? What is contained in the last six chapters? How far do the visions reach? What does [324] the prophet see in the future? What may we know from these guide-posts of the prophet?

2. What history is given in the seventh chapter of Daniel? Give the central theme of the chapter.

3. What remarkable fact is mentioned? What was shown to Nebuchadnezzar? Why? What was opened up to Daniel? Where did the angel of revelation linger?

4. The seventh chapter of Daniel reveals the history of what people? When was this vision given? To what does the giving of this view bear testimony? How old was Daniel? How many years had he been in the court? What testified to the purity of Daniel's life? Who had been shown these things before? Why could the Spirit reveal these things to Daniel?

5. Give the words of Hosea. By what symbols were the kingdoms represented? Of what are winds a symbol? What was represented by the water? What did the beasts represent?

6. How many kingdoms were represented? In what way had the first one been represented to Nebuchadnezzar? How did it appear to Daniel? How had Jeremiah spoken of Babylon?

7. When had Habakkuk spoken of Babylon? What did he say?

8. When Daniel watched the lion in vision, what unnatural position did it take? What was indicated by this change in position?

9. Give Habakkuk's reason for this sudden weakening of the power of Babylon. What unpardonable sin did Babylon commit? When did Daniel witness the overthrow of Babylon?

10. By what symyol was Medo-Persia represented? What was its character? Give the nationality of Darius and Cyrus. Who ruled the kingdom? Who was the leading spirit? What is represented by the beasts? How is Medo-Persia represented in the eighth chap-

ter of Daniel? What portions of Scripture are mentioned as revealing the bear-like nature of Medo-Persia? How many years are covered by the history of the second kingdom?

11. What is said of the third kingdom? What name did the angel give for this kingdom? By what beast is it represented? What is indicated by the four wings and the four heads of the leopard? How is the Grecian kingdom represented in the eighth chapter of Daniel?

12. Of which beast did Daniel wish to know particularly?

13. Describe the fourth beast.

14. What did the angel say of the lives of the beasts? How is this shown in the second chapter of Daniel? How was the same truth represented in the fourth chapter? Explain the way in which these principles have been handed down from nation to nation. What was the condition when the fourth kingdom appeared?

15. What did Rome renew in religion? In education? In cruelty? When did Rome succeed Greece? What were the ten horns? With what part of the image of the second chapter does the fourth beast harmonize? How does the history of Rome differ from that of the preceding nations? Where in prophecy do we find the details of the decline and fall of Rome? By whom and when was it broken into ten parts? Name the ten kingdoms.

16. State Rome's opportunities to receive the gospel. How was light offered to Babylon? To Media and Persia? Did Greece also have an opportunity to receive the light? In what way was Rome especially favored, and how did they treat the light? What judgment came on the nation?

17. Did Roman history end with the division? Quote what is said of the little horn. Give in detail the account of the plucking up of the three horns.

18. Describe the appearance of the little horn.

19. What was the condition of Rome? To what is the rise of the little horn compared? By what name is it known?

20. Why did Babylon and pagan Rome fall? Describe the work of the little horn.

21. What position did Rome hold in the days of Christ? Who preached in Rome? With what results? What gradually crept into the Roman church? What did Paul call it? What was grasped by the church? When was this power assumed? What decree then went into effect? Besides speaking stout words, what was done by the little horn? How much power did it have?

22. Upon what did the little horn lay hands? Give the various means used to keep Europe in darkness for over a thousand years.

23. How long was this power to continue? Give the texts that speak of it. In how many different ways is it spoken of? When did it begin? When was its dominion taken away? Is his power yet destroyed?

24. What besides earthly scenes was shown to Daniel?

25. When was the Saviour crucified? Where was He slain? Where did He go? Of what was the day of atonement a type? Quote Spurrell's translation of the scene.

26. Who abides in the holy of holies? Of what is the throne of God the center? What revolves about it?

27. What is gravity? What is done by it? From whence is all life?

28. What did every offering bring to the mind of God? What will Christ ever retain? With what is the temple filled?

29. Give the words of the Psalmist.

30. Can we comprehend God?

31. When was the door into the holy of holies opened?

32. What is said of the opening of the judgment? Where do you find the only description of the judgment scene? Where is the only prophetic period which marks the time of the judgment? When did the twenty-three hundred days begin? When did they end? What message went forth at the close of the days? How widely was the message preached?

33. When did Christ go in before the Father? Why could this not have been when Christ ascended into heaven? Who accompanied Christ when He went in before the Father? When were the books of record opened? Who has witnessed each sin? Of what does God have a faithful record?

34. Who intercedes for each name? What is written opposite every name that is confessed? Describe the scene that follows.

35. How long has the judgment been in session? What will be decided before its close?

36. Which beast continues after the investigative judgment opens? When does it attract attention? What took place in 1870? While Christ was pleading in man's behalf, what was man doing?

37. Why did Babylon fall? What did Daniel say of the fourth beast? What becomes of the fourth beast?

38. What is said of the fifth kingdom? Who will establish it? Who will possess it? Who will come forth in the [326] first resurrection? Who will be translated? What will become of sin and sinners? What will be blotted out? Who will witness the triumph of truth? What is forgotten?

CHAPTER 9
THE EIGHTH CHAPTER OF DANIEL

1. How long since the vision of the seventh chapter? What subject had often been upon the mind of the prophet? Why did he keep the matter in his heart? What changes had taken place during the two years? How did this affect Daniel? Where was Daniel living at that time? What was the capital of Elam? What was Elam formerly? Who led in the revolt? What had Isaiah foretold? What did Daniel see? Why does this vision begin with Media and Persia?

2. Where was Daniel taken in vision? Describe the ram and its conquests. By what was the second kingdom represented in his previous vision? What is shown by both symbols? What was represented by the uneven horns of the ram? What is the best commentary on the Scriptures? Give the words of the angel.

3. How was the increase of the kingdom represented? In the days of Cyrus, how many provinces were there? How many in the time of Esther? What was the kingdom then called? How was the monarch spoken of? What is said of Xerxes in the eleventh chapter of Daniel?

4. Give the second symbol in the vision. From whence does it come? In what manner?

Describe its appearance. What is said of the fourth king after Cyrus? When was this fulfilled? How large was Xerxes' army? Where was it defeated? What had prophecy foretold?

5. How did Greece attack Medo-Persia? Quote Spurrell's translation.

6. Who were the commanders? What became of Medo-Persia? Why? Who stood by the Persian monarch? What had the nation been in God's hand? Whose example did they follow? Whose fate did they share? What good deed was done by Persia? How is the life of a nation prolonged?

7. Where did the ram and goat meet? Give the historical fulfillment of this meeting. What other defeats followed? What was the result?

8. In what does Alexander stand without a rival? Give a sketch of his early life. What did he proclaim himself? What caused his death?

9. Who directs in the rise and fall of kingdoms?

10. By whom can the Lord save?

11. Will mighty armies always save a nation? Who is the Lord especially watching?

12. Who controls all nations?

13. Give fulfillment of the great horn's being broken. What did the four horns represent?

14. Name the four generals and the territory governed by each.

15. What comes out from one of these horns? How was this power symbolized in the seventh chapter? In the second vision? How does one feel when reading of this power? What was concentrated in this power? What is it said to be? What was brought upon the field of action to counteract the gift of heaven?

16. What did Gabriel say of this power? If our eyes are directed heavenward, what do we receive? What takes possession of those who resist God's love? What is said of the extent of the kingdom? Give what inspiration [327] says of "the little horn." What became of cities that resisted Rome? Give the description of the government given by the angel.

17. How was the great arrogance of Rome displayed? Quote Daniel 8:11.

18. How does God regard His people? Of what did Rome first deprive the Jews? When did Christ come? What did Rome see? With whom did He identify Himself? What did He prove?

19. What did Rome do with Christ? In what condition was paganism? What was its last act?

20. How did Satan work? What crept into the church? Where lay the power of the early church? What was done by Christian mothers? What textbook was used? Were the children left in the pagan schools? Could they eat with the pagans?

21. How and why did Satan put his principles into the new church? What drove out the spirit of life? What fell before the rising power of the hierarchy? What choked the life of the new church? What was taken away? What did Rome nominally become? What is said of the emperor? What decrees were passed? Who attempted to exalt themselves above God? Whose principles were received?

22. How does John speak of the transfer of power? With what is Daniel 8:11, 12 a parallel? Give the work of the little horn of Daniel 7:25. How many times was Daniel shown the twofold history of Rome? Describe each.

23. How did this affect the prophet? Did he understand the time of fulfillment?

Give three definite events that were shown the prophet. How did these scenes pass before him? Who was watching?

24. How long and for what has the universe waited? What do the angelic hosts wonder? Who only knows the time? What is shown by the thirteenth verse? What question was asked by Gabriel? Give his answer.

25. For what did Daniel long? Who appeared before Daniel? What command was given to Gabriel? How was Daniel affected by Gabriel's appearance? With what words did the angel address Daniel?

26. How did Gabriel commence the explanation? In what way did he speak of the two thousand three hundred days? What did Daniel see that caused him to faint?

27. What is taught in the eighth chapter besides the line of prophecy?

28. What gift is to be coveted? What does the study of Daniel's life reveal? What position does Gabriel hold? Give his words to John. To Daniel. Whose attendant is Gabriel? Who formerly occupied his position? Who appeared to Mary? To the shepherds? Who guided the wise men?

29. What did Gabriel bring to Christ? How did he comfort Him? How were the Roman soldiers affected by his presence? Tell of his presence at the Saviour's tomb.

30. Where did the Saviour go? Who comforted the disciples? Which one of the angels has been most closely connected with man? What did he forbid? Is Gabriel one of the Trinity of heaven? How does he count himself? Who communicated with every prophet?

31. Who was Lucifer? Since his fall, how has he used his power? What can you say of false prophets? Who will finally appear as an angel of light? What will be the safety of God's people?

32. Where was Daniel carried? What was [328] shown him? What does the river represent? What are located on the banks of the stream of time? Who presides over the stream of waters? From where was the voice heard? Give the words of the angel.

CHAPTER 10
THE HISTORY OF THE JEWS

1. How much time intervened between the eighth and ninth chapters of Daniel? What were the parting words of Gabriel? Of what did Daniel think while attending to the king's business? Why was he called into the court of Babylon? What calamity had befallen Babylon? What position had been given Daniel?

2. For what did Daniel always find time?

3. What had prophecy said of Cyrus? What was drawing near? What prophecy told of the length of captivity? Over what was Daniel probably perplexed? What did the cleansing of the sanctuary then mean to the Jews?

4. How many times did Jeremiah give the length of the captivity? Give the quotations. What was near?

5. Of what is this prayer an example? What had darkened the vision of many? What relation did they sustain toward the truth of God? How were they personally situated? How did they look upon the journey to Jerusalem?

6. What was strong in the hearts of many? Seventy years after Cyrus' decree, where were many of the Jews? What proportion ever

returned? To whom were they compared? How was the spirit of prophecy received? What did they choose? Did Daniel know of this condition? With whom did he identify himself?

7. Where did he place himself? Give a portion of the prayer.

8. Of whom was Daniel a representative? To whom is his prayer a rebuke?

9. With what words did Daniel approach God? With whom was he acquainted? With what two arms may finite man reach Infinite Love? How was the prayer received? Why are our requests often unanswered? How are we sometimes tested?

10. When did Gabriel touch Daniel?

11. What did Gabriel first mention? Give his words. What was necessary that Daniel might receive the Spirit?

12. Who were God's special favorites? What words were spoken to but few? Who is greatly beloved of the Lord?

13. With which verse does the explanation of the time begin? With what was Gabriel acquainted? Quote Daniel 9:24. How much is contained in this verse? What is said of this verse? What exact date is given? What other important facts are given in the verse? In this interview what part of the two thousand three hundred days was given? What had already been revealed to Daniel?

14. How many years in seventy weeks? What does this period cover? When was it to begin? Into what periods was Jewish history divided? What was accomplished during the first period? To what does the second period extend? What would the one week cover? To what is this last week devoted?

15. What four prophets give us the history of the forty-nine years? For what was Cyrus raised up? What did Isaiah say of him? What was he to do?

16. Where do we find Cyrus' decree? Give a portion of the decree.

17. Could all return to Jerusalem? If they were too poor to go, who would bear the expense? Had there ever been such a decree before? What should Israel have done? What should the [329] exodus have been? How would it have compared with the going out of Egypt?

18. Who watched the preparations? How many had gone at the end of the first year?

19. How did Cyrus feel about it? Who worked to again arouse Cyrus' interest?

20. What was returned to the leaders of the Jews? What work was begun in the second year? What is said of the site of Solomon's temple? Who soon stopped the work? Under what king was the work resumed? How many years was the work stopped? What two prophets now began to prophesy?

21. How had the Jews provided for themselves? What did God want them to do? Who helped them? Who tried to hinder them? What was the result? How was the money supplied?

22. How long was Jerusalem governed by Persia? What was issued in the seventh year of Artaxerxes? Give the six principal points in the decree. What did it establish? Was this a common thing?

23. In what year was this? What period began with this date? What is shown by Ezra 6:14?

24. Who describes the "troublous times" in which the wall was built? What position did

Nehemiah hold? How many years after Artaxerxes' decree did Nehemiah go up to Jerusalem? Who directed the work of building the wall? How did they build?

25. What lessons of Nehemiah should be followed by Christians to-day? Of what is the rebuilding of Jerusalem a fit symbol? Who was responsible for the trouble? What did a few years of rest always bring? How did they treat their own brethren? What is necessary in order to be "free indeed"? What will take place when God's people proclaim liberty among themselves?

26. Quote Daniel 9:25. Give the Greek and Hebrew words for "anointed.' When and with what was Christ anointed? What event closed the sixty-nine weeks?

27. Four hundred and fifty-seven years from Artaxerxes' decree reaches to what date? Twenty-six years added, brings us to what event? Give date of Christ's baptism.

28. For what had the Jewish nation looked? Who controlled the Jewish nation at the close of the sixty-nine weeks? What was the desire of every Jewish mother? Did they know where the Saviour would be born? Who prophesied of John? How long had his voice been heard? How many historical facts established the time of John's preaching? Who came to hear John's preaching? How did John recognize Him?

29. Who was looking for the Saviour? What did John say of him? What did Christ say of the time? In what condition was the nation? What book would have enlightened them? What books, if studied, will warn the world to-day?

30. What two signs were mentioned by Gabriel? How many of the seventy weeks remained? What was done in the first half of the week?

31. What was to take place in the "midst of the week" ? When was this fulfilled? How was this shown in the temple? What became of the sacrificial lamb? Who had withdrawn from the temple? What forever ceased? When did these things take place? How did God still try to save the Jewish people? Give the results. When was Stephen stoned? What resulted from this persecution? How [330] long after this was Jerusalem destroyed?

32. What can you say of the accuracy of the date 457 b. c. ? Give four events establishing it. How does history establish it? In what two ways can you reckon this period?

33. How many of the two thousand three hundred years were explained by Gabriel in the ninth chapter? How many remained? When did the four hundred and ninety years end? When did the twenty-three hundred years end? What events then began to take place?

34. Are any living who helped to give the advent message? How long before 1844 did they begin to sound the message? Who was foremost in this work? What mistake was made? When was this message preached?

35. How did the disappointment affect many? What did further study show? What special light was shown them?

36. To what did the sanctuary spoken of by Daniel refer? By investigating the typical sanctuary service, what was revealed? Whom did they behold in heaven? Of what was the work of the high priest a figure? Upon what work did Christ enter in 1844? In what was William Miller mistaken? In what was he not mistaken?

37. Where are the events between a. d. 34 and 1844 given?

38. What may we expect? What should we do?

CHAPTER 11
THE SANCTUARY

1. What led to the disappointment in 1844?

2. How many sanctuaries are brought to view? What is the first? How many have been permitted to see it? What is the second? How was it built? How long was service held in the second? What did those following the shadow reach?

3. When did the Saviour leave the temple for the last time? What did He say? How did His words affect the people? Although the building remained, what had ceased to be? How did the Father confirm the words?

4. Does the sinner now need a priest to offer his sacrifice? What has been made? Who can accept? What way was now open? What had taken the place of the earthly sanctuary? Where was man's faith now to center?

5. What is the third temple mentioned in the Bible? Of what had the Jews lost sight? Of what did they think when Jesus spoke of His body-temple? What did Jesus say? Give their reply.

6. What comes to those who study the typical work? When these rays are gathered into the body-temple, what do they reflect?

7. What was God's original plan? Who gained possession? Give the result. What was necessary to make the body a pure temple?

8. Why were innocent animals slain?

9. Where did Adam present his offering? What did he see by faith? How did his heart respond? How did nature teach the death of Christ?

10. How were the altars at first lighted? Who first failed to appreciate the sacrifice? Of what did Satan convince him? What was the difference between Cain's and Abel's offerings? Describe Abel's offering. Was it accepted?

11. Describe Cain's offering. Why was it not consumed? What was lacking?

12. Of what are Cain and Abel types? How did the followers of Cain worship? What did they overlook?

13. Anciently what did each family have? [331] What position did the father occupy? What decided who should act as priest?

14. What did Jacob see? Tell the story of Joseph. What was Joseph?

15. Why was the earthly sanctuary built? What did God say? How long before Moses went up into the mountain? How many days did he remain there? What had been lost in Egypt?

16. What did God do to reach man in his fallen state? Of what was the service in the earthly sanctuary a shadow?

17. What was the whole Jewish economy? What was every act in that service? What is this work called?

18. Why did they not see light flashing from sacrificial offerings? Whom did they reject?

19. Follow step by step the work done by the sinner who brought an offering. Give the work of the priest.

20. Describe the ark.

21. Describe the articles of furniture in the first apartment.

22. Where was the blood placed? What was signified by this? What does the sinner behold?

23. Was the sinner forgiven? What does he say of his influence? Where was the blood poured? What does the blood represent? What fact is taught by this act?

24. Who separated the fat from the offering? What was done with the fat? What did this work typify? Why was the burning of the fat a sweet savor to God?

25. What lesson was taught the sinner by the act of separating the fat from the offering?

26. What truth was taught while searching for the fat? To what is the Spirit compared? What did the sinner realize?

27. Describe the offering where the flesh was eaten by the priest. What wonderful truth was taught by this service?

28. What did each offering present? Of what was the incense an object-lesson?

29. How often was the fire replenished? What were the people doing at the time of incense? Give the antitype of the seven lamps. How many are enlightened by the Spirit?

30. What did the table of shewbread represent?

31. What position did the ark occupy, and what did it contain? What names are accepted?

32. Give the significance of the continual burning. What was done with the ashes, and what truth was taught thereby?

33. Mention some things that would call forth questions from the children.

34. What was the design of much of the service in ancient Israel?

35. What question would the children ask in regard to the passover?

36. Why were the stones piled up by Jordan? What would a correct answer to the children's inquiries acquaint them with?

37. Describe the offering for the leper. What change will be made in the air by the blood of Christ?

38. What is said of earth, air, and water? What was typified by the earthen dish containing the blood? By the cedar wood and hyssop dipped in the blood?

39. Of what was the scarlet wool dipped in the blood a pledge?

40. What have we to study? What will be restored through the blood of Christ? With what did the blood of Christ come in contact? How were the two extremes in vegetation represented at the cross? [332]

41. Was there an antitype of the scarlet while His blood was flowing from those cruel wounds? Describe the scene at the cross.

42. What three statements are given in regard to the blood of the world's Redeemer? What is said of him whose sins were as scarlet?

43. What was typified by the various feasts? Give the antitype of the passover and the first-fruits.

44. To what did all the services point?

45. What was the crowning service of the year, and what was accomplished by it?

46. What was revealed to Daniel? When did it begin? What was seen when the ark was opened in heaven? What encircled the fourth commandment? To what did they listen?

47. When did the judgment open? What is the standard in the judgment? What is God's will concerning His people? Of what was the day of atonement a type?

48. How anciently did all know when the day of atonement came? How was it kept? What was the difference between the day of atonement and the weekly Sabbath? What was read from the Sacred Scroll? How was the day spent? What statement was repeated?

49. Give the difference between Gentile and Jewish homes. Give the work of the priest in the temple.

50. Who were represented by the two goats? What was done with the Lord's goat? Give in detail the work of the high priest in the most holy place. Where did he pause as he came out? How did he cleanse the golden altar in the first apartment? For what were the people listening?

51. When was the scapegoat introduced? Describe the part the scapegoat had in the service.

52. Did the congregation behold this service? How did the people feel when they beheld this service? When did they rejoice in freedom from sin?

53. What does the antitype mean to us? What was shown by the day of atonement's being a rest and a fast day?

54. In what time are we living? What are we admonished to do? When the last case is decided, what decree will be issued? Who comes in for a part in the service after every case has been decided?

55. Who will behold the sins laid upon Satan? Where will he spend the thousand years? Where will he go at the end of that time? When will type fully meet antitype? What will then be seen?

56. What is said of the sins of Israel? What will reign forever?

57. What is Christ doing for us? Are you performing your part?

58. What was necessary in the type in order for the work to be of any avail for the people? Who was cut off?

59. Answer carefully each question asked in this paragraph. How many will heed the warning? What will they do?

Chapter 12
Introduction To The Last Vision

1. What is recorded in the last three chapters of Daniel? To what is the tenth chapter a preliminary? To what was Daniel drawing near? How were his last days spent? What had taken place since the events recorded in the ninth chapter? To what was his godly life a rebuke? What did God do to those ungodly men? How was Daniel regarded by Darius? Upon the accession of Cyrus, where did he remain?

2. What had Cyrus done in the first year of his reign? How did he feel regarding [333] the Jews? Why did Cyrus doubt the wisdom of the decree? Whom did the Jews represent? When pardon and freedom are offered, what do they choose? Why was the voice of God dimly heard by the Jews?

3. What two things weighed heavily upon Daniel? At what did he wonder? What was it he could not understand?

4. What did he determine to do two years after the decree? Did he practice total abstinence from food? What did he partake of, and how did he spend his time? What was his purpose? Of what does the spiritual life often partake? How should the soul affect the body?

Where did the prophet go to strengthen his mind? Whom did he take with him? What led the prophet's mind out after God?

5. How long did he thus seek God? As he looked up, whom did he see by his side? How did the vision affect his companions? To what is the countenance of Christ compared? What is the character of one who can bear the light of heaven?

6. How did the eyes of the Son of God appear? How has He promised to "guide thee"?

7. What had Daniel's ears long been accustomed to hear? How did the voice of the Son of God sound to Daniel? How does it sound to ears unaccustomed to heavenly sounds? Who afterward had a similar experience? In what two ways was the same voice heard?

8. How did Daniel feel when he compared himself to Christ? How does he describe his condition? Describe his position.

9. As Gabriel touched him, and lifted him up, what did he say? Describe the touch of Christ's hand.

10. Describe the touch of Gabriel's hand. Who should have this life current in them today? Why did Christ come to earth?

11. How long after Daniel began to pray, was the vision given? Explain the cause of Gabriel's delay. Where had the angel been?

12. Until a nation is rejected by God, who are in the midst of their councils? Who is a constant watcher in legislative halls today? Of what is every just decree the result? Where was this influence at work? What would have been the result if Daniel had ceased to pray at the end of one or two weeks? Quote the promise in regard to

prayer. Why do we not always receive an immediate answer?

13. What did the angel ask the prophet? For what purpose did he say he had come? What is the physical condition of those in vision? When could he speak? Who stood by his side to strengthen him? What did he explain?

14. Can the effect of the Spirit of God on a person be explained? Who speaks through the human instrument? In what condition are the eyes of one in vision? What do they see? When earth's attraction is broken, where are they taken? When a live coal is laid upon the lips, what do they speak?

15. How did Gabriel express his love for Daniel? How did the gray-haired prophet respond?

16. What were revealed? How does man often record events? Why? What class of events are recorded when God writes history? Where is this fact especially noticeable? How does Gabriel give the events of hundreds of years? What does he bring into prominence? How can these events be understood? [334]

17. What books should be studied in order to understand the scriptural history of Persia? To what period is the history carried in these books? When is the record silent?

CHAPTER 13
HISTORY OF THE DECREES

1. Why did the angel begin with the Persian history? When was the vision given? What had Daniel seen in vision? Who is the only authentic Historian? Where is the only unbiased history found? How many unbroken threads are

there in the web of life? What is this? In what way is Egyptian history noted? When and for what is a nation noticed by the Divine Historian?

2. Why did the Medo-Persian kingdom exist? When did it pass from the stage of action?

3. When was the Medo-Persian nation born? Who was the first king? Give his age. Who stood by him during his reign? What opportunity was given Darius? What position was given Daniel? Did Darius know of the true God? How did he respond? How long did he reign?

4. Who worked with the kings of Persia? Give the first words of Gabriel in this last vision. Who can help when God's influence is withdrawn? What emphatic illustration is given?

5. How long had Cyrus been reigning? When had he given freedom to the Jews? Where was the news heralded? What did he offer the Jews? How did they respond? Of what is this a commentary?

6. What was the character of Babylon? What was the nature of Cyrus' decree? Of what is this an illustration?

7. Why were the Jews so slow? What should they have done? Give the result of attending Babylonish schools.

8. If they had been true, what might have been? When was this opportunity offered them? What brought Daniel and his fellows into favor with the king? What might have been established then? What had God always intended? Did Israel do this? What answers the question? What was the result?

9. How was it with those who went to Jerusalem? How did the laying of the foundation of the temple affect the old men? How did the delay on the part of the people affect Cyrus? How long did Daniel fast and pray before his prayer was answered? What were Michael and Gabriel doing during this time? What was Cyrus ready to do had the Jews done their part? Is there any further record of Cyrus? Why was his work but partially accomplished?

10. Who influenced the Jews to delay? What part did Gabriel act? How long did Cambyses reign? How did he spend the most of his time? What is Cambyses called in the Scripture? Who wrote letters of complaint to him against the Jews? Why were they unnoticed? What liberty was still given the Jews? Why did they remain in Babylon? Did they ever wish they had left Babylon?

11. Where was Cambyses slain? Who took the throne? By what name is he known in history? What is his Bible name? How long did he reign? What did he do during this time? Where do we find this letter? Is there anything else recorded of this monarch?

12. How did this letter affect the work at Jerusalem? How did the Jews reason? Whom did God raise up at this time?

13. Give the financial condition of the people. [335]

14. How did God work in Babylon? Who succeeded Smerdis? How is he spoken of in Ezra 4:24?

15. While the Jews were so unbelieving, what was God doing? What did Haggai and Zechariah do? Who next warned the Jews to cease work? What did the leading Jews quote to vindicate their cause? Who wrote to the king, and what was the result?

16. What was seen in this? What command was given to their enemies?

17. What did Tatnai and Shethar-Boznai do? Why was seeming defeat turned into victory? What was the result of God's confounding worldly policy?

18. What warnings were still heard?

19. How long did God keep Darius' heart tender toward His people?

20. Who was watching for the Jews to return to Jerusalem? What was given Zechariah? What opportunity was given Jerusalem? What did Zechariah hear one of the angels say to another? What did God promise for a wall?

21. What words of the Lord were heard? What was embraced in this promise?

22. What did God say should be seen through the whole earth? What remarkable promises were uttered?

23. To what time were their minds pointed?

24. What was the effect of their beginning to build?

25. Who recorded the promise of the latter rain? Study carefully the marginal texts by the promise of the latter rain. What would be in Jerusalem? What did the prophet see in the future?

26. Who was reigning in Persia when these visions were given? Why were these promises not fulfilled in the past? Who are heirs to the same promises to-day?

27. What prophecy was given by Daniel?

28. Who were the three kings that followed Cyrus? Name the fourth king. When did he come upon the throne? Give his Bible name. What book in the Bible is wholly devoted to the Persian history during his reign?

29. When did Persia reach the height of its glory? How many provinces did Persia then rule? What was the capital city? Describe the display of Xerxes' wealth as recorded in Esther. What other feast was similar to this? Describe the furnishings of the palace.

30. What familiar story is mentioned? What was the result of the queen's refusal? Who was Esther? With whom had she lived? Give her character from childhood.

31. What position was held by Mordecai? Give the moral condition of the court. What did Mordecai refuse to do? How were the Jews regarded at this time? What had they failed to do?

32. How long had mercy been extended? Mention the different times when forty years had been given to accomplish a certain work.

33. What decree was issued after the Persians had waited about forty years for the Jews to leave Babylon? What did God permit when entreaty failed? What does God prepare in the midst of persecution?

34. Who had guarded Hadassah? When men failed to represent God's work, whom did he use? How could God use Esther's beauty?

35. Give the import of the decree. How was it proclaimed throughout the kingdom? In what did Satan triumph?

36. Where was the decree first published? What was the effect?

37. How did Esther receive the decree? What did it bring to her? Who joined with her in fasting and prayer? How did she approach the king? What was before her? [336]

38. By whom and how had God prepared for her deliverance?

39. Give the fate of Haman, and the reward of Mordecai. How did the Jews escape? What is a counterpart of Haman's de-

cree? Where will it find many of the professed people of God? How will God's true people be delivered?

40. Why is this record preserved in history?

41. How is the character of Xerxes shown? Why did he muster an immense army? What accompanied the effort?

42. Under whose reign was the final decree issued for the return of the Jews?

43. Where is this decree found? When was it issued? What wonderful prophetic period began at this time? What did Artaxerxes' decree contain?

44. How long was this after the decree of Cyrus? In what year did Nehemiah go up to Jerusalem? How had Ezra suffered? How were the walls built? In what ways did the Jews reform?

45. What proportion of the Jews were saved?

46. What might Jerusalem have become? What power was next mentioned by Daniel? What became of Media and Persia?

47. What is included in the history of the decrees?

48. What do we individually find in the history of Persia? What should we do?

Chapter 14
History of Greece

1. What is contained in the first two verses of this chapter? What history is given in verses 3-13? What was made known to Daniel? What had been difficult for Daniel? In what manner is this last prophecy given?

2. What is said of the words used, and the events selected? In reading the Bible, what two lines of thought are found? How must we seek for the deeper meaning? Of what may the reader catch a glimpse?

3. Why did God give the history of these four kingdoms? What creates an incentive to understand the prophecies? What increases the desire to study the book of Daniel? What is represented by the history of Babylon as a nation? Notwithstanding its splendor, what was it? What was written above the city?

4. Whose daughter was Medo-Persia? Of what did she partake? What is said of her religious principles? What partially checked the wickedness of Medo-Persia? What is revealed in the decree of Ahasuerus?

5. In what did Medo-Persia take an important part? How was it with the Greek nation? What relation did she sustain to Babylon? How is this illustrated in the family relation? Who are the three daughters of Babylon? How do they differ?

6. What nation spans the gulf between the Old and the New Testament? What period was without a prophet? Of what family are the Grecians descendants? Where did they settle? What was developed in this broken country? What did they have in common?

7. To what did their religion bear a close resemblance? How were these forms and ceremonies carried to other nations? What became a model to the Greeks? Where is the origin of everything good and beautiful?

8. By what was the gross idolatry of Babylon and Egypt replaced in Greece? What can you say of these customs? How was the aesthetic taste of the Greeks developed? What

was lacking in their nature study? What did they worship? Give the result.

9. What can you say of their history? Why did they wander in darkness? Of what is their history a reminder? Whom do the worldly students of to-day worship? Upon what are they fed? Of what are they ignorant?

10. Did the Greeks offer sacrifices? How was the spirit of prophecy manifested?

11. What can you say of the Grecian priesthood? What replaced the sacred feasts of Jehovah's people? What did the feasts promote? What did the Grecian games promote? Why did God's people meet together? What was the object of the Grecian gatherings?

12. What history is included in the Grecian history? What can you say of the people? Who was Plato? When did he live? What was combined to form "the traditions" in Christ's day? What was the "science falsely so-called"?

13. With many, what has replaced the Bible? What can you say of Plato's teaching? How did his followers come under the condemnation of Christ?

14. Where do we find the most subtle error? Where was this mixture first found? What was enslaved by Babylon? What was conquered by Greece? Give the effect of this.

15. Give what the angel said of Persia. Of Greece. What is said of Alexander's character and education?

16. When did he begin to reign? What did he do?

17. By what symbol was the third kingdom represented? How long a period was covered by this symbol? What was represented by the wings of a fowl? By the lithe

form and spots of the leopard? With what is Grecian education inseparably connected?

18. Name some of Alexander's conquests. What three gifts were combined in Alexander? How did he seek to win the favor of the conquered races?

19. Describe Alexander's visit to Jerusalem. Who went out to meet him?

20. How did Alexander surprise his army? What was explained to him? Into whose presence was he brought? What message was given him? With what results?

21. How did Alexander gratify his pride? What might he have been? Of what was this the result? What was the outcome of such a choice? Of what is this a commentary?

22. What choice is shown by his doing "according to his will"? How many minds are there in the universe? Name them. When we claim to exercise our own mind, whose mind controls us? What brings liberty? Of what is the Greek philosophy the continuation?

23. Give an account of the struggle for power after Alexander's death. How long did the strife continue? In what way was it settled? What prophecy was thus fulfilled? Which division was first overthrown?

24. How were the divisions reduced to two? When? Quote Spurrell's translation of Daniel 11:5.

25. Give the first two kings of the North, and the first three of the South.

26. What did Gabriel give Daniel? What relation did these nations sustain to the people of God?

27. Explain how Greece was the universal power. What entered every country Alexander had conquered? Show the extent of the Greek

religion, games, education, and language. What city became an educational center? Give the quotation from the Encyclopedia Britannica.

28. Give instances where Israel twice escaped Egyptian bondage? By what were they finally captured? [338]

29. Locate the history of Greece. What can you say of the system of education that God gave? For what did Israel often exchange it?

30. What prepared the Jews to accept Greek teaching?

31. To what extent were the Greek games introduced? What is said of Greek names?

32. Tell of the Saviour's early education. Where were other youths educated?

33. What is a wonder to man? What did God turn to His glory? What was done by Ptolemy Philadelphus? How did this turn to the glory of God? How was man without excuse? What was the household tongue at this time? To what is the word of God compared?

34. What is shown in Daniel 11:3-5 ? What was the enemy's plan? Under this influence what was accomplished?

35. What is found in Daniel 11:6-13 ? In what way did the Greek influence in the northern kingdom differ from that in the southern? Which division carried forward the work symbolized by the leopard and rough goat? What two opposing powers are seen in history? In what way was this manifested in the Middle Ages?

36. What fact is revealed by history? What nations have trouble? In what direction have universal powers gained conquest?

37. In spite of all this, what was attempted? Quote Spurrell's translation of Daniel 11:6. What can you say of this verse? How long before its fulfillment was it written? Relate the history that fulfilled this verse.

38. Give the history that fulfilled verses 7 and 8.

39. Did the trouble cease at this time? Who held much of Syria? When? Who undertook to regain this territory? Describe the sons of Callinicus and give their names.

40. What two kings began to reign about the same time? Give the character of the southern king. What was the result of Antiochus' invasion of Egypt?

41. What did Ptolemy attempt? Who prevented it? What was the result? What might have been during this period? Why did the Jews locate in Palestine? Where were they? If they had done their duty, what would have been the result?

42. What should have been an object lesson' to the Jews? Where should the youth have gone for an education? Who should have been teachers? What did Israel seek?

43. Between whom was peace concluded? How long did it last? What did Antiochus design? What was he made to realize?

44. What power is introduced in the fourteenth verse? What is said of Grecian struggles after this time? How was the power of Greece perpetuated? What is her shrine? What can you say of that power to-day? How long will it continue?

45. What choice is offered the Israel of to-day? How may eternal life be gained? What course will bring death? Why? What is the motive power of God's system? What is exalted by the Greek system?

46. Why has eternal truth always shown on the pathway of men? When does Greek

philosophy and skepticism come forth in full force? What is the only safeguard?

CHAPTER 15
THE FOURTH KINGDOM

1. What power is introduced in the fourteenth verse of the eleventh chapter? How far did Gabriel follow the history of Greece? [339] What prevailed in the once mighty empire of Alexander? Of what did the angel of prophecy speak? How was the fourth kingdom introduced?

2. How was every word given? Is there any significance in the introduction of what was to become the mightiest kingdom on earth? What was it to be to the people of God? How was Rome represented in the seventh chapter? What were its characteristics? What was this power to speak? How did this affect the prophet?

3. What did Daniel see in the next vision? From whence did the little horn spring? How was this kingdom described? What was to be its character? What attitude did it assume toward Christ? What is meant by establishing the vision?

4. Putting all these thoughts together, what do we see? What did each nation have, and why is it here recorded? Of what was Babylon an example? What did her religion counterfeit? What was the result of this? Of what was Medo-Persia a type? What is said of her laws? How were the heads of this despotism kept in check?

5. Wherein was Greece different from the two preceding nations? How did she gain control? When Babylon was overthrown, and Medo-Persia was no more, where was Greece?

6. What is said of the fourth kingdom? How is Rome represented in Revelation 13:2? What united in this kingdom? What are the principal points in the history of any nation? What was the character of Rome? Why was the time of the supremacy shortened?

7. In what year did Ptolemy Epiphanes fall heir to the throne of Egypt? Who planned his overthrow and the division of his empire? What power arose to prominence before the prophet's eye? Had Rome been in existence before? How far back does the traditional history of Rome date? What prophet began to prophesy about the time Rome was founded? Who founded Rome? What was the character of the Romans? In the establishment of a strong central government, who aided the people? What beast received a seat, power, and great authority from the dragon?

8. What must the student recognize in each nation? When Satan found he had failed in the history of Babylon, Medo-Persia, and Greece, what did he attempt? What city did he choose? What can you say of his plans? What did Satan hope? How long will his efforts last?

9. By what was Rome first ruled? What was spanned by Greek governments? Who demanded representation in the Roman government? How long did the kings rule? Who reigned for the next two centuries? In whose hands did the government finally rest?

10. How does God rule? Who are representatives in the councils of heaven? Why was Satan admitted to this council? What did he attempt to do in Rome?

11. How did Rome begin her career as a conquering nation? How was her consti-

tution developed? How did she acquire her territory? Locate and name a rival city. How long did Rome fight for supremacy? With what result? How does Ridpath express the policy of the government?

12. What was Rome doing while she hovered over Carthage? What nation was made one of her provinces? What was the result? What was forbidden? What was this state of things called? [340]

13. Who were sold in the slave markets of Rome? What became a proverbial expression for anything cheap? What policy scheme is mentioned? A few years later, what became of the Macedonians? What is said of the Grecians? From what were the Romans relieved? What was this called?

14. What family was still bearing sway in the Eastern world? Who proposed to unite with Philip V. of Macedon? Who interfered? What happened to Antiochus in the battle of Magnesia?

15. Who controlled Egypt? Why? What is said of the Roman army and the extent of its power?

16. What is said of the republic of Rome? What is impossible when nations depart from the principles of true liberty of conscience? Is this true in individual experience? When only is true liberty known?

17. What does this line of policy demand? What can you say of the Roman army?

18. State what is said of the power of the Senate.

19. What did tradition make the Romans? What does the inspired penman say of this? Who came to Rome as the Prince of Peace?

20. What relation did the religion of Rome sustain to the government? What was the one all-absorbing institution? What is necessary to become great? What took the place of character?

21. What did the form of religion do in Rome? What were some of the leading features of the papacy? Who was deified? Give an illustration of this.

22. Who was the highest religious officer during the reign of paganism? What paved the way for the papal hierarchy of later days?

23. What was borrowed from Greece?

24. For what did it train a class of citizens?

25. Of what is Roman law the basis? Of whom is the Roman lawyer the forefather?

26. How many plans have God and Satan? What are they? What is all history? What is national history?

27. What do students often forget? To what is national history compared? What should be remembered?

28. At what point did Gabriel call attention to the fourth kingdom? In what condition was the republic? What is said of this transition period between the republic and the empire? As the republic lost its power, who composed a corporation? Who controlled the money? Who had the army? Who was the master mind?

29. What countries were conquered by the Roman army? Who entered Jerusalem? What was made known to him? How did Pompey enter the city? Where did Rome now stand? When was this?

30. Who chose Palestine as the home of the Jews? What was God's will concerning His people during the Roman supremacy? With what had God intrusted His people? What

was the object of God in bringing different nations to the Jews? If the Hebrew race had been true to its appointed duty, would the history of the world have been changed? Who came to Jerusalem? Why? What was the result? Why?

31. During what rule did Rome again enter Egypt? Who requested Pompey to visit Egypt to settle difficulties? What became of Pompey? Give an account of Caesar's visit to Egypt.

32. Have we any record that Caesar ever acknowledged God as the Ruler of the nations? By whom was he fascinated and corrupted? What does the seventeenth verse describe? [341] What is said of the character of Egypt?

33. After leaving Egypt, where did Caesar go? What was the famous dispatch he sent to Rome? What did he do on his return to Rome?

34. What is said of Caesar? What was granted to the citizens of many cities? What did he grant to all scientific men of whatever nationality? What were found among his papers after his death? How did he die? What did Gabriel say he would do? Why was heaven watching?

35. When did Julius Caesar come to an untimely death? What became of republicanism?

36. Who died shortly after this? What became of Antony? Who alone remained? What does Gibbon say of this? Whose ambition leveled every barrier of the Roman constitution? What power did the provinces gladly welcome? Who restored the Senate to its former dignity? When are the principles of a free constitution irrevocably lost? Who was proclaimed emperor of Rome?

37. What is Augustus called in Daniel 11:20?

38. What was the condition of the world at this time? How extensive was the territory of this government? Why did Satan exult? What did this moment of quiet resting precede?

39. Why did Mary and Joseph go to the little town of Bethlehem? What was most favorable to Christ? Whom had Satan opposed since the rebellion in heaven? How did Christ come into the world? Who had often tended his flocks on the plains of Bethlehem? What did the shepherds hear? What had the wise men been reading? What did they see? What did they know? How was it with the rest of the empire?

40. Give at least ten facts regarding Bethlehem.

41. What is said of the story of Bethlehem? How many knew of the birth of Christ?

42. How much is given concerning Augustus? What had he unconsciously done?

43. Why was Cyrus called to the throne? Of what was Caesar Augustus an agent? Who was to be born in the city of David?

44. Who was reigning during the most of the life of Christ? How does Gabriel describe Tiberius? What is said of him? What began to manifest itself? What entirely ceased? What right did the emperor usurp? What did the governors of Judah reflect? What was the condition of the Jews when the time drew near for the Saviour to appear? Upon whom did they base all their hopes? What did they expect He would do? What was Satan's studied plan in all this?

45. What did he seek to do in Babylon? What did he hope to do through the Medo-Persian kingdom? What did he do through the teachings of Greece? What did this lead men to forget? In what did a few have faith? What was John the Baptist's work?

46. While Tiberius was reigning and planning, what was the Man of God doing? Who watched Him? Who attended and shielded Him, from the enemy? What did they finally do to Christ? Who was responsible for it? Who upheld them in the act? If the Jews had not put Christ to death, who would nave done it? Who nailed the Son of God to the cross?' With whom did they join hands?

47. Name the representatives from the quarters of the globe that stood near Christ in H is last hours. Who helped bear the cross? What did [342] the Roman soldiers say? What was typified by the darkness that shrouded the dying form of Christ? What did the light that shown about the tomb when the Son of God came forth, typify?

Chapter 16
The Mystery of Iniquity

1. What had been tested? In whom did eternal truth dwell? How did the death of Christ affect Satan? Looking forward to His crucifixion, what did Jesus say? After Satan was cast out of heaven, with whom did he meet from time to time? What had these unfallen beings questioned? What did they witness? Since Satan was cast to the earth, how has he worked?

2. How and where was the gospel preached? How long did it take to warn the world? What was the result of the persecution in Jerusalem? What barrier did the gospel break down?

3. What was the result of the spread of the truth? What has been the greatest drawback in Christian experience?

4. What was the character of the love of the first church? How and for what purpose did mothers watch their children?

5. What did the pagans notice in the new sect? What is said of the Christians and their worship?

6. What had the enemy of all truth sought to do? What was the condition when Christ came? What did Satan do to deceive the Son of Man? How was Christ tempted? What dwelt in mortal clay? What was broken by His resurrection? From the foot of the cross, whom did God choose? For what purpose?

7. What did outward pressure fail to do? What examples are given? What nations have attempted to overthrow the truth? What new plan was devised by Satan? Of what plan is this a repetition?

8. What did Paul write to the Thessalonians concerning the working of this power? Of what is it a description?

9. What crept into the pure church? Who lay in the Christian garb? With what did the mystery of Christ come in contact? Who only is safe from deception?

10. When did the mystery of iniquity begin its work? From this period onward, of what power does history speak? How did the mystery of iniquity work? What is said of the distinction between kings of the North and of the South? What two sides of this controversy are manifest?

11. What is said of the "Church of God"?

12. What characteristics mark the true church? How has God honored them? What has been offered every denomination? What is

the effect of rejecting truth in nations and individuals? Who fill the vacancies? How long will this succession be kept up? Who will enter the Eternal City? When was this struggle revealed to Daniel? What does the history of Rome become?

13. To whom were the most details given? What is said of the church of the first century? What is said of the church of the second and third century? For how many centuries were Christianity and Paganism in open conflict? How did it affect the followers of Christ?

14. What is said of Rome in the third century of the Christian era? What made it hard for the emperors to control affairs? Where was the authority? What pressed the Roman empire on every side? What did [343] Diocletian conceive? Whom did he associate with him to accomplish this purpose? Who were associated with the Augusti?

15. Who was the Caesar of the western division of the empire? When was Constantine confronted by bitter foes? What is said of his policy?

16. With whom did Constantine make a league? What did Constantine outwardly acknowledge at this time? Under whose name did he now fight?

17. What does Gibbon say of the use of the cross?

18. What had replaced the humble followers of Christ?

19. What was complete in the days of Constantine? Whom did Constantine conquer, and over what did he sit as sole monarch? How did he treat the Praetorian guard, the senate, and the people?

20. Give the substance of the extract from Gibbon. Upon what are these words a

sad commentary? How does Constantine's life compare with the pagans?

21. Who made the first religious law in the Christian era? What noted edict was passed by him in 312 ? In what year was the first Sunday law passed? What council did he convene in 825 ? What was done by this council? How did the conflict which then began affect the church? Of what was this a great object lesson?

22. What followed in the wake of his reign? What did he leave to his heirs? State what is said of Constantinople. When was the city founded? How long was it from the founding of the city to the victory of Octavius over Antony at Actium?

23. Of what was this new policy the outworking? What had the kingdoms of the past followed? What was the central thought with them? With whom did this policy change? What was enthroned in the place of paganism? What is said of Christianity at this time? What does Gibbon say hereafter the historian will describe? 24. How is the work of the devil described?

24. What were the results of Constantine's work?

25. What is said of the council of Nice?

26. By what has the Christian world been torn asunder? What can you say of Alexandria? Who was Athanasius? Who was Arius?

27. What two powers met on the battle-field when Constantine contended for the throne of Rome? Where was a more deadly conflict? What early Fathers adopted the philosophy of the Greeks, and applied it to the study of the Bible? Where did higher criticism have its birth? Of what was it the result? Of what is it a revival? Give the result of introducing Greek philosophy into Christian schools.

How did this affect the Roman world, and what did it establish?

28. What two leaders came from this teaching? What is said of the disputed points over which they wrangled? For what purpose was the council of Nice called? Who called this council, and was present in person? What creed was recognized as orthodox?

29. What began when this creed was announced and published to the world? Did this check the spread of Arianism? Where was the doctrine popular? What was the faith of the Vandals? What other nations believed the Arian faith? Where did they settle? Into what countries did Arianism spread? What was the faith of the Emperor? Who became the champion of the Catholic cause? When?

30. What was to become of three of the [344] divisions of Rome? Where does this part of the history begin in Daniel 11?

31. What is said of Justinian's reign? To what is the success of Justinian due?

32. What noted warrior favored the Catholic faith? Under pretence of protecting the dethroned Hilderis, what was done? How was he confirmed in his work? What did the bishop say in prophetic tones? For what purpose was this "holy war" determined?

33. State facts in regard to both armies. Give the result of the conflict. What faith triumphed?

34. Describe the triumph granted Belisarius.

35. Who plotted against the government and the general of Justinian? Why? What is said of the wars of Justinian?

36. What may be taken as an illustration of the extermination of the other two kingdoms? Between what years was this accomplished?

37. What was the taking away of the "daily"? When was the papacy established? Who established the new capital? How was Rome left? What gave birth and power to the papacy? When was the seed sown by Justinian harvested? What did this support?

38. What is the striking feature of this history? What principles did the laws of this emperor contain? What does Fischer say? What laws became the basis of national laws to-day? What religion is the recognized religion of most countries to-day?

39. What two men, above all others, were instrumental in forming the papacy and giving it civil power? What contest was the means of enthroning the papacy? How long did it rule the world?

40. What was crushed during this time? The "Dark Ages" were ushered in at what date?

CHAPTER 17
THE WORK OF THE MYSTERY OF INIQUITY

1. What is an important date in Jewish history? What stands as a mile-post in the Christian church? What event made the former date important? What prophetic period began at this point? What did the latter date witness? What prophetic period began in 538 A. D.? What is said of the little horn of Daniel 7 during this period? To what date are we brought in the thirty-first verse of Daniel 11?

2. Did the papacy develop in a short period? What other powers illustrate the man-

ner of the rise of the papacy? Who gave his power, seat, and great authority to the papacy? What two Roman emperors were conspicuous in preparing the way for the rise of the papacy? What event prepared the way for the papacy to be seated on the Tiber? How was the authority of the papacy gained? What did each of the four kingdoms have? Where did paganism and Christianity mingle their waters? Where did the papacy have its birth? Who was its mother? Describe its growth. What did Christians do with the Bible? Give the result.

3. What was introduced into the Christian church? Why? Which commandment was dropped from the decalogue? Which was divided to make the number ten? What is the fourth commandment? How was it altered? How was the Bible treated? What was the result?

4. Who was the head of the church, and how was he exalted? What had taken place even before this? Mention [345] eight facts given in regard to the work of the papacy.

5. What settled over the world? When the word of God was banished, what was extinguished? What was the noontide of the papacy?

6. How long a time was allotted to the power that was to speak great words against the Most High? Why was its time shortened? What kind of bondage was this for the church? What little companies were found?

7. To what days could the Waldenses trace their history? What were they? What did the power upon the throne change? What had Gabriel told Daniel? Who watched each one who gave his life?

8. What is said of the deliverance of the church from bondage? To what did it give birth? How does this compare with the deliverance from other bondage?

9. In what chapter of Revelation is this deliverance mentioned? What is there stated? How were the bands broken which Satan had placed around the truth? What is said of the Bible during that period? Were there schools for the masses? What is said about books, papers, and physicians. What became of those who dared to advocate learning? Whom did God use to help deliver His people? Where were their schools established? What was taught in those schools?

10. What did Wycliffe accomplish? When? To whom is he compared? To whom did Wycliffe give the Gospel? By what name were his followers known? How were they treated? Who was it that brought Protestantism to America?

11. Who lifted up their voices against the papacy in Bohemia? What German monk proclaimed liberty of conscience? Where did he first find a copy of the Bible? Was Rome able to extinguish this light?

12. What became the lesson book for the German nation? Who assisted Luther in this work of reform? What place became noted as the seat of their principal school? Who were educated and sent forth before the death of Luther? To whom was the word of God opened? How was it with Rome during this onward march of the truth? How many nations of Europe received the light? How was America founded?

13. Had every nation accepted the Reformation what would have been the result? What was God offering to all these nations? Who was offered the grand opportunity of returning from Babylon to Jerusalem? What was repeated? How

was it treated? What is the result of a nation's rejecting the principles of the Reformation?

14. What country is an example of such a history? What had been proclaimed in her borders? What verses in this eleventh chapter were exactly fulfilled in her history?

15. What does Scott say in the "Life of Napoleon," concerning France in 1793? In what sense does France stand apart in the world's history? Of what was this the logical result? What is atheism in the individual?

16. Who was rejected? What was substituted?

17. Describe the unveiling of the "Goddess of Reason." Of what was it the result? .

18. What are men doing when they give private interpretations to the Divine Word? Whom do professed Christians follow in doing this? Where may the result of such worship be read?

19. What two institutions had their origin [346] in Eden? How were they treated in France?

20. What road was France travelling? What does the worship of human intellect bring? What took place in 1798? What tells the story of destruction? Of what is this entire history an object lesson? .

21. What stared France in the face? Who saved the nation?

22. To what did the Reformation in Germany in the sixteenth century strike a death blow? What nation became the battleground between papal tyranny and Protestantism? What does absolute monarchy always accompany? What principle is assumed by any nation when the light of truth is accepted?

23. What knew no bounds in France? Who held two-thirds of the land? Who issued warrants for arrest and imprisonment by his sole authority? What prevailed in every province?

24. In what country were the principles of the Reformation put into practice?

25. When France had reached this state, who then appeared? What was the controlling element? Who were powerless? What was the pope forced to do? What did Napoleon organize? Follow Napoleon from Malta to Aboukir. To what position was Napoleon chosen in 1799? What constitution did France attempt to copy? What was established in France? What did the cause of France represent?

26. What does the historian say of the reforms of Napoleon? What was secured by non-Catholics? Who made the pope a prisoner? When? What prophecy was fulfilled at this time?

27. Toward what did the reform of Napoleon tend? When was he proclaimed emperor? From whom did he receive his crown? What was the result of the partial acceptance of the truth? Is this true individually?

28. Of what was the establishment of the principles of the Reformation in the United States the result? To whom is the struggle of France a warning?

29. What two kings again contended in 1798? How is Constantinople recognized by all the nations in Asia and Europe? In the time of the end, what will center about this city?

30. When the papacy was in power what arose? In what form did the new work of Satan come? How much of this world is Mohammedan in faith? Where did this doctrine originate? What country became the center of its influence? What river banks have fed every form of idolatry?

31. In what way did the followers of Mohammed strive to enter Europe? To what country was their influence extended? With what was all Europe threatened at this time? What did the battle of Tours check? Give date. When was Constantinople captured? In whose hands has it since remained? What was one of the greatest checks of the papacy? What led to the discovery of America? Through whom did God work to advance the truth?

32. How did God use the closing of the passage to the eastern world? What often comes from seeming defeat? What is said of the cross?

33. What countries at this time belonged to the Mohammedans? On what site does a Moslem mosque now stand? What is said of the site of the old temple? What countries escaped out of the hand of this conquering power? Who receives an annual tribute from the Turks who pass in caravans on their way to Mecca?

34. What was the ambition of Napoleon? [347] What might this have been? What event was not yet due? What did Napoleon recognize? What other country recognized the same? What has caused constant jealousy among the nations of Europe?

35. Where have the eyes of the world been centered for year? How is Turkey universally designated? What will take place in the near future? Do the Turks understand this? What has the world been brought to realize again and again? What will take place when the Turk steps out of Constantinople? What name has God given to the battle? Who trembled for Turkey? Who came to the rescue, and why? What powers united to sustain the life of the "sick man"?

36. Who are now holding the four winds of strife? For what purpose are they being held? What work is going forward? What nation stands as a guide-post pointing to the work in the heavenly sanctuary?

37. Whose eye is upon the people of God? Can any man tell when Turkey will leave Europe? What will be said when he does go? Who will then return to heaven? With what word? What sentence will then be pronounced? Why was the fate of Babylon, Medo-Persia, Grecia, and Rome recorded? While the world watches Turkey, what should the servants of God watch?

CHAPTER 18
THE CLOSING SCENE

1. How did God regard Daniel? What had God given him several times? What did the last vision cover? Before Gabriel left, what did he reveal to Daniel? What is Daniel? How many times are each of the following expressions repeated: "the time of the end," "latter days," "the end of the indignation," and "for many days"? What were the angel's closing words? How many times by positive expressions is the mind called to the closing scenes of earth?

2. When this vision began, where was the prophet? In what year of Cyrus' reign was the vision given? Through what kingdoms did he carry the mind of the prophet? What was shown of Grecian influence? What was the result of this moulding influence on the fourth kingdom? What did the prophet see on the throne of Rome? Before whom was the darkness scattered? To what is it compared? What

nation became the battle-field between Protestantism and the papacy?

3. What was denied, and what like a pall hung over the country? How was France affected by this struggle? What was shown the prophet? For what were God's people to patiently wait?

4. Whom had the prophet watched intently? What did he see connecting heaven and earth?

5. For how long did this light follow the Jews? What came with the first advent of Christ? What changes took place in the stream of light?

6. What changes took place at the close of the two thousand three hundred days? Into what place did our great High Priest enter? What was revealed to Daniel? What has taken place over and over again? With what is the marred record of man's life covered? What did Daniel know?

7. What are the nations saying? What are they doing? Whom did the prophet see pass through the earth? How long will Christ intercede? When the last soul is saved, what [348] echoes through heaven? What does the great High Priest lay aside?

8. What is then finished? What door is then closed?

9. How must those who are sealed stand in the time of trouble? What makes this period different from all preceding tests? To what is this compared?

10. What words were uttered which will then be uttered by multitudes? What will roll from other foreheads? Why will there be such deep heart searching? What did the mother of Zebedee's children ask? To whom did Christ say that place belonged? Who will occupy the position mentioned by the mother of Zebedee's sons?

11. Who besides the sealed ones will know that probation has ended? From which of the plagues will there be no escape? How does David describe this time of trouble? Who are shielded from the effects of the plagues? How will the mountains and the islands be affected? What took place at the resurrection of Christ? Who were they and what are they said to be?

12. At what time will there be another partial resurrection? Who will be among those who will arise? What will they see? What will become of those who come forth to shame and everlasting contempt?

13. What garments does the Saviour wear? Who are deeply interested in this work? What is the foundation of God's throne? Where will it be hung? Who will see it?

14. What is painted on the threatening clouds? What mingles with all of God's dealings until men utterly turn from Him? What has been seen in the sky over and over again? Have men listened to its voice? What do the heavens declare? What have scientists studied and failed to see?

15. What, from the creation of the world, has told the plan of redemption? Who cannot understand it?

16. Why does Jehovah point us to the stars? Who was it that saw the Christ-star? What have men invented by using God-given ability? Why has God encouraged this effort? With what result?

17. What is said of each teacher of righteousness saved in the Kingdom of God? Who will be the center of all?

18. As Daniel watched, what did he see and hear? Describe the resurrection of the righ-

teous. Toward what place do they pass? Who throws open the pearly gates? What is chanted?

19. What are the words that come from without? What rings forth from within?

20. What does the accompanying host reply?

21. Describe the hundred and forty-four thousand. What calls forth a song of triumph from their lips? What is so wonderful about the singing? What rings through heaven? From whence come the stones that gleam on the Master's crown? To what are the redeemed compared? What completes the circle of perfection?

22. What is their relation to the king? Whose place will the one hundred and forty-four thousand take? Of whom was another company composed? Then who are seen?

23. How many gather around the Father and the Son? As Christ looks upon them, what does He see, and how is He affected? What will He do? From whence come streams of light? Who bow in adoration? Why?

24. Of what is the universe composed? With what is the immensity of space filled? How are they held in their orbits? From whom is their light reflected? How are the planets guided? [349]

25. Of what is all this a type? Of what is it a pattern? How should each company shine? How does God look upon each company of worshipers? What is said of their movements? How should it be in each family?

26. Where will be found the perfection of this system? How are they peculiar? What did the angel say to Daniel? What did the prophet have the privilege of seeing? How is the teaching compared to Christ's teaching?

27. What can you say of the last scene presented to Daniel? How will those shine that are taken from the depths of sin?

28. What was Daniel told to do? What would take place in the time of the end?

29. What can you say of the time of the end? What is said of the law of God, and of the saints in the beginning of the time of the end? What stood full- fledged before the world? What did this freedom lead the angel to say?

30. Mention some of the inventions of the last days. Why does God allow these things?

31. What is marvelous beyond description? What is said of the realms of science? What is God's object in this? What is it that has led to such intellectual and moral advancement? How rapidly are messages sent from city to city? How from continent to continent?

32. How does man look upon these things? How are angels watching them?

33. What has God offered to every nation? Why were the Jews lost as a nation? Upon what condition was the Christian church to inherit the promises made to the Israelites?

34. What will be developed in the time of the end? What will be one great means of their education?

35. What was revealed in the first glimpse given to the prophet Daniel? To whom is he pointed in the last days? How will the people of God in the last days be fortified physically? How will they be fortified mentally?

36. In what period do we now live? What separation will take place? What will be the attitude of the faithful followers of God? To what time was Daniel's attention centered? Who was near the prophet, listening to the record of events?

37. What question was asked by the angel when Gabriel ceased to speak? Who replied? What did he say?

38. How long have angels waited for the completion of this plan? What have they looked for in each generation? When they saw the inhabitants of the earth loiter, what did one cry out?

39. When this period was mentioned by Christ, what did Daniel say? Fearing that he still might be left in doubt, what did he then say? Had any request of this man of God been left unanswered? What was the reply of the angel? What was meant by the time of the end? What would then cease?

40. When did this period of twelve hundred and sixty years begin? What had been changed during this time? What had been bound? What did the persecution tend to do? At the end of this twelve hundred and sixty years, what would be restored? When did this "time, times, and a half" end? What has been circulated since that time as never before? What special light has shone since 1844?

41. How have the truths for this time spread?

42. How did the angel explain the two periods that had puzzled the prophet? What does he say of those who live at the end of the thirteen hundred and thirty-five days? Why will they be blest? What will happen to many? Who will understand? What will some insist upon when the wise understand? What is said of the words of Gabriel and Christ? What two texts are quoted?

43. How was it with the aged prophet? What had been written? How long would the prophecy stand? How long had the prophet done faithful service in the courts of Babylon and Shushan? How did Daniel stand with men? What did God say of him?

44. How will he stand in the last days? Name the three agencies that will give light to guide the remnant church. What two prophets in this sense will stand together? What will guide the faithful few safely through the time of trouble, and prepare them for Christ's coming?

Adventist Pioneer Library

For more information, visit:
www.APLib.org

or write to:
contact@aplib.org

Made in the USA
Columbia, SC
27 June 2023